Published by Macmillan in association with the International Institute for Strategic Studies

Studies in International Security

International Institute for Strategic Studies conference papers

Christoph Bertram (editor)

Robert O'Neill (editor)

François Heisbourg (editor)

Peacekeeping in International Politics

Alan James

Professor and Head of Department of International Relations
University of Keele

MACMILLAN

in association with the
**INTERNATIONAL INSTITUTE FOR
STRATEGIC STUDIES (IISS)**

First published 1990

Published by
MACMILLAN ACADEMIC AND PROFESSIONAL LTD
Houndmills, Basingstoke, Hampshire RG21 2XS
and London
Companies and representatives
throughout the world

Typeset by P & R Typesetters Ltd, Salisbury, Wilts, UK

Printed in Great Britain by
Billing & Sons Ltd,
Worcester

British Library Cataloguing in Publication Data
James, Alan, *1933*–
Peacekeeping in international politics.—(Studies in
international security; 29).
1. Peacekeeping, history
I. Title
341.584
ISBN 0–333–53000–4 (hardcover)
ISBN 0–333–53932–X (paperback)

To Lorna

Contents

PART III: NEIGHBOURHOOD QUARRELS

Introduction: Calming the Neighbourhood   140

PART IV: HIGH-STREET EMBARRASSMENTS

Introduction: Peacekeeping in the High Street   180

List of Maps

List of Abbreviations

ADF	Arab Deterrent Force (in Lebanon, 1976–1983)
ANC	African National Congress (Movement for the liberation of South Africa)
CC	UN Consular Commission (Netherlands East Indies/ Indonesia, 1947–1951)
CIAV	International Support and Verification Commission (UN and OAS body regarding demobilization of anti-Nicaraguan Contras, 1989–)
Domrep	Mission of the Representative of the (UN) Secretary-General in the Dominican Republic (1965–1966)
IAPF	Inter-American Peace Force (Dominican Republic, 1965–1966)
ICCS	International Commission of Control and Supervision (Vietnam, 1973–1975)
ICSCs	International Commissions for Supervision and Control (in successor states of Indo-China: Cambodia, 1954–1970; Laos, 1954–1974; Vietnam, 1954–1973)
IDF	Israel Defence Forces
JC	Joint Commission (regarding Angola and Namibia, 1988–)
JMMC	Joint Military Monitoring Commission (Angola and Cuba–South Africa, 1988–1989)
MAC	Military Armistice Commission (Korea, 1953–)
MACs	Mixed Armistice Commissions (Arab-Israeli, 1949–)
MF	Monitoring Force (Rhodesia/Zimbabwe, 1979–1980)
MFO	Multinational Force and Observers (Egypt–Israel, 1982–)
MNF I	First Multinational Force (Beirut, Lebanon, 1982)
MNF II	Second Multinational Force (Beirut, Lebanon, 1982–1984)
MPLA	People's Movement for the Liberation of Angola
Nato	North Atlantic Treat Organization (1949–)
NNSC	Neutral Nations Supervisory Commission (Korea, 1953–)
OAS	Organization of American States
OAU	Organization of African Unity
Onuc	UN Operation in the Congo (1960–1964)
Onuca	UN Observer Group in Central America (1989–)
Onuven	UN Observer Mission to Verify the Electoral Process in Nicaragua (1989–1990)

PF	Patriotic Front (Movement for the Liberation of Rhodesia–Zimbabwe)
PLAN	People's Liberation Army of Namibia
PLO	Palestine Liberation Organization
PRG	Provisional Revolutionary Government (South Vietnam)
ROC	Republic of Cyprus
SADF	South African Defence Force
SADR	Saharan Arab Democratic Republic (Polisario Liberation Movement's designation of Western Sahara)
SFM	United States Sinai Field Mission (1976–1982)
SLA	South Lebanon Army
SSM	United States Sinai Support Mission (1975–1982)
Swapo	South West Africa People's Organization
TRNC	Turkish Republic of Northern Cyprus
UAR	United Arab Republic (Union of Egypt and Syria, 1958–1961, but also used by Egypt as her name from 1961 to 1971)
UN	United Nations
Unavem	UN Angola Verification Mission (1988–)
Undof	UN Disengagement Observer Force (Israel–Syria, 1974–)
Unef I	First UN Emergency Force (Egypt–France and UK, and then Egypt–Israel, 1956–1967)
Unef II	Second UN Emergency Force (Egypt–Israel, 1973–1979)
Unficyp	UN Peace-keeping Force in Cyprus (1964–)
Ungomap	UN Good Offices Mission in Afghanistan and Pakistan (1988–1990)
Unifil	UN Interim Force in Lebanon (1978–)
Uniimog	UN Iran–Iraq Military Observer Group (1988–)
Unipom	UN India–Pakistan Observation Mission (1965–1966)
UNIT	UN Inspection Team (Iran–Iraq, 1984–1988)
Unita	National Union for the Total Independence of Angola
Unogil	UN Observation Group in Lebanon (1958)
Unmogip	UN Military Observer Group in India and Pakistan (1949–)
Unscob	UN Special Committee on the Balkans (1947–1952)
Untag	UN Transition Assistance Group (Namibia, 1989–1990)
Untea	UN Temporary Executive Authority (West New Guinea/West Irian, 1962–1963)
Untso	UN Truce Supervision Organization (Arab–Israeli, 1948–)
Unyom	UN Yemen Observation Mission (1963–1964)

Acknowledgements

The preparation of this book has brought me many interesting and rewarding experiences, in the course of which I have met a large number of fine people. I have been very privileged. A multitude of individuals, as well as a variety of institutions, deserve thanks for so freely helping me. I am sorry they cannot all be mentioned by name. Their omission from these acknowledgements certainly does not imply a lack of gratitude on my part.

The first set of thanks must go to my own University, Keele. I benefitted from a term's leave under its Research Awards scheme, and the Vice-Chancellor, Professor Brian Fender, kindly gave me the two terms' leave in which the book was written. My colleagues in the Department of International Relations willingly 'closed ranks' during the latter period of leave, for which I am most appreciative.

Much travel has been involved, to see peacekeeping in action and to talk to those responsible for running it. Keele has assisted in that regard. But most of the necessary money has been provided by the Leverhulme Trust, in the shape of a Research Fellowship, and by the Nuffield Foundation, which awarded me several Small Grants. My gratitude to them is indeed considerable.

Librarians, too, have been enormously helpful. I warmly acknowledge the assistance I received at the Library of the University of Keele, and also: in London, at the Libraries of the UN Information Centre, the Royal Institute of International Affairs, the British Museum, and the Foreign and Commonwealth Office; in Washington, DC, at the Library of the Organization of American States; and in New York at the UN Library and the UN Archives. In particular I want to thank Pat Farquhar, formerly of the UN's London Information Centre, and Brian Barrett of the Library and Records Department of the Foreign and Commonwealth Office, who went much out of their way on my behalf. I was also helped by the Office of the Historian at the United States Department of State and the Directorate of History at Canada's National Defence Headquarters.

Many members of the UN Secretariat have rendered great assistance. I must especially acknowledge the help I have so often received from the former Under-Secretary-General for Special Political Affairs, Sir Brian Urquhart, his successor, Marrack Goulding and James Jonah, now Assistant Secretary-General in charge of the Office for Research and the Collection of Information. Other UN officials in New York who have been particularly helpful include: Jean-Claude Aime, Blanca Antonini, Juergen Dedring, General Timothy Dibuama, Issa Diallo, Brigitte Doring, Colonel Dermot Earley, Gus Feissel, Leon Hosang, Leonard Kapungu, F. T. Liu, Iqbal Riza, George Sherry and Hisako Shimura. I also want to express my warm gratitude to May Davidson for the very kind way in which, invaluably, she put me in touch with the right people in the Secretariat.

Outside the UN, General Indar Jit Rikhye and his staff at the International Peace Academy in New York have always dealt very readily with my numerous enquiries, as have the members of the United States Department of State responsible for relations with the Multinational Force and Observers (MFO), notably Robert Krantz and the late Bob Houghton. Leamon Hunt, the MFO's late Director-General, gave generously of his time when I visited him at the organization's headquarters in Rome. Others who gave me valuable assistance include: Zamir Akram at Pakistan's Ministry of Foreign Affairs; Bob Cloete and John Sunde of South Africa's Ministry of Foreign Affairs; Ambassador Rajeshwar Dayal of India; Mario Gonzales and Oswaldo Vallejo at the Organization of American States; Colonel David Leslie of Canada; and Ambassador Velasquez-Diaz of Honduras. Colonel Ned Doyle of the Republic of Ireland deserves a special mention for having responded with huge patience and helpfulness to very many questions regarding his varied peacekeeping service with the UN.

My understanding of peacekeeping has benefitted enormously from being able to spend time with a number of operations. On these field trips I always received the utmost consideration. Many officers and civilian officials deserve my thanks for this, most of all those who were in charge of the operations: Martti Ahtisaari, Special Representative of the Secretary-General, UN Transition Assistance Group (Untag) in Namibia; General Frederick Bull-Hansen, Commander of the Multinational Force and Observers in Sinai; General Prem Chand, Untag's Force Commander; Generals Alexander Erskine and William Callaghan, successively Chiefs of Staff of the Jerusalem-based UN Truce Supervision Organization (Untso); General Gunther Greindl, Commander of the UN Force in Cyprus (Unficyp); General Gustav Hagglund, both as Commander of the Damascus-based UN Disengagement Observer Force (Undof) and as Commander of the UN Interim Force in Lebanon (Unifil); General James Parker, Chief

Military Observer of the UN Military Observer Group in India and Pakistan (Unmogip); and Benon Sevan, Alternate Representative of the Secretary-General at the UN Good Offices Mission in Afghanistan and Pakistan (Ungomap).

I must also mention the spendid help I received in Cyprus from the Chief of Staff of the UN Force, Brigadier Robin Duchesne. In Lebanon the Commanding Officers of three battalions – Colonel Konrote (Fiji), Commandant O'Grady (Ireland), and Colonel Loset (Norway) – went to a good deal of trouble to ensure that my needs were met, and in Namibia Colonel John Crocker (Australia) was particularly kind. My itineraries have always been arranged with care and efficiency, and for this, as well as for providing valuable commentary en route, I am very grateful to, chiefly: Major Andrew Styles of MFO, Major Lorne McDonald of Undof, Major R. I. M. MacArthur of Unficyp, Captain Alan Galt of Untso, Colonel Ben Akafia of Unifil, Major Thomas Lindell of Unmogip and Major Philip Tarakinikini of Ungomap. Frederic Eckhard arranged my appointments with headquarters officials at Untag with considerable helpfulness. Other field officials, among many, who responded most willingly to my queries include: Victor Andreev, Commandant Maurice Canavan, James Connolly, Helen Gadalla, Vladislav Guerassev, Colonel Allan Ingalls, General Thor Johnsen, Colonel K. N. Mehra, Colonel Michael O'Shea, Colonel H. Shariff, Kenichi Suganuma, Tom White and Joe Woods.

Back at Keele, my knowledge of peacekeeping has been enriched through the work of three of my research students – Colonel Peter Harvey, Shafqat Chauhdry and Pauline Dawson. My colleague, John Proops, of the Department of Economics and Management Science, has considerably speeded up the completion of the book by introducing me to word processing and always being willing to guide me through its mysteries. His cheerful patience and encouragement have been much appreciated. In the final stages of putting the manuscript together, Maureen Groppe has, with great efficiency, gone well beyond the call of duty. She has been a veritable rock of support.

The maps in this book have been drawn by Andrew Lawrence, Cartographer in the Department of Geography at the University of Keele. He undertook this large task with huge care, patience and good humour, and I am exceedingly grateful to him. He has worked on the basis of the best information I could obtain, but it must not be assumed that that information is always completely accurate. Nor must it be assumed that the maps represent the views of the states concerned regarding the legitimacy of the boundaries and other dividing lines which the maps portray.

I am indebted to the International Institute for Strategic Studies for its confidence in me as an author, and for the care with which the Director, François Heisbourg, and his senior staff have read my manuscript. In this connection I wish to pay particular tribute to Colonel John Cross for his meticulous editorial work. Barbara Docherty and Keith Povey, too, for Macmillan, have attended to the manuscript very carefully and Macmillan's Belinda Dutton has been helpfully enthusiastic about the book.

Finally, I thank Lorna for the very substantial support which she has given me throughout the work which this book has entailed. Her enthusiasm for its large demands on my time has not been wholly without qualification. But at bottom she has always had a keen concern for the book's progress. And when, at the end, I was flagging, she brought a stern and salutary editorial pen to the final chapter. Partly in recompense, and also as a mark of my deep affection, I dedicate the book to her.

ALAN JAMES

Introduction: The Nature of Peacekeeping

'Peacekeeping' is a term which, in international politics and therefore in this book, is not to be taken literally. As it has come to be used, it does not connote the authoritative and, if necessary, forceful maintenance of peace. Peacekeeping is not, therefore, what might be called a primary activity. Nor is it directly creative in character, in the sense in which the negotiation of agreements is creative. Instead, it refers to the international help which is sometimes sent to an immediate problem area when disputing states wish, at least for the time being, to live in peace. Accordingly, it is an activity of a secondary kind, in the sense that it is dependent, in respect of both its origin and its success, on the wishes and policies of others. In appropriate circumstances peacekeeping can make a valuable contribution to peace – but only if and to the extent to which disputants choose to take advantage of it.

THE CHARACTERISTICS OF PEACEKEEPING

Personnel

The most important characteristics of peacekeeping fall into four sets, the first of which relates to its personnel. Peacekeeping operations are normally carried out by people with military status – chiefly soldiers, but airmen and even sailors may also be involved. Sometimes, indeed, a peacekeeping body is a traditional-looking military force, composed of a number of battalions under the authority of a commander. The battalions will have been detached from or supplied by various national armies, and the commander will have been appointed by and be responsible to the international authority which has arranged the operation. Often this will be the United Nations (UN), but peacekeeping is by no means a UN preserve.

Additionally, peacekeeping may be and quite frequently is conducted by a group of military observers. They will almost always be under international command, and as a rule its members – usually officers of middle rank – will have been seconded on an individual basis from

1

their national armies to serve for a period with the peacekeeping group. It could happen, and sometimes has, that quasi-military peacekeeping tasks – such as checking on force levels – are done by civilians. It may be, too, that civilians will be found on field activities which are complementary to those of the military peacekeepers. But peacekeeping is overwhelmingly, and distinctively, a military responsibility.

There are several reasons for peacekeepers being drawn from the ranks of those who have had military training and who are under, or are willing to return to, military discipline. Such people are available for immediate despatch to trouble spots. As they are familiar with military procedures, they are acceptable to the local military, with whom they will certainly have to have dealings. Military expertise will usually be needed. Tight discipline will be required of those who play, as peacekeepers do, a sensitive role on foreign soil. And it may be that the authoritative approach which can be easily assumed by military officers will prove very useful in a peacekeeping context.

As, following international practice, the term 'peacekeeping' will here be used to refer to the activity of bodies made up entirely or predominantly of military personnel, this book will exclude a number of field operations which are connected (at least ostensibly) with the maintenance of peace, and which some commentators might treat as instances of peacekeeping. Chiefly they are operations of an investigative or conciliatory kind. As such they have more positive tasks than the reactive ones which are ordinarily associated with military peacekeepers. Generally, therefore, they are clearly distinguishable from the bodies which are here categorized as peacekeeping. Sometimes, however, military personnel have been attached to such civilian bodies to engage in specialized work, in which case note will be taken of the operations in question.

Values

Peacekeeping's second set of characteristics is its values. As the term suggests, they represent the guidelines which are central to the whole concept. They thus distinguish this phenomenon from others and give it a clear and distinct identity.

The values of peacekeeping are twofold. The first is that such bodies are non-threatening. Notwithstanding the fact that peacekeepers are military people, they are not, when so employed, in the busines of threatening or using force. Nor does the fact that peacekeeping forces are lightly armed undermine this value. For their arms are solely for emergency use in individual self-defence, for the defence of peacekeeping positions which are under armed attack or, in respect of a minority of operations, for the maintenance of order within a state. Very strict rules are laid down on this matter, and in the normal way a peacekeeper's arms are never used. Moreover, the members of peacekeeping observer groups customarily do not carry any arms at all. Typically they move around or are posted in pairs, and it is judged that they will do their job with maximum effectiveness and minimum danger to themselves if they are unarmed.

The non-threatening nature of peacekeeping bodies has a close, but not a necessary, connection with the other peacekeeping value – that of impartiality. Peacekeepers have the job of giving help in a situation which, in reality if not in immediate appearance, is bilateral, or even multilateral. Given that they are neither empowered nor equipped to enforce a solution, they are going to be trusted by both sides – and therefore be of use – only if they behave with manifest impartiality. This approach will have its basis in the mandate which an operation is given by its despatching authority, and in the orders which the commander issues to his men. If a force or an observer group fails to observe this value it will become little less than an accessory to one side, and a fairly ineffectual one at that. And if at the same time a force abandons its non-threatening posture, it will become a more significant party to the dispute in question. In either event it will have lost its claim to be a peacekeeping body. There may be some merit in its doing so. But those endeavouring to understand its nature will need to remove it from the peacekeeping category, for it will no longer be acting in accordance with the essential and distinctive values of that activity.

These comments are basically as applicable to peacekeeping forces with a mandate to help in maintaining internal law and order as they are to the more usual kind of peacekeeping bodies which operate in situations of recent or anticipated international fighting. Responsibility for the maintenance of order may be given to peacekeepers because its collapse will have international repercussions or because the resolution of a dispute calls for a period of international administration. In either case, a forceful initiative may sometimes be required. Provided, however, that it is taken purely to maintain order, and not to influence the balance of an internal political controversy, it may be seen as an impartial exercise of force. Putting the point another way, resort to force in this context is compatible with peacekeeping if it is done on behalf of a government, or in support of a set of constitutional arrangements, which is generally accepted within the jurisdiction in question as legitimate. In those circumstances, the central authority will be seen, in respect of law and order matters, as above politics, and the use of force towards that end as an impartial activity. In practice, of course, it may occasionally be hard to ascertain whether this criterion has in fact been met. But in principle the matter is clear.

Functions

The third set of peacekeeping characteristics has to do with its functions. The assistance which impartial and non-threatening military personnel can give to disputing parties takes three forms. They are not mutually exclusive, so a single peacekeeping operation could be designed to perform, or just find itself performing, more than one of these functions at the same time. And it is very possible that an operation may, with the passage of time, move forwards and backwards between the various functions.

The first function refers to a situation which has often given rise to the establishment of a peacekeeping operation. It is that of defusion. By offering to get a group of impartial military observers or an impartial non-fighting force to the scene of a crisis, those who have until then been engaged in belligerent activity may find it possible to accept a cease-fire and perhaps to withdraw, using the peacekeepers as a face-saving device. Another possibility is that a crisis which seemed about to break out into war might be prevented from doing so through the interposition of peacekeepers. Alternatively, the arrival of a peacekeeping body may provide interested parties who were thinking of physically involving themselves at the scene of the crisis, or who were thought to be of that mind, with an acceptable ground for desisting. And once the operation is in place it will be able to offer valuable assistance in the settlement of any crises which subsequently develop between the parties.

The second function of peacekeeping is that of stabilization. This is a function which may be fulfilled by a body which, having already helped to defuse a crisis, does not then depart but stays on with a view to maintaining calm. Alternatively, negotiations may take place in a relatively peaceful atmosphere for the despatch of a peacekeeping body to bolster the stability which already exists on the ground. Or the establishment of such a body may simply await the conclusion of a cease-fire or of some other agreement which has a comparable effect. In any event, the function of such a body is then to assist in the maintenance of stability, which may be done in one of several ways.

The peacekeepers may help in the reduction of anxiety; they may contribute to the prevention of incidents; and they may be able to alleviate or remove tension. However they do it, they may be in for a long stay, as such operations seem particularly prone to longevity. This has sometimes led to the claim that they stand in the way of the negotiation of political settlements, diplomatic complacency being induced by the maintenance of calm. The argument, however, is less than compelling.

3   Thirdly, peacekeepers may provide assistance in resolving disputes. On the face of it, this function could seem superfluous: if two states seriously intend to settle a problem, it might be wondered why they see a need for third-party assistance. But that is too simple a view. The achievement of some settlements may depend on peacekeeping help, as when impartial soldiers maintain order during a plebiscite. It is not impossible that states might agree on a disputed area being subject to international government, either as a face-saving device associated with its handover from one state to another, or as a cooling mechanism while negotiations are held regarding its long-term future or, theoretically, as a permanent arrangement. In any of these events the governors will require the support of military men. Even apparently final settlements may not be politically self-executing. In some cases, the suspicion which one erstwhile disputant continues to entertain of the other – and vice-versa – could well point to the desirability of some impartial mechanism which can report to each of the parties whether the other is indeed honouring its promise, for example, to withdraw troops from a particular area. In other instances a settlement might involve long-term arrangements regarding, perhaps, the limitation of forces in or the demilitarization of a certain region, which almost by their nature call for some kind of international supervision by people with military expertise.

Context

The final set of peacekeeping characteristics has to do with the context within which such operations take place. It has four aspects, all of which are necessary for the effective conduct of peacekeeping. The last two, however, are not only necessary but reflect the distinctive nature of the role played by peacekeepers. Together with the two values of peacekeeping, they constitute the very core and essence of the activity which has become known by this name.

Firstly, a competent authority has to take the decision to establish a peacekeeping operation. This might well be an international organization of a universal or quasi-universal kind. But there is no reason at all why regional organizations of a political sort should not act in this way. Nor is there any reason why an ad hoc group of states should not organize a peacekeeping enterprise, nor even why such a task should not be performed by a single acceptable state. Whoever establishes an operation will also have periodically to consider whether to extend its life or to bring it to an end.

Secondly, provisions are necessary. International organizations do not have direct control of the men and money which peacekeeping operations require nor, other than very marginally, of equipment. For these, states must be looked to. A variety of reasons makes it unlikely that there will be huge difficulty in obtaining the desirable number of military personnel, although there may well be a problem over the recruitment of men who have certain kinds of needed expertise. Money, however, could well be a considerable worry, especially in respect of UN operations. The repayment of debts to contributor states is an issue which has led to much embarrassment, this being due to the reluctance or even refusal of many members to pay their assessed shares of the costs of peacekeeping. As yet, financial shortcomings have not led to the winding-up of an operation, but the annoyance of one or two states over this matter seems to have influenced their decision to withdraw their contingents from UN forces.

Thirdly, and all-importantly, there is the issue of the attitude of the host state or states to the presence of a peacekeeping operation. For, peacekeepers are not in the business of using force to achieve their purposes once they have taken up their positions on the ground, nor do they fight their way in to those positions. Peacekeeping, in short, rests on the consent of the state or states on whose territory it takes place. This is seen most clearly at the time of the establishment of an operation. It might be that a potential host is urgently pressed by interested states to accept a body of peacekeepers. But the operation will take place only if the state who is to play host to it formally agrees to do so.

The principle of host state consent also operates in reverse, in that the withdrawal of consent normally requires the withdrawal of the peacekeepers. This statement has meaning on several levels. It gives the accepted legal position, in that unless it has been specifically agreed to the contrary – of which the only instance which comes to mind is that associated with the Egypt–Israel Peace Treaty – the host state has the right to demand at any time that the peacekeepers depart. It points to what in almost every case will be the diplomatic realities, in that states who contribute troops to an operation will very probably insist on their withdrawal if that is the host's wish. It refers with virtual certainty to military and logistical realities, in that the position of a relatively small and (at most) lightly armed body will quickly become untenable when faced with the non-cooperation and hostility of the armed forces and lay authorities of the host state. The statement also makes complete sense in terms of the idea of peacekeeping. For if peacekeepers show a tendency to outstay their welcome, the tool is likely to be less sought after in the future. All states get uneasy at the thought of foreign military men perhaps not leaving when asked. Accordingly, those who appreciate the usefulness of peacekeeping will not want its prospects to be jeopardized by one or two such bodies abandoning a basic principle of the activity.

The last contextual requirement of peacekeeping is the political cooperation of all the immediate parties to the dispute which has given rise to an operation. As peacekeeping is not a threatening activity, it can fulfil its functions only if the parties – whether or not they are all also hosts – extend their cooperation to the peacekeepers, and maintain it. This does not necessarily involve action of a fulsome or unduly overt kind, which in some circumstances might be politically difficult. But all the parties must allow the peacekeepers to get on with their job, and give their genuine cooperation to more or less the degree which is required. For if this condition is not met, the peacekeeping body is not going to be able to serve its purpose.

This point is linked not only with the functions of peacekeeping and its non-threatening character. It also has a very close connection with the other peacekeeping value of impartiality. For if a peacekeeping body receives cooperation from only one side, it is probably going to look somewhat partial – at the least – to the other, no matter how scrupulous the peacekeepers are about their behaviour. Moreover, inasmuch as the peacekeepers' reports and findings will, in these circumstances, be based on complaints and information received from only one side, and on enquiries conducted on the territory of one side, those reports and findings are likely to facilitate the conclusion that the cooperative side is much more injured, and virtuous, than the other. Because of these factors, a body welcomed by only one side is unlikely to make a worthwhile contribution to the defusing of a crisis or the maintenance of stability. Of course, it may still offer considerable advantages to the potential host, but they are not of the sort which are integral to the idea of peacekeeping.

Equally, if one party stops cooperating with an established peacekeeping operation, the operation thereby loses much if not all of its raison d'être, inasmuch as it takes on the look of a finger-pointing rather than a neutral fire-watching exercise. However, there may be good institutional reasons for keeping an operation in being, as it is then a base from which activity could take place relatively easily in the event of any future agreed need for a full peacekeeping role in the area. Additionally, the continuing presence of a peacekeeping body, albeit one which receives cooperation from only one side, may offer some very small obstacle to the outbreak of further violence. However, this sort of context is less than fully tailored for the requirements of peacekeeping.

THE TERM 'PEACEKEEPING'

To speak of the 'requirements' of peacekeeping or of its 'values' reflects the process of abstraction. The term 'peacekeeping' has never formally been given a fixed and detailed meaning by the collectivity of states, and such a development is most unlikely. Instead, what happened was that states, often in their capacity as members of the UN, authorized and embarked on certain activities which, with hindsight, were seen as having certain basic factors in common. It was then possible, and natural, to invent a term to refer, in an overall way, to the activity. Conceptualization had taken place. This occurred in the late 1950s. Once that sort of intellectual development has come about, it is possible to proceed further along the path of abstraction and delineate the key elements of the new activity which has been identified.

This is what has been done in the preceding section in respect of the chief characteristics of peacekeeping. In consequence, it is possible to say of a particular operation that it should be moved out of the peacekeeping category due to its having acted contrary to the basic values of the activity. Or that an operation's peacekeeping credentials have become tarnished because of an important change in the context in which it takes place. This kind of procedure is necessary if the international world (or any societal situation) is to be spoken of in terms of any generality. And as individual events and occasions are so multifarious, generalization is required if the overall character of international relations is to be grasped. To the extent to which there are clear elements of commonality in a variety of separate happenings, it is also firmly in accordance with empirical reality. Fortunately, such commonality does occur to a considerable extent – one instance of which is the activity which has been conceptualized as peacekeeping.

Scholarly work of this kind, however, runs into two loosely-connected problems. The first is that life does not fall neatly into pre-existing categories. In consequence, any abstract scheme of a definitional sort is probably going to encounter difficulties at the margin, raising a question as to whether, on balance, this or that phenomenon should or should not be included within it. And whichever way a particular writer decides the matter, the outcome may, to some, seem strange. In this work, for example, the UN missions of enquiry which went to North Borneo (soon to become Sabah) and Sarawak in 1963 and to Bahrain in 1970 are not considered. Both were non-threatening and both may be assumed to have acted impartially; the first was intended to defuse a small crisis (over the geographical ambit of the new state of Malaysia) and the second to assist in a resolution of Iran's claim to Bahrain; and both went with the consent and cooperation of the relevant states. They thus share many of the characteristics of peacekeeping, as defined above. But they did not include any military personnel, and have therefore been excluded. The argument that a point might have been stretched was rejected, on the ground that to do so would have made it difficult not to open the door to all missions of enquiry, good offices, conciliation, and mediation, so changing the book's character from one exclusively concerned with what has come to be called peacekeeping to one on peacemaking as well.

In general, the anomaly and marginal case problems do not figure very largely in the discussion of peacekeeping. But a somewhat greater difficulty stems from the second of the problems which are associated with the identification of peacekeeping as a distinct type of international activity. It has to do with the fact that whereas scholars try to use definitions and categories with precision, states are under no such professional obligation. Accordingly, if it suits them, as sometimes it does, they have no hesitation in using the term peacekeeping to refer to an activity which is quite unlike that which was identified in the previous section. The reason for this is clear. The term 'peacekeeping' has a very favourable resonance, so that states are glad to use it in their statements and rhetoric in circumstances where, at least superficially, it will look appropriate. It is a way of trying to engender positive feelings, and hence support, for their policies.

This points to a tension between scholarly and political activity. As has been suggested, it is the scholar's job to make sense of the complex world by the process of judicious abstraction. Having done so, he or she is entitled to make judgements about whether or not a particular case is an instance of peacekeeping as that term has come to be used internationally. But it is not for the scholar to tell states how they should use words. And if in the predominant usage of states the term peacekeeping comes to be given a wider sense than that which has been outlined here, scholarly usage should follow suit. For just as it is the scholars' job to describe the world as it is, and not as they would like it to be, so also they must use the terminology which is prevalent amongst states. However, there would then be a case for a sub-term to refer to a clearly distinct aspect of the now-portmanteau term, or for a new and different term for what was previously called peacekeeping. Suggesting such a terminology would be a legitimate scholarly activity.

As yet, however, there is no difficulty in this regard. There is, it is true, sometimes a measure of public uncertainty about the role of force in peacekeeping. But by and large, states and commentators recognize and use the term peacekeeping to refer to a distinct activity of the sort which has been identified above.

PEACEKEEPING IN INTERNATIONAL POLITICS

Peacekeeping is generally (but somewhat inaccurately) linked with the UN. But, as has been mentioned, the concept made its appearance only in the late 1950s, there having been no thought of it in the minds of those who set up the UN in 1945. For on the one hand they anticipated disputes being pacifically settled, along the traditional lines of enquiry, conciliation, mediation, and so on. And on the other they envisaged economic and, particularly, military sanctions being imposed as a means of coping with threats to and breaches of the peace.

For various reasons, some of them internal to the UN but others – the more important ones – relating to the international context in which the UN found itself, this grand scheme for international enforcement has almost completely failed to work. Not only in diplomatic but also in structural terms, the post-1945 world has been about as inhospitable as could be imagined for the arrangements for keeping the peace which are outlined in the UN Charter. Only once, and then in unusual institutional circumstances, has resort been made to it, or something like it: in Korea, between 1950 and 1953, when a multinational army fought in the UN's name to repel the attack on South Korea by the North. But this experience did not produce any enthusiasm for its repetition, and developments since then have not increased the likelihood of a return to the UN's scheme.

Instead, the tool of peacekeeping has proved to be the Organization's most direct contribution to the maintenance of peace, a development which was acknowledged by the award of the 1988 Nobel Peace Prize to the UN's peacekeeping bodies. But, as has been noted, the device has also often been used by other organizations, including those which predate the UN – for certain operations of the inter-War period can, in the light of later conceptualizing activity, be seen as falling within the peacekeeping category. (They will therefore be included in this book.) Indeed, peacekeeping can be seen as little more than a modern application of an ancient arrangement – that of the use of impartial and non-threatening go-betweens. In the past, however, such intermediaries were predominantly employed with a view to securing agreements, and as such did not need to be drawn from the ranks of the military. The diplomatic climate of the twentieth century, however, and particularly of its second half, has encouraged the enlistment of impartial and non-threatening help to implement settlements as well as to obtain them. Furthermore, that climate, until very recently, has been sufficiently inclement as to point, with even greater frequency and urgency, to the use of such help in defusing crises and maintaining truces. Especially in this last capacity, the intermediaries have sometimes found themselves in long-term rather than in very temporary jobs. And the nature of all these jobs is such that military personnel are generally essential for executing them.

The fact that peacekeeping is conducted by military people, together with their commitment in this role to non-threatening and impartial behaviour, can suggest that the activity is above politics. Peacekeeping's general function of helping to maintain peace might also encourage some to reach this conclusion. But this is a very misleading line of thought. Chiefly, it stems from a failure to pay enough attention to the context within which peacekeeping takes place. For while those who do the actual job of peacekeeping are in no way grinding their own collective axe, and are embarked on an enterprise which is widely regarded as 'good', the factors which account for their having been given the job are very much of a political kind.

At bottom, the establishment of a peacekeeping operation represents the decision of a number of states to lend a hand to one or more of their fellows who are in some sort of need or trouble, and a willingness on the part of the potential consumers of peacekeeping to accept it. The maintenance of such an operation depends on the continuing affirmation of all these sentiments. The situation to which they relate, however, bears on no less a matter than the maintenance of peace. It will therefore certainly be seen as having considerable significance by the local parties; and others at some geographical distance from it may very possibly evince a keen interest in the matter. All of them will be looking at it from their individual points of view, which will have been shaped by their own conceptions of what is best for each of them. In other words, it will be seen in a sharp political light. In consequence, it is by no means to be assumed that the responses of all concerned will generally point in the same direction.

So far as the disputants are concerned, it may be that one or both of them (assuming the matter to have a bilateral complexion) are very far from interested in the creation or bolstering of peace, let alone in the presence of a peacekeeping body. Even if a period of fighting has been avoided or brought to a conclusion, either or both of the states concerned may have little enthusiasm for the idea of involving a multinational third party in their affairs. In respect of sensitive issues, outsiders are often unwelcome, and the prospect of playing host to foreign soldiers, however high minded, is usually viewed with particular caution. The possibly adverse domestic repercussions of so doing may weigh with the potential host, and a number of very imaginable international disadvantages will almost certainly enter its mind. A non-host disputant may also be influenced by some of these negative considerations. Thus, when peacekeepers are accepted, it is virtually always the result of their being seen, by those who are to accommodate or cooperate with them, as the lesser of the available evils. Those immediately concerned will have taken their decisions about the suggested operation in the light of its impact on their positions and policies, at both the domestic and international levels, and on balance have decided on a positive response. Peacekeeping's most basic contextual requirement will have been met as the result of calculations which are political through and through.

Some of the other contextual requirements of peacekeeping are also of a powerfully political nature. The question for a particular state of whether it should offer, or accept, an invitation to contribute troops to a peacekeeping body does not usually give rise to political problems. But it may do so. The question of which states should be invited to contribute to a peacekeeping operation, or whose offers should be accepted, is often intensely political. The potential host state may have very strong views on this matter. Formally speaking, it does not possess a veto in this regard. But as a practical matter it can prevent the inclusion of nationalities it does not like, at least so far as serving on its own soil is concerned. Peacekeeping also, of course, needs money. The UN's peacekeeping work has been in financial difficulty almost from the very beginning, chiefly due to the political objections of some states to aspects of certain operations.

It is, however, in relation to decisions to establish (and, usually to a lesser extent, to continue) peacekeeping operations that political factors are both most visible and most important. For without such authorizations peacekeeping will not exist at all. It is true that the existence of such operations also depends on the agreement of the host state(s). But when the establishment of a peacekeeping operation is in issue, the potential host is often in a great predicament, and thus has very little political leeway. Those who have the responsibility of taking the enabling decision, however, may well be considering the matter in circumstances which, while not without urgency, are also multi-faceted. Pressures on and by them may be received and exerted in a variety of directions, making their political situation more complex and open-ended than that of the potential host or hosts.

It may be, for example, that some states who are of consequence in this process may have little or no desire to see the disputants helped out. The UN Security Council is the body which has had most to do with the setting up and continuation of peacekeeping operations, and any one of the Council's five permanent member states is in a position to block the process. They are also well placed to delay the point of decision.

In other circumstances, however, key outsiders may move with considerable speed. Some of them may have individual national interests at stake, which they may see as best protected by the presence of a peacekeeping body. Or a situation may be perceived as about to give rise to a more widespread danger, the curbing of which may lend great haste to the deliberations about a peacekeeping body. In either kind of case, the potential host may find itself under sharp pressure to go along with the idea that a peacekeeping body be established on its soil. In yet other circumstances, there may be a fairly general feeling – which can probably be related to specific political considerations – that the international society as a whole has some responsibility for taking peacekeeping action.

THE ANALYTICAL SCHEME

The fullest perspective on peacekeeping, therefore, is one which places it firmly in the context of international politics. And that perspective is sharpened by a process of categorization which draws the mind's eye to a key political feature of a set of operations (including proposals for operations which failed to bear fruit). In this work it is the broad political circumstances which have given rise to peacekeeping operations which provide the basis for the categorizing scheme, which has five Parts. The case for classifying a particular operation (or proposal) in one group rather than another will be developed when the operation is discussed, attention then also being paid to the other political factors which have influenced an operation's activity and success. An operation may, of course, change its salient political characteristics over the course of its life – although, as a matter of fact, that has not here presented much of a problem.

The first category (Part I) is made up of back-yard operations – those which take place within the sphere of influence of a major power. Given the facts of international life, such operations are likely to be either in the nature of that power's intervention in its tenants' affairs, although in a relatively acceptable form, or activity which is conducted with its blessing and encouragement. On one or two occasions, however, the power's tenants or rivals have succeeded in highlighting embarrassing situations by means of operations which are at least ostensibly of a peacekeeping nature.

Moving away from the hierarchical privacy of the back yard to the more egalitarian intimacy of the clubhouse, the second category (Part II) deals with peacekeeping operations arranged by a group of states to deal with an intra-group problem. To assist one or more of their fellows, and maybe to alleviate their own vexation, the matter is being sorted out within the club. Naturally, if the club is one with members of varying consequence, its more influential members can be expected to take the lead on these occasions, notwithstanding the principle of equality on which it is formally based.

Thirdly, comes the category of neighbourhood quarrels (Part III). These are relatively public affairs, which may also attract a good deal of outside attention. But they do not arouse the proprietarial action of an overshadowing power or the concern of an in-group. Nor do they cause others great embarrassment or alarm. They are just indicative of troublesome residents. The latter may be told rather sharply to behave themselves, and certainly helped to do so. But if they go on bothering the neighbourhood, others are unlikely to lose a lot of sleep. Soundproofing is one thing which the international village does rather well.

When, however, states leave their own localities and associations for the international high street, they sometimes succeed only in doing others, or themselves, a mischief (Part IV). This can cause considerable embarrassment, both to the states concerned and to their friends and fellow club members. Often they have to get home on peacekeeping crutches, perhaps in consequence of urgent advice from interested parties or perhaps in the manner of the prodigal who has come to the end of his resources.

Finally, there are occasions when states behave rather in the manner of reckless drivers at a crossroads, giving rise at least to the possibility of a minor accident and maybe to a much more extensive conflagration (Part V). In these circumstances the other members of the community, with the leading citizens almost certainly to the fore – except for any who happen themselves to be drunk at the wheel – are likely to press strongly for emergency control measures to be taken. Peacekeepers could well be sent to the scene, and may stay on in the hope of exerting a sobering influence at the dangerous crossroads.

These are not just theoretical possibilities. Peacekeeping operations have appeared across the whole gamut of international conflicts, and they are neither particularly sparse in number nor unevenly spread. Parts I, II, IV and V of this book contain almost exactly the same number of Sections and Part III is not numerically far behind. In all, 57 varieties (for some, an evocative number) are considered. Some deal with peacekeeping proposals which were made but not adopted or which are currently under discussion, a few with bodies whose peacekeeping status is doubtful or whose character changed over time, and one with a force whose claim to be engaged on peacekeeping must be rejected. On the other hand, a number of the sections deal with a group of associated operations, so that about 75 individual peacekeeping activities can be identified. Of these no less than five have been established between April 1988 and November 1989, all by the UN: in respect of Afghanistan, Iran–Iraq, Angola, Namibia, and Central America. The Angolan–South African situation also saw the parties setting up two other bodies of at least a quasi-peacekeeping kind. Furthermore, in March 1990 the UN's Central American peacekeeping body was given the additional responsibility of supervising the demobilization of the anti-Nicaraguan Contras. And during the first half of 1990 two more peacekeeping proposals, both of them very extensive, were continuing to receive close discussion – concerning the ending of the war over Western Sahara and the internal conflict in Cambodia.

Many of these bodies were small, and many were in operation for only a limited period. Nonetheless, the wide range of political disputes to which they were sent offers impressive testimony to peacekeeping's flexibility. The quite considerable use which has been made of military people in a non-threatening and impartial way also suggests that states have found the device of value when they wish to wind down the intensity of international conflicts and problems, or even wind them up. In the case studies which follow these issues will be explored.

FURTHER READING

Dag Hammarskjöld, 'The UNEF Experience Report', in Andrew W. Cordier and Wilder Foote (eds), *The Public Papers of the Secretaries-General of the United Nations, Vol. IV: Dag Hammarskjöld 1958–1960* (New York: Columbia University Press, 1974).

Alan James, 'Unit-Veto Dominance in UN Peacekeeping', in Lawrence S. Finkelstein (ed.), *Politics in the United Nations System after Forty Years* (Durham, NC: Duke University Press, 1988).

Alan James, 'Paying for Peacekeeping', in David P. Forsythe (ed.), *The United Nations in the World Political Economy.* (London: Macmillan, 1989).

Alan James, 'Peacekeeping and the Parties', in Indar Jit Rikhye and Kjell Skjelsbaek (eds), *The United Nations and Peacekeeping* (London: Macmillan, 1990) (reprinted in a revised form in *Political Studies*, XXXVIII (2) (July 1990).

Anthony Parsons, 'The United Nations and International Security in the 1980s', *Millennium: Journal of International Studies*, 12 (2) (Summer 1983).

Anthony Parsons and Alan James, *The United Nations and the Quest for Peace* (Cardiff: Welsh Centre for International Affairs, 1986).

Brian Urquhart, *A Life in Peace and War* (London: Wiedenfeld and Nicolson, 1987).

Part I
Back-yard Problems

Introduction: Peacekeepers in the Back Yard

A back yard, in political terms, may be conceived as an area which is widely regarded and locally treated as very much within the sway of an adjacent major power, or group of powers. The central fact about a political back yard, therefore, is that it is viewed possessively by the relevant power or powers. It is in the nature of a sphere of influence or an exclusive region, where there is a marked imbalance of strength. Accordingly, it is an area in which outsiders are expected to respect the controlling position of the dominant state(s). And in the very possible event of a big stick being carried by the leader(s), it behoves outsiders as well as lesser insiders to walk warily and with deference.

It might be supposed that political back yards are not a wholly welcoming environment for peacekeeping which is done in the name of a universal or a quasi-universal international organization. For dominant powers are unlikely to take kindly to the idea of distantly-controlled and politically-variegated bodies of impartial military men establishing a presence within 'their' areas. Such operations might be well-intentioned and fairly harmless, but even the thought of them is distinctly uncongenial. As dominant powers are likely to be well placed within a universal organization, it would be surprising if such bodies made much peacekeeping headway in the more private parts of political domains. The UN's experience supports this expectation.

The 12 back-yard issues which are considered in Part I fall into two clearly distinct categories. Firstly, there are five cases, or groups of cases, which relate to the post-First World War settlement and its immediate aftermath. At this time the victors were able to exercise political control over much of Europe, and by way of settling some of the numerous problems and disputes which arose they had resort to devices which, with hindsight, are recognizably of a peacekeeping kind. It might be thought that the context was hardly that which gives rise to peacekeeping, especially with regard to the operations which are discussed in the first two, generic, Sections (A and B). For here the victors were making arrangements for the drawing of frontiers, and the states directly concerned had little option but to accept what was on offer. Imposition rather than cooperation and consent was the order of the day. But the affected states had given their formal consent to what was to go on, and in international relations generally, and particularly in back yards, consent commonly has less about it of free choice than might be supposed. Moreover, in these cases the victors were on the whole trying to act impartially in implementing their principles, and their peacekeeping agents on the ground were certainly so engaged.

Section A deals chiefly with the frontier delimitation commissions which were set up after the First World War by the Conference of Ambassadors. This Conference was established to interpret and execute the peace treaties between the victorious powers and the defeated European powers, and one such task was to turn some conference-room maps into reality on the ground. The military officers who acted for the Conference in this respect were helping to settle these issues, and so were playing a part in the pacification of Europe. They provide a very useful reminder that the employment of multinational military teams to engage in impartial and non-threatening activity is not an idea which was stumbled on only after the Second World War. Section A also takes note of another form which peacekeeping may take – the administration of territory, in this case of the about-to-be Free City of Danzig.

Section B underlines the point that the phenomenon called peacekeeping has a history which considerably predates its conceptualization. Additionally, Section B has the merit of drawing attention to a rather different type of activity which may be conducted on the basis of what were to become known as the principles of peacekeeping: the use of multinational forces in a law and order role. For in respect of a number of areas the peace treaties provided for the holding of plebiscites so that frontiers could be drawn in the light of accurate intelligence about the wishes of the people concerned. This was to be the job of plebiscite commissions, and for the maintenance of order during these interregnums inter-allied forces were supplied.

The remaining three cases in this first category (Sections C–E) largely have to do with activity of the new League of Nations. The League was by no means the mere mouthpiece of the victorious European powers, but it was nonetheless a 'safe' organ for them to use, or to see used, in the resolution of certain difficulties. One such was the conflict between Lithuania and Poland which focused on the historic city of Vilna (Section C). It led to the establishment in 1920 of a military commission and to a subsequent plan to have a plebiscite which would be watched over by an international force – although in the event nothing came of this scheme, and Poland retained the city. As if by way of compensation, in 1923 Lithuania effectually annexed Memel, which had been administered by the Allies since the end of the War. Meanwhile, in 1921, a League commission of enquiry checked on the withdrawal of Yugoslav troops from Albanian territory (Section D).

The final inter-war case of back-yard peacekeeping is often regarded as a classic example of how an international organization can nip a conflict in the bud. It arises out of the role of the League of Nations in respect of the Greco–Bulgarian frontier dispute of 1925, when military officers were despatched to report on whether the combatants had complied with the call of the League to cease fire and withdraw (Section E). The real political significance of the case emerges, however, only when it is borne in mind that the area was to all intents and purposes in the Anglo–French back yard, and that these two states were at that time the leading members of the League.

The seven cases, or groups of cases, in the second category (Sections F–L) all relate to peacekeeping activity or propsals since the Second World War in the back yard of the United States – in Latin, and more particularly, Central America. In these instances the institution which has overwhelmingly been looked to for peacekeeping help is the Organization of American States (OAS). For most of the period the United States was but one of that body's 21 members, but she was so far and away the most powerful of them that the Organization was most unlikely to be unresponsive to her strongly-held views about what should be done. Effectively, therefore, the OAS was to a large extent under her control. This meant that it could suitably be used by the United States for any peacekeeping initiatives which seemed appropriate.

The possible occasions for such moves were not likely to be entirely lacking, as there were a number of latent border disputes in Latin America, its frontier areas were not always under firm control, and the general position of the United States was that any fighting should quickly be stopped. Generally, too, the Latin American states were committed both to the maintenance of existing borders and to the pacific settlement of disputes. However, on account of the United States' dominance, they were not as a rule over-keen on her involvement, and in some states there was a distrust of the military. Furthermore, many of the states in the region are small, and many frontiers run along difficult terrain. It was therefore perhaps unlikely that there would be a great deal of peacekeeping activity here, or that it would usually be on more than a small scale. But some operations were to be expected, and it is perhaps not surprising that almost all of them relate to the smaller states of Central America and the Caribbean.

Disputes between Costa Rica and Nicaragua gave rise to no fewer than three peacekeeping missions (Section G), the first two of which arose out of allegations by Costa Rica that Nicaragua was plotting to overthrow her government. Another such mission stemmed from Nicaraguan charges of aggression by Honduras (Section H). In a quite separate Honduran–Nicaraguan context a UN peacekeeping mission was being mooted in 1989, an associated non-peacekeeping body was actually sent to Nicaragua, and in a somewhat wider Central American framework a UN observer group was established in November of that year (Section L). Much earlier, a small commotion in Panama attracted peacekeeping attention (Section I), and Honduras's rumbling tension with El Salvador elicited further peacekeeping arrangements (Section K). In South America, border fighting between Ecuador and Peru (Section F) produced at least a token peacekeeping body. But it was the perceived possibility of a political upset in the sensitive Caribbean which gave rise to the only occasion on which a peacekeeping force (as distinct from a body of observers) has deployed in the United States' back yard.

That state had intervened massively in the Dominican Republic in 1965 (Section J), and managed – just – to secure the imprimatur of the OAS for the translation of her force into an inter-American one. This cosmetic arrangement did not carry with it any peacekeeping credentials for the Force. But at more or less the same time the function of the Force began to change in a peacekeeping direction, and within a few more months it had assumed a full-blown peacekeeping role. Sitting alongside this Force was a tiny UN body, which had managed to secure admittance to the Dominican Republic not long after the United States' troops had arrived. Its mandate was to provide an independent report on the much-criticized American enterprise. The UN claims this body – which included a few military men – as an instance of peacekeeping. But on that another view is possible.

A question which presents itself is why there have been no cases of peacekeeping in the other great back yard of the post-Second World War world – that of the Soviet Union in East Europe. The wholesale re-drawing of the political map which took place there after 1919 by no means removed all potential border disputes, and the later espousal – in one way or another – of communism by these states cannot be assumed to have erased national animosities. But thus far they have never required the assistance of a peacekeeping body, not even of the most private, back-yard, kind.

To have admitted the need for such a body would surely have been a bitter pill for these states to swallow, as it would all too obviously advertise the fact that two ideological brethren were finding it difficult to live peacefully together. But the reason why it has not been necessary to take this particular form of medicine is that, prior to 1989, difficulties of the sort which can be ameliorated by the device of peacekeeping have just not arisen in the Soviet back yard. There have been serious worries for the Soviet Union arising out of the wavering political rectitude of some of her satellites. But they were settled, in a manner of speaking, by brutal intervention in Hungary in 1956 and in Czechoslovakia in 1968 – and by the threat of it in respect of Poland in the early 1980s. What might be seen as the more usual sort of international disputes, however, have not appeared.

This is partly due to the tight discipline which the Soviet Union has exercised. But chiefly it reflects the totalitarian nature of the states concerned, which has enabled them to keep all aspects of their national lives under very close control, and to be particularly vigilant at their borders. It must not be assumed, however, that this pattern will necessarily continue. Politics is an any event always full of surprises, and as the more relaxed policies of the Gorbachev regime seep through, with momentous effect, to the lesser members of the bloc there could be upsetting consequences for inter-state relations within the region. In which case the current willingness of the Soviet Union to make use of peacekeeping in the international high street could conceivably be matched by the appearance of a peacekeeping body or two in her own back yard.

A larger question is whether the recent upheavals have altered the political condition of East Europe from that of a back yard to something more in the nature of a clubhouse – and perhaps not even that. An interesting twist was added to this possibility by Hungary's proposal of September 1989 for the reduction of offensive weapons in a 60-mile zone straddling her borders with Austria and Yugoslavia. As of June 1990 it is too early to do other than simply raise this question in a tentative way. But what can be said is that recent events have certainly not made East Europe less hospitable to peacekeeping than it has been in the past.

Section A The Re-drawing of Some European Frontiers After the First World War (1920–1925) and the Temporary Allied Administration of Danzig (1920)

THE NEW EUROPEAN FRONTIERS

The four treaties which brought the First World War to a formal end in Europe re-drew the political map on a truly heroic scale. Many changes were made to frontiers between existing states, some long-dead states were resurrected, and several new ones were created. To translate these pen and ink decisions into frontier lines on the ground, provision was made in each treaty for the establishment by the victorious powers of a number of delimitation commissions. However, detailed arrangements had to be made for the functioning of each of these bodies; it was necessary for them to report back to an organ representing the signatories to the peace treaty from which they derived their authority; and a means had to be found of dealing with the political issues which might well arise in the course of their activity.

To handle all these matters, and many more besides, a Conference of Ambassadors was set up in Paris to act on behalf of the Principal

23

Allied and Associated Powers in all matters concerning the execution and interpretation of the peace treaties. In addition to the French representative, it consisted of the ambassadors in Paris of Great Britain, Italy and Japan – the principal 'allied' powers. It had been assumed that the United States – the power which had been 'associated' with them during the later stages of the war (not allied because of the American antipathy towards alliances) – would also participate. But due to that state's refusal to ratify the treaty with Germany the American ambassador took no formal part in the proceedings.

The delimitation commissions consisted of military officers from each of the states represented in the Conference of Ambassadors (although it is not clear whether Japan played a full part in this aspect of its activities). Some such bodies were necessary to give reality to the re-drawn map of Europe, and the work of the commissions in this respect during the first half of the 1920s was undoubtedly of great value. Among the frontiers, or parts of frontiers, which were dealt with in this way were those of Albania/Yugoslavia/Greece, Austria/Hungary, Poland/Czechoslovakia, Belgium/Germany, Poland/Germany, and Czechoslovakia/Poland/Germany (see Map 1).

From one point of view this activity was rather far from what later became known as peacekeeping, inasmuch as it was based on a series of imposed peaces and took place on the territory of sometimes reluctantly-cooperative states. But settlements rarely emerge without some kinds of pressure, and those who act as hosts to peacekeepers often have some private unease about their presence. Furthermore, formal consent to the new arrangements had been given, and what the commissions were doing in the field was impartially marking out the agreed frontiers.

From another angle, therefore, the delimitation commissions can be seen as having characteristics which are much in line with those of peacekeeping. It happens that the redrawing of frontiers of adjacent sovereign states and the creation of new states out of the metropolitan territory of old ones has gone resoundingly out of fashion since the imposed redrawing of some East European boundaries which arose out of the Second World War. But were it to happen, the necessity of implementation mechanisms along the lines of the delimitation commissions which reported to the Conference of Ambassadors would soon be evident. Whether they were best seen as operating in someone's political back yard – as the earlier commissions certainly were – would depend on the particular circumstances of each case. But it is most unlikely that many would choke over describing them as instances of peacekeeping.

Map 1   Central European frontiers after the First World War

DANZIG

At the negotiations over the peace treaty with Germany there was much discussion regarding Danzig. It was an overwhelmingly German city with about 200,000 inhabitants, but was hotly claimed by Poland on both historical and economic grounds – the latter point relating to the role it could play as Poland's only significant port. The outcome was the compromise decision that the city and the immediately surrounding area should be established as an autonomous Free City, which was to be placed under what was optimistically called the 'guarantee' of the League of Nations.

Pending the negotiation of a treaty between Poland and Danzig to settle the details of their relationship, the territory was to be under the control of the Principal Allied and Associated Powers. On their behalf a senior British diplomat was appointed as its Administrator, and two battalions of Allied troops, one British and the other French, were stationed in Danzig under the command of a British General. This arrangement lasted from February to November 1920, at which date the Free City was constituted and the Allied administration and troops were withdrawn. They had served as a necessary interim means of maintaining law and order whilst the implementation of the principles set out in the peace treaty was being agreed. At a later date their role would almost certainly have been characterized as an example of peacekeeping.

Notwithstanding the provisions which had been made for Poland's rights and interests in the port of Danzig to be maintained and for Danzig's foreign relations to be conducted by Poland, that state was far from satisfied with the outcome. Germany, however, was no less dissatisfied, and as, in time, she began to assert herself in central Europe, the maintenance of the arrangement which was consequential upon her defeat looked increasingly problematical. In 1939 relations between Germany and Poland became the focus of Europe's lurch towards war, and one of the two main issues between those states was the status of Danzig. It was soon reoccupied by German troops.

However, Germany's further defeat resulted in a clarification of the situation in favour of Poland. Danzig was included within the revised boundaries of that state, and renamed Gdansk. The fact that the anti-totalitarian Solidarity movement which emerged in Poland in the 1980s was based in the former Free City may perhaps be regarded as apt.

FURTHER READING

Gerhard P. Pink, 'The Conference of Ambassadors' (Geneva Research Centre, *Geneva Studies*, XII (4–5), February 1942).

H. W. V. Temperley (ed.), *A History of the Peace Conference of Paris* (London: Henry Frowde and Hodder and Stoughton, 6 vols, 1920–1924).

Arnold J. Toynbee, *Survey of International Affairs, 1920–1923* (London: Oxford University Press, 1925).

Section B The Inter-Allied Plebiscite Forces (1920–1922)

As part of their endeavour to draw the boundaries of central and eastern Europe on a national basis, the victors in the First World War made provision in the several peace treaties (or subsequently) for plebiscites to be held in certain areas which gave rise to particular difficulty. They were to be arranged and conducted by inter-allied commisions, which usually were to take charge of the relevant areas for such time as was necessary. In the event, not all the proposed plebiscites took place, but five did occur. In connection with four of them an international force was placed under the plebiscite commission to guarantee public order and ensure a fair poll, and the same end was sought in respect of the fifth by the use of individual military officers.

The employment of international military personnel in these ways were early and rather special instances of peacekeeping, operating in what was then very much the victors' back yard. All the states concerned had formally consented to the holding of plebiscites through their signatures to and ratifications of the peace treaties, and as a practical matter they had little option but to make way for and cooperate with the inter-allied arrangements. It was very possible that the maintenance of order in the plebiscite areas could necessitate the use of force, especially as some of the areas were very far from settled. But provided this was done only to contain competing or disruptive elements, and not to assist one of them against another, it would be in accord with the principles of what later became known as peacekeeping. For peacekeeping takes account of the fact that the impartial maintenance of internal law and order sometimes requires resort to force. And in respect of these disputes, the provision of international forces and officers equipped to meet that contingency was an integral part of the schemes for their pacific settlement (see Map 2).

27

Map 2 Plebiscite Areas under the 1919 peace settlement

SCHLESWIG

This ex-duchy, which had been so complicatedly troublesome to European chancelleries during much of the nineteenth century, now made yet another appearance on the international stage. It was about 2,000 square miles in area and contained about 270,000 people. It had been annexed by Prussia in 1864, and the question in 1920 was whether that act was to be wholly or partly undone. An International Plebiscite Commission composed of the representatives of Britain, France, Norway and Sweden arrived in January, supported by an International Force of 3,000 British and French men – but, because of the failure of the United States to ratify the peace treaty, without the American battalion for which provision had been made in the original plan. A good number of its personnel were naval, as British ships lying offshore formed part of the British-led force. Plebiscites were held in February and March, as a result of which the Commission recommended to the Conference of Ambassadors that the territory be divided between Denmark and Germany. This proposal was endorsed, and in May 1920 the appropriate dispositions were made and the International Force left. Unlike many other territorial rearrangements which were made in consequence of the First World War, this one appeared to be settled for good.

ALLENSTEIN AND MARIENWERDER

This large area in East Prussia, getting on for 6,000 square miles in extent and having a population of about 700,000, was claimed by both Germany and Poland. It lay to the north and north-west of Warsaw, and immediately to the east of the River Vistula, gaining strategic significance from its position on the River. Two Plebiscite Commissions were appointed, each made up of Britain, France, Italy and Japan, and an International Force of about 2,000 was organized in their support. Chiefly, the Force was constituted by British and Italian troops, but there was also a small French contingent. Two plebiscites were held in July 1920. To the chagrin of Poland, the vote went overwhelmingly in favour of Germany in both areas – to whom, accordingly, most of the territory went. Nowadays, however, in consequence of further change in what used to be a politically fluid region (but this time without the benefit of plebiscites), the names on the map read Olsztyn and Kwidzyn.

THE KLAGENFURT BASIN

Austria and Yugoslavia were the claimants to this area, which was about 750 square miles in extent and contained about 125,000 people. The relevant Peace Treaty provided for plebiscites by zones: if the vote in Zone 1 went in favour of Yugoslavia a vote would then be held in Zone 2; but if the first vote was in favour of Austria, no vote would be held in Zone 2, and the whole area would be included within Austria.

Unlike the other Plebiscite Commissions, this one was neither to administer the area directly nor was it to have an international force at its disposal. However, a number of British, French and Italian officers (the Commisson being made up of these states) were to check that the plebiscite was conducted in accordance with the Commission's orders, and watch over the electoral arrangements and the general behaviour of the local Austrian and Yugoslav administrators. As the first voting day – 10 October 1920 – approached, the Commission decided that this was not enough, and asked for Allied troops to ensure a free and fair poll. The Conference of Ambassadors turned down this request, but did send an extra 58 officers, mostly Italian but including some British and French. Thus Allied officers were present at all the polling stations and also at important entrances to the Zone. This proved sufficient, and a smooth vote produced a majority in favour of Austria. Thus there was no need for a test of opinion in Zone 2, and the whole area went to Austria.

UPPER SILESIA

This was by far the most populous, and wealthy, plebiscite area, having about $2\frac{1}{4}$ million people and being about 4,000 square miles in extent. It was claimed by both about-to-be-diminished Germany and resurrected Poland. After much diplomatic in-fighting, the victors' decision was that the issue should be settled by a plebiscite, to be conducted by an Inter-Allied Commission in the presence of an International Force which was to maintain order throughout what was to be a relatively lengthy interim period.

A Franco–British–Italian Commission went to Upper Silesia as soon as the peace treaty came into effect – January 1920 – and included army officers who were put in charge of the local police. While, however, Britain participated in this aspect of the work, she was reluctant to send battalions of troops, so the International Force which accompanied the Commission was composed only of 11,500 French and 2,000 Italian troops. But as the French elements in the Force, in line with their country's policy, showed a noticeable partiality for the Poles, Britain sent 2,000 soldiers to join the Force shortly before the vote was held.

Poland had been confident of winning, but was proved over-confident. For in the March 1921 plebiscite, Germany obtained well over half the votes. This put the Conference of Ambassadors in a dilemma. France spoke up vigorously for Poland's claims, but Britain and Italy responded strongly in favour of Germany. Unable to resolve the matter, the Conference passed it over to the League of Nations Council in August 1921, promising to accept its decision. Waiting journalists laughed incredulously when told of this turn of events. For, quite apart from the spectacle of the great powers deferring to the new-fangled international organization, they very reasonably wondered how the chief members of the Council would agree given that they had failed to do so in their capacity as members of the Conference of Ambassadors. In the event, however, the League Council produced a partition plan for Upper Silesia which worked very successfully. On the division of the territory between Germany and Poland in May 1922, the International Force disbanded.

The problem for the victorious powers in trying to settle this dispute was not that it lay outside their collective back yard, but that the mechanism they first adopted produced a surprising result – which in turn led to major differences between them as to how they should proceed. These differences reflected the keen anxiety of France, even on the morrow of victory, about the potential German threat to her security, and the more relaxed attitude which the other victors were able to take to their defeated foe. More generally, the whole episode was a reminder, in several respects, that no possible development can be excluded from the political realm. And so far as the pacific settlement of disputes was concerned, it underlined the fact that success depends on the cooperation of the relevant parties – notable amongst whom, in this case, were influential outsiders – which cannot be created merely by the employment of a peacekeeping device.

SOPRON

The Treaty of Trianon had provided that this 80-square-mile area on the Austrian–Hungarian border, with a population of about 50,000, should go to Austria. Later, however, it was agreed that the matter

should be decided by a plebiscite. Immediately prior to its being held
in December 1921 an International Force of 450 men was brought into
the area from the Upper Silesian Force. This was perhaps too little too
late, for there were many seemingly justified allegations of malpractice
on the part of the Hungarians which, to many eyes, accounted for the
vote going in their favour. Austria protested, but the Conference of
Ambassadors ruled that the boundary should be drawn in Hungary's
favour. The international soldiers then returned to Upper Silesia, having
spent just four weeks in Sopron. Developments since 1921 have not
favoured the reopening of the question, but in Austria it can still arouse
some feeling.

FURTHER READING

J. W. Headlam-Morley, 'Memorandum respecting Upper Silesia at the Peace
    Conference and the Upper Silesian Plebiscite', printed as Document No
    13 in W. N. Medlicott *et al.* (eds), *Documents on British Foreign Policy
    1919–1939*, First Series, Vol XVI (London: Her Majesty's Stationery
    Office, 1968).
Sarah Wambaugh, *Plebiscites since the World War* (Washington, DC: Carnegie
    Endowment for International Peace, 2 vols, 1933).
See also the Further Reading for Section A.

Section C The Dispute Over Vilna (1920–1922) and the Question of Memel (1920–1924)

VILNA

At the end of the First World War, the victorious powers provisionally assigned Vilna, the historic capital of Lithuania, to that resurrected state, and the new Soviet regime – the former overlord – concurred. But the majority of Vilna's inhabitants were Poles, and Poland (another resurrected state) claimed the city on that ground. She took the matter to the League of Nations which, with the agreement of the parties, established a Military Commission to watch over the provisional boundary line. It was composed of military officers from Britain, France, Italy, Japan and Spain, and persuaded each party to withdraw from the provisional line for a distance of four miles. However, no sooner had this been done than irregular Polish forces marched on Vilna, causing the Lithuanians to flee. The Military Commission came into action once again, negotiating a new neutral zone between Lithuania and Poland's unofficial forces as well as confirming the old one.

The matter now went back to the League, which had to consider it in the light of an increasing Polish tendency to 'adopt' the unofficial occupation of Vilna. A plebiscite was proposed, to take place under the supervision of an international force organized by the League, and on condition that the irregular Polish forces withdrew. Poland was not too happy about this, but gradually warmed to it, no doubt because of the majority of Poles in the city. Lithuania, on the other hand, became less enamoured of the idea, and spoke (as Poland had done elsewhere)

33

of the superiority of the historic over the democratic principle (see Map 3).

Meanwhile, planning for the international force went ahead. Belgium, Britain, France and Spain offered to participate, and six more states were asked to do so: Denmark, Greece, Italy, Netherlands, Norway and Sweden. All responded positively, at least in principle, and it was anticipated that the force would consist of about 1,800 men. However, Lithuania's prevarications accumulated, and to them was added a Soviet objection to the presence of an international force so near her borders. For good measure, Switzerland refused to allow some of the contingents to pass through her territory. As a result the intended contributors began to get cold feet: most of them were in very much a post-War frame of mind and were not disposed to take any risks in respect of a dispute which, by contemporary means of communication, was far away and of which it could certainly be said that their people knew nothing. Thus in March 1921 the idea of a plebiscite was dropped and the matter handed back to the immediate parties for settlement with the assistance

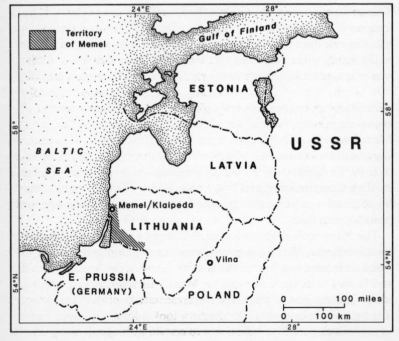

Map 3   The post-First World War territorial settlement in the Baltic region

of a mediator. This meant that Vilna remained in the hands of Poland, who called it Wilno.

The League's Military Commission stayed in the area for a further year with a view to exercising a calming influence. Earlier, its role had been partly that of crisis defusion and partly that of stabilization, and it had achieved a certain amount of success in both respects. However, its success was limited, partly due to the uncooperative attitude of the parties but also because the dispute was on the margins of the victorious powers' back yard. Furthermore, France was particularly reluctant to do anything which would offend Poland. Altogether, the episode reflected the point that peacekeeping can only make a contribution towards the containment or resolution of a dispute if the parties are inclined in that direction. And it underlined the fact that, so far as settlement is concerned, territorial disputes are particularly intractable.

MEMEL

This territory on the north bank of the River Niemen was about 70 miles long and varied between 10 and 20 miles in breadth. Germany was made to renounce her sovereignty over it and its disposition was placed in the hands of the Allied and Associated Powers. The town of Memel was overwhelmingly German in character but the population of the rest of the territory was ethnically Lithuanian, about half of the agricultural population also speaking the Lithuanian language. For economic reasons, too, it was claimed by Lithuania, as the town of Memel was her only possible port. However, Lithuania's boundaries were far from settled, and Memel's administration was therefore taken over by the Allies. On their behalf a French national was appointed as its High Commissioner, and three companies of French troops were at his disposal – acting as what would now be called a law and order peacekeeping force.

The Allies took their time over deciding what to do about Memel. In consequence, their administration of the territory lasted until 1923, when their hand was forced. At that date, Lithuania, having lost Vilna and fearing an adverse decision on Memel, marched in and, after some street fighting, ejected the French representatives of the Allied Powers. The formal disposition of the territory took a little more time, because of a deadlock over Poland's claim to certain privileges in the port. The matter was passed to the League of Nations, and an agreement was reached in 1924 by which Memel became Lithuanian – and was renamed Klaipeda.

POSTSCRIPT

In March 1939 Lithuania was forced to cede the territory of Memel to Germany, the event being marked by the arrival of the Führer himself and the whole German battle fleet. At the end of the Second World War the territory was restored to Lithuania (the town of Memel once again appearing on the map as Klaipeda). But by that time Lithuania had been annexed by the Soviet Union.

When, at the start of the Second World War, Poland was carved up between Germany and the supposedly neutral Soviet Union, Vilna (henceforth known as Vilnius) was restored to Lithuania by the Soviets. But in 1940 the Soviet Union forcefully incorporated Lithuania into her own domain, and after the War Lithuanian nationalism was powerfully discouraged. In the liberal Soviet atmosphere of the late 1980s it has explosively reappeared. Whether Vilnius will re-emerge as the capital of a sovereign Lithuania remains to be seen. It would be a truly remarkable happening. If it did occur, there is also an outside chance that the preceding events would include the actual arrival, 70 years on, of an international plebiscitary team in Vilnius.

FURTHER READING

F. P. Walters, *A History of the League of Nations* (London: Oxford University Press, 1952, 2 vols; reprinted in 1960 and subsequently as 1 volume).

Sarah Wambaugh, *Plebiscites since the World War* (Washington, DC: Carnegie Endowment for International Peace, 2 vols, 1933).

See also the Further Reading for Section A.

Section D   Albania
(1921–1923)

In 1913, the European powers had declared Albania to be a sovereign state, but her independence was far from secure as parts of her territory were eyed covetously by various neighbours. The First World War broke out before her frontiers could be clearly established, and the end of the War found troops from three foreign states on ground which Albania claimed as hers. Italy withdrew, but Greek and Yugoslav forces remained (giving rise to periodic skirmishing). Albania became increasingly dissatisfied with the procrastination of the Conference of Ambassadors, to which the boundary question had been passed, and in 1921 took her grievance to the Assembly of the League.

Here she found much sympathy for her plight and, although the great powers clearly wished to be left to themselves, the Assembly asked the Council to send a Commission of Enquiry to Albania, which it did in October 1921. It was composed of military officers from Norway and Luxembourg (thus permitting it to be categorized as a peacekeeping operation) and a professor from Finland. Its task was to report on the disturbances and supervise the execution of the frontier decision once it had been taken. The Commission was therefore a curious instance of the major powers in their capacity as Council members setting up a body to speed their own action when wearing a different set of hats. For although most League members hoped the Commission would deter aggressive action against Albania, it was also seen as a means of expediting a decision about her frontiers (see Map 4).

However, the achievement of both these goals depended far more on the great powers than on the Commission. And, for whatever reason, they bestirred themselves. A frontier decision was taken; a delimitation commission despatched to implement it; to facilitate this, the parties were told that they should establish a 25-mile-wide demarcation zone (within which the delimitation commission would operate); and Britain called for economic sanctions against Yugoslavia (who had recently made a significant incursion into Albania) if she continued to misbehave. Manifestly, it was not just the frontier but also the powers' back yard which was being mapped out. And the key to that part of the yard was to be looked after by Italy. In words which were rather ominous to an

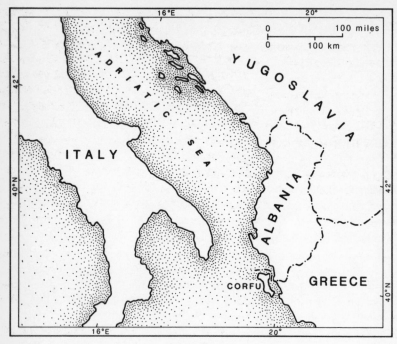

Map 4   Albania

Albanian ear, the powers said that if she ever needed help in the preservation of her territorial integrity, they would favour entrusting that responsibility to Italy.

In this new situation, the terms of reference of the Council's Commission of Enquiry were extended to include assisting in the evacuation of troops from the demarcation zone, checking that Albania's internal peace was not disturbed, and making suggestions for the avoidance of further problems in the area. It thus covered the whole gamut of peacekeeping functions. All the local parties had quickly accepted the decision of the Conference of Ambassadors, so the Commission had an easy task in helping to defuse the crisis by watching over the Yugoslav withdrawal from and the Albanian reoccupation of the territory which the former had occupied. The Commission kept in touch with the delimitation commission, but stabilizing activity was hardly needed. So far as settlement assistance was concerned, the Commission made far-reaching enquiries over the next year or so, and its suggestions played a valuable part in helping Albania to establish herself as a viable member of the international society. However, this could not alter the geopolitical realities of the inter-war period, and in 1939 Italy took advantage of the deteriorating international situation to annex Albania.

FURTHER READING

See the Further Reading for Section A and Walters (1952) in the Further Reading for Section C.

Section E   The Greco–Bulgarian Crisis (1925)

In October 1925 a shooting incident on the Greco–Bulgarian frontier led to two deaths and the threat of a wider conflict, for Greece responded by advancing into Bulgaria. The attacked state appealed to the League of Nations. The then French President of the League Council immediately sent telegrams to both sides, reminding them of their obligations under the League Covenant and exhorting them to stop all forward military movements and withdraw their troops behind their own frontiers. The Council speedily endorsed this initiative, and requested Britain, France and Italy to send military officers to the area to report on how the parties were reacting. The observer group was quickly on the scene and able to tell the Council that the parties were complying with its call.

The Council then asked the group to investigate the incidents which had given rise to the crisis and make their findings available to the commission of enquiry which it was now setting up. In keeping with the brisk pace at which this dispute was being handled, the commission reported within a month, and before the end of the year the Council had adopted its principal recommendations. The parties agreed to go along with them, including the proposal for stationing two neutral officers, of the same nationality, in the area for a period of two years. They were to supervise the reorganization of the frontier guard system on each side of the border, try to avert incidents and settle any which arose, and participate with one officer from each side and an impartial chairman in a conciliation commission to deal with any disputes which could not be immediately settled. These officers were supplied by Sweden. Thus in no time at all this crisis was wound up, and the border relationship of the two states put on a safer footing (see Map 5).

In this process, the use of impartial military officers to stabilize the truce and then to assist in the making and execution of the settlement was undoubtedly of great value. Particularly at the stabilization stage, the situation could all too easily have begun to unravel. But the willingness of the parties to cooperate with them, as well as the parties'

Map 5 Bulgaria and Greece

acceptance of the Council's initial call for the defusing of the crisis, was a very clear reflection of the fact that the dispute took place squarely in the back yard of the leading European powers.

London, Paris and Rome were all agreed that the quarrel should be quickly snuffed out, and with the Treaty of Locarno only a week behind them were in just the right mood to assert themselves in the cause of European tranquillity. There was even talk of sanctions, and the League Secretariat made some unofficial enquiries about the problems involved in the organization of a naval demonstration. But there was no need to move in the direction of enforcement, as what would now be called peacekeeping sufficed. Greece, militarily the stronger of the disputants, was in dire economic straits and suffering from political unrest: thus she was in no position to resist concerted diplomatic pressure from the major powers. Bulgaria had to a large extent been disarmed under the relevant peace treaty, and was diplomatically isolated: a feeler which she put out towards her former ally, Germany, met with no response. She therefore had little practical option but to do as she was told.

Accordingly, with neither party in a position to defy the powers, order could be quickly restored in their back yard. As an important ancillary device in this process, peacekeeping proved its worth.

FURTHER READING

James Barros, *The League of Nations and the Great Powers. The Greek–Bulgarian Incident, 1925* (Oxford: Clarendon Press, 1970).

Section F   The Border Dispute Between Ecuador and Peru (1941–1942, 1955 and 1981–)

An extensive territorial dispute had existed between Ecuador and Peru since their emergence as sovereign states early in the nineteenth century, each making claims against the other. Ecuador's territorial grievance was particularly huge, and in 1941 it led to large-scale hostilities. Peru having established her superiority, a truce was agreed in respect of the western end of the front which provided for a neutral zone varying in width between 20 and 30 miles. The armed forces of both sides withdrew from the zone and military observers from Argentina, Brazil and the United States (who had been active as a mediatory group) watched over it until a substantive agreement was reached early in 1942. This was signed by Ecuador with the greatest reluctance, and in recognition of the need for inter-American solidarity following the United States' enforced entry into the Second World War. It was not therefore seen by her as a real end to the affair (see Map 6).

This agreement was guaranteed by the United States, Argentina, Brazil and Chile – the last-named being included in consequence of her dissatisfaction at not having been involved in the mediatory process. When, therefore, Ecuador complained to the Organization of American States (OAS) in 1955 that Peru was massing troops on her frontiers and that the Peruvian navy was menacing her coastline, the OAS left the matter to the guarantors. They despatched an Investigating Committee to the frontier areas, composed of their military attachés in the two capitals, but after ground and aerial reconaissance the Committee reported that it could find no evidence in support of Ecuador's claims.

In 1981, however, the issue again gave rise to fighting as Ecuadorean troops crossed her south-eastern border into Peruvian territory. The four guarantors put forward a cease-fire proposal, which was soon

43

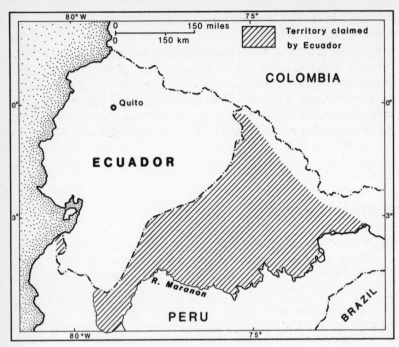

Map 6   Ecuador's territorial claims on Peru

accepted – no doubt in large measure because Ecuador's forces had soon been driven back to their own territory. The guarantor powers then set up a Commission of Military Observers to supervise the disputed area, and their military attachés in Quito (the Ecuadorean capital) assumed this additional role.

The Commission flew over the area, but it is uncertain whether it did anything more. Further clashes occurred, and an agreement was then reached to withdraw troops for a distance of nine miles on each side of the border in the disputed area, and to hold talks in the presence of military representatives of the four guarantors. Subsequently, the border was reopened. However, another brief clash took place in 1984, and the dispute rumbles on, Ecuador's original desire to gain access to the Amazon (via the Maranon) now being sharpened by the supposition that the area might contain oil. But in view of the fact that she is weaker than Peru and that influential outsiders show no disposition to press for a boundary change, her prospects are dim.

This conflict led only to token peacekeeping operations. They may have had a certain symbolic value, given the relative weight of the states who conducted them, but in respect of the 1981 fighting the little that was done was no substitute for the establishment of a full-time observer mission on the ground. It may well be that the situation was not thought to justify such a measure, not least because the fighting took place in a remote mountainous location. But the episode was a reminder both of the attractiveness of the idea of peacekeeping as a means of helping to wind up a conflict and of the need for adequate operational dispositions if a peacekeeping initiative is actually to make such a contribution.

FURTHER READING

Peter Calvert, *Boundary Disputes in Latin America* (London: Institute for the Study of Conflict, 1983).
J. Lloyd Mecham, *The United States and Inter-American Security* (Austin, Texas: University of Texas Press, 1961).
David W. Wainhouse *et al.*, *International Peace Observation* (Baltimore, Md: Johns Hopkins Press, 1966).
Bryce Wood, *The United States and Latin American Wars 1932–1942* (New York: Columbia University Press, 1966).
Bryce Wood, *Aggression and History. The Case of Ecuador and Peru* (Ann Arbor, Mich.: University Microfilms International, 1978).

Section G The Costa Rican–Nicaraguan Disputes (1948–1949, 1955 and 1978–1979)

In the early months of 1948, Costa Rica's conservative regime, which received support from the local communists, was overthrown by forces claiming the democratic principle as the basis of their action. At the end of the year the new regime, just after announcing the dissolution of the Costa Rican army, alleged that the neighbouring police state of Nicaragua had invaded Costa Rica and was plotting the overthrow of her government. It appealed to the Organization of American States (OAS). The United States was concerned at the threat to hemispheric stability, and persuaded the OAS to despatch an investigating committee, to which military advisers were attached. On the basis of its report certain ameliorative calls were made to the disputants, and accepted by them. In consequence they were committed to abstain from hostile acts against each other of both a direct and an indirect kind.

In an effort to ensure that its recommendations were carried out, and to assist as necessary in the process, the OAS sent a Commission of Military Experts to Costa Rica and Nicaragua. It consisted of officers drawn from Brazil, Colombia, Mexico, Paraguay and the United States, four of whom had served as military advisers to the investigating committee. Both disputants promised to cooperate with the Commission, which spent a month in the border areas on each side of the international frontier. It travelled by various means, including foot and horseback, and also made aerial surveys. At the end of January 1949 the Commission reported that the parties' response had been adequate, and it was wound up in February at the same time as the parties signed a pact of amity which had been negotiated with OAS help. The commission had helped to maintain the truce between the parties and given useful assistance in nudging them towards a settlement. However, it was the parties

themselves who had agreed to defuse this relatively minor crisis, and
the fact that the United States was amongst those who favoured this
course must have weighed not inconsiderably with them. For they lived
very much in America's political back yard, and therefore found it
difficult to spurn the advice and the peacekeeping mechanism which
was offered by the Washington-based OAS (see Map 7).

In 1955 there was something of a re-run of the earlier crisis, but at
a much more serious level. The leadership of each country was the
same, Costa Rica made the same complaints about Nicaragua as she
had done six years earlier, and the OAS again appointed an investigating
committee. To calm the situation, the committee devised a plan for
short-term ground and air security zones on each side of the relevant
parts of the border, from which the parties agreed to exclude their
forces. Responsibility for executing this plan was given to the committee's
military advisers, constituted into a Committee (not, this time, a
commission) of Military Experts drawn from the same states as the
main committee: Brazil, Ecuador, Mexico, Paraguay and, unsurprisingly,
the United States. To check on the observance of this scheme, the

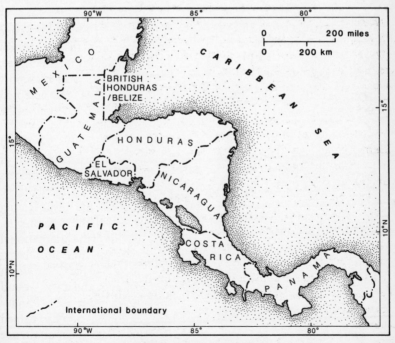

Map 7   Central America

Committee recruited 27 military observers, most of whom came from Ecuador and Mexico, but with a few from Brazil and the United States. They set up observation posts, patrolled, and engaged in aerial surveillance. These peacekeeping arrangements, powerfully backed by the regional squire (who, after her much-criticized part in the Guatemalan affair of 1954 was anxious to re-establish her multilateral credentials), had the desired sedative effect, and the disputants once more promised to behave themselves.

In 1959, however, the activity of anti-Nicaraguan elements in Costa Rica gave rise to further problems betweeen the two states. And in 1977 and 1978 border clashes occurred, again accompanied by (correct) Nicaraguan allegations that the opposition forces in her civil war were both receiving supplies and operating from Costa Rica. As on previous occasions, the matter was taken to the OAS, but that body was reluctant to do much because its members were embarrassed over the excesses of the right-wing Nicaraguan regime. However, towards the end of 1978, and in a rather leisurely way, it appointed a Commission of Civilian Observers to perform the quasi-military and essentially peacekeeping function of watching over the border zone. This Commission submitted several reports over the ensuing six months, saying that its work had made some contribution to the improvement of the situation and that it was appreciated by both sides.

But this activity was little more than a gesture, as in reality the OAS was waiting for the fall of the Nicaraguan government, which took place in the middle of 1979. Its left-wing successors, however, soon lost the sympathy both of other Central American countries and of the United States, and this precipitated a fundamental change in the character of conflict in the region. For the United States now appeared not as a pacifying third party but as the backer of the 'Contra' attack on the new Nicaraguan regime and defender of near-by regimes which were actually or potentially threatened by left-wing rebels. This context was very far removed indeed from the sort which is suitable for peacekeeping. When, however, in the late 1980s the context began to change, the possibility of peacekeeping operations in the area began to be seriously discussed (see Section L below).

FURTHER READING

J. Lloyd Mecham, *The United States and Inter-American Security* (Austin, Texas: University of Texas Press, 1961).

Organization of American States, *Inter-American Treaty of Reciprocal Assistance. Applications. Vol. I: 1948–1959; Vol. III, Part Two: 1977–1981* (Washington, DC: OAS, 1973 and 1982 respectively).

Edgardo Paz-Barnica, 'Peacekeeping within the Inter-American System', in Henry Wiseman (ed.), *Peacekeeping* (New York: Pergamon Press, for the International Peace Academy, 1983).

Jerome Slater, *The OAS and United States Foreign Policy* (Columbus, Ohio: Ohio State University Press, 1967).

David W. Wainhouse *et al.*, *International Peace Observation* (Baltimore, Md: Johns Hopkins Press, 1966).

Section H   The Boundary Dispute Between Honduras and Nicaragua (1957–1962)

With the discovery of possible oil deposits, a long-standing territorial dispute between Honduras and Nicaragua began in 1957 to throw off some dangerous-looking sparks. Armed clashes took place and appeals were made to the Organization of American States (OAS), where the United States called for the ending of hostilities and an early settlement. An investigating committee was despatched to the scene early in May and managed to secure a cease-fire. So as to deal with complaints about its violation (which immediately began to come in) and to prepare plans for the withdrawal of troops, the committee established a Committee of Military Advisers. It was made up of the military assistants who had accompanied the investigators together with others who were specially brought in. All told the Committee consisted of 17 officers from the following nine states: Argentina, Bolivia, Chile, Ecuador, Mexico, Panama, Paraguay, United States (who provided the officer in charge), and Venezuela.

To maintain the truce, the Committee organized a system of ground and aerial surveillance and proposed that a buffer zone be established in the disputed area from which both regular troops (as distinct from border guards) and combat planes be excluded. The parties were persuaded to accept this scheme and thereafter the physical tension between the two was much reduced. The spotlight was now turned on the basic issue, and the OAS secured the agreement of both sides to submit their dispute to the International Court of Justice. To maintain quiet during the lengthy process of international judicial settlement, the parties cooperated in the establishment of a bilateral military commission, and the Committee of Military Advisers was withdrawn. In 1960 the International Court ruled in favour of Honduras (see Map 8).

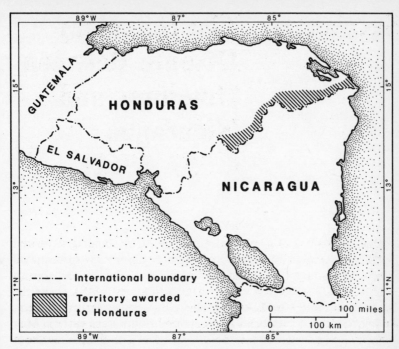

Map 8   Territory awarded to Honduras by the 1960 decision of the International Court of Justice

In this case the cease-fire agreement had gone a long way towards defusing the crisis. Huge numbers of troops were not involved and they were not cheek by jowl over long distances. But there was still plenty of scope for incidents in the rough and contested terrain, and their escalation could by no means be excluded as political tension had been high. In this context, the speedy shoring-up of the cease-fire by the Committee of Military Advisers was of considerable value, as was the Committee's part in its maintenance during the subsequent political discussions. It was a demonstration of the useful functions which could be fulfilled by the device of peacekeeping. And in this particular situation the peacekeepers were assisted by the fact that the disputants were relatively small states quarrelling in the immediate back-yard of a very large regional power who was anxious for an early restoration of peace. This helped to create the favourable political scene within which peacekeeping was able to make its auxiliary but important contribution.

There was also an important peacekeeping postscript, connected with the implementation of the International Court's decision. About 3,500 square miles of territory had to be transferred from Nicaragua to Honduras, and a new 300-mile-long frontier established. Therefore, with the assistance of the five-state Inter-American Peace Committee – which was part of the OAS system – a Honduran–Nicaraguan Mixed Commission was established in 1961. It was given a Mexican chairman and assisted by a number of civilian OAS officials. The representatives to it from the parties were civilians, but both Honduras and Nicaragua appointed army officers as their alternate representatives. Its job, most of which was done in 1961 but which took a further year to complete, was fourfold.

Firstly, it delimited the new frontier, the chairman giving a ruling in respect of one small section on which the parties could not agree. Secondly, where the new boundary did not follow clear natural features, it was demarcated on the ground with markers. Thirdly, the Commission assisted with the transfer of about 4,000 people who wished to stay under Nicaraguan rule. And finally it supervised the withdrawal of the Nicaraguan authorities and the arrival of their Honduran counterparts.

In connection with the last two tasks the OAS officials acted as witnesses and for a brief while lived in areas where incidents might have occurred. There were in fact no serious problems, which at least in part may be attributed to the moderating influence which flowed from the presence of impartial third parties. As at the earlier stage, the overriding condition for this result was, of course, the cooperation of the two disputants. But, as before, the peacekeeping assistance rendered by the OAS made a notable contribution to what has proved to be a lasting settlement of a troublesome boundary problem,

FURTHER READING

Inter-American Peace Committee, *Report to the Eighth Meeting of Consultation of Ministers of Foreign Affairs* (Washington, DC: Pan American Union, 1962).

Inter-American Peace Committee, *Report to the Council of the Organization of American States on the Termination of the Activities of the Honduras–Nicaragua Mixed Commission* (Washington, DC: Pan American Union, 1963).

D. H. N. Johnson, 'The International Court of Justice. Case concerning the Arbitral Award made by the King of Spain on December 23, 1906', *International and Comparative Law Quarterly*, 10(2) (April 1961).

Wayne Earl Johnson, *The Honduras–Nicaragua Boundary Dispute, 1957–1963* (Denver, Col.: University of Denver, unpublished Ph.D. thesis, 1964).

See also the Further Reading for Section G.

Section I   Panama (1959)

The success of Fidel Castro's revolutionary movement in Cuba in January 1959 resulted in many dissident Central American and Caribbean exiles flocking to Cuba. One such from Panama persuaded about 100 Cubans to try to overthrow the Panamanian regime. Their arrival threw the Government into a panic, and it appealed to the OAS. With the United States in support of OAS action, and Cuba disowning the rebel band, an Investigating Committee was quickly appointed. At the same time, member states were asked to supply the Committee with ships and planes for observation and patrol. The United States quickly obliged, Colombia and Ecuador also supplying ships and Costa Rica and Guatemala aircraft. No further invading parties were detected; the rebels were induced to surrender; and the patrols were called off – although not before they had been authorized to stop and investigate any suspicious craft approaching the Panamanian coast.

This speedy and potentially tough response was a reflection of the United States' concern about the extreme left-wing regime which had appeared in her back yard. What actually happened can be seen as a useful defusing exercise of a peacekeeping kind. Had, however, the threat been more substantial, and met by force, the peacekeeping credentials of such action would have been in doubt. For although it would have been taken in support of the maintenance of law and order in a state whose government enjoyed internal legitimacy, it would also have amounted to action against an external predator. Forceful measures of that nature should not be confused with peacekeeping.

For a map, see Map 7 above.

FURTHER READING

See the Further Reading for Section G.

Section J   The United States in the Dominican Republic (1965–1966)

AMERICAN INTERVENTION

In April 1965, fighting broke out in the Dominican Republic between two ideologically opposed groups, and each soon declared itself to be the legitimate government. American citizens were advised to prepare for evacuation; a number of them were shipped out; and many others assembled on the lawn of a hotel in the capital, Santo Domingo, to await their turn. Into this situation, on 28 April, came United States marines and parachute troops, the first time they had been moved in this way since the inauguration of that state's 'good neighbour' policy in 1933. Their function was said to be to protect their fellow citizens, and other foreign nationals, and escort them safely from the country.

However, although the smooth conduct of this operation considerably reduced the number of Americans in the Dominican Republic, American forces continued to arrive, reaching 9,500 by 2 May with another 4,500 on their way. On that day the American President, following up an earlier hint, said that what had begun as a popular democratic revolution in the small Caribbean state was being taken over by a band of communist conspirators. The United States build-up was therefore intended to prevent the emergence of another communist state in the hemisphere – Cuba having already been categorized as such. This explanation was greeted internationally with some scepticism, and in an effort to allay it the names of 58 'Communist and Castroist' leaders were published on 5 May. Unfortunately, the list was found to contain some duplication, which reduced the number of conspirators to 54. This intrepid band was now requiring the prophylactic attention of about 19,000 American troops (see Map 9).

At this date the United States force cannot be seen as having a peacekeeping character. In the first place, the context was entirely

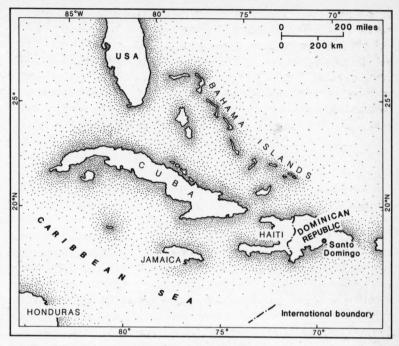

Map 9 The Caribbean

inappropriate. The absence of an invitation may have been excusable, given the civil disorder in which the Dominican Republic found itself, but the cooperation of one side was resoundingly lacking. For, secondly, the clear intention of the American move was to prevent the left wing in the civil conflict gaining the upper hand, by the threat and if necessary the use of superior force. Neither of peacekeeping's core values of impartiality and non-threateningness were therefore being met. And thirdly, even if it were allowed that the function of the force was to defuse a crisis, it was far from generally clear that that crisis was international in nature.

In one sense, however, the very intervention of American troops gave the situation an international colour. And this was increased by a change in the make-up of the force. Almost from the start the United States had made it clear that while the burden was bound chiefly to fall on her, she was anxious that the honour of resisting communism in one part of her back yard should be shared by the other tenants. They did not exactly jump into line. They did agree to despatch an Organization of American States (OAS) committee to try to obtain a cease-fire. But only on 6 May, and then by the barest margin, did they accept that order should be restored in the Dominican Republic through the medium of an Inter-American Force operating under the authority of the OAS. One of those in favour was the Dominican representative who, very conveniently, was speaking for the American-favoured right-wing group. In the absence of this vote, the resolution would have failed to secure the necessary two-thirds support.

Even those who voted for it, however, did not rush to participate. When the Force came formally into being on 23 May it consisted of 250 troops from Honduras, 164 from Nicaragua, 25 Costa Rican policemen, and the American contingent of about 22,000. El Salvador subsequently produced three officers, and from South as distinct from Central America, Paraguay was persuaded to contribute 178 troops and Brazil about 1,150. Brazil provided a substantial part of her own airlift, but that apart, nearly all the transport and supplies for the extra participants came from the United States. In view of her all-round superiority the United States was able to take a generous view on the question of command, and a Brazilian was given the job. A different kind of cosmetic embellishment came with the insertion into the Force's title of the word 'Peace', making it the Inter-American Peace Force (IAPF).

In themselves, however, these developments made no difference whatsoever to the judgement that what was going on in the Dominican Republic was not peacekeeping. The use of that term is justifiable only if the activity in question satisfies the relevant criteria. As a practical matter, there are almost always good reasons for international peacekeeping being done by a body which is composed of military personnel from more than one state. But the mere multilateralization of an intervention does not turn it into peacekeeping, not even if it is done on the authority of an international organization. Nor, on the other hand, is an activity necessarily to be denied the character of peacekeeping just because it is being done by a single state. The number of states involved is irrelevant, as is the name they adopt or the flag under which they operate. But one of the matters which is important is the nature of what they do. And in the Dominican Republic the role of the foreign troops soon began to change, and in a manner which entitled them to claim some peacekeeping credentials.

As might have been expected, the Americans had initially deployed in a way which was markedly unfavourable to the forces of the left-wing group. But, not for the first time (it had happened in respect of Lebanon in 1958 in a situation which had certain clear similarities to that of the Dominican Republic), the United States began to wonder whether she had not been too precipitate in flexing her abundant muscles. As early as the middle of May, before her build-up was complete, she was re-assessing the position on the basis of evidence that the left-wing group was not, after all, in the hands of the communists and, indeed, had wide support. It thus began to look as if what was needed was not so much a defeat for the left as a genuine compromise between the two main groups – and that the role of 'democratic impartiality' which had been formally assigned to the IAPF should be a reality rather than a fiction.

With a view to achieving a political settlement the OAS set up a three-man committee at the beginning of June, one of whose members was a senior and very experienced American diplomat. It proceeded to engage in extensive negotiations with both sides, in the context of a truce which was maintained impartially by the IAPF. The American contingent in the Force had been reduced in size by about half by the end of June, but even so the IAPF was still the dominant military factor in the situation and prepared if necessary to use force. From time to time both sides were – or at least claimed to be – annoyed by the way in which the IAPF prevented each of them from getting at the other. What was taking place was therefore much more in the nature of enforcement than cooperative stabilization. But something of the latter was emerging, and the military personnel involved were trying to be impartial. Unlike the initial American role, therefore, the IAPF now had a clear element of peacekeeping in its activity.

At the end of August an Act of Dominican Reconciliation was agreed, under which a provisional government was to hold office until a new government could emerge from nation-wide elections in 1966. This resulted in a further change in the role of the IAPF, for now it moved to law and order tasks in support of the provisional regime. The situation was still unstable, and sometimes there was considerable shooting. But the Act of Reconciliation was widely accepted, so that the IAPF could be seen not as a confrontational body but, in effect, as the arm of a government which was legitimate in political as well as formal terms. Thus the Force was now unambiguously one of a peacekeeping kind. It gave such aid to the civil authorities as was necessary for the maintenance of order, helped in the recovery of weapons from civilians, assisted in quashing a right-wing plot and a general strike called by the left, and ensured that the military leaders of the contending parties left quietly for foreign posts – a number of them in their country's diplomatic service: one such leader claimed that the 'honour guard' with which he had been provided consisted of the point of an American bayonet! The IAPF was particularly vigilant during the election campaign, which resulted in the installation of a new president on 1 July 1966. The Force, which was now about 8,000 strong, immediately began its withdrawal, which was completed by the end of September. During its 16-month operational period, 27 men had been killed as a result of hostile acts and about 200 wounded.

THE UN's ROLE

From the start of the crisis the matter was vigorously debated in the UN Security Council, where the Soviet Union called for the United States to be condemned and her forces withdrawn. The United States, however, was opposed even to mild enquiries being made in the Dominican Republic on behalf of the UN Secretary-General, and so at first nothing came of these discussions. A large 'Keep Out' notice had been posted by the United States on her back-yard wall.

As sometimes happens, however, an event then occurred which, though of small importance in itself, had significant consequences – in this case enabling the UN to get its foot in the Dominican door. The UN Secretary-General received a telegram from the left-wing faction claiming that as a result of an air attack on its radio station, in which at least two people had been killed, the country's capital was threatened with destruction. This communication had the effect of crystallizing the restlessness which had been growing within and beyond the Security Council at the UN's inaction and apparent helplessness. It also had a numbing effect on those who were opposed to the UN's involvement in the affair, including the United States, who had not yet cast a veto and was reluctant to break this record in a way which would be widely seen as blatantly and suspiciously self-serving. A resolution was therefore passed on 14 May asking the Secretary-General to send a representative to the Republic of Dominica (Domrep) to report on the situation. The United States made the best of a bad job by voting for it, and it was passed unanimously.

In this way a small civilian mission was established in the Dominican capital, and it assumed some of the character of peacekeeping by virtue of the attachment to it of the Secretary-General's Military Adviser, who was assisted at any one time by two military observers from three made available by Brazil, Canada and Ecuador. Its role was to keep an independent eye on what was happening and particularly on the United

States and the right-wing faction, who, in accord with the balance of sympathies at the UN, were thought to be most deserving of critical attention. Put positively, Domrep was conceived as an international amplifier for the weaker side and a moral counterweight to the physical strength of the United States. Much debate followed in the Security Council about the possible extension of Domrep's mandate, including the suggestion that it should supervise the cease-fire. But the United States was implacably opposed to any such scheme, and the UN Secretary-General was also wary of it, as the situation in May 1965 – not least the crisis in which the UN then found itself over the financing of peacekeeping – seemed inappropriate for the organization's wider involvement. Thus nothing of substance ensued.

On the ground, Domrep received a very chilly reception from the United States and, once it came into being, from the American-dominated IAPF. But it could well be that the UN presence occasionally had a restraining effect on the Force, in view of the knowledge that reports which were critical of its behaviour would be given wide attention and much credibility in New York. In this respect, therefore, Domrep did have something about it of the nature of peacekeeping. And insofar as the non-peacekeeping activity of mediation is concerned, the Secretary-General's representative played an important role in encouraging the left wing to move towards a settlement. This, together with the gradual improvement in the situation, resulted in the IAPF taking, in time, a less hostile stance towards Domrep, and cooperation between the two began to develop. But as a whole, and contrary to the UN's claims, Domrep was hardly a peacekeeping mission. Its presence in the United States' back yard was the expression of a political point which that country had felt unable to resist, and not the reflection of a peacekeeping role for the UN in the Dominican crisis. It was the IAPF which, after an unpromising beginning, moved, haltingly, to peacekeeping tasks – and did so under the UN's on-the-spot scrutiny. Once the United States-dominated IAPF had departed there was no further part for Domrep to play in the Dominican Republic. Accordingly, it left in the IAPF's wake.

FURTHER READING

Audrey Bracey, *Resolution of the Dominican Crisis, 1965* (Washington, DC: Institute for the Study of Diplomacy, Georgetown University, 1980).

Yale H. Ferguson, 'The Dominican Intervention of 1965: Recent Interpretations', *International Organization*, 27 (4) (Autumn 1973).

Alan James, *The Politics of Peacekeeping* (London: Chatto Windus, for the Institute for Strategic Studies, 1969).

Aida Luisa Levin, *The Organization of American States and the United Nations* (New York: United Nations Institute for Training and Research, 1974).

Indar Jit Rikhye, *The Theory and Practice of Peacekeeping* (London: Hurst, for the International Peace Academy, 1984).

Indar Jit Rikhye, Michael Harbottle and Bjorn Egge, *The Thin Blue Line* (New Haven: Yale University Press, 1974).

Jerome Slater, *Intervention and Negotiation. The United States and the Dominican Revolution* (New York: Harper & Row, 1970).

David W. Wainhouse *et al.*, *International Peacekeeping at the Crossroads* (Baltimore, Md: Johns Hopkins University Press, 1973).

Section K The Conflict Between El Salvador and Honduras (1969–1971 and 1976–1980)

In July 1969 fighting broke out between the neighbouring Central American states of El Salvador and Honduras. It was sparked off by ill-feeling which arose out of the preliminary rounds of the 1970 World Cup football competition, and thus became known as the 'football war'. But underlying it were long-standing tensions deriving from Salvadorean emigration to and settlement in the much more sparsely populated Honduras. The fighting escalated rapidly and attracted the urgent attention of the Organization of American States (OAS). It appointed a seven-state committee (including the United States) to enquire into the problem, issued calls for a cease-fire and withdrawal, and asked its committee to appoint military observers to see that these calls were complied with. A cessation of hostiities was soon achieved, but it took a tacit threat of sanctions to persuade El Salvador to withdraw. By the end of the month that had been achieved and hostilities had died down.

The OAS now turned its attention to the longer-term stabilization of the situation, and this resulted in a June 1970 agreement between the parties establishing a demilitarized security zone along their common frontier to a depth of 1.8 miles on each side. It was to be policed by military observers drawn from Costa Rica, Guatemala and Nicaragua, whose expenses were to be met in equal parts by the disputants. This arrangement evidently had the desired effect, for in 1971 it was decided that the situation permitted the gradual withdrawal of the observers.

In 1976, however, further clashes occurred. The OAS once more called for a cease-fire, and as an emergency supervisory measure

61

appointed a committee chiefly made up of military attachés. A team of 28 Military Observers soon followed, drawn from 11 Latin American states and the United States, which was given a wide defusing and truce-maintaining role. Once the initial trouble had died down the number of Observers was reduced to 11 (with the parties again supplying the OAS with the necessary funds), and they remained on each side of the border during the subsequent negotiations for a settlement of the dispute. Eventually, in 1980, a treaty of peace was signed and ratified, and the parties thereupon decided that the (costly) observation system was no longer necessary. Accordingly, the Military Observers were withdrawn.

In the ensuing years each party became preoccupied by other urgent matters: Honduras by the conflict in and around Nicaragua and El Salvador by her own deep civil war. But on the basis of their Peace Treaty they proceeded with measures which were designed to reduce tension along their common border. The demarcation of its agreed sections was begun, negotiations took place regarding disputed areas and, in the absence of agreement, the matter was taken to the International Court of Justice. The case began in 1988 and is expected to conclude in 1990.

The decisions of the OAS in relation to El Salvador and Honduras testified to the worth of the idea of peacekeeping as an impartial and non-forceful military activity which can operate effectively provided that the states immediately concerned give it their cooperation. And the peacekeeping arrangements which were actually made on the ground seemed to play a useful role in the restoration and the maintenance of calm. The fact that they were conducted by a body whose largest member, the United States, was in a position to vent effective displeasure in the direction of the two relatively small disputants doubtless added to their efficacy.

For a map, see Map 7.

FURTHER READING

Organization of American States, *Inter-American Treaty of Reciprocal Assistance. Applications. Vol. II: 1960–1972; Vol. III: 1973–1976; Vol. III, Part Two: 1977–1981* (Washington, DC: OAS, 1973, 1977 and 1982 respectively).
Edgardo Pax-Barnica, 'Peacekeeping within the Inter-American System', in Henry Wiseman (ed.), *Peacekeeping* (New York: Pergamon Press, 1983).

Section L   The Peace Process in Central America (1989–)

The coming to power of the left-wing Sandinista regime in Nicaragua in 1979 heralded the start of a ten-year effort to unseat it by its right-wing Contra opponents. Many of the Contras were based in neighbouring Honduras, and received huge amounts of aid from the United States – although the President was often keener on this policy than the purse-string-holding Congress. The war resulted in the death or wounding of, proportionately, very large numbers of people, and helped to devastate the economy – annual inflation in 1988 being said to be more than 25,000 per cent! Not surprisingly, the Government was receptive to nudges in the direction of a settlement from both the Soviet Union and the other Central American states – some of whom also had a civil war problem. But equally, the regime was determined to safeguard the social and political progress it had achieved.

In an endeavour to deal not just with this matter but also with other internal and international conflicts in the region, a series of summit meetings of five Central American Presidents (of Costa Rica, El Salvador, Guatemala, Honduras and Nicaragua) resulted in a multi-sided approach. In the first place, it was agree in February 1989 that plans should be prepared for the disbandment of the 12,000 Contras in Honduras, in exchange for which Nicaragua undertook to implement certain democratic reforms and to hold elections not later than February 1990. The United States was far from happy about this, and pressed hard for the Contras to be kept in being as possible fighting units until after the Nicaraguan elections. At a slightly earlier date her opposition would almost certainly have sunk the scheme. But despite personal pleas by her President the Central American states refused to be deflected, deciding in August 1989 that the demobilization and relocation of the Contras would begin within a month and be completed by the end of the year.

This was quite an ambitious programme, not least because the Contras themselves were not a party to it. To oversee its implementation the Central American Presidents proposed that the UN and the Organization of American States (OAS) establish an International Support and Verification Commission (CIAV being its Spanish acronym). The Secretaries-General of the two Organizations immediately constituted themselves as a skeleton CIAV, but the effort to put flesh on its bones encountered considerable difficulties. The UN Secretary-General insisted that although the operation could work only with the cooperation of the Contras, its personnel would have to be armed and under the authority only of the UN. Any attempt to place a peacekeeping force under two masters was, in his clear view, asking for trouble. The Secretary-General of the OAS, on the other hand, did not welcome the thought of his Organization being effectively side-lined, and began to wonder whether a military operation was really necessary. The outcome of these discussions was a UN Security Council decision of March 1990 that the demobilization of the Contras should be the responsibility of Onuca (see below), to which a Venezuelan infantry battalion was added for the purpose, while their repatriation and the monitoring of their welfare was to be the CIAV's responsibility.

Meanwhile, however, another part of the peace process had moved smoothly ahead. The Central American Presidents had agreed that the Nicaraguan elections should be internationally observed, and there was then some discussion about the possibility of cooperation on this matter between the OAS and the UN. But in the event the two bodies went their separate ways, the UN Secretary-General despatching an Observer Mission (Onuven) to Nicaragua in July 1989, with the Security Council bestowing its blessing on the enterprise later in the month. It began work in August with about 17 personnel, the plan being that that number would be approximately doubled at the end of the year and supplemented by about 120 observers for the February 1990 election – which, surprisingly, resulted in the defeat of the Sandinistas.

Onuven was a civilian body and therefore does not count in its own right as a peacekeeping mission. But it was part of an overall scheme which certainly has peacekeeping credentials, these being chiefly derived from a body which was set up in November 1989. This is Onuca – the Spanish acronym for the UN Observer Group in Central America.

Onuca is a consequence of the calls which have been made for some years at Central American summits for the states of the region, and those outside it, to terminate their support for irregular forces and insurrectionist movements and not to allow their countries to be used for attacks on other states. By 1989 these commitments were hardening, and thus there was a pressing need for some machinery to check on their observance. Here, too, there were early suggestions for a joint OAS/UN operation, but the practical difficulties of this soon resulted in the UN alone being formally approached by the five Central American states. For some time things were held up by Honduras's refusal to cooperate wholeheartedly in any such venture until Nicaragua had promised to withdraw an action she had instituted against Honduras at the International Court of Justice in connection with the latter's aid to the Contras. But by August a satisfactory arrangement had been reached in this respect, enabling the UN to go ahead with the planning for its first unambiguous peacekeeping operation on the American continent (see Map 10).

There were some further delays, but early in November 1989 the Security Council established Onuca for an initial period of six months. Provision was made for 260 unarmed military observers, the first of whom were in place early in December. Thereafter, the plan was for a

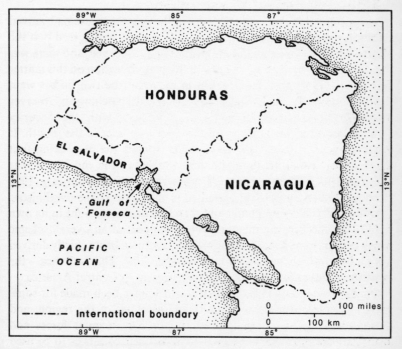

Map 10   El Salvador, Honduras and Nicaragua

phased build-up of the observers, provided that the political situation did not develop so adversely as to make their presence pointless – and hazardous. The initial group of observers came from Canada, Columbia, Ireland, Spain and Venezuela, and were placed under the command of a Spanish General. There were hopes that the Federal Republic of Germany would also provide observers, but constitutional obstacles to this course resulted in her having to settle for the supply of a civilian medical unit and a civilian aircraft. Subsequently, additional observers were supplied by Argentina, Brazil, Ecuador, India, and Sweden, bringing the total number close to the planned figure of 260.

Onuca was conceived as a highly mobile group equipped with helicopters and fast boats (which will increase the size of its military component about 450) as well as vehicles. Canada supplied light observation and light lift helicopters, but difficulties were encountered in securing the naval elements. It had been anticipated that Venezuela would provide them, but that did not happen. Instead, early in 1990, Argentina agreed to supply Onuca with four patrol boats. The land-based observers operate from about 30 verification centres close to sensitive areas. But initially, Onuca's main focus will probably be on the borders of Honduras and Nicaragua and of El Salvador and Honduras, together with the Gulf of Fonseca – which is bordered by these states. Regular and ad hoc patrols are made, as well as investigations of alleged breaches of the non-interventionary promises made by the five regional states, in each of whom Onuca has a liaison office. Its headquarters are in Honduras and its costs are to be shared out among all members of the UN.

Meanwhile, Onuca was already trying to get on with its additional and urgent task of supervising the demobilization of the Contras. Some handed in their arms in Honduras, but the vast majority of those based there returned to join their fellows in Nicaragua. Here, by agreement with the Government, Onuca established seven security zones, each zone being surrounded by a 12-mile-wide demilitarized zone. The 800 Venezuelan troops who had been temporarily added to the UN mission to conduct the demobilization process waited in the security zones to receive and destroy the Contras' arms, but for a while there was an ominous lack of peacekeeping business. Then, however, early in June 1990, it was reported that the process had suddenly got under way in a substantial manner, having been launched by a reconciliation ceremony between senior rebel commanders and Nicaragua's new President.

Upsets may yet befall these plans to assist in ending the war in

Nicaragua and, more generally, to bring a greater measure of peace to the whole region. But they are at least indicative of the flexibility of the device of peacekeeping, and of its possible value. Central America is by no means the only area of the world where civil wars are assisted from outside, and where any professions of repentance on the part of those outsiders is viewed by others with some caution. In such circumstances, peacekeepers can provide an impartial and credible check on what is going on.

The other aspect of these developments which calls for comment concerns the role, or rather the non-role, of the United States. The present evidence in this case suggests that Central America might be in the process of detaching itself from the American back yard and setting up its own clubhouse. Too much must not be read into this as yet unfinished matter, especially as the Contras may not have been the most satisfactory vehicle for conveying American influence into the region. But is could be a straw in the wind.

FURTHER READING

Jan S. Adams, 'Change and Continuity in Soviet Central American Policy', *Problems of Communism*, XXXVIII (2–3) (March–June 1989).

Pat Hayes, 'ONUCA Reconnaissance Mission', *An Cosantoir* 50 (2) (February 1990).

International Institute for Strategic Studies, *Strategic Survey 1988–1989* (London: IISS, 1989).

Ethan Schwartz, 'Central America: Send in the U.N.?', *The InterDependent*, 15 (2) (Spring 1989) (published by the United Nations Association of the United States).

Part II
Clubhouse Troubles

Introduction: Peacekeeping at the Club

States, no less than men, are 'clubbable', although the kind of clubs which are to be found internationally provide only at the margin those purely social facilities which are popular within domestic society. Necessity is the basic international urge, and there is little room for anything else. However, the needs of states are wide-ranging and important, and due to the familiar condition of interdependence a good number of them can be met only through cooperation with other states. In consequence, states often get together on a more or less regular basis the better to satisfy their perceived requirements, and this cooperative activity frequently takes institutionalized form. A further consequence is that those who are banded together in this way become anxious that their relations should not be unnecessarily disturbed, which sometimes leads to the use of peacekeeping devices to sort out certain difficulties which have arisen within a particular clubhouse.

The kind of tension which can occur may bear directly on the purpose of the club, in the sense that the tension's continuation may immediately detract from the efficiency of the cooperative endeavour. Alternatively, it may be that two members of a club fall out on a matter which has no direct bearing on the reason which has brought them within that particular group. Nonetheless, such a dispute may affect their willingness to continue their association within it, so that the resolution of the dispute can quickly become a club matter. Cases of this type presuppose the existence of ties of a relatively close and precise sort. Sometimes, however, states may associate for very general purposes or, almost, simply because they feel that it is appropriate to do so, given some broad factor or factors which they have in common. In such circumstances it is unlikely that the club will be very urgent or demanding in the event of a dispute between two of its members. But nonetheless it is probable that there will be some feeling that pacifying help should at least be offered.

It should be noted, however that at any level the concept of a club – and in this it probably differs from a society – implies a measure of exclusiveness, in the sense that not everyone is eligible for membership. Some criterion of a less than general sort has first to be satisfied.

Accordingly, the United Nations is not a club, as it has become a virtually universal organization. However, this does not mean that the UN cannot be used as a means of assisting a club in the sorting out of one of its troubles, although it is possible – depending on the context and the issue – that some UN members will take exception to such a course, and could be in a position to prevent it.

In dealing with clubhouse troubles, it is to be expected that it will be the more important members who take the lead. They, after all, probably have the biggest stake in its successful operation; they will almost certainly be better placed than other members to do something about an intra-club dispute; even in the egalitarian international context, the generality of club members may well look to their senior colleagues for such an initiative; and the bigger members will very probably conceive themselves as having such a responsibility. This presupposes that in each international club there is a recognition that some members are more important than others, but such a supposition is usually valid.

Ten peacekeeping missions which were designed to cope with intra-club tension can be identified (although at one level one of them was bogus); another was under discussion in 1989; a twelfth, although called a peacekeeping operation, cannot be endorsed as such; and there was one other detailed proposal which, in the event, came to nothing. This last case concerned the efforts of the victors in the Second World War to resolve the claims of two of their number to the city of Trieste and the area surrounding it (Section C). However, the implementation of the peacekeeping scheme ran into a difficulty. As this coincided with one disputant losing the favour of those members of the victorious alliance who were in a physical position to dispose of the territory and with a sudden rise in the stock of the other, the scheme was abandoned and the now-favoured party rewarded with the heart of the territory. The matter had, as it were, been removed from the agenda of one club to that of another, in which only one party was a member. The dispute thereby lost its intra-club character.

Twenty-five years earlier, however, at the end of the First World War, the victorious powers did implement a peacekeeping arrangement to resolve an awkward internal problem. One of their number – and a leading one at that (France) – wanted some adjacent territory (the Saar), but by no stretch of the imagination could the satisfaction of her wish be reconciled with the principles on which the War had latterly been fought. The way out proved to be a form of temporary international government in which the claimant held a privileged position (Section

A). In the same historical period, the club of European states set up a peacekeeping operation in respect of the Spanish Civil War in an attempt to obscure the fact that a great deal of intervening was going on (Section B).

The UN's involvement in clubhouse peacekeeping has thus far been limited to a case which took place at a time when the Organization was very much in the hands of the West, and when the onset of the Cold War encouraged its employment for legitimizing purposes. It concerned the civil war in Greece, a country which was under the wing of the West and troubled by a civil war in which left-wing insurgents were being assisted by three next-door communist states (Section D). The West therefore used the UN to point an accusatory finger at the Communist bloc, hoping, at least in theory, that this would not only bring some diplomatic succour to its club member but also contribute to a lessening of outside interference in Greek affairs.

Two Asian cases fall to be considered in Part II, but one of them – the Indian force which was sent to Sri Lanka in 1987 – can hardly be seen as an instance of genuine peacekeeping (Section L). The other concerns the 1961 Iraqi threat to the new state of Kuwait (Section E). A British force had immediately gone to Kuwait's aid, and was then replaced, in much less threatening circumstances, by a peacekeeping force provided by the Arab League. The League, however, is not a very effective organization, and perhaps partly for that reason makes only one further appearance in these pages – and not a very fruitful one at that (see Part V, Section I below).

The Organization of African Unity (OAU), too, is somewhat lacking in both political cohesion and institutional strength. Its two peacekeeping efforts so far – in respect of a dispute between Algeria and Morocco in the early 1960s and in relation to Chad's internal troubles two decades later (Sections F and G) – have been neither distinguished nor very successful. This helps to account for the fact that the peacekeeping assistance which is envisaged by a 1988 plan for the solution of the Western Sahara problem is overwhelmingly of a UN character (Section M). An additional factor here, however, lies in the OAU's recognition of the group which is fighting against Morocco for the independence of Western Sahara – which has resulted in Moroccan distrust of, and de facto withdrawal from, the Organization.

In respect of Nigeria's civil war of the late 1960s (Section H) an unusual peacekeeping operation took place, in which a group of states sympathetic to the Nigerian regime – a kind of ad hoc Friends of Nigeria club – enquired into allegations of misbehaviour by her Army.

Somewhat similarly, a kind of unofficial Commonwealth force watched over the events of 1979–1980 which brought the civil war in Rhodesia to an end and facilitated the territory's arrival on the international scene as the sovereign state of Zimbabwe (Section I).

The last two instances of clubhouse peacekeeping both relate to the adhesion of Egypt to the small United States Middle East club and to the efforts of its leader to push forward the peace process between Israel and her new associate. As it turned out, this required the playing of a novel peacekeeping role by American civilians in Sinai from 1976 to 1982 (Section J), and the assumption of more extensive peacekeeping responsibilities by the United States from 1982 onwards. For the plan for a UN force to occupy a large buffer zone in eastern Sinai and to check on the execution of important arms limitation promises fell through, because of Arab and Soviet opposition. As a result the United States had to sponsor, organize, and participate in a non-UN force which continues the seemingly permanent association of peacekeeping with the Egyptian–Israeli relationship (Section K).

Section A International Rule in the Saar (1920–1935)

THE PROBLEM OF THE SAAR

When the peace settlement with Germany was being discussed at the end of the First World War, an embarrassing division of opinion arose amongst the victorious allies. It concerned the Saar, which lay to the east of Luxembourg and the immediate north of France. On the face of it, there should have been no question about this region's future, as it was part of Germany and its population of about three quarters of a million was wholly German in both language and culture. However, the Saar's rich coal and iron ore deposits led France to lay claim to it, her aim being both to strengthen herself and weaken German by this adjustment of the international frontier.

At one time such a change would hardly have been remarked upon, provided the other victors could have found equivalent spoil. But in 1919 it was quite contrary to the principles on which the successful states had claimed to be conducting themselves. And Britain in particular -- who felt able to take a more relaxed and positive attitude than France towards 'the German problem' -- was mindful of the political unwisdom of supplying Germany with a grievance so glaring as that which would result from the French annexation of the Saar. A compromise was therefore arranged. The Saar was to be ruled for 15 years by a five-man Commission appointed by the League of Nations Council, and was then to decide whether to rejoin Germany, pass to France, or remain under the League (see Map 11).

The Commission exercised all the powers of government during its 15-year rule, and for the maintenance of order 2,000 French troops were stationed in the territory and at the Commission's disposal. Clearly, their nationality signified the special interest which victorious France claimed in the Saar. But these troops were also playing an international peacekeeping role, in that they were contributing to the pacific settlement of a dispute which had embarrassingly cropped up

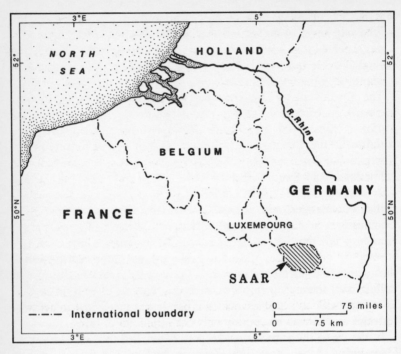

Map 11   The Saar

in the clubhouse of the major powers. In the improved international atmosphere of the mid-1920s, however, their presence was thought to be unnecessary. Thus they were withdrawn in 1927, although the Commission retained the right to recall them in the event of a threat to public order which could not be dealt with by the local police. And to safeguard the Saar's railways, an inter-allied force of 800 men – chiefly French but also containing small Belgian and British contingents – was posted in the Saar in 1927. But it was withdrawn in 1930, as all remained quiet during these three years. Nor was there any subsequent problem.

As the time approached for the Saarlanders to decide on their future, however, the situation changed in a rather ominous way. Hitler had come to power in Germany, and besides engaging in domestic excesses was also, through a branch of the Nazi party, making menacing noises in the Saar. The organization of a free and fair plebiscite suddenly took on awkward and discouraging proportions. Nonetheless, the League went ahead with its preparations, appointing a three-man Plebiscite Commission and receiving promises from the two interested parties that they would engage in neither pressures nor reprisals. Arrangements for the settlement of disputes regarding the plebiscite were made and it was accepted that neutral officials would be employed to oversee the voting. The big question which remained was how order was to be guaranteed in the immediate run up to and during the plebiscite.

The obvious answer was an international force. But not only was Germany opposed to it but also Britain, who would clearly be looked to for a substantial contingent. However, these objections were withdrawn; the League authorized the Commission to recruit an International Force; and one of 3,300 men was quickly assembled. The Netherlands and Sweden each provided 250 troops, and Britain and Italy contingents of 1,500 and 1,300 respectively. The Force had a British commander, and was under the authority of the Governing Commission. No extra costs were to fall on the contributors, as France, Germany and the Saar were to meet those expenses which were not covered by the plebiscite budget. The Force was deployed at key points throughout the territory, maintained a noticeable profile (except on polling day) through marches and patrols, and was highly mobile so as to cope with any problem which arose. It was instructed to act with restraint and always to employ only the minimum of force.

In the event the International Force never had to resort to armed force during the ten weeks that it was in the Saar. On the one hand it built up good relations with the local people, and on the other its visible presence no doubt deterred any who were disposed to upset public order – and by the time of the plebiscite they were very few. In this favourable context the plebiscite went off without a hitch. More than 90 per cent of those who voted (in an almost 100 per cent turn out) opted for the return of the territory to Germany. This took place on 1 March 1935, the day after the Force completed its withdrawal from the Saar.

International peacekeepers thus helped to maintain order during the early part of the time that the Saar was under international government and throughout the plebiscite period. By so doing they made a significant contribution to the settlement of the dispute over the territory's future, and this was particularly true of the International Force of 1934–5. However, it must be noted that the context was notably propitious for the Force. The Saar was already under League of Nations control, so there was no formal difficulty about securing the host's agreement. France, one of the two disputants, had by this time virtually resigned herself to the loss of the territory, and the passive national mood discouraged a confrontational stance towards Germany. And

Germany – the other disputant – decided that the most profitable path for her was to abandon her campaign of propaganda and threats and instead to put on a conciliatory and cooperative face: there was no need to aggravate the situation by shaking the tree if the apple was in any event almost certain to fall into her lap. The ground having been prepared in these ways, virtually all the Force had to do was to turn up.

If, however, it had not been possible to mount the International Force, the dispute could easily have ended much more messily. The Saar dispute therefore provided an early reminder of the valuable secondary role which impartial and non-threatening international bodies are able to play in relation to international disputes. Of course, in these particular circumstances, the clearing up of the Saar problem did nothing to improve overall French–German relations. But with the help of the International Force, one sure source of contention was removed.

POSTSCRIPT

After Germany's defeat in the Second World War, France once again tried to annex the Saar but was once again prevented from doing so by her allies. Instead, in 1947 the Saar was made into an autonomous state, economically linked with France and politically detached from Germany. Seven years later, and in the light of a rapprochement between these two old enemies, a special European status was proposed for the Saar and the possibility of growing economic links with Germany was contemplated. But in 1955, in an internationally-conducted referendum (this time with no need for an international force), the Saarlanders rejected this scheme. What they clearly wanted was to make a second return to the Fatherland. In the very changed international context this was not something which France could resist, and it took place on the first day of 1957.

FURTHER READING

A. H. Burne, 'British Bayonets on the Saar', *Fighting Forces*, XII (1934).
Jacques Freymond, *The Saar Conflict* (London: Stevens, 1960).
C. J. Hill, 'Great Britain and the Saar Plebiscite of 1935', *Journal of Contemporary History*, 9 (2) (April 1974).

H. W. V. Temperley (ed.), *A History of the Peace Conference of Paris*, Vol. II (London: Henry Frowde and Hodder & Stoughton, 1920).

David W. Wainhouse *et al.*, *International Peace Observaton* (Baltimore, Md: Johns Hopkins Press, 1966).

F. P. Walters, *A History of the League of Nations* (London: Oxford University Press, 1952, 2 vols; reprinted in 1960 and subsequently as 1 volume).

Sarah Wambaugh, *The Saar Plebiscite* (Cambridge, Mass.: Harvard University Press, 1940).

Section B   The Spanish Civil War (1937–1939)

INTERVENTION AND 'NON-INTERVENTION'

The Spanish Civil War, which broke out in 1936, witnessed an extraordinary peacekeeping spectacle. The right-wing Nationalist rebels received considerable help from the Fascist regimes in Germany and Italy, at least 40,000 Italian troops and up to 15,000 German troops being sent to Spain. The left-wing Republican government was assisted with supplies by the Soviet Union, and volunteers from that and other countries to the number of perhaps 15,000 were formed into what were called International Brigades in its support.

All this took place, however, in the context of a non-intervention agreement signed at the start of the War by 27 European states, including all the major powers. Furthermore, these states then began to discuss the institution of a system of control, blind eyes being turned on all official sides to what was actually going on. In the early months of 1937 agreement was reached on such a scheme, and it came into force in mid-April. In the theory of the matter, the members of the European club were behaving properly towards a civil disturbance in one of their number, and would themselves keep an eye on the situation to ensure that everyone kept in line.

The control arrangements, which as a whole were run by an International Board headed by a Netherlands Admiral, had three aspects. The French and British (Gibraltarian) frontiers with Spain were watched over from the non-Spanish sides by a team of 135 observers led by a Danish Colonel, and the Portuguese frontier by 140 British observers stationed at her Lisbon embassy (Portugal had been particularly sensitive about a miscellaneous collection of European officers operating on her soil). A team of 550 observing officers, under a second Netherlands Admiral, stood ready to embark some of its members on any ship heading for Spain which was flying the flag of a participating state. On arrival in port the cargo and passengers had to be unloaded under their supervision. Finally, a watch was kept at sea to check on compliance with this last procedure, the patrolling being done by ships from the British, French, German (*sic*), and Italian (*sic*) navies. They could order ships to stop, board them, and examine their papers. But they did not have the right of search. In cases of suspected malpractice, a report would be made to the government of the state in which the ship was registered (see Map 12).

Even on paper this scheme had loopholes (most noticeably the lack of any control of air transport). But, also on paper, it was at least an attempt, and not a bad one, to ensure that the parties to the non-intervention agreement lived up to their undertakings. Had they been so disposed, the control system could have been of value. However, given the blatant interventionary behaviour of certain key states, such arrangements were widely seen as rather farcical (that perception not being obstructed by the pennant flown by the patrolling ships – two black balls on a white background). Unsurprisingly, the scheme had little impact, and it soon collapsed. The Republicans suspected the German and Italian ships of gathering intelligence for the Nationalists, and following attacks on two patrolling German ships, Germany and Italy pulled out of the system. That led France and Portugal to withdraw their permission for the land frontiers to be supervised.

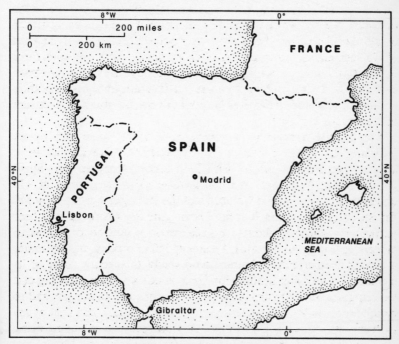

Map 12   The Iberian Peninsula

Britain then proposed the withdrawal of the naval patrols and, instead, the posting of officers in Spanish ports to identify any ships which evaded their continuing obligation to take observers on board. She also proposed the resumption of land supervision. It took a year's further discussion before, in mid-1938, this could be agreed. Quite apart from anything else, however, its rejection by the Nationalists – who by now controlled more than half the coastline – meant that the scheme was worthless. The Republicans were finally defeated in the following year, and in April 1939 the control system was disbanded.

At one level, the whole thing had been a charade, a device used by the club members to pretend, in the face of reality, that real efforts were being made to isolate the Civil War. As some of the leading peacekeepers were also intervening on a very large scale, the system could fairly be said to be bogus. At another level, however, a different conclusion has to emerge. The object of the peacekeeping scheme was to help in preventing the War's expansion into one involving the major European powers, and this purpose was achieved. The desire of Britain and France not to take issue with Germany and Italy was much facilitated, and the last two-mentioned states were happy to operate behind what amounted to a peacekeeping smokescreen. In an indirect way, therefore, the control arrangements helped to stabilize the situation, and so served a peacekeeping function. It was not to be the only time that a peacekeeping body was to operate in this way, but the barefaced poaching by some of the gamekeepers was indeed exceptional.

TOUGHER ACTION

Because of her desire not to get involved in the Civil War, Britain put up with a certain number of Nationalist air attacks (some of the planes probably being piloted by Italians) on her shipping in Spanish ports and their vicinity. When, however, neutral shipping in the Mediterranean began to be attacked by unidentified (almost certainly Italian) submarines, Britain ordered immediate counter attacks. This led to a conference of Mediterranean states at the Swiss town of Nyon in September 1937, at which it was arranged that the British and French fleets, aided in the eastern Mediterranean by the local powers, would patrol the main sea routes. Italy had not attended, but she soon presented herself, and was accepted, as a gamekeeper. The attacks ceased for a while, and completely so after Britain's response to the torpedoing of one of her ships was to say that she would attack any submarine found submerged in the western Mediterranean.

Maintaining peace in an inter-state context through the threat and use of force is an instance of peacekeeping in the literal sense of the term rather than of the phenomenon which is the focus of this book. It is a primary activity, not the derivative, secondary sort which, for better or worse, has come to be called peacekeeping. Italy's participation in the Nyon patrols could perhaps be seen as making them into a cooperative exercise by all the former disputants. But its threatening nature still make it a doubtful candidate for categorization as a (secondary) peacekeeping operation. It might be regarded as such if the submarine predators are regarded as latter-day pirates. But quite apart from the slender factual base for such an approach, there is a question as to whether a public order operation on the high seas is most helpfully treated as peacekeeping (see further, Part III, Section H below).

FURTHER READING

Hugh Thomas, *The Spanish Civil War* (Harmondsworth: Penguin, revised edn, 1965).
Geoffrey Thompson, *Front-Line Diplomat* (London: Hutchinson, 1959).
Arnold J. Toynbee assisted by V. M. Boulter, *Survey of International Affairs 1937. Vol. III: The International Repercussions of the War in Spain (1936–7)* (London: Oxford University Press, 1938).

Section C   The Proposed Internationalization of Trieste (1947–1954)

At the end of the First World War Italy had been awarded the city and hinterland of Trieste, to the great chagrin of the new state of Yugoslavia. At the end of the Second World War Yugoslavia wanted to rectify this matter, and seemed well placed to do so, as her troops were the first of the victors to enter the area. However, following the receipt of what amounted to an ultimatum from her British and American allies, she handed over the city of Trieste and the immediately surrounding territory to them. The leading victorious powers then tried to agree amongst themselves over what to do. Although Italy had entered the War on the German side, she had ended it on the other as a 'co-belligerent'. This was a somewhat dubious status, but it did mean that some notice had to be taken of Italy's views, with the result that the issue was in the nature of an intra-club problem.

Eventually it was decided that most of the region should go to Yugoslavia, but that in the area of the city of Trieste a separate Free Territory of Trieste should be created and placed under the wing of the UN Security Council. The Council was to be responsible for the maintenance of public order, which in the first instance was to be maintained by local police and security services. Armed forces were to be allowed in the Territory only under the Security Council's direction. The Council endorsed this plan in January 1947, and it was confirmed in the Peace Treaty which was signed with Italy in the following month. Pending its implementation the United States and the United Kingdom were to remain in occupation of the northern part of the designated Free Territory – Zone A – and Yugoslavia of the southern part – Zone B. Neither of the claimants were particularly pleased, but there was nothing they could do about it. However, this proved to be far from the end of the problem (see Map 13).

84

The Free Territory arrangement was to come into force on the Security Council's appointment of a Governor for it, but on this key matter the West and the Soviet Union failed to agree. Italy and Yugoslavia were asked to consult with a view to recommending a candidate, but they fared no better than their senior brethren. By 1948 Yugoslavia had lost much Western sympathy on account, generally, of the onset of the Cold War and her membership of the Eastern bloc, and, particularly, of her aid to the communist insurgents in Greece. In respect of Italy, on the other hand, the West wanted to help the Christian Democrats, who were in danger of being overtaken in the general election campaign by the Communist Party. As the communists were under the disadvantage of not being able to take a national line on Trieste, due to their ideological obligation to support Yugoslavia, it was announced by Britain, France, and the United States that the Peace Treaty should be revised to give the whole of the proposed Free Territory to Italy.

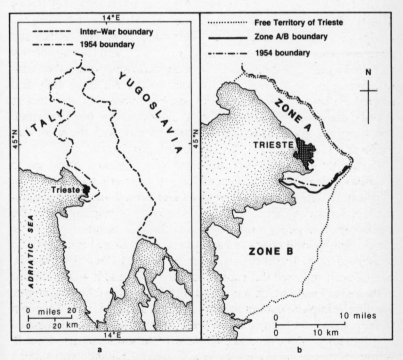

Map 13   (a) International boundaries in the Trieste area (b) The proposed Free Territory of Trieste

This did the electoral trick, but was also the end of the plan for a Free Territory. This scheme was in any event losing its allure in the West because of the role it would give the Soviet Union. That state, however, suddenly discovered a keen interest in Trieste's internationalization, for the expulsion of Yugoslavia from the Soviet bloc in June 1948 meant that the Soviet Union no longer had a land link with the Adriatic through her satellites. Moreover, the Soviets now had no need to worry about Yugoslav susceptibilities. Such was the Soviet Union's new enthusiasm for the idea that she proposed as Governor someone whom she had earlier rejected when he had been a Western nominee. But it was too late. The status quo survived as an interim measure until 1954, when Italy and Yugoslavia were persuaded, subject to a minor rectification in Yugoslavia's favour, to accept it as final. Even the Soviet Union took official cognizance of it.

Thus what had begun as a problem within the victors' club was resolved more or less within the Western club – and was even rounded off by a rare show of unity amongst the leading states of the war-time alliance. In a different perspective, the episode was reminder that although the idea of international government in perpetuity for a disputed area has a certain superficial attraction, there may be considerable difficulties over its implementation. Even if influential states at a distance are able to agree about it, which can by no means be assumed, the immediate claimants may not reconcile themselves to it. It ought also to be remembered that the proposed subjects may be less than enthusiastic about such a scheme which, after all, gives them something of the status of what is now that most unpopular of arrangements: a colony.

FURTHER READING

John C. Campbell (ed.), *Successful Negotiation: Trieste 1954* (Princeton, NJ: Princeton University Press, 1976).

Alan James, *The Politics of Peacekeeping* (London: Chatto & Windus, 1969).

UN, *Yearbook of the United Nations 1946–47* (New York: Department of Public Information, UN, 1947).

Section D   The Civil War in Greece (1947–1954)

During the Second World War Greece was occupied by Germany and the unpopular right-wing government went into exile. At first the British-supported underground movement was led by communists, but subsequently a non-communist resistance group emerged, and in 1943 Britain switched her support to it. She then endeavoured to reconcile the two sides but without much success. In consequence, after her troops landed in Greece in October 1944 they found themselves fighting not only the Germans but also, before long, the forces of the communist movement. The latter came off worst and therefore retired to the north of the country to engage in guerrilla warfare against the restored government and its foreign supporters. Here they soon received a substantial fillip in the shape of assistance from the communist regimes which had been indigenously established in two neighbouring states, Albania and Yugoslavia, and from that which had been installed in a third, Bulgaria, by the Soviet Union (see Map 14).

The situation in Greece was one of the first to come to the new United Nations and led to some inconclusive diplomatic skirmishing – which helped to identify the opposing lines in the emerging Cold War. In December 1946, however, the chief adversaries each thought it worth their while to support the establishment of a UN Commission of Investigation on which every Security Council member was represented. It was an opportunity for the Soviet Union to gain some publicity for her view of events in Greece, but not surprisingly the report of the Western majority on the Commission provided a very different account of what was going on. That was enough for the Soviets, who therefore vetoed a proposal which would in effect have continued the Commission, and another which would have established an observer group on Greece's northern borders.

The Western states, however, realised they were on to a good thing. In March 1947 the United States had declared – in what was to be known as the Truman Doctrine – that she would help any free people

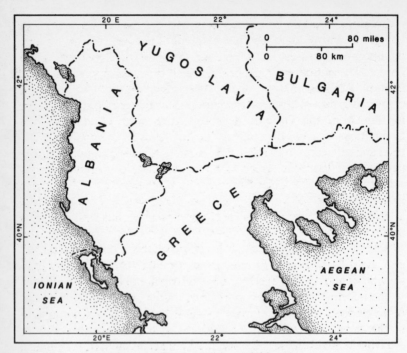

Map 14   Greece and her neighbours

who were resisting attempts by outsiders or armed internal minorities
to overthrow their government. Greece was identified as one of the
Doctrine's first beneficiaries (a sign of Britain's decline as a major
power), and it would clearly be helpful to the United States and her
friends if no less a body than the UN continued to confirm that the
Greek member of the Western club was legitimately in need of help.
Accordingly, the question was transferred from the Security Control to
the UN General Assembly, which was both vetoless and, at that time,
dominated by the West. It obliged in October 1947 by adopting an
American draft resolution which set up a Special Committee on the
Balkans (Unscob) to check on whether Greece's communist neighbours
were, as asked, stopping their aid to the guerrillas and normalizing
their relations with Greece.

Unscob was to consist of the five permanent members of the Security
Council – Britain, China, France, the Soviet Union, and the United
States – and six other states: Australia, Brazil, Mexico, Netherlands,
Pakistan, and Poland. The Soviet Union and Poland, however, refused
to participate, and their ideological associates to the immediate north

of Greece declined the role of co-hosts for a body which was obviously going to censure their conduct. Unscob therefore, except on one unimportant occasion, had to operate solely on the Greek side of the border. The national delegations of which it was composed included military advisers, and the Committee soon decided to set up an organized system of border observation, receiving retrospective approval for this from the General Assembly. Each member state on the Committee was asked to provide suitable persons for this quasi-military task, and all except Australia (then under a left-wing regime) and the new state of Pakistan agreed to do so. About three dozen observers were provided and a Chief Observer divided them into six field teams (plus one in reserve) which, together with necessary supporting staff of a technical kind, were stationed at appropriate points near Greece's northern borders. From these posts they patrolled in liaison with and sometimes in the company of the Greek armed forces, making enquiries into guerrilla activities, frontier incidents, and related matters, and sometimes finding that border clashes took place under their very eyes.

The information gathered by the observer teams provided the bulk of the evidence on which Unscob concluded in 1948, and again in each of the three subsequent years, that the insurgents in Greece were receiving material and moral assistance from her communist neighbours, who were thus endangering peace and security in the Balkans. The Soviet Union replied to this annual chronicle of communist iniquity with a variety of charges, popular among which were Unscob's illegality, its character as a tool of American and British ruling circles, their endeavour to use it for espionage, and its bias in favour of Greece.

That Unscob was biased in Greece's favour is, at one level, indisputable. Certain states were clearly interfering in Greek affairs, and the UN Committee was set up not to consider whether their actions had any justification but, in essence, to point an accusing finger at them. It could be argued that this activity was functionally within the concept of peacekeeping, in that it could have a deterrent effect and so contribute both to the defusing of the crisis and to a form of settlement. But the argument is thin, as there was little ground for thinking that Albania, Bulgaria, and Yugoslavia would be deterred by the prospect or actuality of critical reports from a Western-oriented body, notwithstanding the fact that it was all done in the name of the UN. Furthermore, while deterrence can no more be completely separated from the idea of peacekeeping than it can from many other aspects of life, it is in no way central to it. The context in which peacekeeping manifests itself is marked by at least some kind of cooperation from the parties to the dispute. But in this case there was never any chance of that from the communist states to the north of Greece. For obvious reasons they were opposed to Unscob's existence, and their behaviour towards it virtually never expressed anything other than that negative stance. On this ground too, therefore, Unscob hardly seems like an example of peacekeeping.

Another point which could be made in this connection is that what Unscob itself came to call its observation service was not wholly military in its make-up. For when the Committee decided to set that service up, not all the observers who were supplied to it were drawn from their countries' armed forces. However, some of them were, and all were seen as having the qualifications necessary for this quasi-military task – the British observers, for example, being recently-demobilized military officers. Moreover, before long virtually all of them were military people. It is therefore legitimate to see that the Unscob observer role as having, in terms of its personnel, a military character. Moreover, there is no reason to doubt that the observers acted impartially, in the immediate sense that they simply reported on what they saw. Each observer team did have a political affairs officer from the UN Secretariat among its support staff, but he was not there to keep them on the pro-Greek straight and narrow but to advise them about background matters which were not within their competence. It also appears that although the observers were part of their respective national Unscob delegations, which as a whole would have been under national instructions of however general a kind, the observers were not individually under political instructions. Instead, their responsibility to the UN was emphasized through, for instance, the wearing of (yellow) UN armbands. The need for impartiality and discretion was also stressed, and it seems that their reports to Unscob's headquarters were not tinkered with or slanted in any way but simply attached to Unscob's own reports.

Of course, this approach was greatly facilitated by the fact that there was plently for the observers to see of the sort that Unscob, and the majority in the General Assembly, wanted seen. But it does seem that at this time, when the UN and its members were groping their way towards what later became conceptualized as peacekeeping, the observational side of Unscob's work was evolving towards the idea of a body of independent individuals who owed their loyalty direct to the UN. This was underlined by the fact that, at least from 1949, the observers received a per diem allowance from the UN – a supplement to their individual national salaries – to cover the extra subsistence costs which their work entailed.

By the start of the 1950s the situation in which Unscob was operating had altered in several important respects. Yugoslavia's defection/ expulsion from the communist bloc in 1948 had led to a marked reduction in her aid to the insurgents, and they were also having a much harder time of it in Greece as, with considerable American assistance, the economy improved and the armed forces were strengthened. On the other international side, the Soviet Union evidently had no stomach for a confrontation with the United States over Greece, and she therefore cut her losses. Thus the guerrillas found their support diminishing on every side: an obviously failing cause, like its opposite, has its own momentum. In consequence, it was possible in 1950 to cut the number of observers from 35 to 24. A further reduction followed, and at the end of 1951, on the initiative of Greece, the UN General Assembly decided to wind Unscob up as from early in 1952. Any kind of help is appreciated at a time of weakness, but when the position improves states easily get restive at the presence of international bodies.

However, as a reminder that communists were not to be trusted, the General Assembly also decided, with Greek support, to keep an eye on the situation through the UN's recently-created Peace Observation Commission. It was asked to establish a Balkans Sub-Commission, situated at the UN's headquarters in New York, but with authority to despatch observers upon request and with the consent of the proposed host, to any area of tension in the Balkans. The Sub-Commission, consisting of Colombia, France, Pakistan, Sweden, and the United States, was set up in January 1952. At the request of Greece a small team of military observers, one from each member and a chief observer from Britain, was sent to her border areas and made periodic collective reports direct to the General Assembly. This small team was subsequently reduced in size, and withdrawn in 1954.

In terms of their function and of the context to which they were sent, Unscob and the Balkans Sub-Commission canot be categorized as peacekeeping operations. Rather, they illustrated how the UN could be used by its dominant majority in a finger-pointing Cold War capacity. But on the basis of the professional character of their observers and the way in which they operated, these two bodies can be seen as very much in line with what was to become the peacekeeping tradition. It is also not going too far to suggest that they may have contributed to its development, as they helped to build up experience at the UN as to the way in which impartial and non-threatening military personnel could be best organized and used with a view to the containment or amelioration of tension.

FURTHER READING

John Campbell, 'The Greek Civil War', in Evan Luard (ed.), *The International Regulation of Civil Wars* (London: Thames and Hudson, 1972).

Rosalyn Higgins, *United Nations Peacekeeping. Documents and Commentary. Vol. IV: Europe 1946–1979* (Oxford: Oxford University Press, 1981).

Alan James, *The Politics of Peacekeeping* (London: Chatto and Windus, 1969).

Section E   The Crisis Over
Kuwait
(1961–1963)

The small state of Kuwait at the head of what was then known as the Persian Gulf had been under British protection since the end of the nineteenth century. When this arrangement was brought to an end in June 1961, Kuwait's first taste of international life was very sour: a threat from neighbouring Iraq to 'liberate' what she announced was a part of her domain. This caused concern in a number of quarters, for although Kuwait possessed little by way of either people or territory, she was then the largest crude oil producer in the region and third largest in the world, supplying about 40 per cent of British imports of this key resource. On the basis of a treaty which had been signed with Britain only a week or two earlier, Kuwait asked for help, and about 6,000 British troops, with strong naval and air backing, were quickly moved to Kuwait. Manifestly, they were there to fight if that proved necessary, and were therefore not engaged in peacekeeping (see Map 15).

The arrival of the British force caused much consternation amongst the club of Arab states who, in an unusual unanimity of opinion, set about the task of engineering its early withdrawal. Apart from Iraq, they were also all agreed on the necessity of Kuwait's independence being maintained, not least because of their desire that this valuable economic prize should not fall into Iraq's hands. Britain, for her part, was very willing to go provided that Kuwait's future could be credibly guaranteed. The Arab League therefore agreed in mid-July (Iraq having walked out of the meeting) that it would provide a force to replace that of Britain.

The implementation of this decision was not easy, but by September a Force with a strength of about 3,000 began to arrive in Kuwait. It was drawn chiefly from Saudi Arabia and the United Arab Republic (UAR – Egypt and Syria), smaller contingents being supplied by Jordan, Sudan, and Tunisia. It had the desired short-term effect, in that the British force then left. At this point, however, the Arab League Force, which in theory was designed to take over Britain's job, began to

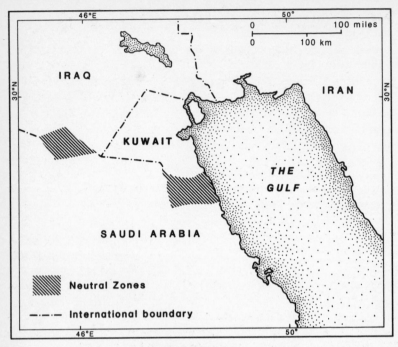

Map 15　Kuwait

disintegrate. The break-up of the sovereign UAR into its two previously and now again-sovereign components led to recriminations in Kuwait, and the withdrawal of Egyptian and Syrian troops. To compensate for this, Jordan increased the size of her contingent. But with Iraq now generally adopting a less belligerent tone, neither Kuwait nor the contributors seemed keen for the Force to remain. By February 1963 it had disappeared, an Arab League plan for a token force to stay behind having come to naught.

Notwithstanding the similar functions which were assigned to them and the rough equivalence in size between the British and the Arab League forces, the latter was not really intended to engage in fighting, and would in all probability have collapsed had it been called upon to do so. It is therefore possible to see the Arab League as having provided a peacekeeping force which served a dual function. Firstly, it was meant to make a contribution to the defusing of the dispute between Iraq and Kuwait by acting as a psychological deterrent to an Iraqi attack. The hope was that even if Iraq had been contemplating armed action to back up her claim to Kuwait, she would hold back because of the presence of the Arab League Force. For an attack in these circumstances would certainly incur the odium of the rest of the Arab world. And even if the Force did not resist, it might nonetheless incur casualities, which could cause Iraq considerable damage of a political kind.

In most situations a peacekeeping force is unlikely to produce this sort of deterrent effect, for if a state has a strong impulse towards war it is unlikely to resist the final step because of the fact that a lightly-armed multinational force is in the area. But this particular case was rather unusual, given an Arab League Force on one side, a potential Arab aggressor on the other, and the fervour with which Arabs at least talk about the strength of the ties by which they are all bound. Especially in view of the doubt which existed about Iraq's determination to go to war, this may therefore have been a rare instance of a peacekeeping type of force making, by its mere presence, the difference between war and peace. For in the event Iraq did not press her claim, and Kuwait benefitted from the show of Arab solidarity in support of her sovereign statehood.

Secondly, however, and perhaps more importantly, the Arab League Force was intended to remove the tension which had arisen between Britain and the Arab states following the assistance which the former had given to Kuwait. It was a matter of dishonour to the Arabs both that one of their number had recalled to her territory the Western imperial state who had only just left it, and that the reason for her doing so was misbehaviour within their own camp. The Force was a means of remedying this perceived slur on the ability of Arabs to handle affairs inside their own club. From Britain's point of view, the Force was a means of enabling her to depart without any loss of face. She saw herself as having done the honourable thing by helping Kuwait, but was ready to stand down in favour of an alternative solution which seemed adequate and satisfied Kuwait. There was no need to examine the fighting credentials of the Arab League Force too closely. It sounded and looked good enough, especially in view of the suspicion that it might not need to be of more than symbolic value, and that was sufficient for a somewhat harassed Britain.

In these ways the Arab League Force helped to defuse the immediate dispute and settle an associated one, albeit rather untidily. It showed two things about the value, in appropriate circumstances, of a lightly-armed multinational force: first, that it can be politically stronger than it looks; and second, that it can assist the members of a club in getting rid of an unwelcome intrusion.

FURTHER READING

David Holden, *Farewell to Arabia* (London: Faber, 1966).
David W. Wainhouse *et al.*, *International Peacekeeping at the Crossroads* (Baltimore, Md: Johns Hopkins University Press, 1973).

Section F The Dispute Between Algeria and Morocco (1963–1964)

On becoming independent in 1956 Morocco laid claim to a part of the Sahara Desert which was then within French Algeria. In 1963, a year after Algeria had secured her independence, Morocco invaded the disputed territory. The Organization of African Unity (OAU) had just been created but Morocco was not keen on its involvement, as Algeria had a strong diplomatic position in Africa, and there were no precedents to nudge her towards using the new body. There was, however, a general view that the dispute should be dealt within the African club, and this led the heads of state of Ethiopia – who was said also to be acting on behalf of the OAU's Provisional Secretariat – and Mali to arrange a meeting with those of the disputants. It took place in October 1963. The outcome was an agreement on a cease-fire, the determination of a demilitarized zone by army officers from each of these four states, and the supervision of both the cease-fire and the zone by a Cease-Fire Commission composed of Ethiopian and Malian officers. The search for a settlement of the dispute was entrusted to an OAU commission (see Map 16).

The cease-fire was soon obtained, and in February 1964 agreement was reached on a 9-mile-wide demilitarized zone. Then, however, and contrary to what seems to have been the original intention, it was agreed by all concerned that the Cease-Fire Commission should disband. But Morocco did not follow this up by leaving the territory she had occupied. In 1965 another agreement, similar to that of 1963, was reached, but was stillborn. Meanwhile, the OAU mediatory commission was also failing to make headway. The matter reverted to the parties, and eventually, in 1970, they set up a joint commission to demarcate the frontier along the lines used in the colonial period. An agreement confirming the work of the commission was signed in 1972, the effect of which was to leave the disputed area in Algerian hands.

97

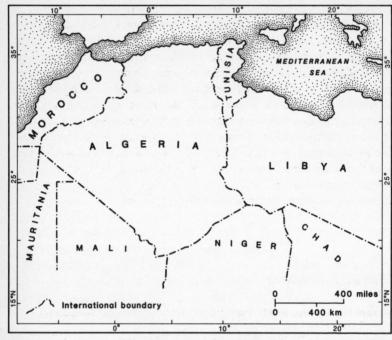

Map 16   Algeria and Morocco

The problem in this case seemed to be that, contrary to appearances, a genuine agreement had not been reached. The scene was therefore unsuitable for the peacekeeping mechanism which had been established. But that mechanism itself was very skimpy and short-lived, and it is just possible that had a larger peacekeeping body made a firmer appearance at the disputed area, the parties would have found it difficult to disown the conciliatory words they had uttered. In the normal way peacekeepers cannot affect policy decisions, but are dependent for their effectiveness on the policy makers. Here, however, policy had, in theory, been laid down, and in a manner which provided for peacekeeping. An opportunity was therefore at hand for a peacekeeping operation to capitalize on the situation. But the provision of just a few officers from two friendly states was hardly a promising base for such a move – and it may be that that had been in the mind of at least one of the parties all along.

There is no reason in principle why peacekeeping should not be conducted on an ad hoc basis by the representative of willing states.

In this case, given the desire of those concerned to allow Africa to look after its own problem, Morocco's distrust of both the Arab League and the OAU, and the fact that the OAU had not properly got going, there was little by way of a practical alternative. But the experience does underline the point that if peacekeepers cannot dress themselves in the colours of a respected institution, and so add to the authority of what they say and do, it is all the more important that the arrangements regarding them should be fully adequate in every respect. Those which were made in respect of the Algerian–Moroccan border dispute could not be so described. Perhaps the outcome would have been the same even if the peacekeeping plans had been satisfactorily comprehensive. But this was one of those rare situations where a more impressive presence on the ground might have made a difference.

FURTHER READING

Hussein A. Hassouna, *The League of Arab States and Regional Disputes* (Dobbs Ferry, NY: Oceana, 1975).

Nathan Pelcovits, 'Peacekeeping: the African Experience', in Henry Wiseman (ed.), *Peacekeeping* (New York: Pergamon Press, 1983).

Saadia Touval, *The Boundary Politics of Independent Africa* (Cambridge, Mass.: Harvard University Press, 1972).

Patricia Berko Wild, 'The Organization of African Unity and the Algerian–Moroccan Border Conflict', *International Organization*, XX (1) (Winter 1966).

Section G The Problem of Chad (1979–1982)

Chad is the fifth largest state in Africa, but for her size has a small population and is very poor. Following independence in 1960, the country was for years rent by factional fighting, and the government never exercised anything like full control over its domain. Indeed, it was often little more than one of the warring groups, notwithstanding the fact that for much of the time it received assistance from France, the ex-colonial power. Here, therefore, was a rudderless sovereign state. But because even her capacity for drift was limited, and there was virtually nothing on board to tempt any raiding parties, Chad was allowed to get on with just making a mess of her own affairs.

In the late 1970s, however, the sub-Saharan members of the Organization of African Unity (OAU) began to take an interest in Chad's problems, spurred on by the fact that the country's northern neighbour, Libya, was doing likewise (and had since 1973 occupied Chad's northern 45,000-square-mile Aozou strip). Early in 1979, at the request of her government and with the agreement of Chad's other neighbours, Nigeria sent a force of 150 men, which was later increased to 800, to assist in the maintenance of a cease-fire and of stability in the area of the capital, Ndjamena. However, things did not go well between the alleged peacekeepers and their hosts (it seems there were faults on both sides), and within a few months the Nigerians were asked to go. Shortly afterwards, an agreement was reached between a number of African states for the despatch of what was called an OAU neutral force, to be composed of 1,500 men from Benin, Congo (Brazzaville), and Guinea. But this came to virtually nothing: only the Congolese arrived, they served no peacekeeping function, and soon left. A further OAU effort in 1980 was completely fruitless (see Map 17).

At this time Libya sent troops into the heart of the country, which resulted in the installation of a pro-Libyan regime. This spurred the OAU itself to produce a 1981 agreement that a 5,000-man peacekeeping force should be sent to Chad to replace the Libyans, part the local factions,

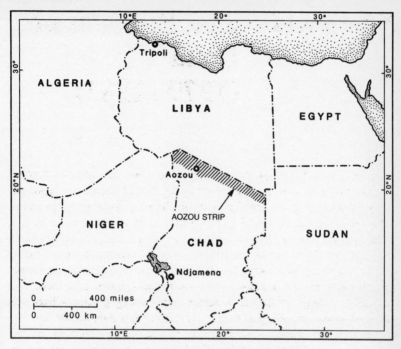

Map 17   Libya's territorial claim on Chad

and pave the way to an internal settlement. The Force was to be drawn from six of its members – Nigeria, Senegal, Zaire, Benin, Guinea and Togo – but in the event troops arrived only from the first three of these states, and the Force therefore never reached more than about 3,500 men. Britain, France, and the United States, all of whom were worried about Libya's ambitions and behaviour, gave help of various kinds to the three contributors. To the surprise of some, Libya, on request of the Chadian government, immediately withdrew her forces to make way for the peacekeepers.

However, both the contributors and the OAU quickly found that peacekeeping was not an inexpensive activity, and that it was something for which the member states were reluctant to pay. The UN was asked for help, but there was little hope of hard cash from that quarter. On the ground, too, the situation was geting more confused and frustrating. The Chadian government turned down OAU proposals for an internal settlement, saying that the country was not an OAU protectorate, but the government was also dissatisfied at not getting more support from the OAU Force against increasingly successful attacks by its internal opponents. In face of this situation, and with the Force already beginning to collapse, the OAU decided in June 1982 on its withdrawal. At this point the Chadian government fell, and its successor asked that the mandate of the Force be extended, but to no effect. By the end of the month it had left.

The despatch of the OAU Force to Chad was a reflection of the view that the African club, in its organizational embodiment (which had existed since 1963), should look after its own problems. Moreover, as the Force, in accordance with the values of peacekeeping, was to be impartial and non-threatening, the decision to mount it did not seem too ambitious. But the Force found itself in a very difficult situation. Keeping factions apart is manageable on a non-threatening basis only if they agree to stop fighting, and it helps a great deal if they cooperate with the peacekeeping force. In Chad neither of these things happened. In consequence, the Force was unable to play a positive role of any significance, and its presence began to be incompatible with its peacekeeping credentials. For in the context of fighting on the relatively small scale which was occurring in Chad, and the lack of a government whose legitimacy was generally accepted, the deployment of a military force was likely to have a partial effect no matter how impartial the conscious behaviour of its contingents. For it was probably going to be an obstruction to the activities of one side or the other, or both, and thus be seen by the stronger party as helping the weaker. The OAU Force did this deliberately, by trying to stand in the way of the advancing rebels. This was justifiable on the ground that the Force was simply doing what it could to stop the fighting. But it took it very close to the margins of peacekeeping, if not over them into the role of a participant. And at the same time the Force was abused by the government for not doing more to defend the status quo.

Nor were the difficulties of the Force confined to the local scene. For it became embarrassingly clear that the institutional context in which the operation was being conducted was also quite inadequate for peacekeeping. The OAU neither possessed nor had access to the financial and logistical resources which were necessary for the support of its Force. Part of the deficiency could be and was supplied by well wishers, but that still left the Organization with a considerable financial responsibility – with which it was just unable to cope. It also appeared that despite adequate-looking paper provisions, the administrative arrangements for the Force were well below scratch.

Altogether, therefore, the Chad Force was not an advertisement for peacekeeping. Its experience underlined the point that running a multinational force is a costly business which also requires efficient backing. It was, too, a reminder that, no matter how strong the political temptation to establish a peacekeeping force – as a sign that an organization is doing something in response to a problem for which it is seen to have some responsibility – there is little operational future for such a force if the local situation is unsuitable for it. Peacekeeping is a secondary activity. It cannot, therefore, create the conditions for its own success, but is dependent on the parties supplying an appropriate context for its work. In Chad such a context was, in the early 1980s, almost completely lacking.

In August 1989, however, Libya and Chad agreed to take their dispute over the Aozou Strip to the International Court of Justice, and Libya also promised to withdraw her troops from the Strip within a year unless a political settlement permitted them to stay. At least on paper, this is the sort of context which is suitable for peacekeeping. Whether it is sufficiently complex or sensitive to justify such an operation remains to be seen.

FURTHER READING

C. O. C. Amate, *Inside the OAU* (London: Macmillan, 1986).

M. C. Dunn, 'Chad: the OAU Tries Peacekeeping', *The Washington Quarterly* (Spring 1982).

Nathan Pelcovits, 'Peacekeeping: The African Experience', in Henry Wiseman (ed.), *Peacekeeping* (New York: Pergamon Press, 1983).

Indar Jit Rikhye, *The Theory and Practice of Peacekeeping* (London: Hurst, 1984).

Henry Wiseman, 'The United Nations and International Peacekeeping: A Comparative Analysis', in United Nations Institute for Training and Research, *The United Nations and the Maintenance of International Peace and Security* (Dordrecht: Nijhoff, 1987).

Section H The Nigerian Civil War (1968-1970)

Throughout 1966 there was widespread disorder in Nigeria, with the Ibo people from its Eastern Region coming under particular attack in other parts of the country. Over a million of them returned home, and in May 1967 the Eastern Region – which for almost a year had been more or less governing itself – declared its independence under the name of Biafra. A bitter civil war began and initially the Biafrans achieved some military success. But at the official international level only one Caribbean and four African states formally recognized the existence of a new sovereign state. In other parts of the continent and beyond, and therefore also at the UN, the official view was that this was an internal Nigerian affair, to which the much-endorsed principle of national self-determination had no application. In consequence, there was no real question of a peacekeeping force being mounted. For quite apart from Nigeria's principled unwillingness to internationalize what she saw as a domestic problem, any such force would have had the effect of hampering the Federal Government's forces and of giving some legitimacy to the weaker rebels. From the Government's point of view, this war was to be one to the finish (see Map 18).

In the West, however, the Biafrans obtained much unofficial sympathy. Nigeria's Eastern Region was predominantly Christian, and good use was made of the international links which were thus available. An effective public relations campaign was also mounted at the secular level, and pictures of starving Biafran children made a big emotional impact. Tales began to spread that the Federal Government's forces had engaged in terror bombing and were bent on genocide. In an endeavour to counter these allegations, the Government, in August 1968, invited four states and two international organizations each to send one observer to inspect Federal military operations in the field. Those approached were Canada, Poland, Sweden, the United Kingdom, the Organization of African Unity (OAU), and the United Nations. All responded positively.

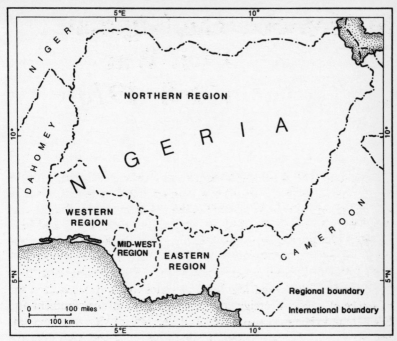

Map 18   Nigeria

The representatives of the two organizations reported individually, but the army officers sent by the four states operated as a team, making joint reports. Some lapses in military behaviour were noted, including a few directed at the observers themselves, one over-zealous officer being so little enamoured by their presence that he threatened an observer with a flogging. But this was an exception to the cooperation which the Observer Team otherwise received. It was present until Biafra's defeat early in 1970, and on the whole reported very favourably on the conduct of the Federal Government's forces.

From one angle this military observer group might not seem a good example of international peacekeeping. It looks like the case of a government getting sympathetic outsiders to give it a favourable report, and so using them just for its own purposes. But there is no necessary reason why self-interested motives should be seen as incompatible with peacekeeping. All states who invite peacekeepers on to their soil, or who cooperate with such bodies, are hoping, in one way or another, to benefit from so doing. They are making use of a certain kind of international help because they deem its employment to be, for them, a desirable (even if the least undesirable) course. Moreover, although peacekeeping normally arises and operates in a bilateral context, there is no reason in principle why it should not relate only to one party to an international dispute if by so doing it can contribute to the creation or maintenance of calm or to a settlement.

There is no ground for thinking that the Observer Team did not operate impartially. Its presence arose out of a conflict which had clear de facto international elements. And although it was not designed to help in the settlement of an inter-state dispute, its activity was arranged in the hope of heading off a looming international problem. For the Federal Government was worried about the possibility of domestic pressure in certain Western states, particularly France (whence, via Gabon, Biafra received some arms), resulting in official action in favour of Biafra. If Biafra had had a firmer international footing, the Team's presence on just one side might have led to complications and recriminations, which in turn could have resulted in its disbandment; indeed, it might not even have been created. But in the circumstances which actually prevailed, it did a job which had much in keeping with peacekeeping of the more usual kind, so demonstrating the flexibility of this international tool.

FURTHER READING

Report of the Observer Team to Nigeria, 24 September to 23 November 1988 (London: Her Majesty's Stationery Office, Cmnd. 3878, Nigeria no. 1, 1969).

J. J. Stremlau, *The International Politics of the Nigerian Civil War* (Princeton, NJ: Princeton University Press, 1977).

Section I The Birth of Zimbabwe (1979–1980)

SUPERVISING THE CEASE-FIRE

The white minority regime in the British self-governing territory of Rhodesia (called Southern Rhodesia until 1963) unilaterally declared its independence in 1965. The declaration was recognized neither by Britain nor by any other sovereign state, but de facto the rebels were in command of Rhodesia for a period of 14 years. However, the regime was harried not just verbally and economically from without, where the UN was in the vanguard, but also physically from within, in the shape of a liberation war waged by black guerrilla groups who were collectively known as the Patriotic Front (PF). Finally, in 1979, an agreement was reached under Britain's sponsorship for a cease-fire and a brief resumption of British rule, during which elections would be held to determine under whose local auspices Rhodesia would move to lawful independence as the sovereign state of Zimbabwe (see Map 19).

As part of this arrangement, provision was made for a Monitoring Force (MF) of about 1,500 men to watch over and do what it could (by way of persuasion, not enforcement) to maintain the cease-fire. This Force was under the command of a Briton who was also the military adviser to the reinstalled British Governor, and Britain had the determining voice regarding its composition. Given her view about the proper way of organizing the transition of power, the bulk of the MF – 1,250 – was British. But as a concession to the PF's wish that there should be substantial non-British elements in the Force, and that ideally it would be under the UN's auspices – which Britain categorically rejected – troops from four Commonwealth states were included: 150 Australians, 74 New Zealanders, 50 Kenyans, and 24 Fijians. The MF thus acquired something of the character of a Commonwealth body, and it is sometimes so described. But as well as being under British control, Britain financed the Force (paying the extra costs of the non-British elements) and provided much of its logistics and transport, receiving help in this last respect from the United States.

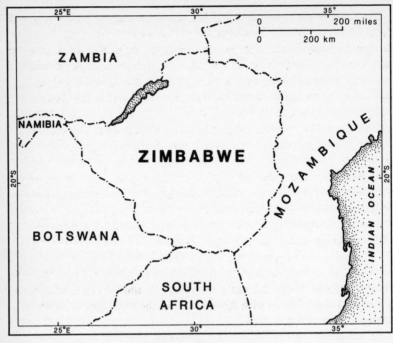

Map 19   Zimbabwe

The cease-fire and associated documents were formally signed on 21 December 1979. By that date advance units of the MF had already arrived in Rhodesia, and it was soon at full strength. It had to use its best efforts to calm any incipient tension and defuse any incidents which occurred. Breaches of the cease-fire had to be reported to the joint cease-fire commission made up of the representatives of the Rhodesian and PF forces, with the Governor's military adviser as chairman, and investigations made on its behalf. Contact had thus to be maintained with the command structure of both sides. So far as the PF guerrillas were concerned, who were widely scattered throughout the veld and whose numbers were somewhat indeterminate, the Force checked on their gathering at rendezvous points and their movement to larger assembly points. With regard to the Rhodesian forces, the MF deployed at their various bases and airfields. It also established itself at border crossing-points to confirm that no improper use was made of them, and maintained liaison teams in the neighbouring states of Zambia and Mozambique.

The small Monitoring Force (MF) was thus very thinly spread, and often found itself in situations of considerable uncertainty and/or danger. In accordance with the peacekeeping principles on which the MF was based (although, in deference to British susceptibilities, the term was never officially used of the Force), its members carried nothing more than personal arms for individual self-defence in the last resort. But perhaps on account of these factors, which meant that the MF was manifestly neither a direct threat to any of the parties nor capable of playing an independent hand, the Force enjoyed a remarkable degree of success. Naturally it encountered difficulties and suspicions. But it soon received a good deal of confidence and respect from those whose activities it was monitoring, and even managed to assert some authority. In consequence it was able to play a truly notable part in defusing the conflict on the ground, maintaining the resultant truce in a complicated and volatile situation, and so providing a sufficiently calm framework for the elections which were central to the settlement of the whole dispute. These were held at the end of February (producing a clear-cut result) and the Force left early in March. A month later Britain cut her constitutional links with Rhodesia, and the new state of Zimbabwe took her international bow.

In contributing to this pacific outcome, the MF was, of course, operating in the context of an agreed cease-fire which was not only accepted by the internal parties but also respected by the neighbouring states (who had been playing an indirect part in the liberation war). Like all peacekeeping bodies, its role was, at bottom, secondary. But this does seem to be one of those relatively rare cases where the assistance of an impartial and non-forceful third party was absolutely essential, rather than merely valuably helpful, for the achievement of the desired result. This was not just, or even largely, due to the bitterness of the war which had been fought over the previous ten years or so, although that did have a bearing on the situation. It was more a reflection of the fact that the arrangement of a speedy and effective cease-fire throughout the ranks of widely-scattered and often loosely-controlled guerrillas would have been almost impossible without a neutral go-between.

At the three-month-long constitutional conference which had led to the agreement on how to settle the Rhodesian dispute, Britain was not at all keen on the idea of involving an international force. For although the dispute had developed wide international ramifications, she still saw it as one for which she had a very special responsibility. Thus she did not warm to the prospect of the establishment of, as she saw it, a multinational group of busybodies. Instead, she suggested that the task of keeping an eye on the cease-fire could well be conducted by some British policemen. There may have been something of the establishment of a bargaining position about this offer, and the outcome was an arrangement which had the appearance of giving the Commonwealth some responsibility for the birth of a state who would have all the qualifications for membership in that club.

Britain's antipathy to the idea of international supervision was understandable in terms of possessiveness, but much less so in the light of the facts of the case. For the situation which would exist in Rhodesia after the declaration of a cease-fire cried out for some sort of impartial military presence. Even the small Force which was eventually supplied was often operating on a knife edge. Anything less, and the grand schemes of the constitutional conference could all too conceivably have come dramatically unstuck. In Rhodesia, therefore, the MF proved the enormous worth of peacekeeping.

THE COMMONWEALTH OBSERVER GROUP

The elections in Rhodesia/Zimbabwe attracted more than 200 accredited observers, from states, international organizations, and non-governmental groups. Pre-eminent among them, however, was the Observer Group organized by the Commonwealth. Its existence was due in no small measure to the Commonwealth Secretary-General, who had to contend with a distinct lack of British enthusiasm for the idea. The Group, under an Indian Chairman, consisted of 11 senior observers, each of whom was accompanied by two assistant observers (three of the latter being military officers). For the actual days of polling 30 supporting staff were added to the Group, which was serviced by a secretariat of about two dozen. Its unanimous verdict was that the elections were free and fair, and that may well have been partly due to the vigilance of this official watchdog.

This was not the only occasion since 1945 on which elections or referenda have been watched over by international teams. The UN has sometimes done so as part of arrangements leading to independence; the Commonwealth has also been used in this context; and once – in Uganda in 1980 – an election was observed by the Commonwealth in an independent state. But the Rhodesian elections of 1980 were the first in which an observer group worked alongside a peacekeeping body. It was not, however, to be the last: the same kind of situation occurred in Namibia in 1989 (see Part IV, Section K below) and in Nicaragua in 1990 (see Part I, Section L above); and it is part of the proposals for the resolution of the problems of Western Sahara and Cambodia (see Section M below, and Part IV, Section L below).

FURTHER READING

Steven Chan, *The Commonwealth Observer Group in Zimbabwe* (Gweru, Zimbabwe: Mambo Press, 1985).

Eighth Report to Heads of Government by the Commonwealth Secretary-General (London: Commonwealth Secretariat, 1981).

J. H. Learmont, 'Reflections from Rhodesia', *RUSI, Journal of the Royal United Services Institute for Defence Studies*, 125 (4) (December 1980).

Henry Wiseman and Alastair M. Taylor, *From Rhodesia to Zimbabwe* (New York: Pergamon Press, 1981).

Section J   The United States in Sinai (1975–1982)

PHASE ONE: 1975–1980

During the early 1970s the wider diplomatic context of the Egyptian–Israeli relationship was transformed. The change was presaged by Egypt's expulsion of Soviet technicians in 1972 which, not surprisingly, led to closer links with the United States. After the traumatic events of the 1973 Arab–Israeli war (see Part V, Section G below), the United States, with Egypt's cooperation, edged the Soviet Union out of the diplomatic picture by masterminding the negotiation of the First Sinai Disengagement Agreement of January 1974. Thereafter a remarkable rapprochement built up between Egypt and the United States, buttressed by huge amounts of American economic aid. This was not, however, at the expense of the traditionally-intimate links between Israel and the United States. In consequence, something in the nature of a patron–client relationship developed between the Western super-power on the one hand and both Egypt and Israel on the other. Egypt had, as it were, become a member of America's Middle Eastern club. This had considerable diplomatic possibilities, in more directions than one.

The First Disengagement Agreement had resulted in a short Israeli withdrawal eastwards across Sinai – relinquishing a little of the Egyptian territory which she had occupied since 1967. Subsequently the United States made efforts to secure a further withdrawal: the two states concerned were situated in an important and volatile part of the world, and if Egypt could be confirmed in the wisdom of aligning herself with the United States rather than the Soviet Union, the prospects for greater stability in the region would, in the American view, be enhanced. But progress was difficult. A major problem was that any such move pointed towards Israel's departure from the Giddi and Mitla Passes, which were of great strategic importance. In time Israel resigned herself to this, but was determined to hang on to the electronic surveillance station which she had built at the western end of the Giddi Pass – which gave

112

her a splendid 'view' of any Egyptian preparations for an attack. An immediate way around this obstacle was found through an agreement that Egypt should be permitted to build an equivalent station at the eastern end of the Pass – looking out to Israel's positions – with the new UN buffer zone being drawn in such a way that it included both stations. However, this was not enough for Israel, and in a notable diplomatic coup she persuaded the United States to supplement the UN's role by placing a number of her nationals in the area. Egypt was not enthusiastic about this idea, but for the sake of the greater good, in the shape of recovering more of Sinai, agreed to go along with it. Thus a Second Disengagement Agreement was signed in September 1975 (see Map 20).

The part of this scheme which involved the United States provided for the establishment of a Sinai Support Mission (SSM). This was to have the status of an independent agency of the American government, based in Washington, with its field organization being known as the Sinai Field Mission (SFM). The latter was to consist of 200 American

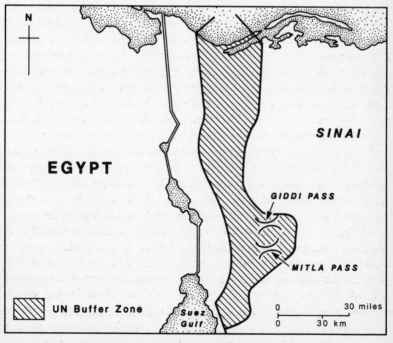

Map 20   The 1975 UN Buffer Zone in Sinai

civilians who, from a base camp and several outstations, and with the aid of sophisticated sensing devices, were to watch over a quadrilateral of about 240 square miles bounded on two of its sides by the Giddi and Mitla Passes. They were also to check that the local parties operated their surveillance stations in accordance with the agreed provisions (see Map 21).

From one point of view the SFM was a superfluous enterprise. For the UN peacekeeping force (and its associated military observers), which was already in the area and was to have a continued role under the Second Disengagement Agreement, was perfectly able to execute the tasks entrusted to the new American body. It is true that Israel, as usual, made capital out of the possibility that the UN force might be withdrawn, or disintegrate, at a time which she found inconvenient. But it was also the case that the United States could not be completely relied on in this respect. From Israel's angle, however, the important thing about the SFM was that it would go as far as possible towards

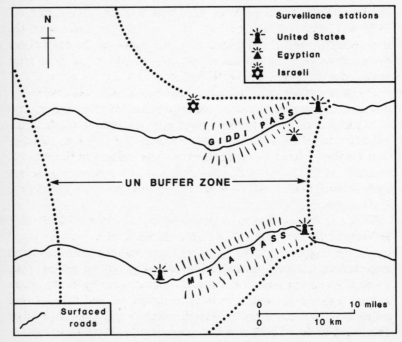

Map 21   National surveillance stations in Sinai after the 1975 Disengagement Agreement

making the United States a de facto guarantor of the disengagement process. Moreover, this guarantee would be much stronger than most, for it would involve the direct stationing of American nationals in the exact spot which would be likely to see intense fighting should Egypt try to win back more of Sinai by force. Thus the members of the SFM were to be cast in the role of arranged hostages: they were to be pledges both of United States' interest in the maintenance of the agreement and of Egypt's commitment to a peaceful relationship with Israel.

Given the United States' anxiety to make further progress with the improvement of Egyptian–Israeli relations, her negotiators were willing to pay Israel's price for her further withdrawal across Sinai – the SFM. The American Congress, however, was far from enamoured of the scheme, not least as it was keenly aware of how the country's recent humilating withdrawal from Vietnam arose out of a situation which had begun with only a small American involvement. It took an emphasis on its civilian, 'technical', character; the giving of a number of detailed assurances about the limited nature of the exercise; and some arm-twisting by the President before Congressional approval was obtained. But by mid-November 1975 the SSM had been established, and the SFM was scheduled to come into operation early in 1976, when the final redeployment of Egyptian and Israeli forces on the basis of the Second Disengagement Agreement was due to take place. After some heroic administrative and logistical efforts the timetable was met.

Over the next four years the actual number of American civilians on duty in Sinai was generally in the region of 160. SFM's top management were required to be government employees, and were seconded on a voluntary basis from Foreign Service agencies. But the other members were employed direct by the commercial firm which won the contract to install and maintain what was referred to as the American tactical early warning system. All the costs of the operation were met by the United States.

SFM's role was that of a peacekeeping observer mission of a technologically-inclined kind. Its members monitored movement in and out of the Egyptian and Israeli surveillance stations, and sometimes inspected the stations themselves, occasionally without notice. They noted all movements into and across the area covered by the American system, reported any improper ones to the parties and the UN, and asked the UN Force to try to keep the local Bedouin out of the way. From time to time the SFM was also used by the Egyptian and Israeli military authorities to pass messages to each other.

This largely passive activity contained no hint of coercion and was done with scrupulous attention to the need for impartiality – to the extent of deciding that the Director's family would live in Cairo and the Deputy Director's in Jerusalem. It was thus entirely in accord with the values of peacekeeping, and was also executing the function of helping the parties to maintain and extend a peaceful relationship. And from them the SFM received full cooperation. Israel had succeeded in involving the United States on the ground in an area about which she had become, in the light of her initial setback in the 1973 War, extremely sensitive. For her part, Egypt came to see the value of maintaining the United States' interest in the peace process and providing her with continuing evidence of Egyptian good faith. When, therefore, in 1977 the United States enquired, at the behest of Congress, about the possibility of replacing some Americans with nationals of third states, both Egypt and Israel firmly resisted such a move. After all, they were both getting what they wanted, and at no financial cost. Thus, although the SFM's personnel were not military, it fulfilled the other criteria of peacekeeping to such an extent that it can legitimately be categorized as that sort of operation.

The SFM had an uneventful life during these years. In its part of the UN buffer zone only 90 violations of the zone's demilitarized status were noted, none of them serious. And in 1979 it looked as though the SFM would soon be leaving as, in accordance with the Egyptian–Israeli Peace Treaty of 1979, Israel was due to vacate the area of the Giddi and Mitla Passes in January 1980. Plans for its removal were well advanced when a development occurred which resulted in it assuming new and different responsibilities.

PHASE TWO: 1980–1982

The Peace Treaty provided for a partial Israeli withdrawal early in 1980 from the territory which she still occupied in Sinai, and a complete withdrawal two years later. Both movements were to be supervised by the UN, which was also to check on the parties' implementation of the detailed provisions of the Treaty regarding zones in which there was a limitation on the size of military forces and the extent of their armaments. So far as the 1980–1982 period was concerned, this involved checking on Egyptian forces and armaments in two large zones (A and B) which covered most of the Sinai Desert, on the demilitarization of a narrow interim buffer zone, and on four surveillance stations (coyly referred to in the Peace Treaty as technical installations) which Israel was permitted to maintain in that zone.

It had been expected, at least formally, that these verification activities would be conducted by the existing UN Force in Sinai (Unef II) and its associated Military Observers from the UN Truce Supervision Organization (Untso). But because of the vociferous opposition of most of the Arab world to the Peace Treaty, the Soviet Union – the close friend of a number of radical Arab regimes – felt obliged to say that she would exercise her veto in the UN Security Council if it was proposed that Unef II's life be extended so that it could play the part for which it was cast in the Treaty. In consequence, the matter was not put to a vote, and Unef II came quietly to an end in July 1979 at the expiration of the period for which its current mandate ran.

Since the First Disengagement Agreement of January 1974, the UN had been entrusted with verification activities in Sinai in respect of zones of limited forces and armaments, and this work had been done by Military Observers from Untso who were attached to Unef II largely for that purpose. Untso's mandate was independent of that of Unef II, and did not require periodic extension by any UN organ. The UN therefore very reasonably suggested that an expanded group of Untso Observers could play the verification role which was provided for in the Egyptian–Israeli Peace Treaty.

Egypt was happy about this idea. Israel, however, would have none of it, notwithstanding the fact that the Treaty provided that neither party would make a unilateral request for the withdrawal of UN personnel and that such personnel could be withdrawn only by a Security Council vote which included the affirmative vote of all five permanent Council members. (This meant that each of these members, three of whom were Britain, France, and the United States, could always veto a proposal for the UN's withdrawal.) Instead, she advanced the argument that Untso would be unable to play the enforcement role envisaged for the UN force – which bore no relation to the facts, as such a role was never anticipated. Clearly, what Israel was after was a continuation of the American presence in Sinai. She was extremely happy with the role the SFM had played since 1976, and was determined to turn the winding up of Unef II to her advantage by pressing for a new American role. It was also an opportunity to discomfit the UN – whose General Assembly so often said very unkind things about her.

As the United States was most anxious that there should be no upset in the implementation of the Peace Treaty's arrangements, for which she had worked so hard, she agreed that the life of the SFM, and its parent body, the SSM, should be extended to comply with Israel's wish. She also agreed, once again, to meet all its costs. Egypt's assent to a new SFM role on her territory was forthcoming, for the same basic reason as that which motivated the United States. Accordingly, it was settled that during the rest of the interim period prior to Israel's complete withdrawal from Sinai, the SFM should conduct the verification tasks which had been envisaged for the UN. On this understanding, Israel did not object to Untso retaining a small token presence in Sinai.

In this way the SFM's main role changed from that of watching and interpreting sensor reports to one of carrying out twice-monthly inspections of Egyptian forces, preceded by a low-level aerial reconnaissance of the area. Each inspection, and its preparatory reconnaissance, involved a number of SFM teams, each team being made up of a United States Government employee (seconded from one of the Foreign Service agencies) and an Observer/Adviser recruited from amongst those with military experience and expertise. The team was always accompanied by an English-speaking Egyptian liaison officer. Additionally, each of Israel's four surveillance stations in the interim buffer zone were inspected on a monthly basis. At the end of each inspection, the SFM supplied each party with a copy of its report, which, where appropriate, would include a note drawing attention to any figures which suggested that a party was deviating from the provisions of the Treaty. Each side was entitled to ask at any time for a special inspection, which was to be carried out within 48 hours of receipt of the request, and five such inspections were held. During this two-year period, the SFM reported 29 deviations from the Treaty, but none of them were serious. Most were corrected by the party concerned or resolved in joint discussions between the parties. Sometimes the SFM's Director was invited to join Egyptian–Israeli meetings to assist in the sorting out of problems (see Map 22).

As in its first phase, the SFM received the full cooperation of both parties, not least because it operated strictly on the basis of the core peacekeeping value of impartiality. During 1980–1982, however, it made a much greater contribution to the pacification of the Egyptian–Israeli dispute than hitherto. For now it was the only peacekeeping body in the area which had a positive role, and that role was a very significant one. Relations between the two parties remained delicate, notwithstanding their agreement on a peace treaty, and there was still a considerable amount of suspicion in the air. It was therefore of the utmost importance that each had good reason to think that the other was keeping its word,

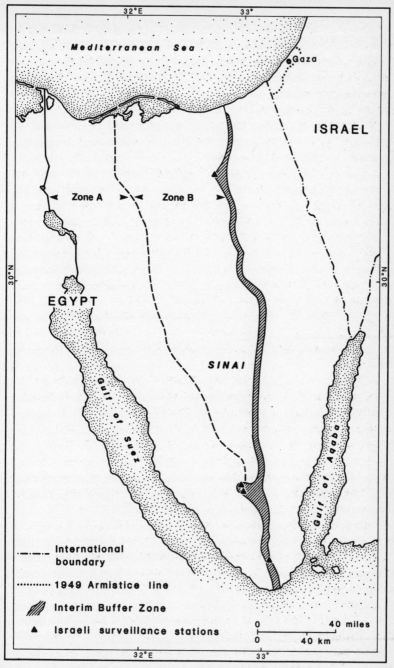

Map 22   The 1979 Interim Buffer Zone in Sinai

Within the map:

Mediterranean Sea

Gaza

ISRAEL

Zone A ← → ← Zone B →

30°N

EGYPT

SINAI

Gulf of Suez

Gulf of Aqaba

30°N

32°E   33°

_._.._   International boundary

....   1949 Armistice line

///////   Interim Buffer Zone

▲   Israeli surveillance stations

0   40 miles
0   40 km

32°E   33°

and particularly that Israel was not given any ground for postponing her departure from Sinai. It is true that the United States was continuing the aerial surveillance flights over the area which she had been making since 1974, and supplying their photographic results to the parties. But this was no substitute for impartial and trusted experts having a close look at what was actually on the ground (which was not always clear or even visible from the air). The SFM was the agency through which such experts were supplied, and through their regular reassurances the parties were encouraged to carry on with the informal peacemaking process. Thus the SFM in its second phase made a key contribution to the continued reduction of tension between two states who, not long before, had been bitter enemies.

Throughout this second period the SFM kept within its continued limit of 200 personnel, generally being about 150 strong. As previously, most of the staff were recruited by the commercial contractor who was responsible for providing what was necessary for the conduct of the Mission, but the top layer continued to be Government personnel seconded from American Foreign Service agencies. Despite the fact that they were all civilians, there can be no hesitation over classifying this second SFM phase as a peacekeeping operation. All its other aspects were resoundingly of a peacekeeping character; and each inspection team always included someone with military expertise. While, therefore, the typical peacekeeping observer mission is one in which military personnel play an untypical military role, on this occasion it was a case of civilians playing an untypical civilian role.

The SFM's work was due to end at the same time as Israel completed her departure from Egyptian territory, which was scheduled for April 1982. As this date approached there were one or two political hiccups, but in the event everything went ahead smoothly and on time. However, although this marked the winding-up of the SFM, the civilian observer role which it had instituted during its second phase lived on, as it was employed by the multinational peacekeeping body, the Multinational Force and Observers (MFO), which now took up duty in eastern Sinai (see the next Section). The SSM and SFM assisted in the planning of the new body, a lot of equipment passed from one to the other, and the MFO drew on the SFM in recruiting some of its senior personnel. This continuity even extended to the MFO adopting the SFM's orange uniforms for its Observers. The political reason for this interlocking was that the MFO, like the SFM, was set up to assist in the improvement of relations between the same two members of the same club, both bodies being engineered by the same club chairman – the United States.

FURTHER READING

N. Bar-Yaacov, 'Keeping the Peace between Egypt and Israel, 1973–80', *Israel Law Review*, 15 (2) (April 1980).

Marshall N. Carter, *The American Presence in the Sinai Desert* (Washington, DC: George Washington University, unpublished M.A. dissertation, 1976).

Edward R. F. Sheehan, 'Step by Step in the Middle East', *Foreign Policy*, 22 (Spring 1976).

United States Government, *Watch in the Sinai* (Washington, DC: Department of State, 1980).

United States Government, *Peace in the Sinai* (Washington, DC: Department of State, 1982).

James M. Wallen, 'The Application of Technology to Peacekeeping' in Hugh Hanning (ed.), *Peacekeeping and Technology* (New York: International Peace Academy, 1983).

Section K Supervising the Egyptian–Israeli Peace Treaty (1982–)

The 1979 Peace Treaty between Egypt and Israel envisaged a continued role for the UN Force (Unef II) which was then based in Sinai, and for its associated Military Observers (see Part V, Section G below). During the run-up to Israel's final departure from Egyptian territory, which was scheduled for April 1982, it was to carry out certain interim tasks. Then, for an indefinite period, it was to do three things. Firstly, it was to occupy a wide buffer zone in eastern Sinai adjacent to the international frontier and the Egyptian shore of the Gulf of Aqaba. Secondly, it was to ensure freedom of navigation through the Strait of Tiran at the mouth of the Gulf of Aqaba, a point which in the past had been the focus of much Egyptian–Israeli tension due to the existence, at the head of the Gulf, of a short Israeli shoreline and port. And finally, it was to check on the parties' compliance with the arms-limitation provisions of the Treaty.

In this last connection four zones were established: Zone C, in which the UN force was to be based, and in which no Egyptian forces were permitted; Zone B in central Sinai, which was to contain no more than 4,000 lightly-armed Egyptian troops; a western Zone A, in which Egypt was limited to 22,000 armed men and specified numbers of weapons and armoured vehicles; and, as a reciprocal measure, a narrow Zone D was established on the Israeli side of the international frontier in which the Israeli Defence Force was restricted to 4,000 persons, with limitations on the number and nature of their weapons and vehicles. In effect, the price which Egypt paid for the return of Sinai was its substantial demilitarization (see Map 23).

This scheme immediately ran into difficulty. As a result of making peace with Israel, Egypt was declared an enemy of the Arab people, and the Soviet Union came to the aid of the outraged Arab states by, in effect albeit not in form, vetoing the proposal that the UN should continue to play a peacekeeping role in Sinai. As related in Section J

122

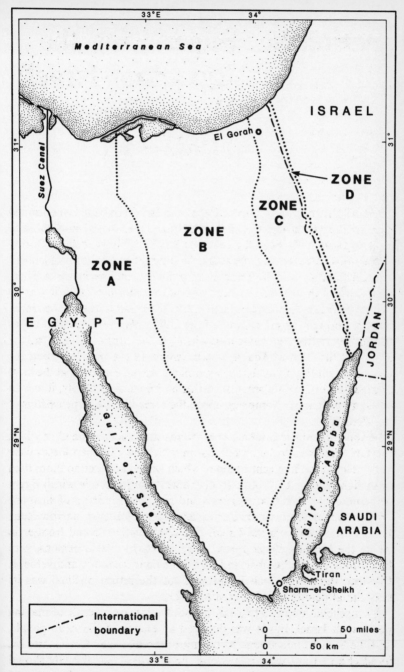

Map 23   Sinai after the coming into force of the Egyptian–Israeli Peace Treaty

above, the American Sinai Field Mission (SFM) filled most of this gap. Two years later, the Soviet Union still found herself unable to permit the implementation of the proposed peacekeeping scheme. The United States had undertaken that in the event of any such hitch she would do what was necessary to provide an alternative multinational force, and Israel made it clear that without such a force she would not complete her withdrawal from Sinai. It therefore fell to the United States to honour her earlier promise, and supply an acceptable solution for the serious problem which was looming in her Middle Eastern clubhouse.

At the time of its negotiation, the United States had emphasized that the Peace Treaty would not result in the deployment of American troops in the Middle East. Now, however, she evidently concluded that as she had to sponsor a peacekeeping force in the area, there was also something to be said for being a participant. This was sweet music indeed to Israel's ears, and doubtless owed something to her prompting. Never much enamoured of the UN, the prospect of directly associating her superpower ally in the security of her southwestern border on a permanent basis brought her negotiators to Washington in strength. Egypt was much less keen on the idea. But, although she could not easily say so, there were some benefits to be had from the involvement of the United States in an arrangement which, as well as providing an obstacle to an Egyptian attack on Israel, would also inconvenience any Israeli plans to attack in the other direction. Egypt could also not forget that she was now a pariah in the Arab world, and was receiving very considerable American aid. She therefore agreed to go ahead with the general plan, and following detailed discussions a Protocol was signed by Egypt and Israel in August 1981, and witnessed by the United States.

It provided for a body called the Multinational Force and Observers (MFO), which was to have its own legal personality, headquarters, budget, flag, insignia, and employees. At its head was to be a civilian Director-General, appointed by the parties for a four-year period who, with the MFO's Commander, was to be responsible for the new body carrying out the functions which the Peace Treaty had assigned to the UN. The parties were not, however, to have a free hand in making these appointments. For an accompanying exchange of letters provided that the Director-General would be an American suggested by the United States, and that that country would also nominate the Force Commander (to be a non-American) if the parties could not agree on one. The United States was also to be closely involved with the MFO in another way, as she undertook to pay three-fifths of its first year's costs, and one-third thereafter, with the parties being equally responsible for the balance. (In 1988 and 1989 Japan made voluntary contributions, cautiously specifying that they were to defray the costs of civilian salaries and food purchases, and in 1989 there were hopes that the Federal Republic of Germany might follow suit.) The MFO's life could be ended only by agreement between Egypt and Israel.

Bringing the MFO to life in the first place, however, proved troublesome. It was to be about 2,500 strong (although it emerged as much nearer 2,700, and remained at near that figure until some reductions in the size of its infantry battalions in 1988 brought the total down to approximately 2,375). This was more or less a straight compromise between Israel's wish for about 5,000 troops and Egypt's expressed preference for none at all. This did not look a large number, but it was not easy to achieve. The parties had, of course, to agree on the contributor states, which immediately excluded those countries – numerous in Africa and Asia – who had no diplomatic relations with Israel. And Egypt did not want any African participants, so as not to stir up divisiveness in the Organization of African Unity about the Middle Eastern peace process. The United States offered to supply one of the three infantry battalions which were to be the MFO's military core, and, using some financial inducements, persuaded Fiji and Colombia to provide the other two. Especially, however, as the United States had also promised to supply a logistics support unit and the (civilian) observer component (the continuation, in effect, of the second-phase activity of the Sinai Field Mission), the MFO was assuming too much of an American look. What was needed, it was thought, was West European participation. The United States had plenty of allies here, but they proved tiresomely reluctant to oblige. For although, in Cold War terms, the United States was their leader, they were not members of her Middle Eastern club, and had a strong wish not to be seen as such.

There were two reasons for this. Firstly, the European Community, mindful of the close American identification with Israel, was trying to distance itself somewhat from the United States in the Middle East peace process, and develop its own distinctive approach. Secondly, the Europeans could not ignore the importance for many of them of Arab oil, and were keenly aware that, due to its link with the Peace Treaty, the MFO was viewed with considerable hostility by much of the Arab world. Moreover, all the Community countries were anxious that they should keep in step on this issue, even though only a few of them might be expected to participate in the MFO. Accordingly, they moved very slowly, and some harsh American words were reported to have been said. Eventually, however, it was announced that Britain, France, Italy and the Netherlands would contribute to the MFO. But now it was

Israel's turn to be awkward. She was unhappy about the European emphasis on the MFO's free-standing, as distinct from its Peace-Treaty-linked, nature, and the United States had to exercise her persuasive powers in yet another direction. But at last everything was sorted out, the planning was completed on time, and the MFO became operational on Israel's final departure from Egyptian territory on 25 April 1982.

The civilian headquarters of the MFO was established in Rome, and its field headquarters at El Gorah, in north-eastern Sinai. Each of its first two Commanders was Norwegian, and they brought some Norwegian officers with them. But formally speaking, Norway was not regarded as a participating state, not even when, in 1989, the MFO's command passed to a New Zealander, but Norway retained a few officers in the MFO. Fiji's battalion is in the northern part of Zone C, Colombia's in the middle, and the American battalion in the south. There is an operational justification for the position of the Americans, as the battalion has its own helicopters, and is therefore better placed than the other two to operate at a distance from the MFO's separate airborne units. But it is also the case that Israel was strongly in favour of this positioning, perhaps reflecting the calculation that in the event of a crisis between herself and Egypt, the Americans would be at a key strategic spot but also largely out of the Israeli line of fire.

The seven non-infantry-suppliers, whose contingents have varied in size between about 20 and 150, are as follows. From 1986 to 1990 Canada provided a helicopter unit (a role which was originally played by a joint Australia–New Zealand unit, but Australia pulled out for domestic political reasons, and Canada then rejected the idea of New Zealand participation in a joint unit with her); France provides some fixed-wing aircraft; Italy supplies the MFO's Coastal Patrol Unit, which, through the medium of three vessels originally commissioned as minesweepers, watches over the Strait of Tiran; the Netherlands deals with signals and provides military police; a training and advisory team comes from New Zealand; Uruguay provides motor transport and engineering units; and the United Kingdom a headquarters unit. Notwithstanding the withdrawal of the Canadian aviators in 1990, Canada continued to participate in the MFO at a low level, providing staff officers and an air traffic control unit.

Within Zone C the MFO's task is to watch over the execution of the obligations which Egypt and Israel have undertaken. More specifically, this entails checking that none of their armed forces (as distinct from lightly-armed Egyptian civil police) are in the Zone, whether on land, in its territorial waters, or in its air space. Towards this end, checkpoints are set up on regularly-used routes and observation posts at other key locations. About 36 such positions are permanently manned (this representing a 1988 reduction from the previous figure of about 45); there are in the region of 40 fixed locations for temporary observation posts (mostly along the international frontier); and other purely temporary observation posts may be set up from time to time. Regular patrolling takes place from these positions on an irregular pattern, on foot and by vehicle, and in the American sector also by helicopter. Thus in a typical week about 150 operational patrols might be conducted.

The MFO's fundamental duty in all these respects is simply to observe and report. Headquarters is immediately informed of anything untoward, but the MFO is not there to physically prevent anything improper being done. Its troops are lightly armed, and may use their weapons in self-defence or to resist efforts to prevent them doing their duty. But as with all peacekeeping missions, the rules regarding the use of force are very restrictively drawn.

The job of the American Civilian Observer Unit, which was established at about 30 strong but reduced to 20 in 1989, is to check on force levels in Zones A, B and D (as well as confirming that there are no Egyptian forces in Zone C). About half the Observers are drawn from the State Department or associated foreign affairs agencies, and the other half are people with military experience. Generally they pair off on this basis and inspect the whole area once every two weeks. An aerial reconnaissance is made prior to each two-week period to plan the detailed verification missions, which then take place on the ground in three- to four-day tours. Inspection routes are to some extent standard, but the Observers also follow some randomly chosen routes with minimum advance notice being given to the parties. A pair of Observers is always accompanied by a liaison officer from the armed forces of the party whose territory is being surveyed. (In all this the MFO clearly draws heavily on the experience of the earlier SFM.) The Observers' reports are passed by the Force Commander to both parties simultaneously, each of whom has the right to request special inspections which must then be conducted within the next two days.

In the event of either party being adjudged by the Force Commander to have violated the Peace Treaty or the Protocol, it is his responsibility to draw formal attention to the offence and ask, as appropriate, that it be rectified or not repeated. All violations are reported to both parties. In practice, however, the Commander deals with many more matters and in more subtle ways than these bald statements imply, for his role is in fact as much diplomatic as military. Thus he tries to assist the difficult process of amelioration between the two former enemies by, for example, never publicizing violations, by arranging trilateral meetings at his headquarters about once a quarter, and visiting Tel Aviv (where the Israeli liaison system is based) and Cairo about once a month. These activities have assumed particular importance as neither the liaison system envisaged by the Peace Treaty nor the re-establishment of diplomatic relations between Egypt and Israel have been as fruitful as was hoped.

At both the diplomatic and military levels, the key to successful operation is a reputation for impartiality. And it is to the MFO's considerable credit that both sides see it very much in this light. Of course, there is some overall difference of attitude to it. Egypt presents herself as the gracious host, accepting limitations on her domestic jurisdiction so as to assuage Israel's worries. Israel has the greater immediate stake in the MFO's presence, and emphasizes the need for it to keep a close eye on Egypt's activities in Sinai. She also touchily insisted on the return home of two Canadian MFO airmen who spoke Arabic. But both states have confidence in it, and a considerable interest in its smooth functioning. Looking to the past, the peacekeeping idea which it represents helped to bring Israel a formal peace with her largest Arab neighbour, and Egypt the return of her land. Currently and in the future, the MFO's presence helps support that peace and the territorial status quo.

The crucial word here is 'helps'. The MFO cannot make Egypt and Israel honour their obligations to maintain peace. But given such a mutual desire – which, broadly speaking, is certainly present – the MFO provides assistance of a subordinate but very valuable kind which helps the parties to implement their pacific disposition. It does so in four ways. The least important is what might be called the atmospheric effects of the MFO's presence and operations, in that it both symbolizes and helps the development of the parties' new attitude to each other. A second, and also lesser, contribution which the MFO makes is through the early warning which it is likely to give of any intended attack by one party on the other. The chief beneficiary here is Israel, but she is not dependent on the MFO in this respect. Quite apart from her own intelligence-gathering work, and the operation of her own electronic early-warning system in Zone D, she also, like Egypt, receives reports of the United States aerial surveillance missions which are conducted over the four Zones. (This agreed practice goes back to 1974, and has nothing to do with the MFO.) However, Israel probably values the

MFO's early-warning potential, both as an additional source of information and because of its international credibility. *Mutatis mutandis*, the same may be said of Egypt.

The third way in which the MFO contributes to the maintenance of peace between Egypt and Israel is through what might be called its hostage effect. For in a marginal situation (as distinct from one which is clearly deemed to require resort to armed force), the multinational make-up of the MFO may help to deter arrogant or reckless behaviour by the armed forces of the parties. Up to a point this consideration is valid in respect of any peacekeeping force, but the particular nature of the MFO makes it more effective in this respect than is usual. For besides having an impressively weighty spread of participants – notably, of course, the United States – all of its contributors have, by agreeing to serve, demonstrated a specific commitment to the Middle East peace process, to any obstruction or physical disturbance of which they can be expected to take particular exception. Service in a UN peacekeeping force, by contrast, often means, at the diplomatic level, not much more than a general interest in stability and a display of loyalty to the UN.

The fourth, and most important, way in which the MFO helps the parties to maintain peace is through its buffer effect. Two previously hostile countries, such as Egypt and Israel, may find that the making of peace does not guarantee the absence of incidents in a sensitive border area, which could conceivably upset their pacific intentions. A demilitarized zone provides part of the answer, putting each country's army at some distance from the other's. But a demilitarization agreement in these circumstances is a fragile edifice if it is left to stand on its own. Creeping violations – a few sentries here, a trench there, a tank somewhere else, and so on – are all too possible, and likely to lead to the growth of anxiety and anger at a rate which is disproportionate to the actual infringements. Accordingly, a neutral force becomes very desirable, as it can watch over and patrol the area in sufficient numerical strength to discourage the parties from dishonouring their obligations. This is what the MFO provides through its presence and activities in Zone C.

Thus far, the MFO has had a very quiet life, and partly because of this and partly to make financial savings a number of reductions were made in its strength in 1989–1990. As of June 1990 its military personnel numbered about 2120. Further economies will be looked for in the early 1990s. These developments reflect the fact that the MFO is operating in a context which, in peacekeeping terms, is first class. Things could hardly have been more favourable for this American-sponsored body, and it has made the most of them. But this does not mean that it will probably soon disperse. For one thing, it is perhaps unlikely but by no means impossible that the peace which Egypt and Israel have made will begin to unravel. In that event, provided neither of them are bent on war, their need for the MFO will be all the greater. But leaving that possibility aside, the previous relationship of the parties, the local hazards which could still materialize, and the continuing – indeed, heightened – Palestinian problem, all suggest that it may be some time before Egypt and Israel feel they can dispense with the peacekeeping assistance which the MFO provides. And for her part, the United States is likely to maintain her very keen interest in the presence of the Force. She wants to keep both Egypt and Israel in her club, and that requires the minimization of incidents and problems between them. In that connection, the MFO plays a highly-valued role.

FURTHER READING

Allan Cooper, 'Multinational Force and Observers – Establishment of the Canadian Rotary Wing Aviation Unit', *Canadian Defence*, 19 (1) (Summer 1989).

Frank Gregory, *The Multinational Force – Aid or Obstacle to Conflict Resolution?* (London: Institute for the Study of Conflict, 1984).

Robert B. Houghton and Frank G. Trinka, *Multinational Peacekeeping in the Middle East* (Washington, DC: US Department of State, Foreign Service Institute, 1984).

Alan James, 'Symbol in Sinai: The Multinational Force and Observers', *Millennium: Journal of International Studies*, 14 (3) (Winter 1985).

John Mackinlay, *The Peacekeepers* (London: Unwin Hyman, 1989).

MFO, *The Multinational Force and Observers* (Rome: Office of Public Affairs, MFO, 1987).

Nathan, A. Pelcovits, *Peacekeeping on Arab–Israeli Fronts* (Boulder, Col.: Westview Press, 1984).

Alfred Pijpers, 'European Participation in the Sinai Peacekeeping Force (MFO)', in D. Allen and A. Pijpers (eds.), *European Foreign Policy-Making and the Arab–Israeli Conflict* (Dordrecht: Nijhoff, 1984).

Mala Tabory, *The Multinational Force and Observers in the Sinai* (Boulder, Col.: Westview Press, 1986).

Section L   India's Peacekeeping Force in Sri Lanka (1987–1990) and her Assistance to the Maldives (1988)

TAMIL UNREST IN SRI LANKA

The flexibility of the term 'peacekeeping', the convenience which this can have for governments, and the public confusion which can thereby arise are all well illustrated by Indian–Sri Lankan developments since 1987.

The South Indian state of Tamil Nadu contains most of the 55 million Tamil people. However, there are also about three million Tamils in Sri Lanka (formerly Ceylon) – about one-fifth of the population. They are concentrated in the North and to a lesser extent in the East of the island, and almost since Sri Lankan independence in 1948 have felt discriminated against by the Sinhalese majority. Serious clashes have occurred since about the mid-1970s, and in the early 1980s the demand emerged for an independent Tamil state – Tamil Eelam. This movement was led by the Tamil 'Tigers'. They received support of various kinds from their ethnic associates in Tamil Nadu, and the situation began to complicate relations between India and Sri Lanka. In July 1987 Sri Lanka asked India – a fellow member in the South Asian Association for Regional Cooperation – for aid in putting the Tigers down. More specifically, the agreement between the two spoke of the despatch of an 'Indian Peace Keeping Contingent' (see Map 24).

The problem which had arisen could reasonably be seen as one within the South Asian clubhouse. But the proposed means for coping with

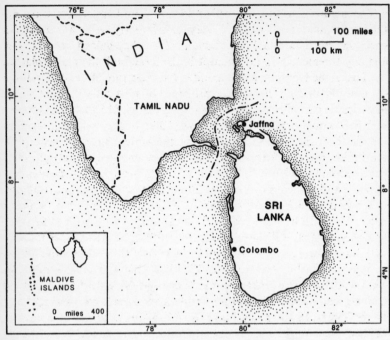

Map 24   India, Sri Lanka and The Maldives

it had only the thinnest connection, if that, with what had come to be
known as peacekeeping. For the Sri Lankan Government was hardly
one which, being generally accepted as legitimate, just needed some
impartial assistance in the maintenance of law and order. Instead, it
was a Government with a rebellion on its hands, of an extent which
was deemed to justify that most extreme of measures – a call for foreign
help. For that reason, the amount and nature of the help which was
furnished went way beyond that which is associated with peacekeeping.
Three thousand troops were initially despatched; within a few months
they had risen to ten times that number; and by mid-1988 were about
50,000 strong. They had armour and tanks at their disposal, and towards
the end of 1987 launched a major offensive against the Tamil rebels.
By this means India succeeded in obtaining rough control over the
north and east of Sri Lanka. But it was only rough; the rebellion
continued; and losses mounted on both sides, 1,000 or so Indian troops
having been killed by September 1989, and more than twice as many
Tiger militants. India had become a clear party to the internal conflict,
and worse was to follow.

The invitation to India provided the non-Tamil opponents of the Sri Lankan regime, particularly a very-far-left party, with an attractive basis on which to attack the Government. They gained ground, and anarchy threatened. In an attempt both to outflank them and placate the Tigers, the Government demanded the departure of the Indian force by the end of July 1989. The principle of host-state consent is an inextricable part of peacekeeping, but India refused to go, on the ground that that would expose the Tamils who had worked with her force to the wrath of the Tigers. The deadline therefore came and went, with the Indian force still firmly in place. Never engaged on recognizably peacekeeping tasks, it had, from the Sri Lankan angle, become an army of occupation. Two months later, after much wrangling, India agreed to suspend her operations against the Tigers, and also gave a qualified promise to withdraw her troops from Sri Lanka by the end of the year – a date which was later advanced to March 1990. Some token withdrawals were begun; the process was then stepped up; and by the revised deadline all the Indian force had left. But it had also ominously been reported that as part of her preparations for departure, India was training and equipping an army drawn from Tamils who are opposed to the Tigers. In the event, however, the Tigers took effective control of their areas of Sri Lanka, and the outbreak in June 1990 of heavy fighting between them and the Government's forces led to fears of a renewed civil war.

The term 'peacekeeping' undoubtedly carries a satisfactory political resonance, both in its own right and because of the specific connotations it has acquired since the late 1950s. It is not therefore surprising that states try to turn it to their advantage. But its use in this, very inappropriate, Sri Lankan situation has unfortunately created some uncertainty about the phenomenon to which it refers. On the positive side, however, the experience of India's interventionary force may perhaps serve as a cautionary reminder that there is no real half-way house between the use of troops in a non-threatening, peacekeeping mode, and their employment in battle.

THE MALDIVES

With in the region of 190,000 people, the Maldives is by no means the world's least populous sovereign state – about 12 states lie beneath her in the population league. But her people are spread over 202 tiny islands, and there are about 1,000 more uninhabited ones in the Maldivian archipelago. Maintaining the security of this state against external predators could therefore present a considerable problem.

In November 1988 a mercenary force of about 200, reportedly organized by a Maldivian businessman based in Sri Lanka, landed in the capital and tried to seize power. The Maldives Government appealed to India for help, and an airborne force of about 1,000 paratroopers was despatched with naval vessels in support. The attempted coup was quickly crushed. As it seemed to have had no domestic support, the measures taken against it can be seen as in the nature of law and order activity on behalf of an internally legitimate government. India's move in this case is therefore much closer to peacekeeping than her contemporaneous action in Sri Lanka. But no loud claims were made to that effect, and the expedition is properly distinguished from peacekeeping on the ground that the effort to upset the Maldives Government had no international ramifications. If it had had such a colouration, there might also well have been argument as to the international impartiality of India's action. But as it is the episode is best seen as simply a case of help being extended by one state to another.

FURTHER READING

Dennis Austin and Anirudha Gupta. *Lions and Tigers. The Crisis in Sri Lanka* (London: Centre for Security and Conflict Studies, 1988).
John Bray, 'Sri Lanka: things fall apart?', *The World Today*, 45 (8–9) (August–September 1989).
James Manor (ed.), *Sri Lanka in Change and Crisis* (London: Croom Helm, 1984).
Kumar Rupesinghe, 'Sri Lanka: Peacekeeping and Peace Building', *Bulletin of Peace Proposals*, 20 (3) (September 1989).
Deepak Tripathi, 'India's Maldives mission and after', *The World Today*, 45 (1) (January 1989).

Section M The Problem of Western Sahara (1988–)

Spain withdrew from Western Sahara early in 1976, having agreed that Morocco should have the northern two-thirds and Mauritania the rest – this being a recognition of their historic links with the territory. However, the indigenous but Algerian-backed Polisario movement also laid claim to it on behalf of the newly-announced Saharan Arab Democratic Republic (SADR), and embarked on guerrilla warfare. This, together with a change of regime, encouraged Mauritania to renounce her share of the post-colonial spoils in 1979, but Morocco was in earnest. She extended her claim to the whole territory and supported it vigorously. Committing huge resources to her campaign, she began the construction of a sand (and electronically-equipped) wall across the desert to safeguard that part of Western Sahara which she controlled, including an area of rich phosphate deposits. The wall was successively pushed outwards, and by 1988 contained most of the former colony (see Map 25).

This intra-African problem has from the start attracted the attention of the Organization of African Unity (OAU), and as early as 1978 it was proposed that there be an African-supervised cease fire and a UN-controlled referendum, with a later suggestion that the referendum be organized by the OAU. However, Morocco was wary of Polisario's demand that she withdraw prior to the vote. No doubt she was apprehensive about the possible impact on its conduct of the fact that the diplomatic tide was turning against her – half the OAU's members having recognized SADR by 1980. The consequential issue of SADR's admission to the African club resulted in its paralysis for a while, and almost in its break-up.

In the mid-1980s, however, relations between Algeria and Morocco began to improve, and with Saudi Arabia and the United States (both of whom looked favourably on Morocco) also urging a settlement, the pressures were building up on both sides to reach an accommodation. The UN was a more promising peacekeeping instrument than the OAU,

135

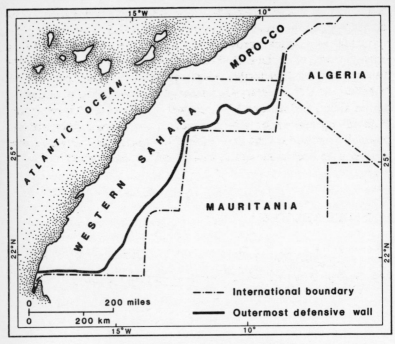

Map 25   Morocco in Western Sahara

in terms both of its expertise and of its acceptability, and in 1988, after
lengthy negotiations, it came up with a plan. The proposal was that
the UN, through a Special Representative of the Secretary-General
should, in effect, control Western Sahara for a transitional period. The
Representative would have a security unit at his disposal to maintain
law and order, and in cooperation with the OAU would be responsible
for the arrangement of a referendum in which the people would be
asked whether they wanted independence or integration into Morocco.
UN military observers would watch over a cease fire and the sites at
which the Moroccan and Polisario forces would gather during the
period of de facto international administration.

At the end of August 1988 this scheme was accepted in principle by
both sides, and then given a fair wind by the Security Council. But a
year later the parties had still not agreed on the all-important details,
not least on the way in which the voting roll was to be compiled, and
on the extent of the reduction in Moroccan troops prior to the
transitional period. Polisario seemed to be the side which was dragging

its feet, and there were other indications which suggested that Morocco felt relatively confident about the outcome of the UN programme. This circumstance perhaps partly accounted for the occurrence, after a lengthy truce, of serious clashes in October and November 1989, resulting in at least the further postponement of the peacekeeping plan. However, the UN Secretary-General continued his efforts to nudge the parties along, and in June 1990 renewed talks between Morocco and Polisario opened under UN auspices. If the dispute does not get peacefully resolved on the basis of the UN's proposals, very extensive use will have been made of the tool of international peacekeeping.

FURTHER READING

International Institute for Strategic Studies: *Strategic Survey 1988–1989* (London: IISS, 1989).
Toby Shelley: 'Desert War – The Obstacle in North African Unity', *Gulf Report* (November 1988).

Part III
Neighbourhood Quarrels

Introduction: Calming the Neighbourhood

A neighbourhood has a character which is intermediate between that of a back yard or a clubhouse on the one hand and a high street or a crossroads on the other. It lacks the air of privacy which attends the first two locations, and also the very public associations of the second pair. Yet to some degree it enjoys the nature of both. It is an area for which the residents are chiefly responsible, but it may attract the attention of outsiders, for several reasons. They may take an initiative regarding a neighbourhood out of a sense of public spirit or obligation; or because its affairs are impinging somewhat awkwardly on their own; or they may just respond to a request for help. In practice, of course, external activity directed towards a neighbourhood may not emerge in as clear-cut a fashion as these remarks suggest. But there is a perceptible distinction between the kind of concern which a neighbourhood elicits and the behaviour which is typical in respect of the more proprietarial and open contexts which were referred to above.

In international politics, neighbourhood quarrels have not given rise to as much peacekeeping activity as the problems which have occurred in other metaphorical locations. For that the reason is not hard to find. It does not lie in a paucity of disputes between those who are geographically contiguous, nor in the peculiar belligerency of such disputants. It is due rather to the connectedness of international matters. Thus when neighbours quarrel they may immediately arouse the interest of others on account of both of them being located within the same back yard, or club. Alternatively, international activity may ensue because one of the parties is causing some of its associates serious embarrassment. Or the quarrel may present a threat to the general international peace of such proportions as to give it the nature of a dangerous crossroads. In any of these events the 'neighbourhoodness' of the issue is, as it were, overridden by the more compelling character of its wider political context.

This is just another way of saying that life internationally, as elsewhere, and probably more so, is lived at more than one level. In this book's political analysis, the allocation of a dispute to one category rather than another has been determined by what is conceived to be the level which most influences its outcome. As pairs of states are nowadays rarely able to get on with a quarrel entirely on their own, it is not surprising that the number of disputes which fall to be considered in Part III is fewer than in Parts I, II, IV and V. Moreover, when states do quarrel without the attentions of concerned outsiders, it is not over-likely that one or both of them will eventually see virtue in recourse to international peacekeeping. Such measures are generally seen as only the lesser of two evils, and in fact are often accepted chiefly in consequence of external pressure.

Even in respect of the eight cases which are discussed in Part III (which could also be seen as arising out of no more than five quarrels or issues), third-party pressures were by no means absent. For, as has been indicated, outsiders may take an interest in a neighbourhood quarrel out of a sense of duty. This is not usually the most imperative of international motives. But if it is unlikely to involve onerous consequences, as in the case of a call for peacekeeping or for behaviour which might point in that direction, it may sometimes be indulged. The great powers, more particularly, may be responsive to the idea that they have an overall responsibility for the maintenance of peace. And the UN was based on this very assumption. The unreality of this scheme – so far as the joint enforcement of peace was concerned – was soon manifest. But the general idea was in the international air, and circumstances provided some early opportunities for trying to act on its basis – but in a manner which was far less dramatic and costly than had been originally intended. To put it differently, what would later be called peacekeeping made two small appearances on the international stage.

First, however, came a non-event, in the shape of a high-minded proposal that the UN should solve the competition for Jerusalem by placing it under international administration (Section B). It soon proved, however, that the city was not available for placement. But then, following sharp calls by the Security Council for some temporary ends to the Arab–Israeli fighting, UN truce and armistice observers were despatched to the field in 1948 and 1949 (Section C). The organization which was thus begun is still in existence. But the conflict in question was before long to assume the aspect of something much more threatening than a neighbourhood quarrel, so that the UN's peacekeeping activity in relation to it since 1967 is discussed elsewhere (Part V, Section F below).

At more or less the same time and in much the same way, another UN observer mission was begun, which is also still in existence. It arose

out of the war between the two new states of India and Pakistan over
Kashmir (Section D). Like the Middle Eastern quarrel (at that time),
this was a dispute which was not entangled in the emerging Cold War.
Accordingly, the Security Council was in a position to call for a cessation
of fighting, and it supplied military observers to help in the stabilization
of the situation. A decade and a half later, another war between the
same two states, over the same issue, was dealt with in much the same
way (Section E). But then the major powers acted less out of a sense
of responsibility than because their own relationships were being
complicated by the war.

In respect of neither of these issues were peacekeeping operations
mounted out of a feeling of great anxiety or immediate concern. The
parties were nudged and helped by and large because it was the
appropriate thing to do. Had they chosen to go on fighting, and provided
that no very dramatic outcomes were in sight, third parties would
probably not have lost much sleep. In the case of the Iran–Iraq War
which began in 1980, even nudges were lacking. The rest of the international
society, and the great powers in particular, were quite content to see
these two neighbours setting about each other in a vigorous but not
very consequential way. One humanitarian gesture was made in an
effort to limit civilian casualties (Section F). But apart from that
third parties only really got moving late in the day. And when in 1988
the war was called off, it was chiefly because of the weariness of one of
the parties. An observer mission was then established to help the
quarrelsome neighbours live in peace (Section G).

In a rather similar manner, a territorial dispute between Colombia
and Peru in the early 1930s was allowed to take its course (Section A).
Even the United States was content more or less to stand on the sidelines
– not because the war's continuation suited her but because she was
in a rare self-denying period so far as intervention in her back yard
was concerned. However, when domestic developments in one of the
parties opened the way to a settlement, the European-oriented League
of Nations, no less, stepped in to resolve the issue by engaging in a
miniscule piece of international administration.

Naval peacekeeping has not so far been fully experienced. But its
discussion was stimulated by the overflow of the Iran–Iraq War into
the waters of the Gulf, and the argument for it is superficially enticing.
For if a neighbourhood quarrel adversely affects the interests of third
parties in an area where they are fully entitled to be – on the high seas
– the question arises as to why the seas should not be policed to ensure
the safety of neutral shipping. However, even law and order operations

on land are very tricky for peacekeepers. The degree of strength which is available may be insufficient, which may be another way of saying that the situation is unsuitable for peacekeeping. Or, if it is sufficient, it may all too easily be used in a manner which oversteps the peacekeeping mark. At sea, the first problem is perhaps unlikely to occur, but the second is by no means improbable. If, therefore, 'peacekeepers' do make their appearance on the high seas, it may well be found that the enterprise on which they are embarked is different from that which has been advertised (Section H). To say that is by no means necessarily to downplay the importance of what is being done. But it may have to be distinguished from peacekeeping.

Section A The Dispute Between Colombia and Peru over Leticia (1933–1934)

From the perspective of the post-Second World War years, it is all too easy to assume that because Latin America lies in the geographical back yard of the United States its conflicts will receive the close and if necessary dictatorial attention of the continent's great power. This, however, fails to notice that in the late 1920s the United States, perhaps partly in remorse for her earlier policies, put away her big stick for a couple of decades and instead developed the policy which was conceptualized in 1933 as that of the good neighbour. It was marked not just by an unwillingness to use armed strength and material inducements in Latin America but also by a keen desire to avoid even the appearance of diplomatic pressure. Exhortation and an impartial mediatory role was now to be the limit of American leadership. When, therefore, in 1932–1933 her mediatory efforts in respect of a dispute between Colombia and Peru proved unsuccessful, she withdrew in a very docile way and seemed glad to leave the matter to the League of Nations, going so far as to attend the meetings of the Advisory Committee which had been established by its Council.

The dispute concerned the district of Leticia, which had been ceded to Colombia by Peru in 1922. It gave Colombia direct access to the main stream of the Amazon, and was prized accordingly. However, in 1932 Colombian officials were driven out by some freelance Peruvians, and Peru felt obliged to give them the state's backing. The ameliorative efforts of Brazil and the United States were rejected, as was a League of Nation's proposal. Tension rose, some fighting took place, and it looked as though a full-scale war was about to develop (see Map 26).

145

Map 26   Leticia

Then, however, in April 1933 the Peruvian President was assassinated, and his successor was of a more conciliatory frame of mind. This resulted in the League putting forward a revised version of its earlier proposal, which was accepted by the parties. Peru had by then become uncomfortably aware of her military unpreparedness and the onerous cost of a war, and Colombia was satisfied with the League's scheme. For it provided for a League Commission to take charge of the town of Leticia in Colombia's name for not more than a year. The Commission was to maintain order with the aid of a force of its own selection, paid for – together with the Commission's other expenses – by Colombia, and it was known that the force would consist of Colombian troops seconded to the League. Peru asked that this last fact be not officially communicated to her. She also managed to save some face in the important matter of flags. Much had been made at home of her promise never to haul down the Peruvian flag at Leticia. The flag pole in question, with the flag still flying, was therefore uprooted and taken across the river to Peruvian territory, where it was reinstalled.

In this way the League of Nations came, in June 1933, to assume an administrative role. Its Commission consisted of an American (another sign of that country's benevolence towards the League), a Brazilian, and a Spaniard, and had up to 150 Colombian troops at its disposal. The League's blue and white flag flew over Leticia (alongside that of Colombia), and the League's troops wore armbands bearing the lettters SDN (for Société des Nations) on their Colombian uniforms. As planned, the Commission stayed for a year, and its period of rule was uneventful. Nothing had been said, however, about what was to happen at the end of the year, and negotiations between the disputants went unpromisingly. Preparations for war were recommenced, but shortly before the Commission was due to leave an agreement was reached which recognized that Leticia was part of Colombia. Thus, when the League's Commission wound up its affairs, the town of Leticia, together with the surrounding district, was formally restored to Colombia.

It had been anticipated from the outset that this would be the eventual result, which was why the League's role was acceptable to Colombia. But the relative smoothness with which it was achieved was in all probability due to the device of temporary international administration. For it was much easier for Peru to withdraw in favour of the League pending a final agreement than it was for her to make a direct transfer of the area to her recent foe. Especially as the final result was still theoretically in doubt, this was a respectable and face-saving procedure, and one which facilitated Peru's later assent to Colombia's resumption of authority in Leticia. By acting as a temporary go-between while tempers cooled and negotiations were held, the League therefore made a significant contribution to the pacific settlement of the dispute. Its key members had no direct interest in the matter, which also meant that they had no difficulty in authorizing a minor patching-up operation – especially as it involved them in little inconvenience and no cost. They could not, or, like the United States, would not march Peru away from Leticia. But, given her eventual willingness to withdraw, they were able to assist her departure in a way which would later be described as peacekeeping.

FURTHER READING

J. Lloyd Mecham, *The United States and Inter-American Security* (Austin, Texas: University of Texas Press, 1961).

F. P. Walters, *A History of the League of Nations* (London: Oxford University Press, 1952, 2 volumes; reprinted in 1960 and subsequently as 1 volume).

Walter L. Williams, Jr, *Intergovernmental Military Forces and World Public Order* (Leiden: Sijthoff; Dobbs Ferry, NY: Oceana, 1971).

Bryce Wood, *The United States and Latin American Wars* (New York: Columbia University Press, 1966).

Section B The Proposed Internationalization of Jerusalem (1947–1950)

In connection with Britain's proposed withdrawal from Palestine (see Section C below), the UN General Assembly said in November 1947 that the large prize of Jerusalem (and its surrounding area, including Bethlehem) should go to neither of the groups who were gearing up for war but should have a separate and permanent international status. The UN Trusteeship Council was asked to prepare an appropriate statute for the city. It proposed that that Council (where there is no veto) should appoint a Governor to administer Jerusalem on behalf of the UN, that the city should be demilitarized, and that law and order should be maintained by a special police force responsible to the Governor and recruited outside Palestine. The Jews were far from happy about the idea, but went along with it as part of a package which offered them their own state. The Arabs, however, would accept nothing less than a Palestinian Arab state with Jerusalem as its capital.

The fighting which broke out in May 1948 between the newly-proclaimed Israel and her Arab neighbours resulted in the division of Jerusalem: its newer parts ended up in Israel's hands and the old city, which contained virtually all the places holy to Islam, Judaism, and Christianity, in Jordan's. The UN continued to espouse the scheme whereby the whole city would be placed under an international regime. But both Israel and Jordan were now determined to hang on to the parts which they had won by force of arms – which earned the latter the wrath of her fellow Arabs, who had become sudden converts to the internationalization idea. In 1950 Israel proclaimed Jerusalem as her capital, and Jordan formally annexed all the territory she held on the West Bank of the River Jordan. There were international reservations

149

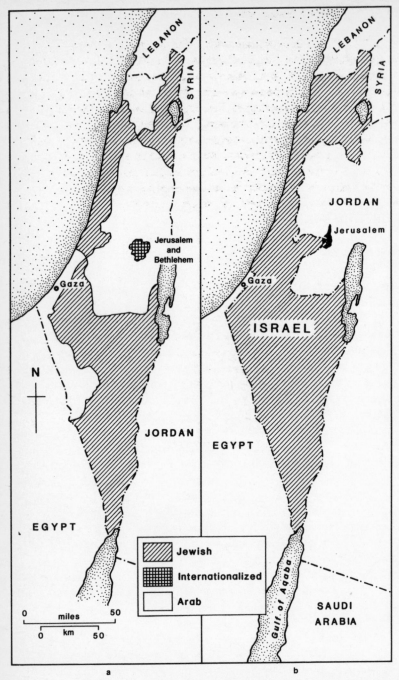

LEBANON

SYRIA

Jerusalem
and
Bethlehem

Gaza

N

JORDAN

EGYPT

LEBANON

SYRIA

JORDAN

Jerusalem

Gaza

ISRAEL

EGYPT

Gulf of Aqaba

SAUDI
ARABIA

Jewish
Internationalized
Arab

0   miles   50

0   km   50

a

b

Map 27   (a) The UN proposals for the partition of Palestine (b) Armistice lines
after the 1948–1949 Arab–Israeli War

about both these announcements. But that was where, in practical terms, the matter rested (see Map 27).

When Israel drove Jordan out of the old city of Jerusalem in 1967 there were hopes in some quarters that an international regime might at last be established for the city. But the Israelis would have none of it. For them to let go of Jerusalem, their hands would have to be wrenched apart.

FURTHER READING

Alan James, *The Politics of Peacekeeping* (London: Chatto and Windus, 1969).
George Kirk, *The Middle East 1945–1950* (London: Oxford University Press, 1954) (in multivolume series, *Survey of International Affairs 1939–1946*, ed. Arnold Toynbee).

Section C Sedative Efforts Regarding the Arab–Israeli Dispute (1948–1967)

THE FIRST ARAB–ISRAELI WAR

The fierce conflict in British-held Palestine between Arabs and Jews, each striving to establish themselves as the obvious successors to the colonial regime, resulted in Britain taking three major decisions in 1947. First, the UN was asked to produce a solution; second, Britain was in any event going to leave; and third, she was not going to try to enforce a proposal which was not acceptable to both disputants. The problem was, of course, about the most intractable which could be imagined. But Britain's response to it clearly signified that she was no longer the world power of former years.

The UN General Assembly's proposal that Palestine should be partitioned was totally rejected by the Arabs, and Britain's departure in May 1948 was marked both by the proclamation of the state of Israel and by the invasion of the vacated area by a number of disunited Arab states. Although by this time the war-time alliance of the Soviet Union and the United States had been replaced by deep suspicion, in respect of the First War of Palestinian Succession they showed a more or less united front, which was shared by the rest of the Council. There were some differences of attitude to the parties: each of the two superpowers had a lot of sympathy for Israel, the Soviet Union for ideological and the United States for domestic political reasons; while Britain was more inclined to favour the Arabs, seeing them as her protégés. All Council members, however, were chiefly anxious to curtail what was seen as a neighbourhood quarrel. This was not because it threatened any of their important interests – provided neither side was in danger of complete defeat – nor because it was thought to have dangerous escalatory properties. But it was taking place in a sensitive area; the larger powers saw it as disorderly conduct on the part of awkward but minor elements; and it ran counter to the UN's commitment to a more peaceful world. In these circumstances the Security Council was just the body to deal with the matter, and it spoke quite toughly. Furthermore, it provided for the international supervision of its demands, thus beginning what has proved to be a continuously close association between the Arab–Israeli dispute and UN peacekeeping.

On 29 May 1948 the parties were called upon to order a four-week truce and to permit its supervision by the UN. They complied. At the insistence of the United States, and with a view to excluding the Soviet Union from the scene, Military Observers were sought only from Belgium, France, and herself. The Soviet Union objected, but to no avail. About 100 unarmed officers were quickly moved to the scene and, by observing, investigating, and persuading, helped the first truce to work fairly well. They identified their temporary status by wearing UN armbands on their national uniforms, the distinctive blue beret not being used by UN peacekeepers until 1956.

Hostilities broke out again at the end of the four-week period as the Arabs did not wish to give the Israelis more time to entrench themselves. This led the Security Council on 15 July to order, no less, an indefinite truce, provide for its supervision, and imply that stronger measures would be taken if the parties were recalcitrant. The fighting stopped, and this time about 300 officers, from the same states, were brought in to watch over the truce. Later they were supplemented by about the same number of enlisted men. They tried to maintain calm at the opposing front lines in the same ways as before, and also tried to observe the large hinterland to check whether men and material were being moved in a way which, contrary to the terms of the truce, would alter the military balance. Undoubtedly the Observers' presence contributed to the settlement of many incidents and the avoidance of others. But the underlying situation was most unstable, and a number of very serious breaches of the peace occurred as attempts were made, chiefly by the Israelis, to 'tidy up' the military lines and so pave the way to an outcome which would be favourable in both political and strategic terms.

Given the instability of the truce, the Security Council decided in November to call for armistices to be established. Negotiations were begun early in 1949 with a UN official as mediator, and by July General Armistice Agreements had been signed between Israel and each of her four Arab neighbours. All the Agreements referred to the groups which had helped to maintain the two truces as the UN 'Truce Supervision Organization' (Untso), as if it had already been so named and had an ongoing existence, and the Agreements relied on Untso for some aspects of their functioning. In August the Security Council therefore authorized the continued service of such military personnel as were necessary for the implementation of the Armistices. It also reaffirmed that part of its earlier truce resolution which had ordered a cease-fire, and instructed Untso to do what it could to maintain it. In this way Untso obtained an additional basis for its work which was independent of the Armistices and, in theory, of the parties. It could claim that it was acting on behalf of the Security Council and therefore of the UN as a whole, expressing the world's wish for peaceful relations between Israel and the surrounding Arab states.

UNTSO's ROLE, 1949–1967

It had been envisaged that the armistice regimes would be a brief interlude between the suspension of hostilities and treaties of peace. In the event they were often precarious affairs which were mutually accepted for up to 18 years – at which date the first Arab–Israeli peace treaty was still 12 years away. Moreover, the suspicion and hostility which accounted for this also found reflection in the early and widespread breakdown of most of the schemes for the joint operation, with international assistance, of the Armistices.

Mixed Armistice Commissions (MACs) had been provided for in each case, with a senior Untso member as chairman. They were to look into claims and complaints about the application and observance of the Agreements and, if appropriate, take decisions on them. However, an MAC as a whole could conduct an investigation only if this was agreed by both of the parties and the chairman. In the absence of unanimity, the investigation was carried out by Untso Observers alone. Due to the prevailing military and political situation (the Arabs refusing to recognize Israel), unanimity was rare. Thus the MACs could hardly ever operate as complete units in the field or take a unanimous (and therefore effective) decision on the basis of Untso's investigations. Complaints, however, flooded in from both sides in respect of three of the Agreements (that between Israel and Lebanon being the exception). In consequence, the meetings of three of the four MACs became opportunities for the exchange of often bitter allegations rather than a means of settling common problems. The result was that for practical purposes these MACs were one by one abandoned – and in time all four were denounced by Israel. The UN, however, has always regarded each of them as still formally in existence (other than, since the 1979 Peace Treaty, that between Egypt and Israel), so they are available for resuscitation.

Notwithstanding the breakdown of three of the MACs, Untso continued to exercise, so far as possible, the functions assigned to it under the Agreements, as well as those which flowed from its independent mandate. There were four aspects to its peacekeeping role. Firstly, it made its own investigations of incidents, which may in a small way have discouraged the cheek-by-jowl armies from engaging in provocative behaviour. Secondly, Untso took various stabilizing measures. For example, it urged the making of local commanders' agreements, sometimes successfully. It made a little progress in getting disputed lines demarcated. It made some arrangements for the division and cultivation of land in one of the demilitarized zones which the Armistices had established. It watched over a neutral zone. It escorted convoys to two enclaves. And it managed to get some fixed observation posts set up on three borders. Without these activities it is virtually certain that the various fronts would have been much more unstable.

Untso's third, and most important role, was to try to defuse the many incidents which nonetheless occurred. For this was an area where shooting could very easily break out, and could almost as easily get out of hand. The overall situation was tense; the opposing armed forces were in close proximity; infiltration was encouraged by Egypt, until 1956, and was not discouraged by Jordan; and the demilitarized zone on the Syrian border and the neutral zone on Jordan's gave rise to no end of trouble. There were thus ample opportunities for the outbreak of firing, and once it had begun neither side was likely, of its own accord, to take the initiative in bringing it to a definite end. This, however, was just what Untso's Military Observers could do. Indeed, it became almost a matter of routine, in such circumstances, for Untso to propose a cease-fire to each side's MAC delegates, or sometimes to the local commanders, and even to suggest a time for it. And by getting Observers to the scene of trouble as soon as possible, Untso could both try to encourage either the conclusion of a cease-fire or the honouring of one which had already been agreed. In the event of a repeated failure to obtain a cease-fire, or in a particularly serious case, it was possible for Untso's Chief of Staff (as its head is called) to intervene at governmental level. In these ways fighting was brought to an early conclusion in countless instances. Had it not been, the possibility of escalation even to the point of full-scale war could not have been excluded.

Fourthly, Untso was an important means of contact between states who were not in diplomatic relations. This was valuable not just at the political level but also at the humanitarian – facilitating, for example, the handing over of people and animals and the taking of measures to control locusts and malaria.

This work, of course, dealt only with the symptoms of the Arab–Israeli dispute. But Untso was intended to deal only with symptoms. The root of the problem had to be addressed by the parties themselves. It was theoretically possible for them to be encouraged in a conciliatory direction by urgent representations from outside, but whether they would be disposed to hearken to such calls was open to question. Even the likelihood of telling representations being made was much reduced when, towards the middle of the 1950s, the Soviet Union began to espouse the Arab cause, as that put each superpower on a different side of the dispute.

In terms, however, of trying to keep the intense local enmity in check, Untso did an enormously valuable job between 1949 and 1967. It was far from receiving outward signs of gratitude for this work, Israel being particularly obstructive towards Untso and even, in the view of some, arrogant. This may have been the outcome of two superficially opposing factors: her feeling of military superiority in relation to the Arab states and her anxiety about her long-term strategic viability – an anxiety which was also fuelled by the bitter historical experience of the Jews. In any event, Israel often put difficulties in Untso's way, besides falling out very seriously with two of its Chiefs of Staff. But it is likely that at bottom she was glad to have Untso there, and the Arabs almost certainly were. For it was probably essential for the maintenance of overall stability – which, for most of the time, was what both sides wanted. If war was actively sought – as it was by Israel in 1956 and 1967 – Untso could do nothing about it. But short of that situation, its impartial presence was a huge help in preventing unwanted conflagrations.

For its first half-dozen years after 1949, Untso was made up of about only three dozen Observers. Then it grew to about 60; by the end of the 1950s it was double that size; and it increased at one point in the mid-1960s to about 140. Its original practice of looking only to Belgium, France, and the United States for military personnel was quietly dropped in 1953, and in 1966 the Observers were drawn from 12 states – but none of them from the Eastern bloc. Its headquarters throughout this period was in the old British Government House in Jerusalem, which was within the neutral zone established by the Israeli–Jordanian Armistice Agreement. That zone was to disappear in 1967, and for the next six years Untso was to operate along different front lines, and in a very different political context from that which had given it birth (see Part V, Section F below). But its headquarters remained in the same building – and is there still.

For a map, see Map 27b above.

FURTHER READING

N. Bar-Yaacov, *The Israel–Syrian Armistice* (Jerusalem: Magnes Press, 1967).

Odd Bull, *War and Peace in the Middle East* (London: Cooper, 1976).

E. L. M. Burns, *Between Arab and Israeli* (London: Harrap, 1962).

M. R. Cannon, *The UN Truce Supervision Organization in the Arab–Israeli Conflict* (Oxford: University of Oxford, unpublished B. Litt. thesis, 1975).

Carl von Horn, *Soldiering for Peace* (London: Cassell, 1966).

E. H. Hutchinson, *Violent Truce* (New York: Devin Adair, 1966).

Paul Mohn, 'Problems of Truce Supervision', *International Conciliation*, 478 (February 1952).

W. Andrew Terrill, 'The Lessons of UNTSO and the Future of UN Truce Supervision', *Conflict*, 9 (1989).

United Nations, *The Blue Helmets* (New York: UN Department of Public Information, 1985).

Section D   The Problem of Kashmir (1949–   )

Shortly after India and Pakistan became independent in 1947, fighting broke out between them over the large princely state of Jammu and Kashmir (here referred to as Kashmir). It was overwhelmingly Muslim in population, but its Hindu ruler had agreed, albeit with an important qualification, that it should accede to India. The matter was brought to the UN, where there was a general disposition to make some contribution towards the restoration of peace between these two important new states, neither of whom was seen as a supporter of one side or the other in the emerging East–West conflict. A Commission was therefore appointed to investigate and mediate, and it obtained the parties' agreement to a cease-fire which was to come into operation on 1 January 1949. At the same time the Commission acquired a military adviser and, to enable him to report on the observance of the cease-fire, the UN furnished him with a few dozen military officers drawn from the armies of a number of member states. They watched over the cease-fire, prevented minor incidents from getting out of hand, and, following the delineation of the cease-fire line in an agreement of July 1949, assisted in its demarcation (except in the remote and difficult Siachen Glacier region). In this way Kashmir was divided between India and Pakistan, supposedly on a temporary basis pending a plebiscite, and birth was given to the peacekeeping body which, a couple of years later, was detached from the UN's mediatory activity and became known as the UN Military Observer Group in India and Pakistan (Unmogip) (see Map 28).

PHASE ONE: 1949–1971

Besides prohibiting a renewal of hostilities, the cease-fire provided that the troops of each side should not advance within 500 yards of the line, and that there should be no increase in forces or defences throughout

158

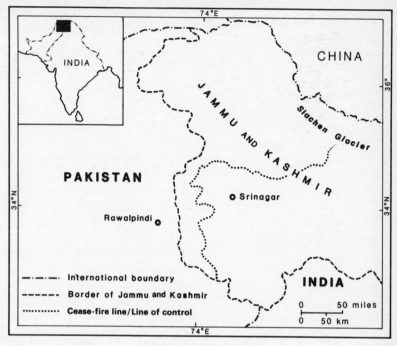

Map 28   Kashmir

Kashmir. The line itself was about 500 miles long, and often ran along difficult terrain. Thus Unmogip, which in general was only between three and five dozen strong, had a large task on its hands. It dealt with civilian infringements of the line, investigated complaints and adjudicated on them, and prevented minor incidents from escalating into more dangerous situations, this last being its most important function. It also reported to the UN Secretary-General on each side's compliance with the arms-limitation terms of the cease-fire, as Unmogip was given access to secret information regarding the identity and disposition of Indian and Pakistani forces in Kashmir. To undertake these tasks, a number of field stations were established – about half a dozen on each side – and by being based at one of these stations for two to three months, each Observer became well acquainted with 'his' sector of the cease-fire line. Moreover, to prevent the development of too close an emotional attachment to one side, each Observer's tour of duty was, in principle, equally divided between both sides. Unmogip's headquarters was also rotated at six-monthly intervals between Srinagar in Indian-held Kashmir and Rawalpindi in Pakistan.

In these ways Unmogip gave notable assistance in the maintenance of relative calm in Kashmir. In part this was due to the professionalism of its Observers and the reputation which they acquired on both sides for impartiality. They did not carry arms, and the small teams in which they operated always consisted of a mix of nationalities. These nationalities had, in the usual peacekeeping way, to be acceptable to the parties, and this resulted in the phasing out of American Observers at India's request following Pakistan's entry into the Western alliance system in 1954. But this issue did not usually give rise to difficulty, and during the first phase of Unmogip's activity, no fewer than 14 states provided Military Observers for Unmogip, four of them also, at various times, supplying aircraft. The expenses of the Group were included in the UN's regular budget and assessed on the members in the normal way, but each side contributed generously towards Unmogip's local costs.

It was also, of course, the parties who, at bottom, enabled Unmogip to play such a worthwhile role. For while the issue of Kashmir gave rise to frequent tension, and was regarded on each side as a matter of national honour, neither was constantly thirsting for war over the question. Thus, for most of the time they were very willing to cooperate with Unmogip in its peacekeeping work, and so provided the favourable political context which was essential for its success. Moreover, there was nothing particularly provocative about the position of the cease-fire line itself, and the national armies on both sides were both well disciplined and usually anxious that quiet should be maintained. In these circumstances, there is a question as to whether Unmogip was necessary for the maintenance of peace. Probably it was not, especially after the initial settling-down period. But undoubtedly it was a considerable help.

When, however, an Indo–Pakistani war threatened, whether over Kashmir or some other question, there was virtually nothing which Unmogip could do, or could be expected to do, to avert it. Thus the entry of armed infiltrators into Indian-held Kashmir in August 1965 led to brief but full-scale hostilities in the following month (see Section E below). Six years later, events in what was then East Pakistan led to civil war, and Indian intervention at the end of the year. The short war which followed resulted in the emergence of East Pakistan as the sovereign state of Bangladesh, and also precipitated some fighting in Kashmir – which, for Unmogip, proved to have some large consequences.

PHASE TWO: 1972–

The line at which fighting was halted in Kashmir in December 1971, and which was confirmed in an Indo–Pakistani agreement of July 1972, was in some small respects different from that which had been set out in 1949. Before long, India seized on this as an opportunity to try to ease the UN out of its involvement with Kashmir. Unmogip's functions, said India, derived from the 1949 agreement, which had now been superseded by the 1972 agreement. Accordingly, the UN body no longer had any role to play in Kashmir, and she would soon be asking for its withdrawal.

In fact she has not done so, doubtless mindful of the critical interpretation which some quarters would put on such a request, and also of the possibility that a draft resolution to that effect might not secure the necessary number of votes in the Security Council, or even be vetoed. Moreover, she has continued to provide accommodation and transport for the Observers on her side of the line, and to receive Unmogip's headquarters every six months. But ever since 1972 India has ignored Unmogip as an operational body. She no longer complains to it about Pakistan's violations of the cease-fire; she does not allow the Observers to conduct investigations on her side of the line; and she has placed severe restrictions on their freedom of movement. Border problems which arise with Pakistan are dealt with on a strictly bilateral basis. In India's view, the future of Indian-held Kashmir is no longer alive at the international level. She has settled for her half of the loaf.

Pakistan, however, as the party with a continuing grievance – for she feels that she has a very strong claim to the whole of Kashmir – unsurprisingly argues in the contrary direction. She claims that Kashmir is still very much an unsettled international issue, and sees Unmogip's presence as tangible evidence of that position. She therefore says that the 1949 agreement is still valid, and that the new line is but the old one with some changes. In consequence, Unmogip is seen as still having a role in the maintenance of calm along the whole of the line of control, and she therefore complains to it in the pre-1972 way about any perceived Indian infringements of the cease-fire. It follows that she continues to cooperate with Unmogip as before, and gives it every facility for the investigation of her complaints.

In this sensitive situation, Unmogip no longer formally checks on the levels of forces and armaments in Pakistan-held Kashmir. But on the basis that one party cannot unilaterally abrogate an ongoing agreement, Unmogip continues to respond, to the best of its ability, to Pakistan's frequent complaints about cease-fire infringements. Investigations are conducted – but on the Pakistan side only; judgements are made as to whether or not a violation has taken place, or stating that the investigation was inconclusive; each result is passed on to Pakistan; and periodically they are also transmitted to India – who studiously ignores them. Thus the Observers on the Pakistan side lead an active and challenging life, but their postings to the Indian side entail a lot of inaction and a corresponding amount of boredom. As of December 1989, Unmogip had 35 Military Observers drawn from the following eight countries: Belgium, Chile, Denmark, Finland, Italy, Norway, Sweden, and Uruguay. The Chief Military Observer at that time was from Ireland. They were backed by about 20 civilian international staff from the UN Secretariat.

From 1972 until the end of 1989 the line of control was generally quiet, and the incidents which occurred were chiefly of a 'routine' variety. But as India no longer cooperates with Unmogip, this stability can hardly be attributed to the UN's peacekeeping role. It could be that the Indian troops are a trifle more cautious from time to time, because of the investigating role of the UN Military Observers, but it is unlikely that the latter are a weighty sedative factor in the situation. Overwhelmingly, Unmogip now serves to back up Pakistan's claim about the continued existence of an international dispute, and as a possible means of legitimizing her complaints about specific instances of Indian misbehaviour. In fact, however, Pakistan makes virtually no public use of Unmogip's findings, perhaps fearing that India would retaliate by banning Unmogip from her part of Kashmir.

The question therefore arises as to whether there is any point in the UN maintaining Unmogip, either in its present shape or at all. Undoubtedly, Kashmir is still a possible Indo–Pakistani flashpoint, and it could also easily get embroiled in any fighting which might occur on the recognized international frontier. In any such event, the presence of Unmogip could be of use – but that is hardly a sufficient justification for its retention. Unmogip could also provide a basis for any expanded peacekeeping activity in respect of India and Pakistan which might be required of the UN in future, and it is certainly the case that having such a basis makes things far easier than setting up a new operation from scratch. But that possibility does not amount to a convincing case for keeping Unmogip in being. Unmogip is undoubtedly useful as a kind of training ground for officers who might go on to serve in other peacekeeping operations. But it is not essential for the purpose, quite apart from the questionable propriety of maintaining it for that reason.

The strongest argument for maintaining Unmogip is that not to do so would give the clear appearance of submitting to India's unilateral claim that Kashmir is over and done with as an international issue. Many states consider that Pakistan still has a legitimate grievance about Kashmir, or at the least that her case deserves a hearing. It is also seen as a dispute which, in the light both of its history and the wish of one of the parties, properly interests the UN. Unmogip is tangible evidence of that interest – notwithstanding the fact that its current peacekeeping value is virtually nil.

The conclusion which follows from this is that the function just discussed could perfectly well be served by a much scaled-down Unmogip. For example, one field station on the Indian side, with static Observers, would maintain a sufficient foothold there. On the Pakistan side, a small team of observers could make a recurring tour of the line of control, perhaps investigating complaints as it went along – for there is no urgency about so one-sided an activity. In these ways the general international interest in the matter would be advertised, but at less cost than now, and with no real peacekeeping pretensions. Peacekeeping operations can be extremely valuable, but only where the parties are willing to cooperate with them. Where, as in Kashmir, that essential condition is not fulfilled, there is no point in maintaining a peacekeeping facade. However, given the highly disturbed condition of Indian-held Kashmir during the early part of 1990, and the threat which this presents to Indo–Pakistani relations, it is most unlikely that the UN Security Council will favour a thinning out of Unmogip's already scanty personnel.

FURTHER READING

Pauline Dawson, *The United Nations Military Observer Group in India and Pakistan (UNMOGIP) 1948–65, with a Postscript on the Impact on UNMOGIP of the Indo–Pakistan War of 1971* (Keele: University of Keele, unpublished Ph.D. thesis, 1987).

Rosalyn Higgins, *United Nations Peacekeeping 1946–1967. Documents and Commentary. Vol. II: Asia* (London: Oxford University Press, 1970).

Alan James, 'Recent Developments in United Nations Peacekeeping', *The Year Book of World Affairs 1977* (London: Stevens, 1977).

Sylvain Lourie, 'The UN Military Observer Group in India and Pakistan', *International Organization*, IX (1) (February 1955).

Section E   The Withdrawal of Forces After the Indo–Pakistani War (1965–1966)

THE 1965 HOSTILITIES

Pakistan's attempts to spark off a revolt in Indian-held Kashmir in August 1965 led to violations of the cease-fire line by both sides. (For the background to this, see Section D above.) Pakistan then launched a full-scale assault across the line, to which India responsed by invading (what was then West) Pakistan at several points. Thus the two states were at war not just in Kashmir but also along the 1,000-mile-long international frontier (see Map 29).

The crisis attracted a good deal of ameliorative attention, not least from the two superpowers, both of whom felt that its continuation might cause them some embarrassment. For each had close links with one of the belligerents – the Soviet Union with India and the United States with Pakistan – but had also been trying to improve her relations with the other. A number of other states, too, while having not direct interests in the matter, were unhappy about the fighting. This was particularly true of Britain and some fellow-Commonwealth states. In a rare show of unity, therefore, the UN Security Council issued two calls for a cease-fire, and on 20 September went so far as to 'demand' that one took effect two days later and that forces be subsequently withdrawn. In view of the amount of displeasure they were arousing, but also for other reasons, the parties agreed to call off their war.

The Security Council had also asked for the supervision of the cease-fire and withdrawal. The UN already had an observer mission on hand in Kashmir – Unmogip, see Section D above – and the parties got into a subtle and perhaps trivial argument about whether it could be employed for the new requirement beyond as well as within Kashmir. Pakistan refused to agree to this, and a separate body was therefore

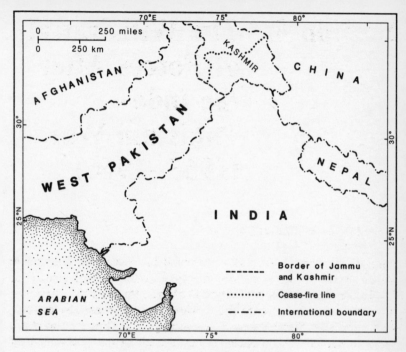

Map 29   India and West Pakistan

set up, the UN India–Pakistan Observation Mission (Unipom), which consisted of 90 unarmed Military Observers from the following 10 states: Brazil, Burma, Canada, Ceylon (now Sri Lanka), Ethiopia, Ireland, Nepal, Netherlands, Nigeria, and Venezuela. (Two Eastern bloc states were also asked to provide Observers, but after some hesitation declined.) In an attempt to mollify India's feelings, which had also been upset by earlier talk of the possible despatch of a 1,000-man force to the area, the UN emphasized that the whole withdrawal would be treated as a single operation.

It was, however, some time before the withdrawal could get under way, as Pakistan was reluctant to make any move until she had obtained some concessions in relation to her basic grievance regarding Kashmir. But India flatly refused to discuss the subject in the context of the winding down of the war. All Pakistan could therefore get in return for her promise to withdraw, given at a meeting in Tashkent in January 1966 at which the Soviet Union played the unaccustomed role of honest broker, was a bland agreement by India to continue meetings on matters of direct concern. It proved worthless.

Meanwhile, Unipom, and also Unmogip in Kashmir, had been playing an important defusing and stabilizing role. The cease-fire was at times a very tenuous affair, with some units seeming not to be fully under control and some local commanders trying to improve their positions by edging forwards. On bad days each side submitted hundreds of complaints about the other's violations of the cease-fire, and clashes often occurred, occasionally of a serious character. When fighting broke out Unipom and Unmogip tried to persuade the relevant commanders to restore the cease-fire. They also tried to reduce the likelihood of such developments by negotiating agreements for tactical readjustments in localities where the disposition of forces was particularly provocative. The Observers also engaged both sides in negotiations for a no-firing agreement, a limitation on aerial activity, and a ban on test firing in the vicinity of the front lines, with eventual success in each case. In such ways as these the UN's peacekeepers undoubtedly exercised a valuable cooling influence, clearing the way for the parties to move on to the withdrawal of forces.

In an effort to make progress in this direction, the UN Secretary-General asked the Commander of the UN Force which sat between Egypt and Israel to visit the area to negotiate plans for withdrawal. Pakistan accepted the idea, but once again it appeared that Indian susceptibilities had been insufficiently catered for, and it was only after the General had discovered pressing business in Gaza that the scheme could be put into operation – with a different General. He was able to announce, five days after the Tashkent agreement had sorted out the political problem, that guidelines had been agreed to resolve the military one. Agreement on the detailed ground rules followed, and by the end of February, with the assistance of Unipom and Unmogip, each side's army was safely back on its own soil. Unipom's disbandment followed, with a financial flea in its ear in the shape of an Indian announcement that as the victim of aggression she could be expected neither to help pay for it nor for the extra costs which Unmogip had incurred in the aftermath of the war. Like most UN observer groups, Unipom and Unmogip were financed from the Organization's regular budget, and in due course India witheld the appropriate proportionate sums.

THE 1971 HOSTILITIES

Unipom's success was a direct reflection of the favourable context in which it operated. The Security Council was most anxious to calm the situation down through the use of a peacekeeping mission; the parties were willing to receive the mission; and, albeit sometimes hesitantly, they cooperated with it. When India and Pakistan next went to war, in 1971, they did so in a very different political context, with the result that the UN's role was negligible.

Following an East Pakistan declaration of independence in March 1971, the Pakistan Army engaged in what, by all accounts, was a policy of brutal suppression. India grew increasingly restive at this (to which a flow of refugees into India from East Pakistan made its contribution), and Pakistan worried about the possibility of Indian intervention. Pakistan therefore asked several times that UN observers be posted on the East Pakistan–India border, or even just on the Pakistani side, but to no avail. India was naturally opposed to this, and had the backing of the veto-holding Soviet Union. This circumstance was also the reason why the Security Council could not reach a decision when India sent her troops into East Pakistan in December (and almost immediately recognized its independence under the name of Bangladesh). Within a couple of weeks the war was over. Pakistan had broken – or been broken – up.

The affair underlined the point that peacekeeping measures are of full use only when all the immediately involved parties are anxious to maintain peace. In such circumstances, peacekeepers can play an important derivative role. But if that condition is not obtained, peacekeeping is at best of limited value – as a face-saver, maybe, or an impartial reporting body – and at worst is completely irrelevant.

FURTHER READING

Shafqat Hussain Chauhdry, *United Nations India–Pakistan Observation Mission, 1965–1966* (Keele: University of Keele, unpublished Ph.D. thesis, 1979).

Andrew W. Cordier and Max Harrelson (eds), *The Public Papers of the Secretaries-General of the United Nations, Vol. VII: U Thant 1965–1967* (New York: Columbia University Press, 1976).

Robert W. Reford, 'Unipom: Success of a Mission', *International Journal*, 27 (3) (Summer 1972).

Robert Jackson, *South Asian Crisis: India–Pakistan–Bangladesh* (London: Chatto and Windus, 1975).

Section F Military Attacks on Civilians in the Iran–Iraq War (1984–1988)

A few years after the outbreak of the Iran–Iraq War, concern began to be expressed at the UN about what appeared to be deliberate military attacks on purely civilian targets – Iraq seeming to be the chief offender. The Secretary-General therefore began discussions about an arrangement which would both examine any allegations of such happenings and, it was hoped, discourage their occurrence. Perhaps because of her distrust of the Security Council, Iran was not keen on the idea of on-the-spot military teams, whereas Iraq suggested that several be established in each state. The result was a compromise, the Secretary-General announcing in June 1984 that he was setting up a UN Inspection Team (UNIT) in each capital. Each Team was to consist of three Military Observers (seconded from Untso) and a civilian official, the Observers being drawn from four acceptable states: Austria, Finland, Ireland and Sweden.

This small defusing operation got off to a smooth start, but was soon in trouble. An inspection conducted in Iran confirmed that two villages seemed to have been deliberately attacked, whereas two inspections in Iraq produced non-committal reports. Iraq's enthusiasm for the UN arrangement waned, and early in 1985 it in effect broke down amidst mutual recriminations as to who had sabotaged it. Thereafter Iraq both declined to ask for inspections and refused to grant safe conduct for any which were formally requested by Iran (this procedure being a feature of this particular scheme). Informal inspections could still be, and sometimes were, conducted, but nothing could be said about them.

As public reports were of the essence of this operation, there was little point in keeping the UNITs at their original level. In the middle of 1985, therefore, each was reduced to one Observer and one civilian, and in 1986 a single Observer was left on his own in each capital. The inspection scheme had become simply a holding operation – a base from which something might be built if the UN was asked to engage in other peacekeeping activity in relation to the War. This is what happened, as the UN military presence in each capital was of considerable value in the planning for the Observer Group which was set up after the 1988 cease-fire (see Section G below). At this point the UNITs were disestablished, having been of more peacekeeping use in preparing for their successors than they had been in their own right. Each party had in fact been chiefly interested in them as possible suppliers of damning material about the other. The chance that they might have had some humanitarian benefit justified their establishment, but they never had any real peacekeeping significance.

For a map, see Map 30 below.

FURTHER READING

'Iran and Iraq Accept Secretary-General's Appeal', *UN Chronicle*, XXI (5) (May 1984).

Section G   Supporting the Iran–Iraq Cease-fire (1988–   )

The war which broke out in 1980 between Iran and Iraq seemed, on the face of it, tailor-made for strong UN calls for its cessation, followed by a tidying-up peacekeeping operation. To outsiders, hugely important issues did not seem to be at stake. Fighting was going on in a sensitive area, and threatened to – and later did – spill over into an even more sensitive one. The two combatants were non-aligned, and neither superpower was closely linked with either of them. Losses were considerable. And a decisive military outcome seemed unlikely. However, it was not until 1987 that the Security Council got around to demanding a cease-fire, and a further year was to go by before Iran – originally the injured party but latterly the more stubborn one – decided that the going was getting too tough.

The basic reason for the Security Council's inactivity was that for most of its members, and especially the leading ones, the continuation of this neighbourhood quarrel was rather convenient. Iran in the full flush of her 1979 Islamic revolution had presented an alarming prospect. Her local preoccupation in the 1980s was therefore not without benefits, and the fact that Iraq was also being discouraged from other mischief was not seen as a bad thing.

But in mid-1988 it was suddenly announced that the war was at an end, and the Security Council immediately busied itself with consequential matters. It had agreed the year before that an observer mission would be necessary to firm up a cease-fire and supervise the withdrawal of forces to their own territory. A mission was now sent to the area to make detailed plans, and on 9 August the Council unanimously established the UN Iran–Iraq Military Observer Group (Uniimog) for an initial period of six months. The two superpowers helped with the required transport, and by 20 August, the day on which the cease-fire came into effect, Uniimog was on the spot and ready to begin its first patrols. Its parent body might have been sluggish while

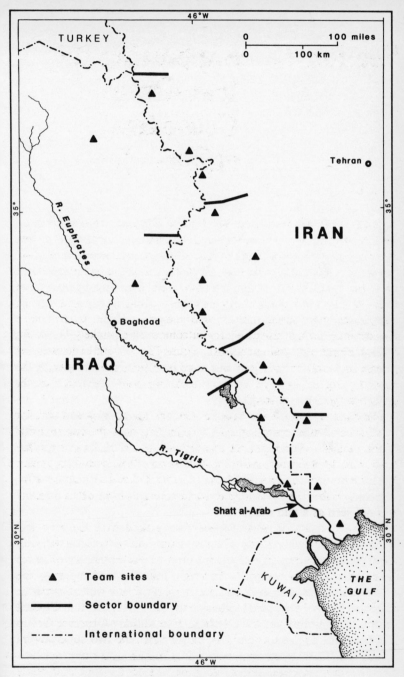

Map 30   UN positions on the Iran–Iraq border

the war was on. But once it was over the UN moved very smartly (see Map 30).

At Uniimog's core is a body of about 350 unarmed Military Observers, initially drawn from no fewer than 26 states – one-sixth of the total UN membership. The states are: Argentina, Australia, Austria, Bangladesh, Canada, Denmark, Finland, Ghana, Hungary, India, Indonesia, Ireland, Italy, Kenya, Malaysia, New Zealand, Nigeria, Norway, Peru, Poland, Senegal, Sweden, Turkey, Uruguay, Yugoslavia and Zambia. A large Canadian signals unit was part of Uniimog for a few months to set up its communications, the running of which was then passed to the Group's international civilian staff. Uniimog also includes an air unit, a military police unit, and a medical section, bringing its military personnel to 403 as of March 1990. This number was expected to increase somewhat through an expansion of Uniimog's air unit. And there would be a further small expansion if the parties are able to agree that a Uniimog naval unit should patrol in and near the Shatt al-Arab – the waterway which, for some distance inland from the head of the Gulf, contentiously forms the Iran–Iraq international frontier. Uniimog's initial head (the Chief Military Observer) was a Yugoslav General, and the Group has two headquarters, one in each capital. Its costs are shared out among all UN members in agreed proportions.

If Uniimog worked on the basis of its prospectus, it would probably fulfil all three of the major peacekeeping functions. For although reference is made in its mandate to it monitoring the cease-fire after each side has withdrawn to its own territory, it is perhaps unlikely that such a withdrawal will take place until a fair amount of progress has been made towards a settlement of the various issues in dispute. With-drawal, supervised by Uniimog, may therefore be associated with at least a partial resolution of the conflict. As of June 1990, however, that development seems at least a little way off.

Meanwhile, Uniimog engages in the tasks of defusion and stabilization along an often zig-zag cease-fire line about 900 miles in length, which leaves Iraq in occupation of more Iranian land than vice versa. Topographically, it ranges from mountainous terrain in the north, which can be traversed only by mule-back or on foot, to marshes in the south which require the use of boats. The UN Observers in the field are deployed in four sectors on the Iranian side and three on the Iraqi, each sector controlling a number of team sites, which are located as near the cease-fire line as possible.

One of Uniimog's first jobs was to secure agreement on the exact position of each side's forces when the cease-fire came into effect, so as to reduce the likelihood of later argument as to whether it had been violated. This was not always easy, but had by and large been achieved within a few months. Where the opposing forces were in dangerous proximity – in one case they were separated by only 10 yards – Uniimog tried to persuade them to withdraw to less provocative positions, sometimes with success. And where confrontations resulted from actual or alleged breaches of the cease-fire, the Observers tried to get those involved to take defusing measures. If an on-the-spot solution could not be reached the matter would be referred up the chain of command. Large numbers of allegations of cease-fire violations were in fact made – about 2,000 in the first five months – but most of them were of a minor nature or unconfirmed by Uniimog. Those that were confirmed consisted chiefly of the movement of troops or the establishment of positions forward of the cease-fire lines or of works to strengthen defensive positions. In February 1989 Uniimog reported that the number of complaints was diminishing, but also that in some areas tension remained high or was even increasing.

The chief way in which Uniimog tries to introduce more stability into the situation is by advertising its presence as an impartial body which is charged by the UN with overseeing the cease-fire. Its Observers patrol regularly, in twos and usually by vehicle, to check that the side to which they are assigned is observing its obligations. In the context of the agreed cessation of hostilities this has some deterrent effect, and also enables local commanders to let off steam in a harmless way. If appropriate, complaints can be taken up by the Observers with their counterparts on the other side, either by radio or through a meeting in no-man's-land. Uniimog has also tried to build up confidence, and thus stability, between the two sides by arranging for the exchange of war dead and such prisoners as each side will release, and by helping in the arrangement and execution of locust spraying along the cease-fire line. Towards the same end the Observer Group has also made efforts to set up a mixed military working group, but as of June 1990 recriminations between the two sides had prevented the start of its meetings.

At a wider level, the UN has arranged a number of meetings between the foreign ministers of Iran and Iraq in an endeavour to make progress towards a withdrawal of forces and a settlement of the overall dispute. However, as of September 1989 it has not been possible to reach agreement even on some apparently more immediate matters let alone the larger issues. In these circumstances, Uniimog could be in for a long stay. Already, in its first 22 months, it has made a very substantial contribution towards the firming-up of the cease-fire which, after a long and extremely bitter war, was even more fragile than many such arrangements. Some escalatory developments have been nipped in the bud; calming-down action has been taken on numerous occasions; and a degree of stability has been fostered along much of the cease-fire line. Without Uniimog, it is highly likely that the cease-fire would have frequently broken down, and possible that full-scale war might have been resumed.

It can by no means be assumed that Uniimog's continuing presence between the forces of Iran and Iraq will be accompanied by progress towards a full settlement between the two states. In which case some might well be heard saying that the existence of a peacekeeping body provides the parties with an excuse not to wind down their dispute – or at least is something of a discouragement to their doing so. As in earlier instances where this kind of remark has been made, its validity is extremely doubtful. It is just a fact of international life that some disputes are enormously hard to settle, and a development in that direction is, if anything, likely to be obstructed rather than encouraged by frequent border clashes. Peacekeepers need not therefore worry that they are somehow standing in the way of peace. And by helping in the maintenance of calm, they are doing something which is widely regarded as of considerable value in its own right.

It happens that the middle-term prospect for a settlement of the Iran–Iraq conflict is brighter than that for some other disputes which have attracted the services of peacekeepers, as in this case it is leadership rather than territory which is crucial. But in the short term, and provided that each side maintains its commitment to the cease fire, Uniimog will have the opportunity to engage in a lot of important peacekeeping work.

FURTHER READING

Shahram Chubin, 'The last phase of the Iran–Iraq war: from stalemate for ceasefire', *Third World Quarterly*, 11 (2) (April 1989).
J. Duggan, 'Iran–Iraq – a Solution in the Resolution', *An Cosantoir*, 48 (10) (October 1988).
Ford Foundation, *The United Nations and the Iran–Iraq War* (New York: Ford Foundation, 1987).
Alan James, 'The United Nations and the Gulf War', *Naval Forces*, IX (VI) (December 1988).

Section H   The Question of Naval Peacekeeping

Peacekeeping activity is not much needed in respect of naval confrontations. The self-contained nature of ships, the tight control which is exercised over the use of their armaments, their mobility, and the fact that they chiefly operate on the high seas, where ships of other states have an equal entitlement to sail, all result in there being little call for peacekeeping facilities. The effective implementation of orders to end a conflict at sea is unlikely to require the help of third parties. The resulting situation can easily be stabilized by unilateral measures. And navies are not usually involved in the activity which is necessary for the resolution of international disputes.

Occasionally, however, naval elements have been given peacekeeping employment in connection with terrestrial problems. As part of the notional attempt to discourage the involvement of outsiders in the Spanish Civil War, naval patrols were instituted (see Part II, Section B above). During the latter part of the first truce in the initial War of Palestinian Succession (see Section C above), the UN had one French naval corvette and three United States destroyers at its disposal, and was thus able to patrol the coastal waters of Israel and the neighbouring Arab states. When West New Guinea/West Irian was administered by the UN to facilitate its transfer from the Netherlands to Indonesia, the need to safeguard international order in that aqueous and untarmacadamed part of the world resulted in the Pakistan Navy manning nine vessels which were transferred to the UN by the Netherlands (see Part IV, Section B below). To execute its obligation to ensure freedom of navigation through the strategically-significant Strait of Tiran (a former flash point in the Arab–Israeli conflict), the Multinational Force and Observers (MFO) makes use of a few converted Italian minesweepers (see Part II, Section K above). Panama's affairs once attracted a naval patrol (see Part I, Section I above). Fast patrol boats are being used by the UN Observer Group in Central America (Onuca – see Part I, Section L above). And the UN Observer Group which is watching over the Iran–Iraq cease fire may deploy a

175

small naval unit in the contentious Shatt al-Arab (see Section G above).

Notwithstanding the use of the word 'ensure' in the MFO's mandate, most of this activity is of a purely watchdog kind. Other than in the rather uncommon case of West New Guinea, naval patrols have been instituted just to keep an eye on the situation, and by so doing to discourage, it is hoped, destabilizing behaviour. If any such behaviour nonetheless occurs, local calls can be made for its discontinuance, no doubt with an air of authority. But only in the Panamanian situation was it intended to follow through such calls, if necessary, with the use of naval force to prevent improper goings-on. In other words, the peacekeeping activity has been of the usual non-threatening sort, based on the premise that the parties are cooperatively inclined.

The question arises whether there is any naval analogy to the less usual form of peacekeeping, where force may be used not just in self-defence but as a means of helping to maintain order in a state whose government is generally viewed (by the populace) as legitimate. In those circumstances, and provided that the stability of the domestic scene bears on an international dispute, the display of force comes within the category of peacekeeping. The reason for that is because force, or its threat, is being used impartially in the sense that it is not intended to have any impact on the local political balance. It represents what might be called 'normal' governmental activity in the interests of law and order.

It might be thought that a preparedness to use force to safeguard shipping in a neighbourhood where fighting has spilled over onto the high seas could be regarded as analogous to the situation just described. Action in support of the principle of the freedom of the seas seems eminently of a law and order kind. But it is unlikely to fall into the category of peacekeeping because of the probability that it will have some independent effect on the conflict in question. If, for example, mines have been laid along a particular route, the layer has presumably set them there with a view to damaging its adversary, either directly or indirectly. Their clearance will therefore be in the interests of the state at whom they were aimed. All the more so is it the case that if neutral shipping is directly attacked, that is because the attacker believes that the other side is benefitting from it. Again, therefore, action by third parties to defend such shipping will be to the advantage of one side and the disadvantage of the other.

This was by far the most important reason why nothing came of the frequently-heard suggestion that, in respect of the Iran–Iraq War, a

UN force should be organized to protect shipping the Gulf. Given the Security Council's failure to name an aggressor, the force would have had to act against all attacks on neutral shipping, which would almost certainly have worked to the disadvantage of Iraq. However, the major powers, for their own reasons, while not particularly wanting Iraq to win, very much wanted her not to lose. Accordingly, instead of sponsoring a UN force, they each made individual arrangements to protect their own ships.

On rare occasions force may be used at sea in what might be seen as a public order manner but not in relation to an international conflict. This could occur following threats to shipping from vessels which do not have, or at least do not advertise, allegiance to any state. Piratical activity (still to be found in the South China Sea and adjacent waters) is a case in point; sea-based terrorism of a freelance kind could perhaps become of contemporary relevance; and maritime drug-running certainly takes place. On one (unconvincing) interpretation, the measures taken following the Nyon Conference of 1937 against submarine predators in the Mediterranean fall into this category (see Part II, Section B above). A case which clearly does so is the search for mines in the Red Sea by American, British, French, and Egyptian naval elements in mid-1984 after a number of ships had been so damaged. But as issues of this nature do not threaten peace between states, it does seem a trifle odd to refer to action taken in connection with them as peacekeeping. The issue of public safety can be easily distinguished from the bolstering of peace, and perhaps it should be.

Naval action which had a rather different public order aspect, and did concern a kind of international dispute, arose out of the UN's condemnation of Rhodesia's 1965 Unilateral Declaration of Independence. All UN members were called on to institute an embargo on the export of oil and petroleum products to the rebel regime, the chief route for which was a pipeline running from the Portuguese port of Beira in Mozambique to landlocked Rhodesia. When, therefore, two oil tankers appeared off Beira in 1966 with cargoes thought to be bound for Rhodesia, the Security Council called on Britain to prevent, if necessary by force, the arrival in Beira of vessels reasonably believed to be carrying oil for Rhodesia. This led her to establish a blockade – the Beira Patrol – which was at first maintained by an aircraft carrier and then by two frigates with support from long-range aircraft. The patrol was discontinued in 1975 with Portugal's grant of sovereignty to its East African territory – which, unlike its former superior, was disinclined to help Rhodesia.

The problem with this case, however, is that if it is seen as action on behalf of the collectivity of states in a public order matter, in that measures were taken to undermine an illegal white minority regime, it does not bear on an inter-state dispute. This raises a question as to its peacekeeping status. But if it is regarded as, de facto, an international dispute, the use of force in support of one side excludes it from the category of peacekeeping.

The conclusion to be drawn from this somewhat rag-bag collection of cases is that naval analogies to law and order peacekeeping operations within the state are unlikely often to occur. Even in a domestic context such operations are not common and sometimes, besides being difficult, offer the temptation to exceed the impartial bounds of peacekeeping. At sea, there is no real equivalent to the two situations which may give rise to domestic law and order operations. The first is where, as part of an international deal, territory needs to be administered with the aid of a peacekeeping body. By definition, the high seas can hardly be bargained over in this way. The second is where an inter-state conflict looms in consequence of a certain sort of threat to internal order. At sea, however, such threats to order as occur almost always come from states themselves, rather than individuals and groups. If the latter do present a problem, a question arises as to whether an operation to deal with it is most helpfully regarded as an instance of peacekeeping.

None of the remarks in this Section are meant to suggest that action taken in support of order on the high seas is either unnecessary or improper. The only point which emerges is that while peacekeeping operations may sometimes include a naval element, it is unlikely that operations of a substantively maritime nature will often fall clearly within the bounds of what has come to be called peacekeeping.

FURTHER READING

Alan James, 'The United Nations and the Gulf War', *Naval Forces*, IX (VI) (December 1988).

Part IV
High-street Embarrassments

Introduction: Peacekeeping in the High Street

As well as conducting business in their back yards and clubs, states also have much to do in the high (or main) street of the international society. Here they have dealings with all those whom they do not meet in their more restricted contexts and associations, so that, as in a town, the high street is a very important location. And, as domestically, some members of society are much more noticeable in the centre of town than others, usually the weightier ones but also those who are particularly vocal or who wish, in one way or another, to make something of a splash. Generally, states will be about their individual affairs when they are abroad in the high street, but – and again the domestic comparison is apt – it is not unknown for them to move about in groups or even gangs.

Sometimes, states' conduct in the high street is such as to cause embarrassment – either to themselves or to their friends, or to both. This may occur as the result of positive moves on their part – intervening in the concerns of others, for example. Or they may be making a passive nuisance of themselves by outstaying their welcome in particular places. At the domestic level, individual misbehaviour of this sort can be dealt with by calling up the police. But mobs are not so readily coped with, and organized activity of a deliberately disobedient kind may be far beyond the resources of the local constabulary. Internationally, each unit is a highly organized group, and there is no semblance of a central authority to call for order. Moreover, states are notoriously touchy: reluctant to heed advice, often obstreperous in face of inducements and pressures, full of pride, and ever-conscious of their image. In consequence they do not find it easy to withdraw from enterprises to which they have set their hands, even when they realize that a mistake has been or is being made. Seemingly, the admission of error is, for states, a cardinal sin.

In these circumstances the tool of peacekeeping can be enormously helpful in getting a state off an embarrassing hook. It is relatively easy to arrange and offers the malefactor several very important advantages. It should enable such a state to depart in good order and with at least the appearance – due to peacekeeping's non-threatening nature – of

180

going of its own volition. The international and perhaps elevated-looking auspices under which the peacekeeping operation takes place may facilitate a decision to withdraw. Further, the actual tasks of the peacekeepers may supply a state with a justification for going, along the lines – almost certainly spurious – that they will carry on where it left off. Alternatively, a state may seek independent verification of its good faith in executing an agreement. With these face-saving or kudos-gathering opportunities, a state may find it much easier to withdraw from an uncomfortable position, and may well be pressingly encouraged to do so by embarassed international friends or from within political circles at home.

It might be supposed that peacekeeping would be chiefly resorted to in this high-street context by great powers who were getting their lesser friends and associates out of trouble: the equivalent of senior members of the family bailing out some of the younger ones after their late-night excesses. But at the international level it usually takes strength to get into the kind of situation which leads to serious embarrassment. In consequence, none of the ten peacekeeping operations and the two peacekeeping proposals which fall to be considered in Part IV relate to the activity of a very small state. And only two concern the policies of smallish or small to medium states – both dealing with the Netherlands' reluctant withdrawal from her colonial East Indies. The first of these operations helped to defuse the crisis and in its settlement (Section A), and the second, as well as doing likewise, also played an internal stabilizing role (Section B).

Of the remaining operations and proposals, two arose out of the belligerent threats or activity of quite substantial medium powers, and a third out of the policy of a strong regional state. The first of these resulted from inter-communal strife in the non-aligned state of Cyprus, which, at the end of 1963, produced a serious likelihood of intervention by Turkey in support of the Turkish–Cypriot minority (Section G). To avert this, and also, therefore, the possibility of counter intervention by Greece, hasty prophylactic measures were taken at the instance of the Western alliance, and before long were replaced by a UN peacekeeping force.

The other case of this kind was the Falklands crisis of 1982 (Section H), which was precipitated by Argentina's invasion of Britain's small and remote colonial dependency. Here the embarrassment of the state which really counted – the United States – was somewhat muted, which may partly account for Argentina's refusal of the peacekeeping withdrawal route which was offered to her. In consequence, Britain went ahead with the forceful recovery of the territory. The third case arose out of South Africa's long determination to hang on to the former League of Nations mandated territory of South West Africa (Namibia) (Section K). In the late 1980s, however, she decided, in face of regular and universal condemnation, that enough was enough – and agreed to leave with the aid of a large and long-planned peacekeeping operation.

All the other seven peacekeeping operations which dealt with a high-street embarrassment bear in one way or another on the activities of the five permanent members of the UN Security Council – the great powers of 1945. Each one of them has sought or been willing to receive the help of a peacekeeping body to extricate itself from a situation of considerable embarrassment – and the list therefore includes the two superpowers. This is a mark both of the depth of the difficulties in which they found themselves and of the usefulness of the device of peacekeeping. For no state likes having to make use of an international helpline, and the major powers could be expected to find it particularly distasteful. But needs must when the Devil calls.

By far the biggest and best-known of these operations is that which arose out of the Suez crisis of 1956 – and led to the distinctive concept of peacekeeping (Section F). A UN Force was established as a means of getting Britain and France out of their ill-judged intervention, and having defused the crisis the Force stayed on to stabilize the Egyptian–Israeli border. Two years previously, the creation of three International Commissions had assisted France out of her East Asian colonial possessions in Indo-China (Section D). And the year before that an ad hoc international body had arranged the withdrawal from Burma of troops belonging to the army of Nationalist China – which, after her mainland defeat, had set up a regime on the off-shore island of Formosa, but still sat in China's UN seat (Section C).

The International Commissions in Indo-China had been set up both to defuse and settle the crisis, but at least in respect of Vietnam the reference to a settlement was little more than a gesture. And in time the United States came, more or less, to take France's place in that country, but with no greater success. In 1973 she too made an ignominious departure – with the way to it being eased by an agreement on the creation of a peacekeeping body (Section E). It proved of no use as a settlement mechanism on the ground, but was undoubtedly important in helping the United States to think in terms of withdrawal, and therefore played an important role in defusing that significant aspect of the crisis.

Two high-street peacekeeping bodies which were established in 1988, together with a proposed third, chiefly concerned the activity or policy of the Soviet Union. The suggestion that this might happen would, only a few years before, have received short shrift. But under that country's liberalizing regime of the late 1980s, agreement was reached on a withdrawal of Soviet troops from Afghanistan (Section I) and of Cuban (proxy) troops from Angola (Section J), with small UN observer groups keeping an eye on both operations. A parallel agreement regarding Angola provided for the departure of South African troops and the forces of the African National Congress, and here too a small verifying mission was set up (Section J). The Soviet Union also supported the idea that a peacekeeping operation should be established in connection with the departure of Vietnamese troops from Cambodia, where they had had maintained a puppet regime for 10 years (Section L). It would be going too far to say that the Vietnamese were Soviet proxies, but they were certainly in Cambodia with Soviet support and encouragement. In this case, however, due to disagreement among the Cambodian factions, the peacekeeping proposal had to be put on one side, at least for the time being.

In respect of Afghanistan and Angola the UN was asked to do no more than verify that the agreements were being honoured (and as of June 1990 the Angolan operation is little more than half way through). But the Soviet Union's relatively relaxed attitude to the idea that UN military observers should check on her abandonment of two rather embarrassing adventures had a double significance which could exceed the not inconsiderable usefulness of the UN's immediate tasks. Firstly, it promisingly emphasized the Soviet Union's generally more cooperative approach to peacekeeping issues. And secondly it suggested to others that being watched over by a peacekeeping body need not be seen as demeaning. Too much should not be read into these comments, as states always take decisions in the light of how their interests can best be prosecuted or defended in the particular circumstances of the day. But these recent developments could be interesting straws in the peacekeeping wind.

Section A The Netherlands' Last Stand in her East Indies/ Indonesia (1947–1951)

After the Second World War, the Netherlands experienced great difficulty in regaining control over her East Indies, which had been occupied during the War by Japan. For on the Japanese defeat, the indigenous Indonesians had declared their independence and made good de facto progress towards that goal. The Netherlands' attempt to quell what was seen as a rebellion resulted, first in 1946 and again in 1947, in the matter being brought to the UN, and over the two and a half years following the second occasion there was a lot of UN activity in relation to the Indonesian problem. First, in 1947, a Good Offices Committee was established, and then, in January 1949, a Commission for Indonesia. The Commission marked an appreciable stepping up of pressure on the Dutch, as it was charged with the conduct of negotiations for the creation of a sovereign Indonesia. This event took place at the end of 1949, but the UN Commission stayed on until 1951 to watch over the implementation of the agreements for the setting up of the new state (see Map 31).

In all these matters the United States played a key role, as was seen in the fact that she was chairman of both the Committee and the Commission. At first she took a moderate line towards the Netherlands. This was not unconnected with her growing concern about a Soviet threat to Western Europe, and the possibility that a collective defence organization might be required. The Netherlands was not a large state, but in strategic and political terms it was quite important that she be persuaded to keep in step with the United States. Then, however, in response to tough Dutch action in Indonesia the United States started getting tough herself, as the Netherlands' high-street stand was beginning to embarrass her.

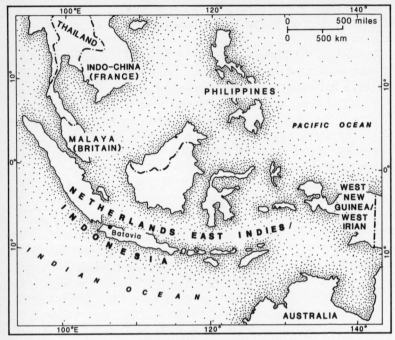

Map 31   Netherlands East Indies/Indonesia

From the American perspective, East and South East Asia can just as
easily be seen as West and South West Pacific – and partly for this reason
it is a region in which the United States has long had a keen interest.
In the late 1940s it was causing her considerable worry. The Communist
movement was doing very well in China, and not at all badly in
Indo-China and Malaya. The prospect of Communist guerrilla activity
in Dutch-held Indonesia could not be ruled out, and was far from
alluring. Accordingly, the United States came to the view that an early
settlement of the Indonesian problem in favour of the independence
movement was necessary. Indonesia would be one of the world's more
populous states, and would also have considerable economic potential.
The American hope was that if sovereignty was secured with American
assistance, the new state might not look too badly on the West.
The United States still did not wish to upset the Netherlands more
than was necessary, and certainly not to humiliate her. But plans for
a North Atlantic treaty were well advanced and the Netherlands would
be unlikely to withdraw from the scheme on account of an American-
inspired reverse in the East. And given the overall situation, some Dutch

displeasure had to be afforded. The UN Commission for Indonesia was therefore used to pressure the Netherlands towards withdrawal, and with success.

Throughout the UN's handling of the Indonesian case its mediatory endeavours were supplemented by operations of a rather different kind – which, a decade later, would have been called peacekeeping. This activity was directed partly towards defusing the crisis, and partly towards its settlement. Both types of operation reflected the predominant American with to minimize instability in the region and to get a firm settlement. The first aspect of this work began in August 1947, when the Soviet Union proposed to the Security Council that a commission made up of all Council members go to Indonesia to supervise a cease-fire. Her draft resolution received the necessary seven votes, including that of the United States, but it was not adopted because of a French veto – which was probably cast to prevent Soviet field activity in what, from one point of view, was still a colonial situation. (Within a year all the Western powers would automatically be lining up against any such proposal.) Instead, a Commission was established made up of those Security Council members with career (as distinct from honorary) consuls in Indonesia's capital, Batavia – soon to be known as Djakarta: Australia, Belgium, China, France, the United Kingdom, and the United States.

The peacekeeping functions of this Consular Commission (CC) were executed by military observers supplied by each of its member states. Within a month of its establishment in August 1947, 27 officers were at its disposal. Due, however, to some misunderstandings about the nature of the commitment, they had dwindled to 15 by the end of the year. But then they rose to 55 early in 1948, and to a maximum of 63 in August 1949 when an agreement to end hostilities was signed. Thereafter their numbers declined, and they finally withdrew at the same time as the UN Commission for Indonesia wound up its activities in 1951. All of China's observers departed earlier, in May 1949, owing to the critical internal situation of their country.

The exact status of the CC in relation to the UN was never exactly clear. In consequence, it was equally unclear whether the military observers were agents of their own states or of the Security Council, or both. During the life of the Good Offices Committee, the Netherlands met almost all the CC's costs. But by the time the UN Commission for Indonesia was set up the observers were more generally seen as working for the UN, which therefore paid their expenses and raised the required money on the Organization's regular budget. The link with the UN was also manifested by the letters 'UN' being inscribed on armbands worn by the observers and on their vehicles and flags. They may thus be seen not only as falling within the category of peacekeeping but also, on the assumption that from the start they were serving the UN, as the earliest instance of the Organization's involvement in this role.

In its initial crisis-defusing role, the CC was first asked to report on the extent to which the Security Council's call for a cease-fire was being honoured. The point of this request was not just to secure information but also to encourage the parties to comply with the cease-fire call. The hope was that they would be so encouraged by the knowledge that impartial third parties were keeping an eye on their behaviour, and commenting on it both to their individual home states and to the UN. Later, the CC was asked to make its services available to both the Good Offices Committee and the Commission for Indonesia in connection with their mandates to help the parties maintain a cease-fire. This it did by, as before, reporting on compliance, and also by assisting in the settlement of incidents and by liaising between the military forces of the two sides. In the nature of its being, the CC could do these kinds of things only when the parties were willing to cooperate with it. They, and particularly the Dutch, were not always of this frame of mind. But when they were so disposed – and at the end of 1948 the United States had made it clear to the Netherlands that she had to give way – the CC was an exceedingly valuable peacekeeping tool.

Once a settlement had been agreed, the CC again proved its worth by assisting in the implementation of its terms, so contributing to the smooth handling of a number of sensitive matters. Notable among them was the evacuation of 35,000 Indonesian soldiers from behind the Dutch forward positions, the handover of the capital city to the Indonesians (they had lost it to the Dutch in the fighting at the end of 1948), the carrying into effect of the final cease-fire, and the repatriation of Dutch forces following the transfer of sovereignty. Given the suspicion which each side entertained for the other, they might have found considerable difficulty in dealing successfully with these issues had they not had the assistance of impartial third parties who possessed the required expertise. The work of the UN's military observers therefore considerably reduce the danger of the settlement breaking down.

Although at this early stage the full potential of the device which was to become known as peacekeeping was not appreciated, nonetheless the ground was being prepared, both here and in two other observer operations, for the emergence of the first UN peacekeeping force in 1956. And in time the UN was to give further peacekeeping help to

Indonesia and the Netherlands, as certain business which was unfinished in 1949 threatened to cause serious trouble in the early 1960s.

FURTHER READING

Sydney D. Bailey, *How Wars End* (Oxford: Clarendon Press, two vols, 1982).

Rosalyn Higgins, *United Nations Peacekeeping 1946–1967. Documents and Commentary. Vol. II: Asia* (London: Oxford University Press, 1970).

Alan James, *The Politics of Peacekeeping* (London: Chatto and Windus, 1969).

Alastair M. Taylor, *Indonesian Independence and the United Nations* (London: Stevens, 1960).

David W. Wainhouse *et al., International Peace Observation* (Baltimore, Md: Johns Hopkins University Press, 1966).

Section B The Transfer of West New Guinea/West Irian from the Netherlands to Indonesia (1962–1963)

DUTCH WITHDRAWAL

When, in 1949, the Netherlands had formally withdrawn from her East Indies in favour of what now became the new state of Indonesia, one territorial matter had been left on one side: the disposition of West New Guinea. Dutch control was to continue pending negotiations about its future, which were to be completed within a year. However, they were not so completed, and during the 1950s relations between the two states gradually deteriorated because of this issue.

At the end of the decade the Netherlands began to realize that time was not on her side. There was talk of a wind of change blowing through Africa, and it was manifested by the arrival in the UN in 1960 of no fewer than 16 new African states. Clearly, the balance of voting power in the General Assembly was going to turn against the Netherlands on the issue of whether negotiations on West New Guinea should be reopened. Worse, at the end of 1960 the candidate who won the United States presidential election quickly made it clear that his administration would be much more sympathetic towards Third World states than his predecessor's had been. In this new light, West New Guinea began to look like a political as well as a financial liability.

The Netherlands' response was to speed up the process of political development in her colony and to try to get the UN's imprimatur on what she was doing. But the UN was now taking its cue from Indonesia who, being alive to the legitimizing possibilities of any kind of UN mission, was opposed to the Organization becoming involved in West New Guinea in any capacity other than that of liquidator. Even a 1961 Netherlands' offer to place the territory under the UN's rule until its people were sufficiently developed to decide their own future was spurned. Those people, said Indonesia, were Indonesians, and had therefore already exercised their right of self-determination. With a view to helping history catch up with her conception of reality, Indonesia began to land infiltrators in the territory, mobilized her armed forces, and spoke of the possible seizure of West New Guinea by force. Meanwhile, the United States ostentatiously absented herself from the 1961 inauguration of a central representative body in the colony. She also, in response to an Indonesian threat to involve the Soviet Union, said that she was in favour of the issue being the subject of mediation. Clearly, as in the late 1940s, the future of the Netherlands empire in this region was becoming an embarrassment to the United States.

The Netherlands got the message. In January 1962 she announced that she was ready for unconditional talks with Indonesia and that she had no objection to the involvement of a mediator. She favoured the UN Secretary-General or a member of the UN Secretariat, but Indonesia wanted an internationally unencumbered American. The upshot was that the Secretary-General appointed an American to act as his representative – but he was widely seen as the unofficial representative of the United States. The negotiations were not easy, and were marked by further Indonesian intervention in West New Guinea. But now the Netherlands was in no position to take umbrage, and an agreement was signed on 15 August 1962. It made liberal use of the device of international peacekeeping.

In the first place, with a view to defusing the crisis, UN personnel were to watch over the cease-fire between the Dutch and the Indonesians, and settle any incidents which occurred. A team of 21 military observers was quickly assembled to do this job, a large part of which consisted of transmitting the news of the ending of hostilities to the 1,500 Indonesian troops who were scattered throughout the territory. It was also the observers' task to establish a non-military supply line to these men, and to secure their concentration in selected places. With the cooperation of both sides, all these things were done in about a month, and the UN thus made an effective contribution towards the abatement of tension. The military observers were drawn from the armies of Brazil, Ceylon (now Sri Lanka), India, Ireland, Nigeria, and Sweden.

Secondly, the UN was to assist in settling the dispute by playing a law and order role. It was to assume the administration of West New Guinea for a temporary period of at least seven months, and at the end of the UN's administration the territory was to be transferred to Indonesia. The world organization was thus to be the intermediary through whose hands the territory was to pass on its way from its previous owner to the successful claimant. This was a very important role, as it enabled the Netherlands to save a lot of much-needed face. It meant that the indignity of a direct transfer to its long-time adversary would be avoided – and also the danger of upsets along such a hazard-ridden route. The uncertainty about the exact period of time for which the UN was to act as administrator also assisted the Netherlands, in that it permitted her to present the arrangement as one which was not entirely cut and dried. Furthermore, the agreement provided that Indonesia would continue the education and development of the people, and permit an act of self-determination before the end of 1969 in which the people would decide whether or not they wished to remain with Indonesia. In preparation for it, UN experts would be based in the territory as necessary, and would be increased a year prior to the act of self-determination so that the UN could effectively assist and participate in the exercise.

Thus, whatever her private views about the strength of these provisions, the Netherlands could say in public that she had got a good deal for the inhabitants of the territory: their democratic rights were being safeguarded to the maximum extent possible in the circumstances. Accordingly, she could leave with a good conscience. In fact, of course, she was being hustled out, and without much regard on the part of her hustlers as to what the people of West New Guinea wanted. The important thing for some of those who were pressing for her departure was simply to get rid of her, and so end this vestige of colonialism. For others, notably the United States, the matter of most importance was to avoid fighting between a Nato member and a leading Third World state – one who had also been very prominent at the inaugural, 1961, meeting of Non-Aligned states. In this process the UN was to play a key role, in that it allowed the Netherlands to go with good grace and with the minimum of disturbance. At last this festering crisis, which was beginning to look rather nasty, was to be lanced.

The UN assumed the administration of West New Guinea on 1 October 1962 – the first time that the Organization had been entrusted with such responsibilities. Its Temporary Executive Authority (Untea) – in which 32 nationalities were represented – had, on virtually no notice and in a short space of time, to adapt the territory's institutions from the Dutch to an Indonesian pattern, arrange a smooth administrative take-over, and prepare the people for change. It was doing this in one of the world's most primitive areas – it was estimated that more than one-third of the inhabitants were not yet subject to any central control – which no doubt made its task easier in some respects as well as more difficult in others. However, its essential role was relatively simple: to hold the administrative fort for a short while so that the territory could be quietly passed from Dutch to Indonesian control. This Untea did, and there is no doubt that the transfer was greatly eased by the fact that it was indirect and conducted by a sympathetic intermediary.

During its administration of West New Guinea, Untea was provided with a Security Force on which it could rely for the maintenance of public order. For this the UN turned chiefly to Pakistan (Malaya having said that she was unable to do the job), who was politically acceptable to both sides. She was a member of the Western alliance system, which satisfied the Dutch, and yet was also, like Indonesia, both Asian and Muslim. Pakistan therefore supplied the ground forces of the Force, amounting to about 1,500 men, and also 110 men for its navy. This last consisted of vessels transferred to the UN from the Netherlands to provide transport and to carry out patrol duties. The Force was completed by air transport units supplied by Canada and – the country with a very keen interest in the whole affair – the United States. The Security Force succeeded in maintaining public order without difficulty, as only a few incidents were reported during its time in West New Guinea, none of them very serious.

When the agreement of 15 August 1962 had been signed by Indonesia and the Netherlands, the UN Secretary-General had said that the second phase of Untea's administration – which was to begin on 1 May 1963 and continue for an unspecified period – would be as short as possible. Indonesia was very soon making it clear that in her view there need be no second phase at all, and indeed that the first phase could be curtailed. The UN insisted on remaining until 1 May, but had no reason to prolong its stay. Untea's life, like its function, was always envisaged as very limited, and once all the Dutch troops and administrators had gone, and arrangements were being made for their replacement by Indonesians, events might just as well take the speediest course. Thus Untea's second phase was omitted or, in the view favoured by the UN, reduced to a matter of hours. This interpretation was possible because it had not been specified at what time on 1 May the first phase was to end, and the actual handing over of authority took place at

12.30 p.m. on that day. Hence honour was satisfied on both sides, and the UN's first experience of government was brought to a harmonious conclusion. It had also been conducted without any financial problems, as all the costs of the three peacekeeping activities were shared equally by Indonesia and the Netherlands.

Thus Indonesia was given what she regarded as her rightful inheritance, and West New Guinea became West Irian. The Netherlands brought her long connection with the East to an end. And the United States in particular and the West in general was relieved of what was becoming an unattractive embarrassment in an increasingly important part of the international high street. All this was done in ways which illustrated both the versatility and the usefulness of peacekeeping. The device was not an essential technical element in the resolution of the crisis, for the direct transfer of West New Guinea from the Netherlands to Indonesia was not at all a theoretically impractical proposition. It would have carried the risk of incidents and would have been an untidy operation. But it could have been done. However, it would have been a most humiliating course for the Netherlands, and she was most unwilling to follow it. If, therefore, she was to withdraw, it was politically necessary that she should not herself hand over her colony to her former adversary.

The use of the UN in a temporary governmental capacity was an admirable solution to this problem. The parties might have found it hard to agree on anyone else to do this job, and if they had so agreed the state so chosen might have been reluctant to cooperate. The UN however, was acceptable to both disputants, and willing to involve itself. This, together with the provisions of the agreement regarding self-determination for the West New Guineans, allowed the Netherlands both to capitulate to Indonesia and to leave with a sufficient measure of self-esteem. Had she not been enabled to do both these things, it is conceivable that she would have fought on, at least for a while. The peaceful settlement of the dispute, therefore, was not only facilitated by Untea and its Security Force, for whom the way was prepared by the UN's military observers: it may also have been partly dependent on the possibility of their presence in West New Guinea.

In the events leading to a settlement, however, the opportunity of using the UN as a temporary government for the territory was not a decisive factor. The Organization would probably have been prepared to assist in this way at any time during the dispute. But its involvement depended on the agreement of the parties – a legal requirement in the case of the Netherlands and, at least during the latter part of the dispute, a political requirement in the case of Indonesia. And an accord between them was reached only when the Netherlands increasingly found herself out on a military and a diplomatic limb. Militarily, her situation in West New Guinea was worsening, and diplomatically she was becoming unpleasantly isolated. In this last connection, the way in which Portugal received relatively little sympathy and no practical help when India marched into the Portuguese colony of Goa at the end of 1961 must have been chilling. Almost immediately, the Netherlands decided that, provided it could be done in not too mortifying a way, she would cede West New Guinea to Indonesia. At that stage – but only at that stage – the UN was able to render significant assistance, underlining the point that with a willing host and cooperative parties peacekeeping can be an enormously useful tool.

POSTSCRIPT

Although Indonesia had agreed that an act of self-determination should be held in West Irian before the end of 1969, there could have been no expectation either of Indonesia relinquishing the territory or of her being pressed to do so, whatever the act revealed. The anti-colonialists regarded the matter as closed; so did the Eastern bloc; and the West was not looking for trouble. What, in the prevalent view, the principle of self-determination entailed was the break-up of empires, not the dismemberment of new, non-white states: there were too many insecure members around for that.

On Untea's departure, some UN experts did remain in West Irian. But not for long, and over the next few years Indonesia's behaviour and some of her statements suggested that there was not much chance of the act of self-determination ever being held. However, the country's (new) rulers must have realised that this sort of line was not going to do them any good in the world at large, and also that it was probably quite unnecessary. Thus in 1969 the act went ahead, under the eyes of a representative of the UN Secretary-General. It was arranged by the government in what was said to be Indonesian style, those who were deemed to represent the people being gathered together in councils and asked publicly to pronounce themselves as to whether they wished to remain with Indonesia or not. There was a heartening 100 per cent endorsement of the status quo. At the UN some African states murmured about how it had been done, no doubt thinking that South Africa might warm to the use of this sort of arrangement in respect of

South West Africa/Namibia. But in general the member states welcomed the chance at last to get this matter out of the way. In this the Western members concurred. For in less than a generation, traditional colonialism had become not an honourable responsibility but an aggravating embarrassment.

For a map, see Map 31 above.

FURTHER READING

D. W. Bowett, *United Nations Forces* (London: Stevens, 1964).

William Henderson, *West New Guinea: The Dispute and its Settlement* (South Orange, NJ: Seton Hall University Press, 1973).

Justus M. van der Kroef, 'The West New Guinea Settlement', *Orbis*, 7 (1) (Spring 1963).

Paul W. van der Veur, 'The United Nations in West New Guinea: a Critique', *International Organization*, XVIII (1) (Winter 1964).

Yearbook of the United Nations 1969, vol. 23 (New York: UN Office of Public Information, 1972).

Section C   The Withdrawal of Chinese (Nationalist) Troops from Burma (1953–1954)

Following the defeat on the Chinese mainland of the National (or Kuomintang) Government in 1949 and its re-establishment on the offshore island of Taiwan (or Formosa), a number of its troops made their way into Burma and created a base for themselves near her border with Thailand. This was an area where Burma was already having trouble from Karen rebels, and she now alleged that they were being assisted by the Kuomintang forces. She took her complaint about the foreign military presence to the UN General Assembly and received a lot of sympathy, but little else. She therefore turned to the National Government's friend and protector, the United States, for whom the matter was becoming, in a small way, something of an embarrassment. For here was one of her clients (who still occupied China's permanent seat in the UN Security Council) giving a third world state a very reasonable cause for international complaint (see Map 32).

What the United States did was to set up a Joint Military Committee composed of the representatives of Nationalist China and Burma – the immediate disputants – and of Thailand and herself as interested and friendly parties. Its task was to consider ways and means of evacuating the Chinese troops. The United States and Thailand appointed their military attachés in Burma's capital, Rangoon, to represent them, and the Committee quickly got down to work. Burma soon withdrew in protest at what seemed to her the insufficiently urgent approach of the Chinese representative, but that did not noticeably hamper the Committee's activity. It arranged a cease-fire; made evacuation plans; persuaded Nationalist China to support and expedite them; and dealt

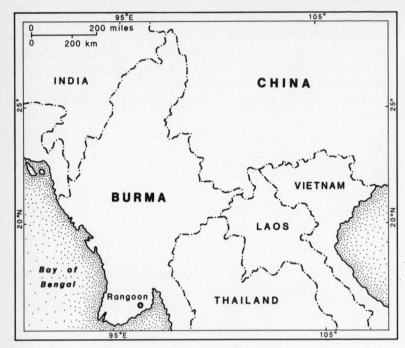

Map 32   Burma

with their execution. The United States provided the necessary logistic backing for the operation and a good deal of the cost, Nationalist China and Thailand also making some financial contribution. Within a year about 7,000 troops and dependants had been removed, those who remained being disavowed by their government.

In this way a problem which was irritating for Burma (and could have become so for Thailand), and which was doing no good at all for America's image, was to a large extent removed. In the context of sufficient cooperation from both directly-involved parties and the push of the United States, the matter could confidently be left in the hands of a free-standing peacekeeping mechanism for defusing and settlement – at least to the extent to which it was susceptible to international amelioration. Had the problem occurred at a later date, when the UN was more fully into the business of peacekeeping, it might well have been handled by the world organization. But this affair showed how the tool of peacekeeping could be used successfully in an ad hoc way by a group of interested states. That was not a bad precedent, as it pointed to the wide availability of the peacekeeping device. Moreover, in this particular case the United States was glad to get the matter out of the way in a relatively private manner – clearing the high street of some troublesome sojourners in the dusk rather than in the full light of day. It was not the end of Burma's internal problems. But stripping them of their international aspect had at least resulted in their significant diminution.

FURTHER READING

D. W. Wainhouse *et al.*, *International Peace Observation* (Baltimore, Md: Johns Hopkins Press, 1966).

Section D   The Withdrawal of France from Indo-China and its Aftermath (1954–1974)

Like the Dutch in their East Indies, the French found at the end of the Second World War that reasserting control in the territories which were collectively known as Indo-China was not a straightforward task. Communist-led independence movements had grown up during the Japanese occupation, and, especially in Vietnam, could not be fully quashed. Early in 1954 the military situation in Vietnam became critical, with France on the verge of a humiliating defeat, and at one or two points it seemed as if the United States might intervene in support of her ally. However, opinion in the United States was not enthusiastic about this prospect; Britain was opposed to it; and in France herself the idea of a negotiated peace was gaining in attraction. An international conference was therefore called at Geneva to discuss the matter. It opened in May, and was attended by the five great powers (China being represented by the Communist regime which had been firmly established on the mainland since 1949), the three territories of Indo-China (Cambodia, Laos, and Vietnam), and the chief independence movement – the Viet Minh.

From the Western point of view, the immediate business of the conference was to extricate France from the morass in which she now found herself, which had become a considerable embarrassment in the very middle of the high street. Moreover, it was not conceived only in colonial terms, as the Viet Minh was seen as spearheading a Communist threat to all of south-east Asia. The conflict had thus increasingly assumed cold war overtones, and there was talk of the 'domino effect' of a Communist success in any one area. It therefore became even more urgent for the United States and the West to salvage as much as possible from the affair.

This was a difficult task, as much ground had already been lost, particularly in Vietnam. But the West did not come out of the conference too badly. France, it is true, agreed to renounce her authority in all three territories. But on the other hand, the Viet Minh was to withdraw its forces from Cambodia and Laos, and the indigenous insurgents in those two territories were to make their peace with their now-sovereign governments – which could be expected to display a Western orientation. Only in Vietnam was ground formally relinquished by the West, the country being temporarily divided along the seventeenth parallel, with the Communist regime to the North and the pro-Western regime to the South. Elections were to be held throughout Vietnam in 1956 with a view to reunification. However, even this bare recognition of reality was too much for the United States, who regarded the outcome as a Communist victory. She therefore refused to sign the Final Declaration of the conference, which meant that it went totally unsigned (see Map 33).

However, that did not obstruct the signature at the end of the conference of bilateral cease-fire agreements in respect of each of the three Indo-Chinese territories. But there was a major problem with regard to the implementation of these agreements in that it could by no means be assumed that they would be self-executing. The war which they brought to an end had been long and bitter, which meant that even the maintenance of a cease-fire would probably not be straightforward. A lot of complex troop movements were also to take place, which would be a somewhat fraught procedure in any post-war context, and particularly so in this one. Furthermore, the intention was that military and political stability would be created in the area – but East and West had no trust in the good faith of the representatives of the other camp. Much time was therefore taken at the Geneva conference in the discussion of arrangements for trying to ensure that the agreements were honoured. The result was the establishment of three International Commissions for Supervision and Control (ICSCs).

There was no real question of these bodies being set up under the UN's auspices, as China's seat in that Organization was occupied by the rump Chinese regime on Formosa. The UN – very much controlled by the West at this time – had also recently declared (mainland) China to be an aggressor in Korea, so adding insult to injury. Accordingly, the ICSCs were virtually free-standing bodies, each being composed of representatives of Canada, India, and Poland. Canada was a member of the Western alliance system; Poland came from the Eastern bloc; and India stood aloof from both these groups, following a policy which

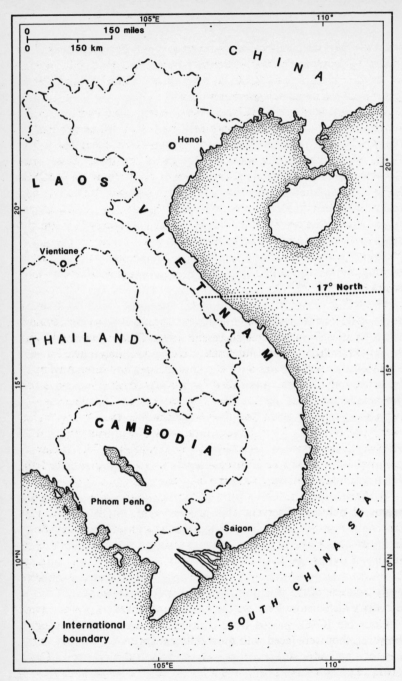

Map 33   Cambodia, Laos and Vietnam

was then known as neutralism – later to be called non-alignment. This balancing arrangement was underlined by the fact that India was to be the chairman of each ICSC, to head their secretariats, and was to provide all the necessary communications.

The ICSCs were led by civilians, who generally were members of the foreign ministry of the state concerned, but by far the larger part of the ICSCs' staff was drawn from various branches of the military. The ICSC for Vietnam was always the biggest of the three, at its peak (towards the end of 1955) numbering about 1,500. In all three ICSCs Indians predominated, as they had the major administrative and technical responsibilities. In respect of the ICSCs for Laos and Vietnam it was provided that the costs would be shared equally between the signatories to the cease-fire agreements – i.e., France and the insurgents. But these provisions were subject to some amendment, and, at least in respect of the Vietnam ICSC, the whole financial situation soon became very troublesome.

The ICSCs' functions were twofold. Firstly, they were to assist in defusing the crisis in Indo-China, and then their job was to help maintain the truce in each of the three successor states. There is no doubt that so far as the first of these functions is concerned they played a very valuable role, as there was a lot of calming down and disentangling to be done. Initially what was called for was an effective cease-fire and disengagement. That had to be followed within 300 days by the regrouping of many units and their withdrawal to their 'home' areas. A demarcation line along the seventeenth parallel in Vietnam, and an associated demilitarized zone, had to be established. The release of prisoners of war and civilian detainees was to take place. And the existing military balance had to be maintained.

With the help of the ICSCs, principally through their fixed and mobile teams of military observers, this process went, on the whole, very smoothly. For on the one hand, impartial assistance was being offered in the execution of a wide-ranging and sensitive agreement. And on the other, all the parties had an interest in the ending of the immediate crisis on the terms which had been agreed at Geneva. It was an excellent early example of the worth, in an appropriate context, of the kind of activity which, before long, was to be conceptualized as peacekeeping.

Once the ICSCs passed from defusing the crisis to stabilizing it, however, they were faced with quite different sorts of situations. In the case of Cambodia, which had been least disturbed by the Indo-China crisis, there was very little for the ICSC's members to do after the end of 1955. For the country was sufficiently stable and united for there to be no truce for the ICSC to maintain. Canada therefore favoured winding up the Cambodian ICSC, but this idea was not endorsed elsewhere, not even by the host state. Instead, therefore, the Commission was wound down to a symbolic size. It continued in this form until, late in 1969, Cambodia asked it to leave. It was formally brought to an end on 1 January 1970.

In the case of Laos, the situation was less straightforward, but hardly very serious. Pathet Lao insurgents continued to control the northern part of the country and occasional skirmishes were reported, interspersed with talks – in which the Laotian ICSC played a useful mediatory role. These culminated in the holding of elections in 1958, in which the Pathet Lao participated and as the result of which two of its members entered the government. The ICSC was then asked to leave, but as Poland was not keen on this, it instead adjourned *sine die*. The situation had not, however, been resolved, and in 1962, in connection with the international conference over the neutralization of Laos, the Commission was reconvened. It remained in being throughout the 1960s, but appeared to make little contribution to a situation which was not only often confused but also increasingly a fully-fledged civil war of its own. Moreover, there was considerable intervention in this conflict by those who were involved in the war in neighbouring Vietnam. The impotence of the ICSC was marked by the withdrawal of the Canadian delegation at the end of 1969, Canada's representation at meetings of the Laotian ICSC being undertaken by a member of her delegation to the Vietnam ICSC. In 1973, as hopes rose for a peace settlement in Laos to accompany that which had been arranged for Vietnam, the Laos Commission was revived, with Canada again playing a full part. However, it was unable to make a useful contribution and ceased to function in 1974.

In Vietnam the ICSC found itself in a situation which exposed all the limitations of peacekeeping, and which also drew attention to the peculiar hazards of this particular peacekeeping enterprise. As early as July 1955 South Vietnam made it clear that she had no interest in the proposed country-wide elections. Doubtless the government shared the widespread view that the communists were the more likely to win. Instead, the efforts of the South were bent in the direction – quite contrary to the assumptions and arrangements of the Geneva conference – of building up a self-contained state. In this she assumed, correctly, that she could rely on the support and provisioning of the United States. In the early 1960s this began to take the form of a substantial military presence, as the United States saw South Vietnam as a free-world ally who needed help against the subversion of the Communist North. By 1966 the number of American service personnel in the South had reached a quarter of a million, and no less than half a million just three years later. The Vietnam War was fully under way.

In this context there was very little the ICSC could do to help in the maintenance of peace. Its value in this respect was dependent on the pacific intent and cooperation of the parties. But by the 1960s the always hostile North and South were in effect fighting each other. There was thus no truce to maintain and no local disposition to create one. The ICSC remained a symbol of the aspirations of the Geneva conference of 1954, and could also be seen as a possible basis for reactivated peacekeeping activity in the event of an improvement in the political situation. Meanwhile, it declined in size in keeping with its reduced workload, and by the early 1970s its staff were in the region of 300 – only one-fifth of the 1955 number.

There was, however, an additional twist to the role of the ICSC during these years, which arose out of its status and composition. It could be seen as having a quasi-independent personality arising either from the agreement on the cessation of hostilities which set it up or from the conference at which this agreement was negotiated, the co-chairmen of which were Britain and the Soviet Union. But its exact status was very uncertain, and also little considered. There were thus no independent behavioural demands on the Commission's members arising from this quarter. This had the consequence of opening an already-ajar door even wider to the ICSC being influenced by its national composition. For a very significant fact about the Commission was that its staff were drawn from the diplomatic and military ranks of three politically-balanced states. It was possible for the individuals concerned to see themselves as playing independent roles, especially when all the parties were cooperating with the ICSC. But it was unlikely that such attitudes would be maintained, and even less likely that all three states would allow their representatives to maintain them, if the local political situation fragmented. And so it proved. The Poles made the running in clear partisanship; the Canadians, with occasional misgivings and hesitations, followed suit; and the Indians sometimes seemed to be responding to the current direction of India's foreign policy.

Especially in the light of the absence of an independent organizational buffer, and of the composition of the ICSC, such a development was hardly surprising. But it did mean that, certainly from the late 1950s, the Commission could not be regarded as an instance of peacekeeping. It could be argued that the several ICSC members were doing no more than see events through their individual ideological and political prisms, and that in this sense they were all still behaving impartially. But it is an unconvincing argument, on both a priori grounds and in the light of the evidence. Impartiality had effectively been abandoned, which meant that the ICSC was no longer a peacekeeping body.

This conclusion can be supported on a consequential ground: that the ICSC was no longer engaged on a peacekeeping function. For Poland was manifestly bent on using the Commission on behalf of 'her' local cold war side to point an accusatory finger at the other; and at the opposite end of the political and ideological spectrum Canada was soon doing more or less the same. In these circumstances, peacekeeping had been thrown out of the window. At its beginning the ICSC for Vietnam had done good work of that kind. But by the time it was terminated in 1973 it had long since lost any claim to be engaged in peacekeeping.

FURTHER READING

James Eayrs, *In Defence of Canada. Indochina*: *Roots of Complicity* (Toronto: University of Toronto Press, 1983).

Fred Gaffen, *In the Eye of the Storm* (Toronto: Deneau and Wayne, 1987).

John S. Hannon Jr, 'The International Control Commission Experience and the Role of an Improved International Supervisory Body in the Vietnam Settlement', in R. A. Falk (ed.), *The Vietnam War and International Law*, Vol. 3 (Princeton, NJ: Princeton University Press, 1972).

Douglas A. Ross, *In the Interests of Peace* (Toronto: University of Toronto Press, 1984).

Ramesh Thakur, *Peacekeeping in Vietnam* (Edmonton: University of Alberta Press, 1984).

Section E   The United States' Exit from Vietnam (1973–1975)

Despite the support of half a million American troops, and the heavy American bombing of the North, it had become abundantly clear by the end of the 1960s that the South Vietnamese government was unable to destroy the communist insurgency. In effect, therefore, the world's richest and, on paper, most powerful state was going down to defeat. The new, 1969, administration in the United States drew the obvious conclusion and began to look for a way of extricating itself from this imbroglio. At first, it tried to impose terms on the North and the (rebel) Provisional Revolutionary Government (PRG) in the South. But this approach made no headway, and the agreements which were eventually signed in Paris in January 1973 provided for little more than a cease-fire and an American withdrawal within 60 days.

One of the other things which it did provide, however, was an International Commission of Control and Supervision (ICCS) of the cease-fire – a new version of the old ICSC for Vietnam, which now came to an end. It was composed of four states: Canada (who was more or less press-ganged into service by the United States) and Indonesia, both of whom could be expected to be sympathetic to South Vietnam; and Hungary and Poland, who could certainly be expected to take the side of the PRG and the North. The chairmanship of the Commission was to rotate. Unanimity was required for all decisions – although the members could make their individual views known. Each member was to supply 290 individuals for the Commission, half of whom were to be military officers for the international control teams. And each member, besides paying the salaries of its nationals, was to make a minimal financial contribution to the Commission's costs, the rest being met equally by the four parties to the cease-fire.

It was widely assumed, however, that the cease-fire was no more than an intermission – to allow a face-saving American withdrawal – in the

207

dedicated Communist campaign to take over all of Vietnam. In which case there would be no real stabilizing role for the ICCS – a conclusion which received overwhelming support from its composition, structure, and procedure. In fact, the ICCS was almost entirely a cosmetic device to increase the political acceptability of the United States' abandonment of South Vietnam. And while the device had an international bearing, it was chiefly directed towards the American public. Its role in these respects had a dual aspect.

Firstly, in the period leading up to and immediately following the Paris agreements, emphasis could be – and was – placed on the proposed control machinery with a view to suggesting that a real cease-fire was to come into being. Why else, it was implied, was such trouble being taken over the supervisory arrangements? The United States was not abandoning South Vietnam to the Communist wolves, but was setting up a properly supervised agreement. She could therefore leave with a clear conscience. Secondly, if things did go less than well for the South after the Americans had left, some of the Commissioners could be looked to for evidence in support of the claim that the Communists were cheating. It would then be too late for the United States to do anything about it on the ground. But she would be better placed to argue that it was the iniquity of the other side which was upsetting an agreement which the United States had reached in good faith, and with an eye to the best interests of South Vietnam.

In this second respect the United States was handsomely rewarded. For the anti-Communist zeal of the leader of the Canadian delegation on the Commission was almost embarrassing in its extent. But as the cease-fire provisions were virtually ignored by every side, including the United States (who continued to supply the South), the Canadian government lost patience with the Commission, and withdrew at the end of July 1973. There was then a hiatus in the ICCS's field activity while a replacement was recruited. Iran (at that time ruled by the pro-Western Shah) stepped forward into this role. But as the fighting increased, there was nothing worthwhile for the ICCS to do in the way of peacekeeping. Instead, each pair of Commission states did what it could in verbal defence of its local side – and was condemned for it by the other. Towards the end of 1974 the situation in South Vietnam resulted in another suspension of the Commission's activity, and it also found itself in financial difficulty as North Vietnam refused to pay her share of its costs and the PRG said it could not afford to do so. In the following year the victory of the PRG and North Vietnam brought the life of the ICCS to an end.

As a peacekeeping exercise, the ICCS was in all respects bar one never even a starter. The detailed arrangements which were made for its operation looked right, but the context was all wrong, for the key parties were in no way disposed to defuse the crisis let alone maintain a truce or move towards a settlement. Furthermore, the Commission's composition and structure in any event encouraged partiality rather than impartiality, and in this particular context they guaranteed it. But the reality was that the ICCS was meant to operate in the peacekeeping mode only as a means of enabling the United States to abandon a very embarrassing position in the international high street with a certain amount of outward dignity. As such, the ICCS served its purpose.

There was, however, little dignity about the final American departure from the South Vietnamese capital, Saigon (soon to be re-named Ho Chi Minh City), on the day that the Communist victory was completed – 30 April 1975. Her embassy had to be evacuated by helicopter, with marines keeping angry crowds at bay, and the building was stormed after the last helicopter had left. A 20-year enterprise of immense cost and embarrassment had both come to naught and ended ignominiously.

In neighbouring Laos, too, Vietnamese-supported Communists were soon fully in control, leading to the withdrawal of the last remnants of the peacekeeping Commission which had been set up in 1954. But in Cambodia, where Communists also came forcefully to power, the ruling group was soon in serious dispute with their ideological brethren in Vietnam. They looked to China for support, besides embarking on a horrific internal policy, which came to an end only when Vietnam invaded the country at the end of 1978. In connection with Vietnam's departure 11 years later, it was proposed that the emergence of a government representing all Cambodian factions should be facilitated by a substantial UN peacekeeping operation. However, the country's internal divisions were too great to permit an agreement on the matter, so the UN plan had, at least temporarily, to be put on one side (see Section L below).

For a map, see Map 33 above.

FURTHER READING

David Cox, 'The International Commission of Control and Supervision in Vietnam, 1973', in Henry Wiseman (ed.), *Peacekeeping* (New York: Pergamon Press, 1983).

Gareth Porter, *A Peace Denied* (Bloomington, Ind.: Indiana University Press, 1975).

Section F   The Anglo–French Debacle at Suez and its Aftermath (1956–1967)

The nationalization of the Suez Canal by Egypt on 26 July 1956 set off a crisis which erupted three months later in a triple invasion of Egypt. First Israel crossed into the Sinai Desert and headed for the Suez Canal. Then, ostensibly in an effort to safeguard the Canal, but really (and in collaboration with Israel) with the intention of seizing it, came Britain and France. These two powers had long been dominant in the Middle East, but their 1956 adventure was to mark the end of their sway. No sooner had they landed at the northern end of the Canal at Port Said than orders were being issued to cease fire. In this Britain took the lead. The decision was a result of a bitterly divided country, strong opposition to the venture in the Commonwealth and at the UN and, above all, the anger of the United States. This anger was expressed not only in diplomatic terms but also in economic ones, in that heavy American selling was forcing the pound towards devaluation.

It is also the case, however, that at the very least Britain was helped towards this decision by the fact that the UN had just established an Emergency Force (Unef) to watch over the cessation of hostilities. That last phrase is indicative of the basic point that the Force was not designed to pull the combatants apart. Instead, its arrival and operation was dependent on the absence of fighting. And when a cease-fire came into effect at midnight on 6–7 November, the first members of the Force were ready to arrive. However, they could not enter Egypt for another week as the host state needed certain assurances about the character and composition of the Force. Once Egypt was satisfied the Force took up its positions, and in little more than two months had been brought to a size of 6,000 officers and men drawn from 10 of the 24 UN members who had offered to supply contingents. These 10 states were: Brazil, Canada, Colombia, Denmark, Finland, India, Indonesia, Norway, Sweden, and Yugoslavia (see Map 34).

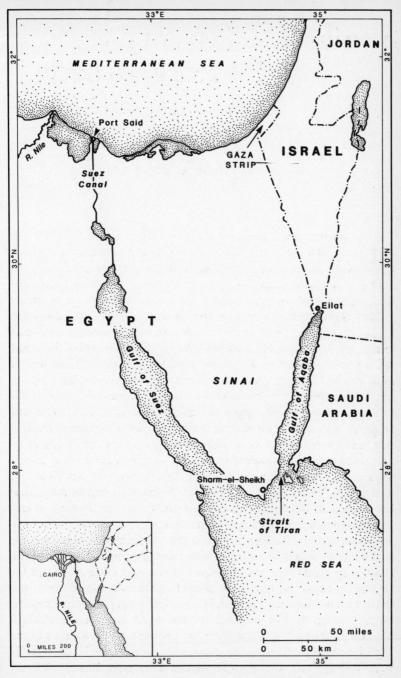

Map 34   Suez, Sinai and the Gaza Strip

DEFUSION

The role of Unef (later known, to distinguish it from its successor, as Unef I) in persuading Britain and France to cease fire and then to withdraw was chiefly and overwhelmingly that of a face-saver. For it enabled those for whom such a belief was important to envisage Unef as an alternative means of securing the alleged Anglo–French goal of separating the combatants. Moreover, the Force also provided some superficial evidence in support of the British and French claim that they had been honourably engaged from the start, having acted in the international interest and always with a willingness – nay, a desire – to leave the moment the UN was able to discharge its responsibilities. Before long this reasoning was extended to include the suggestion that they had always hoped to galvanize the UN into just the kind of life which it was now displaying: honest citizens had risked, and encountered, denigration with a view to rousing the dormant police.

The reality behind this brave face, however, was that two major Western states were virtually being frog-marched away from the scene of their crime by their leader, to whom they had given huge offence. They had acted without consulting her; they had done so on the eve of a presidential election in the United States; they had damaged the American campaign to recruit more uncommitted states to the alliance system of the West; they had distracted attention away from the Soviet invasion of Hungary which was just taking place; they had enabled the Soviet Union to make the mischievous suggestion that the two superpowers should intervene jointly in Egypt to discipline the miscreants; and they had supplied countries who were disposed to criticize the West with a grand opportunity to make general diplomatic hay out of the episode.

While, however, these feelings were little disguised, the United States also recognized that, as their major ally, she had to help Britain and France to get off the hook on which they had succeeded in impaling themselves, and that this process had to have a certain outward dignity. Canada – faced with what she saw as the appalling prospect of a rift between the United States on the one hand and Britain and France on the other – had already floated the idea of using the UN for this purpose. It was immediately endorsed by the United States, who also supplied an appropriate draft resolution. Canada presented it to the General Assembly – the Security Council having been left behind in this process due to the presence there of the veto-wielding malefactors – and it was quickly passed. The UN Emergency Force had been born.

The speedy defusing of the Suez crisis was therefore very much due to the direct pressures and institutional activity of the Western superpower, who was exceedingly anxious to get rid of the large embarrassment which had suddenly developed at a central position in the international high street. In this process the creation of Unef was a very important factor, as it permitted Britain and France to call off their enterprise without too much loss of face. However, the declaration of a cease-fire did not bring the crisis to an end, for in the heated and entangled situation which existed on the ground there was always the possibility of a resumption of fighting. This draws attention to another of Unef's peacekeeping contributions: its stabilizing role after the cease-fire and prior to the departure of the major invaders.

It did this by taking up positions between the Anglo–French forces on the one hand and the Egyptian forces on the other, so reducing the possibility of incidents and armed clashes. Complaints that the cease-fire had been violated were investigated by Unef, and in this way grievances were lessened. It made arrangements for the exchange of prisoners and enquired about missing personnel, all of which had a calming effect. In part of the Port Said area it took over responsibility for maintaining order, in conjunction with the local authorities, so as to decrease the chances of angry confrontations between the population and the Anglo–French forces. In these impartial ways the peacekeeping force helped to abate tension. Its contribution in this respect was exceedingly valuable, particularly so during the days immediately following its arrival, when the situation was highly charged.

RESOLUTION

The main reason for the establishment of Unef, however, was to facilitate the withdrawal of the invaders. In this respect its function was to assist in the resolution of the immediate crisis. Reference has already been made to the way in which the Force provided Britain and France with some very tenuous reasons for leaving. In fact, and in keeping with their general position, they did not fall over themselves to go, and were soon expressing disenchantment with Unef's impartial stance. Some bitter comments were also made about the attitude of the United States having become harsher after the cease-fire than before. But by this very token there was little future in Britain and France trying to prolong their stay, and early in December they announced that their troops would all be withdrawn within three weeks.

Unef played a very useful role in this process, which was naturally somewhat fraught. There was the double danger that some departing soldiers might engage in a final defiant flourish, and that some members of the Egyptian Army might decide to help them on their way. There was also the possibly tricky problem of the transfer of authority to local administrators as territory was vacated. Unef helped to get around these problems in two ways. Firstly, it positioned itself around the grouping area as the final withdrawal took place, so lessening the chance of incidents. And secondly, it maintained smooth continuity in respect of security and public services by taking over these functions from the departing invaders and then immediately passing them over to the Egyptian authorities. Thus the UN Force helped to ensure an uneventful Anglo–French withdrawal. It was not, of course, directly instrumental in getting them to go. But it was a factor of some importance in that process, and provided valuable aid in the smooth implementation of that decision.

Unef assisted the third invader's withdrawal in a similar fashion, and this was its main function in respect of Israel as the enterprise had not involved her in any loss of face. Early in November she had intimated that she would relinquish control of Sinai only in return for guarantees regarding Egypt's future behaviour. But, with American prodding, Israel soon abandoned this position and, with Unef's help, retraced her steps across much of Sinai. However, in January 1957, she dug in her heels with regard to withdrawal from the Gaza Strip and Sharm-el-Sheikh.

The Strip was fertile and heavily populated, and had been the main centre for the organization of the officially unofficial commando (*fedayeen*) raids into Israel which had recently become an increasingly serious source of tension. It had also been the scene of by far the greatest number of official incidents which had taken place between the two countries since the Armistice of 1949. Israel was most anxious to deny Egypt its use for such aggravating purposes. The case of Sharm-el-Sheikh illustrated the same concern. Because of Egypt's denial of passage through the Suez Canal to ships going to and from Israel, the only direct sea route between Israel and points east and south was via the port of Eilat, which lies on a very small strip of Israeli territory at the head of the Gulf of Aqaba. However, the Strait of Tiran, which forms the narrow entrance to the Gulf from the Red Sea, can easily be controlled from Sharm-el-Sheikh, and since 1950 Egypt had used her position there to close the Gulf to Israeli trade. Israel was determined to break this blockade, and proposed that a detachment of UN troops should be stationed at Sharm-el-Sheikh. With regard to Gaza, she suggested its demilitarization under an Israeli administration.

Israel's idea regarding Sharm-el-Sheikh found general acceptance, and Egypt was willing to go along with it. But on Gaza the most that Israel could obtain was a UN decision that its peacekeeping force should be on the Armistice Demarcation Line which ran around much of the Strip. This did not satisfy her, and she prevaricated, trying to enlist American support for her hopes. But the United States simply urged Israel to get out and keep her fingers crossed. Then, when she still refused to budge, the American President publicly threatened to support UN sanctions unless Israel complied with the Organization's demand that she completely withdraw from Egyptian territory. In view of this Israel decided that the game was up, and by 8 March 1957 all her troops were back behind her own borders.

STABILIZATION

When Unef was established there had been some talk about the possibility of it helping to pave the way for a settlement of the deep dispute between Egypt and Israel. But the problem which was foremost in the minds of its creators was the defusing of the crisis which had been precipitated by the Anglo—French—Israeli invasion. It may therefore be doubted whether many of them anticipated that, when the invaders had left, the Force would pitch its tents at the Egyptian—Israeli border and give every sign of anticipating a long stay.

But that is what happened. The United States was anxious that tension be minimized in this dangerous region, but was much less well placed to influence the situation than she was in some other parts of the world. Accordingly, she welcomed the suggestion that Unef should be kept in the area to help in maintaining quiet, and the other Western powers concurred, as did a number of smaller states. The Soviet Union and her friends, however, were not at all keen on the idea. They were acutely aware of their minority position in the UN General Assembly which, having established Unef, was responsible for it, and of their lack of 'representation' in the Force. They also spoke movingly about the gross infringement of Egypt's sovereignty which the presence of the Force would entail. But it emerged that Egypt was unworried by the prospect, and instead was impressed by the possible advantages of having a multinational UN Force between her and her evidently much stronger adversary.

The General Assembly thus gave the necessary authorization. Israel would not allow Unef to straddle the border, and as the Force was not in the business of imposition it settled down just on the Egyptian side. Along most of the Armistice Demarcation Line, which ran for a distance of about 35 miles around the perimeter of the heavily populated Strip, observation posts were established, each of them visible from the next on the principle that the Line should be under constant surveillance. Elsewhere in the Strip, and along all of its border at night, this principle was implemented by way of foot and mobile patrols.

Along the international frontier between Egypt and Israel, which extends from the south-eastern corner of the Gaza Strip to the head of the Gulf of Aqaba and measures about 117 miles, the rugged terrain and absence of a settled population led to a different form of activity. Some field observation posts were established, but Unef's watch was chiefly based on ground patrols supplemented by aerial observation. Finally, at the entrance to the 100-mile-long Gulf of Aqaba, a small detachment was placed on static guard duty at Sharm-el-Sheikh, opposite the Strait of Tiran.

Unef was only very lightly armed. In dealing with infiltrators or other border incidents its personnel were instructed to use minimum force and not to fire except in self-defence. Anyone trying to cross the border from the Egyptian side, or approaching it in suspicious circumstances, could be apprehended, as could anyone who had crossed from Israel. Such people were, after interrogation, to be handed over to the local authorities. The latter cooperated with the Force by prohibiting movement at night in Gaza within a zone of 300 yards to the rear of the Demarcation Line, and by allowing locals into the zone by day only for agricultural purposes. Moreover, Egypt did not reintroduce her armed forces into Gaza – although the build-up of Palestinian fighters in the Strip during the 10 years that Unef was there somewhat nullified the effect of this decision. With regard to the international frontier in Sinai, an agreement was reached whereby no armed Egyptian personnel were allowed within one and a quarter miles of the frontier by day or within three miles by night. Thus, although it was never formalized, Unef was able to establish something in the nature of a buffer zone between Egypt and Israel.

Within the first two years of Unef's life, Indonesia, Finland and Colombia withdrew their contingents, Finland possibly doing so in deference to the Soviet Union's view about the operation. This resulted in an expansion of some other contingents. But over the years the Force was sporadically reduced in size, so that at its withdrawal in May 1967 it was at little more than half its initial strength. This was clearly influenced by the difficulties which the UN was having in getting some of its members to pay their share of the costs of the Force. But it was also a reflection of the fact that for virtually all of Unef's life the Egyptian–Israeli border was remarkably quiet. Incidents occurred fairly frequently during the few months immediately following its arrival at the border. But in August 1957 there was a marked drop, only five being reported, and thereafter the number remained at about this level, none of them being very serious. The Force was thus able somewhat to diminish the intensity of its observation and patrols, and so reduce its manpower, without lessening the effectiveness of its work.

The quiet which prevailed in Gaza and Sinai during these years was often attributed chiefly to the presence of the UN's peacekeeping force. It was perhaps to be expected that UN Secretaries-General should not undervalue the work of Unef. But the Organization's chief administrative officer was by no means alone in speaking in these terms: journalists, politicians and academics all made similar observations on numerous occasions. And there is no doubt that, up to a certain point, their assessment is valid. For the Force made a very important contribution to peaceful relations between Egypt and Israel in two of the three most usual ways in which it is open to such a body to help in the maintenance of stability along an international dividing line.

Firstly, peacekeepers can play a key role in the prevention of incidents, and very much did so in this particular case. For the presence and disposition of Unef meant that the armed forces of the two sides were no longer in visual contact. This was a great improvement on the previous situation, when incidents could – and did – easily arise between hostile and trigger-happy troops who found themselves in close proximity. But besides preventing incidents which arose out of provocative direct contact, Unef was also a considerable discouragement to cross-border forays of an official kind. The Force could not have prevented the passage of raiding parties. But its presence greatly reduced the temptation to despatch them. For quite apart from the international criticism which would have been directed at cavalier treatment of the UN's peacekeeping force, such enterprises would also very probably have led to embarrassing physical incidents with its members. In turn, this could have jeopardized the continued presence of the Force. For even if the UN itself did not withdraw it, the calling home by contributor states of their troops could have had the same result. As Egypt and

Israel were both anxious for it to stay, it followed that they could no longer indulge themselves in the manner to which they had become accustomed.

Furthermore, the presence of Unef was also a considerable discouragement to the small commando-type raids which, prior to 1956, the Egyptians had been in the habit of making. These were not official acts, but there is no doubt that they received governmental support. Now, however, there was not only a vigilant third party at the border, which made apprehension a real possibility, but Unef's presence could be taken, correctly, as implying that the former policy was out of favour. Anyone caught trying to cross into Israel would therefore be uncertain of his reception when handed over to the Egyptian authorities. It is thus very plausible to see a direct correlation between Unef's presence and the reduction in infiltration which ensued. This drastic lessening in the provocation given to Israel was important, for it was that which had given rise to the occasional large-scale acts of retaliation which only underlined and, if anything, deepened the hostility between the two states. Hence, by acting as an obstruction to such incidents, Unef helped very materially to maintain peace.

The second way in which peacekeepers often help to maintain a truce is by cooling tempers when incidents have taken or are taking place, or when tension has risen to a dangerous level. However, the situation on the Egyptian–Israeli border was so calm throughout the time that Unef was positioned there that the Force was never called upon to play this role.

Peacekeeping's third stabilizing role at a border is that of reducing anxiety. The knowledge that the peacekeepers will be making routine reports to their superiors may marginally diminish the worry which one or other, or both, of the parties have about being the object of a surprise attack. For if there is alarm in the reports, the addressees – for example, the UN Secretary-General or the states who contribute troops – can be expected to make some pacifying moves.

Over and above this possibility, however, a peacekeeping body may play an anxiety-reducing role through its mere presence. In the case of Unef, whatever might have been said about the exact legal relationship between Egypt and the Force, there could have been little doubt that in the event of it no longer being welcome on Egyptian soil, it would leave. Thus its maintenance at the Egyptian–Israeli border, and even more importantly, the absence of a question about that matter, was a possible indication of Egypt's willingness to keep tension low. In turn, the Force's presence may well have helped to reduce Israel's anxiety about the situation, for in the event of minor problems she had, prima facie, no reason to believe they were the harbingers of more serious trouble. Equally, Unef's presence meant that interested outsiders had less cause to get jittery whenever the scene was somewhat disturbed. Of course, both sides were fully aware of the possibility of a surprise attack through Unef's lines, so that its presence was no reason for a lack of vigilance. But inasmuch as the Force was a kind of pledge of good behaviour, it may have helped to introduce a little extra calm into the situation.

So far as the resumption of full-scale hostilities was concerned, however, Unef was no more a significant deterrent than any other peacekeeping body could ever realistically be. It may have had some very minor effect of this kind: going to war through the positions of a multinational peacekeeping force would probably have had some adverse diplomatic consequences; and the fact that such a force could furnish credible reports of how the conflict had broken out would not have been a pleasing prospect to a potential aggressor. But these would have been very small considerations in relation to the question of whether to go to war. If, on other grounds, the answer to that question was clearly positive, neither Egypt nor Israel would have been deterred by the presence of the UN Force.

What Unef did not do during its 10 years on the Egyptian–Israeli border, therefore, was to keep the peace. Rather, it helped these two states to implement their temporary disposition to live in peace. It was a derivative rather than a substantive obstruction to the worsening of the situation, making a secondary rather than a primary contribution to peace. But that is not at all to say that it was of little importance. Without Unef anxiety in the area might well have been appreciably higher, and it is very probable that there would have been border incidents. For even if both sides had been pacifically inclined, the proximity of hostile troops and the disposition of unofficial fighting groups to make their mark would almost certainly have resulted in clashes. In these circumstances, escalation could all too easily have taken place, and a serious confrontation have developed. The consequence could very conceivably have been that that parties would, willy-nilly, have found themselves at war. Accordingly, Unef can be given credit not only for having played a significant role in the defusing and immediate resolution of the Suez crisis, but also for having made a contribution of great importance to the maintenance of a very quiet truce between Egypt and Israel from 1957 until 1967. The attitude of the parties, however, and particularly of Egypt, meant that the situation was no more than a truce.

WITHDRAWAL

After the Suez war, the Arab neighbour who gave Israel the most formidable trouble was Syria. Egypt (known as the United Arab Republic from 1961 to 1971, but referred to here by her traditional name) was now holding back; Lebanon, as always, was most anxious to keep her border quiet, and at this period had no difficulty in doing so; and while numerous incidents occurred on the long Jordanian border, they were not usually of great significance. Syria, however, was another matter altogether, more unstable and extreme than any of Israel's other neighbours, and during the early months of 1967 tension between the two states reached a high level. Raids and assaults from both sides increased. It began to look as if Israel might respond in a large way, although, contrary to what Egypt was to claim, it is most questionable whether she was planning a full-scale invasion of Syria. However, the situation produced a military agreeement between Egypt and Syria, and gave rise to a dramatic and far-reaching series of events.

The first sign of this occurred on 16 May, when Unef's Commander was told by the Egyptian Chief of Staff that Egypt's forces were already concentrated in eastern Sinai. He was asked to order Unef's immediate withdrawal from the border. In response, the UN Secretary-General, U Thant, said that there could be no question of the UN force just standing aside for the duration of the crisis and in an area which was convenient for Egypt. On the following day, UN troops in Sinai found Egyptian units deployed in their vicinity, and in two cases between their camps and the frontier. And on 18 May, by which time there were 20,000–30,000 Egyptian troops at the frontier, UN troops were forced out of two of their observation posts. The same day brought a formal request from Egypt for Unef's complete withdrawal. After consulting the troop-contributing states, Thant reluctantly complied with this request, the Force ending its operational role on 19 May. (Its complete physical extrication from the area, however, took another month.) On 22 May Egypt reinstituted the blockade of the Gulf of Aqaba, which was for Israel a sufficient reason for going to war. She stayed her hand for a brief while, both to see if international pressure could lift the blockade and to make it clear that she had not behaved precipitately.

But then, on 5 June, she began a series of crushing blows which resulted, within six days, in the Israeli occupation of all of Sinai, of the Syrian Golan Heights, and of all Jordanian territory to the west of the River Jordan.

For having agreed with such apparent readiness to the request for Unef's withdrawal, Thant was very heavily criticized. And after the outbreak of the Six Day War, some observers more or less said that it was his responsibility. This is absurd. Thant was, after all, responding to a request from a member state, so that even if there is a direct link between the withdrawal of Unef and the War, the responsibility for it must at the very least be shared with Egypt. However, the argument in favour of the existence of a direct link is faulty. Egypt's subsequent closure of the Gulf of Aqaba to Israeli shipping was a much larger step in the direction of war; the international society's failure to mobilize effective pressure to secure its reopening was another such step; and the final step was Israel's own decision in favour of an all-out war against three of her Arab neighbours. Her feeling of claustrophobic encirclement was understandable. But the ultimate choice of war was hers, as was the type of war on which she embarked.

Such connection as does exist between the withdrawal of Unef and the outbreak of war has to do with the withdrawal being part of a chain of events which culminated in war. It is certainly the case that had the UN Force been in place, Egypt would presumably not have closed the Gulf of Aqaba, and without that there would hardly have been a war in June 1967. The question therefore arises as to whether the chain could have been broken when the withdrawal of the Force was sought. There are four grounds on which the case for withdrawal can be based. The first three were often referred to by the Secretary-General in justification of his action, and the fourth could not have been far from his mind.

The first is legal, and can be summed up by saying that as Egypt's consent was necessary for the Force to arrive, the withdrawal of the host state's consent necessitated the withdrawal of the Force. A contrary and more subtle legal argument can be constructed, but not one which is more convincing. Secondly, there is a functional argument. Unef had, since March 1957, been acting as a buffer, of sorts, between the disputants. Now one of them had pushed it away and stood directly opposite the other. The whole object of its being was thus nullified, and there was no point in keeping it in place. This is entirely convincing, as is the third argument. It is that, as a practical matter, it was not possible to maintain a small, non-fighting force in Egypt against the wishes of that state: its movement, supply, and rotation could all have been easily interfered with; such a situation could also have been dangerous for its individual members; and two contributor states had immediately made it clear that they would not allow their men to remain if the host wanted the Force to leave. Unef might therefore have faced more than one sort of disintegration if it had tried to stay on. Finally, there is the cogent political argument that the likelihood of the UN being asked to engage in future peacekeeping operations would be much reduced if potential hosts had reason to think that the peacekeepers might not leave when asked.

However, while the case for compliance with Egypt's wishes is overwhelming, there is still a question as to whether it was necessary to comply so quickly and so unresistingly. Two things might have been done. Firstly, Thant might have tried to persuade Egypt's President Nasser to change his mind. He did intend to make such an appeal, but was pressed by Egypt's Foreign Minister not to do so: such a request, he was told, would be sternly rebuffed. Nonetheless, he might still have gone ahead, even to the extent of making an immediate visit to Cairo. Not much would have been lost by such a venture. Secondly, he could have taken the issue to the UN General Assembly, which had established the Force. It is almost unimaginable that the Assembly would have gone against Egypt's clearly expressed wish in this matter. But some time would have been gained, and the way might have been opened for a face-saving Egyptian retreat. It did not look as if Egypt was, on her own initiative, spoiling for a war with Israel. And if Israel could have been persuaded to give some guarantee of pacific intentions with regard to Syria, Egypt might conceivably have backed down.

However, the great powers were divided in their Middle Eastern allegiances, and therefore not in a position to bring joint pressure on both disputants in the cause of peace. Israel was not in any frame of mind to offer the sort of guarantee regarding Syria which either that state or Egypt would have seen as satisfactory. And Egypt would have found it very difficult indeed to go back on her request for Unef's withdrawal. Only the previous month Syria had sneered at Egypt's failure to give help during an Israeli attack, and for years the question had been loudly asked in the Arab world as to why Egypt cowered behind the shield of Unef. Having now publicly indicated that the UN Force stood in the way of Egyptian succour for Syria and, by implication, for any other Arab state in distress at Israel's hand, Egypt would have been in very considerable trouble – domestic, possibly, as well as diplomatic – if she had agreed that Unef could, after all, stay on her soil. With his demand that the Force go, President Nasser had broken out of some of the frustrations which had been besetting him in his relations with his fellow Arab states. It is very difficult indeed to imagine that he might have been persuaded to withdraw the demand. Much the more likely outcome of any attempt to make him do so would have been a hardening of his position.

It is thus most improbable that a different UN response to Egypt's request would have broken the chain of events which led to the Six Day War. The peacekeeping role of Unef was dependent upon both Egypt and Israel wanting a quiet border, and its ability to influence their wishes in this regard was virtually non-existent. In May 1967 a decisive change took place in Egypt's policy, and it was that, not the withdrawal of the UN Force, which precipitated a crisis. Nor is it at all likely that the flow of the crisis could have been stemmed by the UN trying to get President Nasser to change his mind. Egypt may not have been calculating on a war with Israel, and was not chiefly responsible for it. But hers was the first step towards it. In face of this decision, after a ten-year interval, to live dangerously once again, Unef's usefulness was at an end.

FURTHER READING

Sydney D. Bailey, *How Wars End*, Vol. II (Oxford: Clarendon Press, 1982).

Winston Burdett, *Encounter with the Middle East* (London: Deutsch, 1970).

E. L. M. Burns, *Between Arab and Israeli* (London: Harrap, 1962).

Andrew W. Cordier and Max Harrelson (eds), *The Public Papers of the Secretaries-General of the United Nations. Vol. VII: U Thant 1965–1967* (New York: Columbia University Press, 1976).

Alan James, 'U Thant and His Critics', *The Year Book of World Affairs 1972* (London: Stevens, 1972).

Indar Jit Rikhye, *The Sinai Blunder* (New Delhi: Oxford and IBH, 1978).

Gabriella Rosner, *The United Nations Emergency Force* (New York: Columbia University Press, 1963).

Brian Urquhart, *Hammarskjöld* (London: Bodley Head, 1972).

Section G The Turkish Threat to Cyprus (1964–)

When Cyprus became a sovereign state in 1960 it did so on the basis of a constitution which provided a number of safeguards for the Turkish-Cypriot minority. This group made up about one-fifth of the country's population of about 600,000, almost all the remainder identifying very closely with Greece. However, the arrangements which were intended to balance the interests and allay the anxieties of the two linguistic and cultural groups gave rise only to mutual resentments and recriminations. These came to a head in the latter part of 1963 when the Greek-Cypriot President Makarios proposed certain constitutional amendments. Fighting broke out in December, which set alarm bells ringing vigorously in a number of quarters.

The Government of Cyprus, dominated by Greek Cypriots, feared that Turkey would intervene on behalf of her cultural compatriots, and the mainland Turks had already engaged in some menacing sabre-rattling. It was widely supposed, however, that any such event would precipitate counter-intervention by Greece, who, notwithstanding her military and logistic inferiority, would be politically unable to abandon the Greek Cypriots to her traditional enemy. That prospect sent shivers up Britain's spine, for more than one reason. She was a formal guarantor of the 1960 constitution, and had troops on the island of Cyprus in two military bases (which remained British territory): it would thus be difficult for her not to intervene. Cyprus was also a member of the Commonwealth, and might make a claim on Britain's help on that ground. But both Greece and Turkey were Britain's allies in the North Atlantic Treaty Organization (Nato). The prospect of their fighting each other in a strategically sensitive area was bad enough, but the thought of having to try physically to pull them apart was even worse. And an intra-Nato war, on the soil of a non-aligned state, was also virtually the last thing which was wanted by the leader of the alliance, the United States – not just because of its international implications but also because a presidential election was to be held at the end of

1964. From the point of view of the Western alliance, therefore, what had erupted was a high-street embarrassment of the very first order (see Map 35).

Initially, and with the consent of the host state and of Greece and Turkey, British troops endeavoured to maintain the peace, and on the basis of the parties' cooperation this activity had some success. But the situation was very fragile, and Britain had neither the stomach nor, maybe, the resources to shoulder the job indefinitely. Others, in Britain's view, should share both the responsibility and the honour of preventing the fuse to this particular powder keg being lit. The idea of a Nato force was explored, but rejected by Cyprus, who feared that it would lean in the Turkish rather than the Greek direction. In this she was supported by the Soviet Union, who spoke up as champion of small states who were threatened with interference by loitering Western powers. Reluctantly, therefore, but with last-minute haste so as to gain a procedural advantage, Britain and the United States took the matter to the UN Security Council. Here, after much backstage discussion, it was unanimously agreed on 4 March that a peacekeeping force should

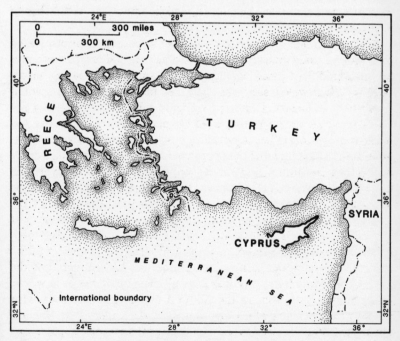

Map 35   Cyprus and her neighbours

be set up to try to prevent fighting, maintain order, and assist in the restoration of normal conditions.

THE FIRST PHASE: 1964–1974

Getting the UN Peace-keeping Force in Cyrpus (Unficyp) together was not, however, the easiest of tasks, as some suitable states refused to participate, and others sought explanations or assurances of various kinds. Sweden, for example, did not want to be the only neutral state in the Force, and Ireland wanted to be sure that she would not find herself involved in a partitioning exercise. Nor did all the problems arise with the potential contributors. Cyrpus, to obtain something of a balance between Nato and non-Nato participants, insisted that Danish and Norwegian troops must not both be included. But at the same time she made the achievement of a balance more difficult by refusing to have coloured – or at least African – contingents in the Force. Turkey, too, is said to have raised her voice against the inclusion of contingents from the Third World. There was also a general worry about financing as, due to a UN financial crisis (which had arisen out of its peacekeeping activities), the contributor states, together with the host, were to be liable for all the costs not met by voluntary donations. However, much of this apprehension was removed by some early financial promises, not least from Britain and the United States.

But the major difficulty related to the conditions under which the Force would have to operate. A resumption of fighting between the Greek and Turkish communities could be no means be ruled out, and in that event the military intervention of their mainland backers was always very possible. That could mean danger for the participating troops and embarrassment for their governments, arising from both domestic and international sources. Moreover, quite apart from large-scale fighting, outbreaks of sporadic shooting were very likely, for the situation was emotionally charged and large numbers of the male population were armed. There was also the consideration that the UN's hard and unpleasant task might last a good deal longer than the three months for which it was initially scheduled – and getting out of the Force would assuredly be a lot harder than getting in.

However, by the end of March it was possible for Unficyp to be declared operational. Unusually for a permanent member of the Security Council, Britain was a contributor to the UN Force, being joined by contingents from Canada, Denmark, Finland, Ireland and Sweden.

Britain also contributed an air unit, and Austria a field hospital. This made up a total force of something in excess of 6,000 men, including a group of about 175 civilian police drawn from five states. The police remained stable in number throughout Unficyp's first phase, but over these ten years (with the life of the Force being regularly extended for short periods) the military component of Unficyp declined to rather less than half its initial size. In part this was due to an improvement in the security situation and in part to financial pressure. However, its national composition remained much the same, the only changes being the arrival of an Austrian infantry batallion in 1972 and the departure of the Irish battalion in the following year.

Throughout the first phase of its life Unficyp engaged in a considerable amount of humanitarian work. But at the political level, its role was exclusively in the field of stabilization, for by the time it arrived the crisis had been largely defused. And at no time was there even the sight of a settlement in the implementation of which it could have assisted. Efforts were going on in this direction, but to no avail. Unficyp's task, therefore, was to try to keep things quiet, both as a desirable end in itself and in the hope of preparing the way for an agreement. Its contribution in this respect illustrated the chief ways in which a peacekeeping body can assist in maintaining calm.

In the first place, Unficyp did what it could to prevent incidents. Following the disorders of December 1963, thousands of Turkish-Cypriots had uprooted themselves from mixed villages and the smaller Turkish-Cypriot hamlets to concentrate in larger groups. This led, in some parts of the island, to the establishment of what were in the nature of opposing front lines; and in the capital, Nicosia, a very clear division existed between the northern, Turkish-Cypriot part of the city and the southern, Greek-Cypriot, part. In such places, Unficyp tried to place itself between the opposing military positions; and where local cease-fire lines were agreed, as in Nicosia along what became known as the Green Line (the term deriving from the colour in which the line was first drawn on a map), the Force demarcated and watched over them. Where neither of these things were possible, it set up observation posts nearby.

Unficyp also entered into negotiations for its own occupation of disputed points, for the dismantlement of fortifications, and for the demilitarization of some provocative forward positions. One notable success of this kind was the defortification of the areas of direct confrontation in Famagusta, which was completed in January 1966. Unficyp patrolled towns and villages which were particularly sensitive, and maintained a presence on main roads. Following the closure of the

Nicosia–Kyrenia road to Greek-Cypriot traffic, it secured its reopening (in October 1964) under the exclusive control of the UN Force. At the non-military intercommunal level, which was little less explosive than the armed confrontation, the UN civilian police also contributed to incident prevention. With a view to preventing the humiliation of Turkish-Cypriots, they accompanied some Greek-Cypriot police patrols and set up posts at potentially troublesome points.

When incidents did occur, Unficyp endeavoured to interpose itself so as to prevent more serious developments. In the event of isolated shooting, it might order those concerned to lay down their arms – although if they refused the UN troops were unable to do anything about it, and even if they complied Unficyp had no right to confiscate their arms. If bluff of this kind failed, Unficyp tried to bring fighting to an end by persuasion and negotiation at the appropriate level. This temper-cooling activity was much needed during the first year that the Force was in Cyprus, and was often, in local terms, successful. In conjunction with its incident-prevention work, Unficyp thus helped to reduce much surface tension, and even made some contribution to the third aspect of stabilization: the reduction of anxiety.

But the underlying tension between the two communities hardly abated. In consequence, the Force had no real success in persuading the parties to scale down their military confrontation. A major crisis occurred in 1967, focussing on Ayios Theodhoros, which brought Turkey to the brink of intervention. Restraint was urged from a variety of quarters, far the most telling voice being that of the United States. Thereafter, the situation appeared to improve, as Unficyp resumed its work of maintaining the truce and so helped to prevent scenes in the international high street which the West would have found enormously embarrassing.

There is, in fact, little doubt that the role of the Force was of great significance in keeping the two Cypriot communities from each other's throats. For even had their leaders wished it otherwise, conditions in Cyprus were such that, without the presence of a peacekeeping force, violence was just about unavoidable. The two communities had become deeply suspicious of each other; the division between them was imperfect; and arms and ammunition were widely distributed. In these circumstances incidents were well-nigh inevitable, and their escalation hardly less so. Thus the situation was tailor-made for, at the least, widespread civil disorder and very possibly a resumption of civil war. This would have carried ominous international implications. The condition for nipping such developments in the bud was the presence of an impartial third party. Unficyp fulfilled this role, and so made a very significant contribution to the maintenance of peace.

As with all peacekeeping bodies, however, the UN Force was playing only a secondary part. It was, with the cooperation of those concerned, guarding against accidental war, and in an accident-prone region. But the basic decisions regarding peace and war remained with the principal actors: the Cyprus government and the Turkish community on the island, and Greece and Turkey beyond. If any of these four decided on a showdown, or on action so provocative as to precipitate one, Unficyp would be unable to prevent it. That was clear from the very beginning, and was proved to be so by the events of 1974.

THE SECOND PHASE: 1974–

On 15 July 1974, the Cyprus National Guard, under the leadership of mainland Greek officers and at the instigation of the military regime in Greece, attempted a coup. Very soon the death of President Makarios was being proclaimed – an announcement which, as was said in another context, proved to be 'greatly exaggerated'. Fearing that these events might lead to the union (*enosis*) of Cyprus with Greece, Turkey invaded Cyprus, and occupied a wedge-shaped northern area. A cease-fire was then declared and in Greece the military regime fell. But Turkey decided that nonetheless she should complete her conception of a proper job in Cyprus, and on 14 August resumed her advance. Over the next two days she obtained control over the northern third of Cyprus, the line of division soon becoming ominously known to the Greek Cypriots as the 'Attila Line'. They insist that this represented the Turkish code name for the invasion, but Turkey says it was called the Peace Operation.

These happenings resulted in the immediate displacement of between a third and a half of the Greek-Cypriot population (about 200,000 people) who sought refuge in the south, and about 40,000 Turkish-Cypriots moved in the opposite direction. Over the next few years almost all the remaining Greek and Turkish Cypriots moved to 'their' part of the island, making Cyprus both culturally and politically divided. In 1983 the northern part declared itself to be the sovereign Turkish Republic of Northern Cyprus (TRNC), but only Turkey has taken formal note of that event. The (Greek-Cypriot) government of the Republic of Cyprus (ROC) continues to claim that it speaks for all the territory with which the state of Cyprus was born, and this claim receives virtually universal recognition. A political settlement has not been lost through want of trying, but seems no closer than it has ever been.

In consequence of all this, Unficyp found itself in a very different position to that which had resulted in its creation 10 years earlier. Instead of having to cope with an internal problem which had immediate international ramifications, the Force found itself in the middle of an international problem. It had no mandate to operate in this context, but the UN Secretary-General told it to get on with the job of trying to stabilize the new situation. The Security Council did not dissent from this development, and by periodically extending the life of the Force since then may be taken to have endorsed it. And there is some ground for thinking that Britain, at least, was much in favour of, and may have urged, this pragmatic UN response.

She was, after all, a guarantor of the 1960 constitution who, in the hour of need, had not intervened in its support. At the least, therefore, she could be expected to encourage a third-best response. And although the Western nightmare of a Greco-Turkish war had also not occurred, there could be no firm expectation that Greece would continue to stay her hand in the event of a further Turkish advance in Cyprus. Even if she did, and Turkey took over all of the island, the possible strategic advantage which would thus accrue to the West could be far outweighed by the possible strategic loss, in the shape of the departure of Greece from Nato, and the certain diplomatic disaster which a further Turkish advance would represent. The West therefore had every reason to support the continued peacekeeping involvement of the UN as, on a reverse ground, had the Soviet Union. For although she would make much diplomatic hay out of a complete Turkish takeover, she would also probably see the outcome, in strategic terms, as a gain for Nato. The Soviet Union was also inclined in favour of Unficyp as that was very much the policy of the non-aligned ROC. China, too, since abandoning in 1981 her studious detachment from all peacekeeping matters, has marked her interest in stability in the eastern Mediterranean by voting for Unficyp's continuation.

The Soviet Union has not gone so far, however, as to contribute towards the costs of the Cyprus Force. She is now, under President Gorbachev, hugely more forthcoming on the financing of UN peacekeeping operations than hitherto. But she probably continues to see Unficyp as chiefly a means of helping the West, and therefore its financial responsibility. Other states seem to take the same view, and even a leading Western state – France – did not put her hand in her pocket for Unficyp until March 1990. The result is that the UN is about eight years behind in reimbursing troop-contributing countries the extra costs of their involvement. This factor may help to account for Finland's withdrawal of its contingent in 1977, and was certainly influential in Sweden's decision to withdraw in 1987. This brought the Force down to just four main contributors – Austria, Canada, Denmark and the UK – the last three of whom are members of Nato. Its composition, together with the greatly improved relations between the super-powers, resulted in 1989 in the first-ever appointment of a Nato national (a Canadian) as Unficyp's Commander – this also being the first occasion since the early 1960s that such a national was chosen to lead a UN force.

The need for economy which is consequential upon Unficyp's financial problem has also contributed to reductions in its size. The crisis of 1974 brought an increase to about 4,000 men, but since then it has diminished to about half that number, having 2,091 military personnel in November 1989. The change in Unficyp's role has also drastically reduced the need for civilian police, who at the same date numbered only 35. Their chief job is to provide police services in the area between the front lines of each side.

UNFICYP'S PRESENT ROLE

So far as the major Turkish offensives of July and August 1974 were concerned, there was nothing which Unficyp could do. It was neither intended nor equipped to resist an army on the march – and if it had been it would not have been an instance of peacekeeping. But Unficyp was able to make some contribution towards defusing the crisis. Its presence here and there marginally stemmed the barbarity of a conflict which had marked civil war overtones. It provided valuable help in firming-up the two cease-fires which were declared. And it persuaded local commanders to let it take over Nicosia Airport as a UN Protected Area. Turkey then wanted to go back on this agreement, and it looked as though she might try to turn Unficyp out. Strong messages passed from New York to Ankara; the UN Force at the Airport was reinforced, and troops from every contributing country included; the media was alerted; and Britain reinforced her air strength at her Sovereign Bases, flying conspicuously over the Airport en route. This went well beyond peacekeeping. But it was an opportunity for the UN troops to stand firm on a new status quo, and for Britain and the United States to shake their fists at Turkey in a relatively safe way. Turkey backed down, and the Airport has since remained in UN hands. But as the parties failed to agree on how it should be used, it has become derelict – a mouldering testimony to inter-communal strife.

It was not long before calm was restored to Cyprus, as the cease-fire lines became and remained stable. Unficyp once again entered the business of stabilization, but not now by way of watching over law and order throughout the state. Instead, it plays a buffer role in the area between the two front lines which runs across the whole of Cyprus for a distance of about 110 miles, including the Protected Area at Nicosia Airport. In width this UN zone, as it is colloquially called, varies between 20 yards and four miles and in all covers about 3 per cent of the land area of Cyprus, including some of its most valuable agricultural land (see Maps 36 and 37).

In this buffer zone Unficyp has established a string of observation posts, numbering 146 in November 1989, of which 54 were then permanently manned. With the use of night-vision devices, the Force can keep a permanent watch on the cease-fire lines. The zone is also patrolled, sometimes by foot but usually by vehicle. Since 1986 an all-weather

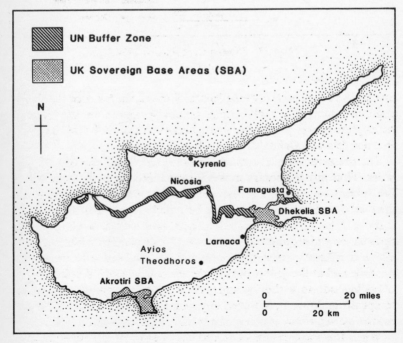

Map 36   The UN Buffer Zone in Cyprus

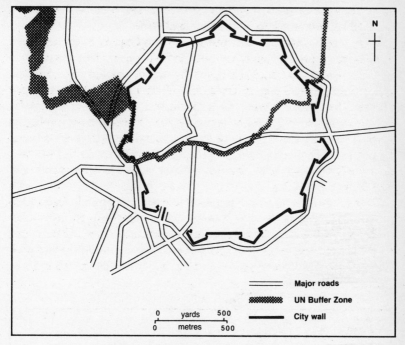

Map 37   Nicosia since August 1974

track has run along the whole length of the zone. A Force Reserve of armoured cars can be called up as necessary, and an air unit of small helicopters makes a valuable contribution to the ability of the Force to observe and monitor the status quo.

The preservation of the exact status quo is at the core of Unficyp's work. Thus any temporary moves forward into the buffer zone will be the subject of protest, and the dismantling of any new fortifications forward of the cease-fire lines will be called for – almost always with success. Attempts at the improvement of positions at the front is also resisted, on the ground that they would be provocative. Here, too, the Force is generally successful. Such matters are dealt with as soon as possible and at the lowest possible level, so as to make it easier for the offending side to withdraw and with a view to keeping the political temperature down. If, however, any such efforts fail, the matter can be moved up the chain of command to the necessary level.

When this incident-prevention work takes place outside Nicosia, it is usually the Force itself which identifies any breach of the status quo as well as calling for its correction, as the forces of each side are generally some distance away from each other. Also in these areas, Unficyp has encouraged the resumption of farming by the landowners of each side, and has gone to some lengths to ensure that this activity is neither a security risk to the other side nor perceived as one. In Nicosia itself, however, incidents can and do occur directly between the parties, as the distances between the front lines are very short and positions are heavily fortified. This is the main flash point in Cyprus, and it is here, therefore, that temper-cooling activity is frequently required and usually employed with quick success. With a view to preventing incidents, Unficyp has from time to time proposed a neutral area or the mutual unmanning of various positions, and in April 1989 a limited pull-back of forces was agreed. But nothing has yet come of UN proposals for formal investigations and reports on troop and armament levels, as each side sees such developments in practice likely to favour the other. In consequence, each party gets periodically alarmed by its own figures about the military strength of its opponent, which does nothing to alleviate the atmosphere of acute suspicion which exists in Cyprus.

But at a day-to-day level, it is undoubtedly the case that Unficyp helps to reduce anxiety, which in turn reinforces the stability of the truce. Thus it has become almost a working assumption in Cyprus that such incidents as occur will be settled, and that the truce will be maintained. At bottom this reflects the facts that Turkey and the TRNC are happy to sit on what they have got, and that the ROC recognizes both her own military incapacity to eject the Turks and the political unlikelihood of getting substantial armed help for this purpose from Greece. It must not be assumed that the parties will always act rationally on the basis of these positions: as always in politics, the situation could change with dramatic and surprising suddeness. But insofar as calculations are possible, the cease-fire in Cyprus does seem very secure. This is not due to Unficyp. But within the context of the parties' current policies, the stability which exists has a great deal to do with the presence of the UN Force.

Basically, this is a consequence of the prophylactic effect of having a buffer zone under the effective control of a peacekeeping force – one which, by definition and in practice, is a threat to neither side and can be relied on to behave impartially towards both. If it were not there, minor cease-fire violations would almost certainly occur, which would very likely lead to bigger ones. This could easily result in the area between the lines being messily swallowed up by the adversaries in a process which would have dangerously escalatory potential. Even if the rough status quo was maintained, the existence of a direct armed confrontation, and the absence of any independent temper-cooling device, would probably put the situation under constant threat. And although both sides might wish to avoid another war, they could nonetheless find themselves being carried along in that direction by the sheer momentum of highly-charged events. Accordingly, Unficyp can be seen as playing a very valuable stabilizing role, through its part in diminishing the likelihood of incidents and dampening any which do occur.

Those who, for whatever reason, are uneasy at the presence of the UN Force, tend to respond to this analysis in one of three ways. The first, which is not often explicitly presented these days, is that it would be no bad thing if the parties did fight it out, in that that would lead to a final settlement of the problem. A pecking order would be clearly established, and everyone would know where they stood. However, the fact of the matter is that, even if it was once so, it is no longer the case that arms are acceptable as a final arbiter. Especially where territory and the democratic rights of those who live on it are concerned, neither the parties directly involved nor even bystanders subscribe to the view that might makes right. The response of the international community to the Turkish invasion of 1974 and to the subsequent proclamation of the TRNC is sufficient evidence of that. Furthermore, in this particular case there is no disposition on either side to go to war. The ROC would no doubt like to do so if she felt strong enough, but that essential condition is lacking and does not look like being supplied in the foreseeable future.

The second critical response to Unficyp's presence is that it has come to stand in the way of a settlement. The argument is that the urgency of the search for one, by both the parties and interested outsiders, is much reduced due to the day-to-day stability which is being maintained by the UN Force. It is therefore suggested that a firm time-limit should be placed on its presence. This, it is said, would concentrate minds wonderfully. It is an argument which has been quite popular about peacekeeping generally, and understandably so, as it is almost a law of politics that the degree of attention a problem receives is in direct proportion to the amount of trouble which it threatens. And the case to which the argument has been most often applied is that of Cyprus. That, too, is understandable, given the 25-year life of the Force and uncompromising attitude of the disputants. The argument was, for example, hinted at very clearly by Sweden in 1987 when she was explaining why she planned to withdraw her contingent from the Force. But the prescription which the argument supplies is seriously deficient, in both general and particular terms.

The general point is that some disputes, of which territorial disputes are the prime instance, are just not soluble by, in effect, threatening to expose the parties to the full consequences of their own intransigence – not least for the reason that it is rare for them to be equally and urgently worried by that prospect. And even if they were, it does not follow that both of them would be willing to settle for something in the nature of half a loaf. Pride and political survival might well stand in the way of that. These comments are illustrated by the particular case of Cyprus. For there is no evidence to suggest that the absence of the UN Force would encourage a more conciliatory frame of mind on either side.

The third possible response of a critical kind to Unficyp's presence is surprisingly little heard. It is that if the parties want to maintain stability – as they clearly do – they should see to it themselves. This would have been enormously hard, if indeed possible, in the pre-1974 situation. But in the presence of a clear dividing line across Cyprus, the parties could go a long way on their own towards minimizing instability. Detailed agreements could, in principle, be reached regarding the delineation and demarcation of cease-fire lines, and on the status and use of the area in between. Even without such arrangements, which would present considerable difficulties for the ROC, it should be possible, through sensible self-denying measures and strict discipline, to secure a high degree of calm, and to prevent the escalation of any incidents which did occur – at least in most cases. Undoubtedly, Unficyp greatly reduces the incentive to embark on such measures.

The adoption of this course, however, and the withdrawal of Unficyp which it implies, would be to live dangerously. For it is exceedingly improbable that the situation would be as secure without the UN Force as it is with it. Human nature and politics would almost certainly combine to produce incidents and retaliation. Escalation and even a general conflagration might follow – no matter how determined the parties were, in principle, on the maintenance of quiet. That would not be in the interest of either of the authorities in Cyprus, or of their international backers. And it would greatly displease the Western alliance – which sees Unficyp as a premium which has to be paid to reduce the danger of an irritant once again becoming a very considerable embarrassment. In short, all concerned are most anxious that avoidable risks should be avoided. The consequence is that Unficyp is definitely not a candidate for early retirement.

FURTHER READING

James M. Boyd, 'Cyprus: Episode in Peacekeeping', *International Organization*, XX (1) (Winter 1966).

Glen D. Camp, 'Greco-Turkish Conflict over Cyprus', *Political Science Quarterly*, 95 (1) (Spring 1980).

Michael Harbottle, *The Impartial Solider* (London: Oxford University Press, 1970).

House of Commons, Foreign Affairs Committee: Third Report, Session 1986–87: *Cyprus* (London: Her Majesty's Stationery Office, 1987).

Alan James, 'The UN Force in Cyprus', *International Affairs*, 65 (3) (Summer 1989).

Norman MacQueen, 'Ireland and the United Nations Peace-keeping Force in Cyprus', *Review of International Studies*, 9 (2) (April 1983).

Robert McDonald, *The Problem of Cyprus* (London: IISS, Adelphi Paper 234, Winter 1988/9).

James A. Stegenga, *The United Nations Force in Cyprus* (Columbus, Ohio: Ohio State University Press, 1968).

Kurt Waldheim, *In the Eye of the Storm* (London: Weidenfeld & Nicolson, 1985).

NOTE

Regular public reports are made by the UN Secretary-General on almost all the Organization's current peacekeeping operations.

Section H   The War over the Falkland Islands/Islas Malvinas (1982)

Early in April 1982 Argentina executed a successful invasion of the British colony of the Falkland Islands. She had long laid claim to the territory, as well as to some other small British islands in the South Atlantic, but the advancement of her case in so dramatic and unorthodox a fashion was a great surprise in every quarter. Britain immediately made it clear that if the Argentinians would not leave, she proposed to eject them, and set about organizing an expedition to what, for her, was a very distant part of the international high street (see Map 38).

Diplomatic efforts to avert the looming armed conflict were by no means wanting. In this the United States took a lead, as she was embarrassed both by Argentina's military initiative and by the prospect of that important Latin American state being at war with one of the leading members of the Western alliance. However, the United States was herself in the awkward position of having political commitments to and some sympathy for both sides, and as a result the expression of her embarrassment was somewhat muted. Elsewhere, at least in the rhetorical level, Argentina received considerable diplomatic support, and she therefore sat tight. Britain, for her part, felt no compunction about refusing to accept anything less than the clear prospect of Argentina's withdrawal. Thus the United States' mediatory efforts came to nothing.

Meanwhile, at the United Nations the Secretary-General quietly established a task force to work on contingency plans in case the world organization was asked to contribute towards a peaceful resolution of the conflict. And as May began, the initiative passed openly to him. An intensive series of negotiations ensued, which focussed on the possibility of the UN playing an administrative role in respect of the Islands while negotiations for a final settlement took place. This plan gradually assumed the following shape. There would first, under the supervision

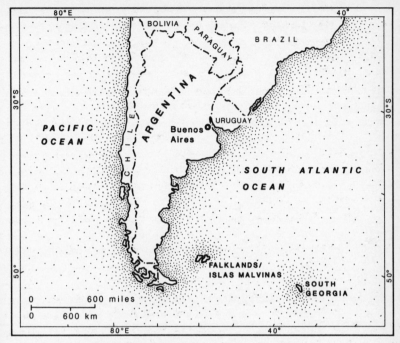

Map 38   The Falkland Islands/Islas Malvinas

of UN Observers, be a mutual withdrawal of forces – of Argentinian troops from the Islands and of Britain's advancing naval force. The UN would then administer the territory for a period, flying its own flag. Small liaison offices would be established on the Falklands by the contending parties, and on these offices their respective flags could be flown. Argentina and Britain would then enter into negotiations under the Secretary-General's auspices with a view to reaching agreement by the end of the year.

Neither side seemed optimistic at the start of these talks, nor keen on the idea of the UN's involvement on the ground. But as negotiations progressed the points of difference narrowed, and it began to look as if the UN might be able to play an intermediary peacekeeping role. Differences about certain important aspects of the plan remained, but progress had undoubtedly been made. Britain therefore proposed a draft agreement which incorporated the essence of the ideas which had been developed regarding the help which the UN could give. The counter-proposal from Argentina, however, was seen by Britain as, in essence, a rejection of her own draft. The British invasion therefore went ahead, and by mid-June had been successfully completed.

It was not the mere idea of temporary UN administration of the Falklands which stook in the way of an agreement. Rather, it was, on the one hand, Britain's insistence on firm guarantees against Argentina being able to turn the interim period unfairly to her advantage and, on the other, Argentina's reluctance to lose all the advantages of having seized the Islands. What Britain wanted was a restoration of the previous situation in everything except the immediate governing authority, the maintenance of the status quo during the UN's rule, and a clear timetable for bringing that rule to an end – with Britain reassuming authority in the absence of an agreement to the contrary. But what Argentina wanted was to amplify her voice on the Islands during the time that the UN administered them, and to go a long way towards ensuring that the negotiations did not have to be brought to an early and, for her, an unsatisfactory end. Put more bluntly, Britain's aim was to use the interim period to show that the islanders sought a restoration of British rule, and Argentina's aim was to use the period to build up the case for the transfer of the territory to her.

In these circumstances it is not surprising that the UN's scheme came to naught. Interim international administration is a fine device in situations of two kinds: where, in effect, a state has accepted that she must abandon a territory, but wants a face-saving cover for her departure; or where both parties to a territorial dispute are willing, however reluctantly, to risk an unfavourable – a 100 per cent unfavourable – outcome. But in this particular case Argentina chose not to make a face-saving exit, and each party was willing to let the UN step in only on terms which pointed to an outcome favourable to herself. This was a recipe for deadlock.

Putting the matter in a wider political framework, neither Argentina nor Britain had embarrassed their important friends to such an extent that those friends were determined to put a stop to what was going on. This was not a re-run of Suez for Britain, and it was not Argentina's Suez. Nor did either principal come to feel sufficient embarrassment about her own action as to induce her to look for an escape route. Indeed, the situation was quite the contrary, each side being so convinced of the justice of the cause as to be willing to fight for it – although whether Argentina had bargained for that at the start of the affair is another question. If the immediate political context had developed in a more pacific direction, peacekeeping could have worked. But here the necessary requirement of an overriding desire on both sides to avoid a war proved to be lacking.

FURTHER READING

Anthony Parsons, 'The Falklands crisis in the United Nations, 31 March–14 June 1982', *International Affairs*, 59 (2) (Spring 1983).

The Times, 21 May 1982.

United Nations Information Centre, London, *Secretary-General of the United Nations Reports to the Security Council on the Situation in the Falklands (Malvinas) Islands on 21 May 1982*, BR/82/13 (22 May 1982).

Section I The Soviet Withdrawal from Afghanistan and its Aftermath (1988–1990)

THE AFGHANISTAN SETTLEMENT

In the 1980s the Soviet Union found herself embarrassingly bogged down in Afghanistan. That state had never been part of the Soviet bloc, but not unnaturally the Soviets took a close interest in the affairs of this strategically interesting neighbour. At the end of the 1970s her left-wing regime seemed to be in need of propping up, and the Soviet response was to intervene in strength. About 100,000 Soviet troops went down the international high street and into Afghanistan; a new and compliant president was installed (his predecessor being executed); and Soviet advisers assumed operational control in nearly all governmental ministries. It proved an exceedingly ill-judged venture. The Afghanistan Army more or less disintegrated. The Soviet troops were harried at many points by the Mujahidin – the numerous, but far from united, guerrilla opponents of the Soviet presence and the puppet regime. And at the UN the Soviet Union went down to resounding annual defeats as the General Assembly called, in effect, for a Soviet withdrawal (see Map 39).

In line with the very first of these resolutions, passed in 1980, the UN Secretary-General appointed a representative to look into ways of promoting a peaceful settlement. He held numerous rounds of talks with the interested parties, both in their capitals and at Geneva. Besides the Soviet Union and Afghanistan, they included Pakistan and Iran, as about five million people (getting on for a third of Afghanistan's population) had sought refuge in these states from the huge destructiveness which the long war in Afghanistan had entailed. Pakistan was also the base for much of the Mujahidin activity.

242

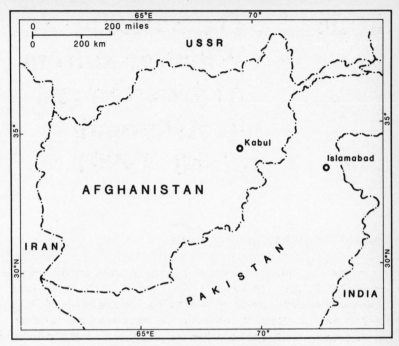

Map 39   Afghanistan and Pakistan

The stumbling block to an agreement was the question of Soviet withdrawal. Despite her immensely superior firepower, she was manifestly not winning the war, which made it very hard for her to agree to go. Furthermore, there was a general expectation that the Kabul regime which she was supporting would collapse immediately after her departure, which would therefore rub nothing but salt into what would in any event be an extremely sensitive political wound. On the other hand, the Soviet Union's presence in Afghanistan was not doing her any kind of good, and there was little evidence that staying on was going to be of much help to her Kabul protege. It was a predicament with striking resemblances to that which had faced the United States in Vietnam some years before.

In the case of Vietnam, moves in the direction of withdrawal were only begun with a change of administration. Likewise in the case of Afghanistan, it took the advent in 1985 of a new leader – Mr Gorbachev – for the nettle seriously to be grasped. He immediately said that the Soviet Union was committed to a political rather than a military solution – presumably having been encouraged in this direction by assurances that the Kabul regime would, with Soviet aid, have a good chance of survival. And after many more talks, he announced, in February 1988, that if an agreement could be reached between Afghanistan and Pakistan, Soviet troops, now thought to number in the region of 115,000, would withdraw. A draft agreement between these two states had existed for some time, but at this point Pakistan began to make difficulties. They were overcome as the result of an understanding between the two superpowers that it was open to them to continue supplying arms to their Afghan associates on the basis of what the United States called 'positive symmetry' (the Soviets having rejected the concept of 'negative symmetry'). A last-minute hitch over the seating arrangements at the Geneva signing ceremony (a problem not new to that city) having been overcome, four agreements were signed on 14 April.

Two of them were between Afghanistan and Pakistan, one dealing with mutual non-interference and non-intervention and the other with the return of refugees. A third was a declaration (called a 'guarantee') of non-interference by the Soviet Union and the United States. And these two states witnessed an agreement between the other two on the 'Interrelationships for the Settlement of the Situation Relating to Afghanistan'. This made reference to a quite separate agreement between Afghanistan and the Soviet Union providing for a phased withdrawal of the latter's troops over a nine-month period starting on 15 May. And it provided that a representative of the UN Secretary-General would lend his good offices to assist in the implementation of the accords. Towards that end a UN team of unarmed military officers, no fewer than 10 and more more than 50, were to be stationed in Afghanistan and Pakistan to check, at the request of any of the parties or on their own initiative, on any possible violations of the Geneva Agreements and to assist in their execution.

THE SOVIET WITHDRAWAL

In this convoluted way the UN Good Offices Mission in Afghanistan and Pakistan (Ungomap) was born – although, in what proved an unfounded concern for Soviet sensitivities, the Security Council's formal authorization for its establishment was not sought until six months later. Further complications were immediately to hand. For inasmuch as the Afghan–Soviet agreement on the withdrawal of Soviet troops was not one of the Geneva accords, some observers took the apparently reasonable view that Ungomap had no authority to watch over it. However, it had been understood from the beginning that the UN would monitor the Soviet withdrawal, just as the need for a more general system of verification had been recognized, and thus what was arguably a deficiency in the agreements gave rise to no problems. The Soviet Union was now anxious to rid herself of the Afghan incubus as soon as possible, and had therefore accepted the Pakistani and American requirement that there be some respectable means of checking on whether she was in fact getting out. For their part, Pakistan and the West appreciated that the Soviet Union needed some check on the Pakistani undertaking to stop giving assistance to the Mujahidin. It was, after all, the least that the Soviets could do for the government which they were now leaving so conspicuously in the lurch.

A 50-man team of military officers drawn from existing UN operations was quickly in place. Led by a Finnish general, they came from Austria, Canada, Denmark, Fiji, Finland, Ghana, Ireland, Nepal, Poland, and Sweden. The UN paid them a daily allowance (on top of their continuing national salaries), and Afghanistan and Pakistan agreed to meet the cost of the local facilities and services which were needed. The Mission's other expenses were to be met from the UN's regular budget. For civilian support, Ungomap relied on about 30 officials from the UN Secretariat. Two sets of headquarters were established, one in Islamabad and the other in Kabul.

In some Western circles there was considerable doubt concerning the likelihood of a full Soviet departure within the agreed time, and the ability of Ungomap to do anything to speed them on their way. But the Soviets not only began to leave as promised but soon went out of their way to cooperate with the UN observers, realizing that they were a means of showing to an often sceptical world that the Soviet Union was honouring her word. This led to the establishment of two Ungomap outposts on the Afghan–Soviet border and one at an air base near the border. Because of security considerations, the Soviets did not always provide the UN with their withdrawal plans in advance. But in that case they advised Ungomap of their movements after the event, and invited it to check that they had really gone, sometimes providing transport for the purpose (Ungomap having no aircraft of its own). The UN officers were also able to check on the number of departing troops at the border crossing points or at the airport. The Soviets were equally forthcoming in relation to the media. Clearly, the Soviet Union had nothing to hide. And precisely on schedule, on

15 February 1989, she announced that the last Soviet soldier had left Afghanistan, which was confirmed by Ungomap.

This activity is a good example of the way in which the UN can be called on for peacekeeping help of a settlement-assistance kind. The parties had come to an agreement which was built around a Soviet withdrawal. For each side's peace of mind and also for wider international considerations, independent confirmation that the agreement was being respected – or a ground for alleging that it was not – was highly desirable. That did not require much by way of manpower, for the key element in the arrangement was highly visible. It would have been possible, in theory, for the parties to have proceeded without the UN's peacekeeping involvement. But in terms of the political requirements of the situation, it would have been hard to do so. Accordingly, Ungomap supplied a minor but nonetheless important element in the total package.

The sometimes encountered observation that Ungomap was too small to make any real difference to the situation is therefore based on a mistaken premise. There was never the remotest question of the Soviet Union being frog-marched out of Afghanistan. What Ungomap was established to do, essentially, was to confirm that the Soviet Union had left Afghanistan, and that it did – giving rise to the first occasion on which a super power, or even a major one, had wholeheartedly cooperated with a peacekeeping operation. In this way, Ungomap gave significant help in extricating the Soviets from their embarrassing deployment into the international high street, and in winding up a major international trouble spot. While in one sense Ungomap did not do much, in another it thus did a lot.

AFGHANISTAN–PAKISTAN RELATIONS

Ungomap's main peacekeeping work was now done. But in addition to watching over the Soviet withdrawal it also had, from the beginning, the task of checking on the execution of all the Geneva Agreements, and in particular the promises of Afghanistan and Pakistan not to interfere in each other's affairs. For this reason its officers were based more or less equally in Afghanistan and Pakistan. And it was to remain on hand to assist with any problems at least until January 1990 – two months after the date on which the mixed commissions arranging and supervising the return of the refugees were due to complete their work. It had, however, been officially anticipated that after the Soviets had left Afghanistan Ungomap could be reduced in size   and its military officers had in fact been reduced from 50 to 40 by February 1989 (but without any reduction in the number of states from which they were drawn). No doubt this reflected the widespread assumption that without the Soviet presence the Kabul regime would fall, so permitting a great improvement in Afghan–Pakistan relations and a smooth return of the refugees.

However, the Government – bolstered by large Soviet supplies – did not collapse, and recriminations between it and Pakistan continued. Whether or not, as Afghanistan alleged daily to Ungomap, Pakistan was directly interfering in Afghanistan, she certainly was most sympathetic towards the Mujahidin rebels, permitted them to use her territory as a rear base, and allowed arms and supplies to move across it into Afghanistan. For her part, Pakistan frequently complained to Ungomap that Afghanistan was interfering in Pakistan, and about the continuous Soviet support for the Kabul Government.

In respect of this situation the never more than 50-man-strong Ungomap was, operationally speaking, in an almost impossible position. There was in any event an inevitable time-lag between a complaint and a subsequent enquiry, giving plenty of opportunity for tracks to be covered. If there was anything to hide, it was not to be expected that either Afghanistan or Pakistan would be over-enegertic in facilitating enquiries – for, after all, they were also the accused. Additionally, on the Pakistan side much of the 900-mile-long border was in the autonomous, and dangerous, Tribal Areas, which tended to delay matters still further. And in Afghanistan the security position never permitted much by way of investigation (with the result that following the Soviet withdrawal Ungomap's Kabul headquarters were overstaffed). Investigations of specific (and therefore investigable) complaints were conducted, in both Afghanistan and Pakistan, but Ungomap found it possible to comment on them only in terms of degrees of probability. And there is no reason to think that this activity had any significant deterrent effect on the outside support which was being received by each side in the war in Afghanistan.

This situation was, in fact, totally unsuitable for peacekeeping. For none of those concerned in the civil war were at all disposed to make peace except on terms which the other side found wholly unacceptable. The Mujahidin, for example, would have nothing to do with a Soviet suggestion of April 1989 for a cease-fire supervised by a UN force – a typical weaker-party ploy. There was thus no real agreement for Ungomap to monitor. Both sides found the UN body of some marginal value, as they could advertise their complaints to it and Ungomap's inability to produce firm findings against them as signs of their good faith. This activity was also a way of letting off steam, and additionally it was possible to use Ungomap as something in the nature of a scapegoat – implying that if only it did better the situation would improve.

In this last cause, Afghanistan called on Ungomap in April 1989 to establish a number of posts immediately on the Pakistan side of the border, in addition to the Mission's two outstations in Pakistani cities adjacent to it. Pakistan agreed to three such posts – and in return (unsuccessfully) requested additional posts in Afghanistan to monitor Soviet activity. But Ungomap was no more equipped to make any worthwhile contribution to closing the Afghan–Soviet border than it was to doing likewise in respect of that between Afghanistan and Pakistan, and neither Pakistan on the one hand nor the Soviet Union on the other were willing to see Ungomap built up with that in mind. These tit-for-tat requests thus only underlined the point that while the parties were able to use Ungomap in a propaganda context, it was hardly helping in the maintenance of peace. And with the moving of the spotlight from the clearing up of an embarrassment in the international high street to the patrolling of a locally-dangerous crossroads – but one at which the leading locals were not at all disposed to modify their aggressive manner of driving – Ungomap's peacekeeping relevance was called sharply into question.

As it happened, for about the first year of its life the UN had always been at pains to say that Ungomap should not be seen as a peacekeeping operation. Its very name points in a mediatory rather than a peacekeeping direction, and Ungomap went so far as to discourage its military personnel being described as 'observers'. This approach may partly have stemmed from the fact that when Ungomap was first mooted the Soviet Union was far from enamoured with UN peacekeeping. But another part of the explanation lay in the UN's own internal politics, in that Ungomap was neither negotiated by nor did it initially become the responsibility of that section of the Secretariat which handles peacekeeping operations. There is no question, however, that Ungomap's supervisory role in relation to the departing Soviet troops, and also the investigatory role which was assigned to it by the Geneva Agreements, were wholly typical of peacekeeping.

After February 1989, however, the impracticality of this last task was thrown into high relief. And by that time Ungomap had already assumed a clear mediatory role. For in November 1988 the UN General Assembly had asked the Secretary-General to help in the establishment of a broad-based coalition government in Afghanistan, and he turned to Ungomap's top civilian and military officials for the undertaking of this task. This gave Ungomap the right, which it did not have under the Geneva Agreements, to make official contact with the Mujahidin. Its change of operational emphasis in the direction of mediation was further signified by the replacement, in May 1989, of the General at the head of Ungomap's military side by an officer of lower rank.

As Ungomap approached its scheduled end (January 1990) an argument developed in the UN Security Council about its future. The Soviet Union was anxious for it to continue at least for six months, seeing it as a means of keeping an eye on the involvement of Pakistan (and, rather less directly, of the United States) in Afghanistan. The Afghan Government in Kabul was naturally of the same mind. But by the same token, the United States, with Pakistan's concurrence, proposed that Ungomap simply be allowed to expire. However, she did not want to risk vetoing its extension, as that would too blatantly suggest that she and Pakistan had a lot to hide. Nor did she wish to do anything which might help to undermine Mr Gorbachev's internal position in the Soviet Union, which was beginning to look somewhat hazardous. For the same reason, the Soviet Union also wanted to avoid a confrontation, and in the overall atmosphere of superpower cooperation a compromise was arranged, Ungomap being extended for two months with an unchanged mandate.

When, however, the matter was reconsidered in March 1990, the United States successfully insisted that the time had come for Ungomap to be brought to an end. The continuing existence of a diplomatic problem was recognized by an agreement that the UN Secretary-General's Representative in Afghanistan and Pakistan would remain in place. And the military ramifications of the situation were also acknowledged, in that 10 army officers from Ungomap were assigned to the Representative so that he could have access to independent military advice. But as a peacekeeping body Ungomap was adjudged, through no fault of its own, to be no longer giving value for money. And quite right, too. For a vigorous and well-fuelled civil war is no place for a peacekeeping operation.

If, however, the situation improves, it could be that a further peacekeeping body might make an appearance in Afghanistan. For it was being said in June 1990 that the Soviet Union and the United States had reached agreement on certain principles for a settlement of the problem, which included a role for the UN in the supervision of elections. But the superpowers were not at that stage agreed on the position of the Soviet-backed Kabul Government prior to and during any such elections. And even if this hurdle were to be overcome, it was unclear whether the Kabul regime would fall in line with Soviet wishes, and even less clear that the United States would be able to 'deliver' the various factions of the Mujahidin. As always, successful peacekeeping depends, basically, on the willingness of the local parties to cooperate with the peacekeepers, and therefore, in a sense, with each other. In Afghanistan in mid-1990 there was very little sign of the spirit of compromise.

FURTHER READING

Selig S. Harrison, *Paths to Peace in Afghanistan* (New York: International Peace Academy, 1989).

Rosanne Klass, 'Afghanistan: the Accords', *Foreign Affairs*, 66 (5) (Summer 1988).

D. S. Leslie and R. G. Elms, 'United Nations Good Offices Mission in Afghanistan and Pakistan: Lessons From a Peacekeeping Experience', *Canadian Defence*, 19 (1) (Summer 1989).

P. J. McHale, 'UNGOMAP – A New Venture for Peace', *An Cosantoir*, 48 (10) (October 1988).

Amin Saikal, 'Afghanistan: the end-game', *The World Today*, 45 (3) (March 1989).

Amin Saikal and William Maley (eds), *The Soviet Withdrawal from Afghanistan* (Cambridge: Cambridge University Press, 1989).

Section J The Cuban and Other Withdrawals from Angola (1988–)

When Portugal finally left Angola in 1975, three guerrilla movements were competing for control of the whole country. At the instigation of the Soviet Union, and with her logistic and financial support, Cuba sent about 20,000 troops to support the left-wing MPLA group, and in the following year it came out formally on top. However, the South African-supported Unita remained in control of about one-third of Angola, and the civil war rumbled on. To provide the government with much-needed assistance of various sorts, the Cubans remained, and a decade or so later were reported to have doubled in number.

In part, the Cuban presence reflected that state's desire to play a leading role in the politics of the Third World. But chiefly she was a proxy for the Soviet Union, who wanted to prop up regimes of an appropriate ideological and political hue. However, the use of her own troops for this purpose would have been bothersome in several respects, not least on account of the danger of a higher level of confrontation with the West. She therefore opted for the role of paymaster to the willing Cubans. And as Cuba was in any event heavily reliant on the Soviet Union for economic support, the venture did not seem to involve an undue degree of risk for the Soviets (see Map 40).

In terms of helping the Angolan government to exercise authority over all of the country, however, Cuba's involvement was very far from a success. Unita remained in control of much of the south and east, benefitting not only from South African but also from American support. And the country as a whole, under the physical impact and financial demands of the civil war, declined from relative prosperity to extreme poverty, its huge mineral potential going largely untapped. Moreover, in the more liberal and conciliatory atmosphere of the

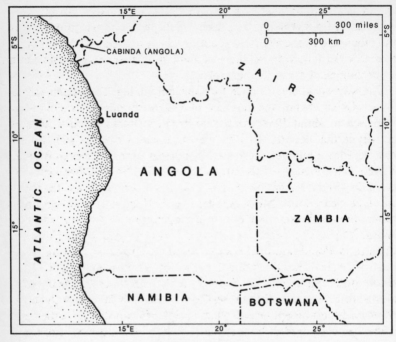

Map 40   Angola

Gorbachev era, the indirect Soviet presence in Angola began to look somewhat out of place. It was not a major embarrassment, but it was becoming a minor one. And there was another reason of a more immediate kind which led to its reconsideration.

In the early 1980s, discussion of the South West Africa/Namibia issue had involved the concept of 'linkage': South Africa would withdraw from Namibia if Cuba withdrew from Angola, and this was a position to which South Africa held tenaciously. But it was not until 1988 that she seemed to be in earnest about withdrawing from Namibia. This prospect had considerable appeal to the Soviets. For, quite apart from the attraction of seeing South Africa on the retreat, there was every reason to believe that the government of an independent Namibia would be sympathetic towards, and valuable for, the Soviet Union. In this light the Cubans in Angola looked distinctly expendable. Their departure would, it was true, weaken the MPLA government. But as South Africa's withdrawal from Namibia would also involve her withdrawal from Angola, Unita, too, would be weakened. On balance there was little doubt that Namibian independence, linked with a Cuban withdrawal from Angola, would be clearly in the Soviet interest. On the other side of the political equation, there was equally little doubt that a Soviet failure to facilitate Namibian independence would have repercussions of a very embarrassing kind.

The way was therefore open for some bargaining. To strengthen the Soviet/Cuban hand, the number of Cuban troops in Angola was increased to about 50,000, and they began to hamper South African activity in that country. In June they even won what was widely seen as a significant military success against South African forces in Angola – their first for more than ten years. Provided South Africa felt she could do without retaliation, the route to a face-saving Cuban withdrawal was now clear. South Africa desisted – in both military and economic terms she was feeling the strain of her operations in Angola – and in August 1988 a cease-fire was declared between Angola and Cuba on the one hand and South Africa on the other. Further talks were to be held regarding the timetable for the linked questions of Cuba's withdrawal from Angola and South Africa's from Namibia. Meanwhile, South Africa was to withdraw her forces from Angola, and both states confirmed their acceptance of the principles for an overall settlement which had been agreed the previous month in New York. One of these provided, in effect, for the ending of South Africa's support for Unita and of Angola's permission for the African National Congress (ANC) to use Angola as an anti-South African base.

THE JOINT MILITARY MONITORING COMMISSION

In the interests of maintaining the cease-fire and of maximizing conditions for an orderly South African withdrawal from Namibia, the August 1988 agreement (called the Protocol of Geneva) set up what became known as the Joint Military Monitoring Commission (JMMC). It was intended to assist in stabilizing the Angolan–Namibian border between the departure of South African troops from Angola (they had left by the end of August) and the as-then-undetermined date on which the transition process in Namibia would begin. Daily meetings, on a rotational basis, were held at the border between middle-ranking military officers representing Angola and Cuba (jointly) on the one hand and South Africa on the other. Every second week a higher-level military meeting was held, also at the border, and there was provision for meetings at foreign-ministry level as necessary. As befitted its brokering role in the whole peace process, the United States had observer status in the JMMC, and was thus present as a kind of continuing mediator.

To provide the JMMC with eyes and ears, it was arranged that the parties would establish a number of posts along the border, from which, by observation and patrolling, a watch could be kept to check on the honouring by each party of its non-interventionary promise. Eleven such posts were envisaged, each of them having a 'leg' on both sides of the border. However, it was not until October that a start was made on setting them up, and in the event only eight were established, on account of Unita controlling the area (at the eastern end of the very long border) in which the remaining three were to be located. At each leg of each post a platoon-sized group of about 20 men was based, so that by the point at which the system was fully operational – January 1989 – several hundred military personnel were involved in the peacekeeping work of the JMMC. The operation offered the unusual spectacle of peacekeeping tasks being conducted not by outsiders but by the parties themselves.

By the beginning of 1989, however, it had been agreed that South Africa's withdrawal from Namibia would begin on 1 April 1989, so a start had soon to be made on deactivating the posts and winding up the JMMC machinery. This had been done by the end of March. But then the system was temporarily reactivated to help cope with the crisis which occurred at the very outset of the Namibian transition process (see Section K, below). Once that task had been completed, the JMMC was finally wound up in mid-May.

In respect of the 1 April crisis, the JMMC was a valuable source of information about what was actually going on on the ground. Prior to that point it assisted in maintaining stability along the Angolan–Namibian border, and was able to do so because both parties stuck to their bargain. In consequence, the ANC fighters had to move out of Angola in a northerly direction (to Uganda and Tanzania), and Unita was largely deprived of South African support (although it still received help from the United States). This Angolan–South African cooperation was not just reflected in the close contacts which were established through the JMMC but was also valuably encouraged by the very existence of that body. For its members were two very unlikely-looking partners, between whom a measure of trust needed to be built if the remarkable conciliatory developments in southwestern Africa were to receive a fair wind. The experience of working together in the context of the JMMC helped Angola and South Africa to develop confidence in each other. In this way the JMMC provided a most worthwhile bonus on top of its more usual, and very helpful, peacekeeping tasks.

THE ANGOLA VERIFICATION MISSION

Meanwhile, in late 1988, with the United States continuing in the role of a pressing mediator, discussion had turned to the timetable for Cuba's withdrawal from Angola (together with the linked issue of South Africa's withdrawal from Namibia). Not unnaturally, the issue of verification arose. As the UN was to play a big peacekeeping part in Namibia's transition to independence (see Section K, below), it was appropriate that it should also contribute to the solution of this associated matter. In December 1988 the Security Council therefore established an Angola Verification Mission (Unavem) to check on the implementation of an agreement under which Cuban troops were to make a phased withdrawal from Angola over a two-and-a-half year period.

Unavem, which established its headquarters in Luanda, was made up of 70 military observers and 22 international civilian staff. The observers, as usual of officer rank, were drawn from ten states: Algeria, Argentina, Brazil (who also provided the Chief Military Observer), Congo, Czechoslovakia, India, Jordan, Norway, Spain, and Yugoslavia. Unavem is given advance notice of all Cuban departures and (rotational) arrivals, and they are checked by teams at five outstations in ports and airports. Additionally, two mobile teams make periodic inspections to confirm that no Cubans have been illicitly left behind in the southern part of the country. Unavem's costs are assessed on all UN members on the basis of a special scale.

This was another example of the way in which the tool of peacekeeping can assist in the settlement of international disputes. The Soviet Union wanted to relieve herself of what was becoming something of an embarrassment in the international high street. But for South Africa (the other main party to the dispute) to go ahead with her linked withdrawal from both Angola and Namibia, she needed some appropriate means of checking that the Soviet proxies were keeping to their side of the bargain, as well as a promise that the ANC would leave Angola. It would not have been beyond the resources of her own intelligence system to keep a close eye on the departure of the Cubans. But any adverse reports from such a source would have carried little credibility beyond South Africa, and would therefore have been a poor basis on which to mount any critical observations or retaliatory measures. What was needed, therefore, was an independent and impartial verification arrangement. South Africa had no respect for the UN as a political organization. But a multinational team of military officers, albeit under UN auspices, could be more or less trusted to say what they saw. Unavem was therefore established.

Unavem's task is very straightforward – little more than a counting job. Indeed, from an operational point of view military men might hardly seem to be required. But quite apart from their immediate availability, the fact that Unavem has to deal with the Angolan and Cuban army authorities points strongly in the direction of military personnel, as does the need for some expertise in the identification of military equipment. It might be, however, that some reduction in the number of Military Observers will prove possible. Certainly, the Mission's first year has gone very smoothly, Cuba having withdrawn about 31,000 troops by the end of 1989 at a rate somewhat in excess of her own timetable. By providing international verification of this activity, Unavem is playing a secondary but nonetheless important part in the interlocked process which provides not only for Cuba's withdrawal from Angola, but also for a solution of the long dispute over South Africa's presence in Namibia.

FURTHER READING

Gerald J. Bender, 'Peacemaking in Southern Africa: the Luanda–Pretoria tug-of-war', *Third World Quarterly*, 11 (2) (April 1989).

G. R. Berridge, 'Diplomatic Procedure and the Angola/Namibia Accords, 1988', *International Affairs*, 65 (2) (Summer 1989).

S. Neil MacFarlane, 'The Soviet Union and Southern African Security', *Problems of Communism*, XXXVIII (2–3) (March–June 1989).

Section K   South Africa's Withdrawal from Namibia (1989–1990)

The former German colony of South West Africa is rather bigger than France and the United Kingdom combined, but is very sparsely populated, having no more than about one and a quarter million inhabitants. After the First World War it was taken from Germany and administered by South Africa as a League of Nations Mandated Territory. South Africa was anxious to include it within her own domain, and after the Second World War refused to convert it into a UN Trust Territory (League Mandates generally being transformed into UN Trusts). Before very long this became one of the grounds on which she was regularly condemned by large majorities in the UN General Assembly, and in 1966 the Assembly purported to terminate South Africa's right to govern the territory. The International Court of Justice upheld the legality of this act in 1971, by which time South West Africa had been renamed, by the UN, as Namibia. By that date the UN had also appointed a Council to administer it and prepare it for independence, but the Council was unable to secure access to the territory for which it was supposedly responsible.

In 1978 a detailed plan for the settlement of the dispute was conditionally accepted by South Africa, but although some additions were made to the plan at later dates her conditions could not be satisfied. Some doubted whether they were meant to be. The 1980s saw no respite to the anti-South Africa campaign, and even the conservative regimes of the United Kingdom and the United States felt unable to give her public support. When, therefore, late in the decade a great improvement in superpower relations resulted in peace beginning to break out, seemingly all over, South Africa at last decided to withdraw from Namibia. Internationally, her position there was a huge embarrassment, as all other states now saw the territory as part of the international high street. The cost of staying on was becoming onerous, due to the long, externally-based struggle of the South West Africa People's

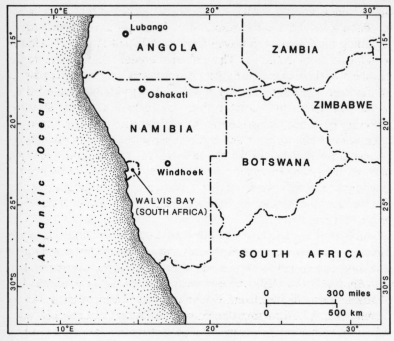

Map 41   Namibia

Organization (Swapo) to eject her. South Africa's relations with the
West might be improved by her departure, and those with African states
could hardly get worse. And there were some positive possibilities in
having a weak neighbour who could be helped much more by her than
by the other states of the continent. Taking the opportunity, therefore,
to link the issue with the withdrawal of Cuban troops from Angola
(see Section J, above), a trilateral agreement was signed in New York
on 22 December 1988 by which South Africa agreed to resurrect the
ten-year-old plan. The process of South African withdrawal and the
concomitant move towards Namibian independence was to begin on
1 April 1989. This scheme was quickly approved by the UN Security
Council (see Map 41).

THE JOINT COMMISSION

At one of the numerous meetings which led to this notable development,
it had been agreed (in the Protocol of Brazzaville of 13 December)

that a Joint Commission (JC) should be established to serve as a forum for discussion and for the resolution of any problems which arose regarding the Cuban withdrawal from Angola and the South African withdrawal from Namibia. These three signatory states were to be members of the Commission; the United States was to participate as an observer – reflecting her key role in the negotiations which led up to the settlement; the Soviet Union was to have a similar status – reflecting both her changed international policies and the improved international atmosphere; and upon independence, Namibia was to become a full member of the JC. It began to meet monthly, rotating between the (then) three member states, but subsequently its regular meetings declined to two-monthly intervals, and then to once a quarter. But it could hold ad hoc meetings, and before long a few such meetings proved very necessary.

The JC was essentially a diplomatic mechanism. But, moving in the direction of peacekeeping, a partly-military Intelligence Sub-Committee was soon established to keep an eye on military aspects of the overall plan. And in October 1989, in response to worries about the possibility of Angola-based fighters from Swapo's People's Liberation Army of Namibia (PLAN) disrupting the Namibian electoral process, a further sub-body, with a fairly clear peacekeeping character, was set up. It had two aspects. A small verification group was set up in northern Namibia, at Oshakati, consisting of Angolan military representatives and some non-military South Africans (non-military because at this time no South African military were permitted to be at large in Namibia). Cuban military people came for any meetings, as did American and Soviet military personnel, and if an investigation was decided upon it was conducted by all five states, accompanied by an Untag representative. On two occasions the JC's verification group went to Angola.

The second aspect of the Intelligence Sub-Committee's sub-body was an evaluation group which met in Namibia's capital, Windhoek, the composition of which was partly military. It was designed to deal with any matters arising from the work of the verification outpost of Oshakati, and also with any day-to-day ground-level questions which bore upon the smooth implementation of the settlement which had been agreed for Angola and Namibia. Once the Namibian elections of early November 1989 were over the Oshakati peacekeeping outpost was wound up, but regular meetings of the evaluation body in Windhoek continued to be held. The UN Group in Namibia participated in them, as did a representative of the Provisional Namibian Government which emerged from the elections.

These sub-bodies of the JC performed largely routine but nonetheless worthwhile tasks, and generally the Commission led to useful informal contacts at several levels, all of which helped to maintain the confidence of the erstwhile adversaries in the comprehensive peace process which was under way in southwestern Africa. The Commission is to continue in being until Cuba has completed her withdrawal from Angola (the scheduled date for which is July 1991). But it could be that its dissolution will give rise to some bilateral or trilateral spin-off of a stabilizing kind.

THE TRANSITION ASSISTANCE GROUP

It had been supposed that Namibia's transition from South African rule to sovereign status would take about a year. During this period South Africa was to retain authority in Namibia, and was therefore responsible both for the maintenance of law and order and for the conduct of the elections leading to independence. But South Africa was to be closely watched and in some respects controlled by a Special Representative of the UN Secretary-General, whose central task was to ensure that a constituent assembly was freely and fairly elected. The assembly would then draw up a constitution on the basis of which the sovereign state of Namibia could be proclaimed.

An essential aspect of this scheme was the provision of assistance for the Special Representative in the shape of a multi-layered peacekeeping operation – the UN Transition Assistance Group (Untag) – which he headed. Based in Windhoek, it had a civilian and a military component, the former being threefold. The first civilian activity involved the establishment and operation of a network of regional and district offices throughout Namibia to explain what was going on and to assist in the much-needed process of internal reconciliation. Untag's information role was also pursued through radio broadcasts, television slots, advertisements, and the distribution of leaflets. For this very important activity and also the general administration of Untag, a staff of about 450 international officials were mustered, representing no fewer than 91 of the UN's 159 member nationalities. (Getting on for half of this staff were women, which was a matter of some congratulation within Untag.)

Secondly, to oversee all aspects of the complex and sensitive electoral process, about 850 electoral supervisors were obtained from 27 member states. Additionally, for the actual election period (voting was to take place over five days, from 7 to 11 November), more than 500 members of the UN Secretariat were recruited from outside Namibia for electoral duties, and about 350 men from Untag's military component were also pressed into this civilian task (which they therefore executed in civilian clothes). They were deployed at all the 215 fixed and 143 mobile polling stations to watch over the conduct of the election by the local, South African-controlled, administration.

Thirdly, to keep a close eye on the local police and generally watch over their maintenance of law and order, 500 police monitors – professional policemen seconded by their states – were recruited. In June 1989, as the result of allegations of intimidation, it was decided to double this number, and in October a further 500 police monitors were brought in. All 1,500 remained in Namibia until the end of the transition period. They were drawn from 25 of the UN's member states and, except in rare circumstances, were unarmed.

UNTAG's MILITARY COMPONENT AND FUNCTIONS

On the military side, it had been originally anticipated that Untag would need 7,500 men, the bulk of whom would be made up by seven infantry battalions. Subsequently it was thought that one of the battalions could be held in reserve. When, however, in 1988 the detailed financial planning for Untag was done, the five permanent members of the Security Council (who would be responsible for most of Untag's costs) discovered that further and substantial economies could safely be made. A joint demarche to the UN Secretary-General followed, asking for a large reduction in Untag's military component. The Secretary-General was unconvinced, and was strongly supported in his doubts by the Non-Aligned members of the UN. But money talked, and a revised plan was advanced which provided for 4,650 military personnel.

At the core of this component were three enlarged infantry battalions of about 850 men each. They were supplied by Finland, Kenya, and Malaysia, with Bangladesh, Togo, Venezuela, and Yugoslavia (who had also agreed to supply battalions) holding their men in reserve. These troops were armed, but in accordance with the values of peacekeeping, were under orders to use force only in self-defence, and then always at the minimum level. (In the event, Untag fired a shot in anger only once – when some of its Kenyan troops came across an armed robbery.)

Additionally, Untag had a military observer element made up of 300 officers, provided by the following 14 states: Bangladesh, Czechoslovakia,

Finland, India, Ireland, Kenya, Malaysia, Pakistan, Panama, Peru, Poland, Sudan, Togo, and Yugoslavia. In accordance with UN peace-keeping practice the observers were to be unarmed, but it was later agreed that in certain circumstances they might be authorized by Untag's Commander to carry weapons. (As events transpired no such authorization was ever thought to be necessary.) The logistic element of Untag was to consist of about 1,700 troops. They came from Australia, Canada, Denmark, Italy, Poland, Spain, and the United Kingdom. Additionally, there was to be a headquarters staff, drawn from the existing contributors, of about 100. Switzerland provided a civilian medical unit (the first time this non-UN member had played an integral role – albeit a non-military one – in a peacekeeping mission) and the Federal Republic of Germany also supplied some civilian elements for Untag's logistic units.

Untag was thus made up of military men from no fewer than 20 states. Putting this team together was sometimes a delicate matter. One notable absentee was Sweden – almost ever-present in UN peacekeeping missions but on this occasion vetoed by South Africa on account of her vocal sympathies for the anti-apartheid movement. She was replaced by Poland – a somewhat ironic happening in view of South Africa's attitude to communism. Nigeria, too, was blackballed. South Africa also objected to Canada, but was persuaded to change her mind, and was satisfied about the response to certain questions which she raised about the appropriateness of Australian participation. The approval of Swapo, which the UN had long treated as the only legitimate spokesman for Namibia, was also sought regarding the national military make-up of Untag, but no problems emerged from that quarter.

The tasks to be performed by Untag's military component fell into four broad categories. In the first place, it had to watch over or monitor (to use the UN-preferred term) the virtual demilitarization of Namibia. This activity had a number of aspects, much of it concerning the South African Defence Force (SADF). About 30,000 SADF personnel were in Namibia, and during the first three months of the transitional period they were to be progressively reduced, under Untag's supervision, to 1,500. Those then remaining – the Merlyn Force as it was called – were to be confined to two bases, with a very close UN eye being kept on the base perimeters and the (non-operational) movements of SADF men outside the bases. Immediately after the elections the Merlyn Force was also to be withdrawn, under UN supervision. Vacated military installations were to be watched over by Untag until they could be handed over to the government of an independent Namibia. Additionally, a close check was to be kept on about 1,000 SADF personnel who conducted civilian tasks in Namibia – chiefly dealing with aviation movements but also engaged in some teaching and medical work.

Untag had also to monitor the demobilization, by the end of June 1989, of the South West Africa Territory Force, including its largely autonomous counter-insurgency unit known as Koevoet, and its various 'ethnic forces' and citizen units. The arms, ammunition, and equipment of such groups were to be handed in and guarded by Untag until the assumption of power by an indigenous and independent government.

Untag's second main military task concerned the maintenance of law and order. The South African Administrator-General retained general responsibility for this important function, so Untag had no immediate overall role in the matter. But certain specific tasks of a law and order character fell to the UN's military component, such as the guarding of vital installations in the troubled northern area of Namibia – for example, ones having to do with communications and with the supply of water and power. The UN soldiers had also to protect the entry points and reception centres which were established for the Namibian refugees – about 40,000 of them – who were returning to the territory for the election. In certain sensitive areas, Untag soldiers went on joint patrols with the Group's police monitors. Untag had also to check on the cessation of all hostile acts throughout Namibia, in accordance with the formalizing on 1 April 1989 of the de facto cease fire which had come into effect in August of the previous year. Further, by patrolling and otherwise showing the UN flag, Untag provided general support for the maintenance of law and order. This last task was particularly important in sensitive areas, such as those where there were a number of white farmers.

Thirdly, although it was not part of its formal mandate, Untag's military component, as is usually the case with peacekeeping forces, played a much-valued humanitarian role. For example, it helped with the supply of water, engaged in certain engineering works of benefit to the local communities, and provided some medical assistance.

Fourthly, Untag's military component had to do what it could to ensure that throughout the transition process Namibia was insulated from external influences. This had two aspects. One involved border surveillance. In the West and South, on the borders with the South African enclave of Walvis Bay and with South Africa proper, this task was executed by Untag's Military Observers. In the West, three 'static' observation posts were established, which were manned on a 24-hour basis, while a further area was patrolled from a fourth post. In the

South there were six such 'static' posts and four 'mobile' ones. Watching over Namibia's relatively untroubled border with Botswana in the East was the responsibility of the Kenyan battalion, which patrolled along some parts of it (as well as having duties in much of the rest of Namibia). In the North, where most Namibians live, the much more difficult border with, chiefly, Angola but also with Zambia, was divided between the Finnish and Malaysian battalions. The Malaysians were responsible for the surveillance of its western part and the Finns of its eastern section. They engaged in ground and air patrols, conducted investigations, and set up temporary border posts as necessary.

The second aspect of Untag's insulation function involved activity in Angola, to the north of Namibia, where much of the Swapo struggle against South Africa's control of Namibia was based and organized. It had been agreed in 1980, as part of the early plan for South Africa's withdrawal from Namibia, that a demilitarized zone would be established to a depth of 31 miles on each side of Namibia's northern borders. Untag was to operate freely in the zone, and (it had been further agreed in 1982) would check that the remaining Swapo fighters in Angola and Zambia stayed in their bases. However, in view of the August 1988 cease-fire agreement between Angola and Cuba on the one hand and South Africa on the other, and an associated agreement which provided for the withdrawal of Swapo forces in Angola to the north of the sixteenth parallel (to which, however, Swapo was not a direct party), the idea of a demilitarized zone was dropped. Instead, it was agreed that Untag would just monitor the work of the Angolan authorities in relation to Swapo (by this time there were no Swapo based in Zambia). However, for reasons which may have had something to do both with a lack of full cooperation from Angola and Swapo and with a lack of despatch on the UN's part, this aspect of Untag's work was, to all intents and purposes, not in operation at the start of the transition period on 1 April. This may have contributed to the unfortunate happenings which began on that date.

THE CRISIS OF 1 APRIL 1989

It was anticipated that Untag would have a life of 12 months. This commitment to a limited-term mandate was something of a novelty in UN peacekeeping. Nonetheless, the cost of the proposed operation was considerable – at an expected $416 million it was about half the amount of the UN's regular budget. In view of the UN's parlous financial condition on the one hand and the controversy which surrounded various aspects of South Africa's proposed withdrawal from Namibia on the other, there was a reluctance to make any firm arrangements to move Untag personnel to Namibia before the UN General Assembly had authorized the necessary expenditures. In turn, this had to await the final go-ahead from the Security Council. The Council delayed giving this until mid-February 1989, largely on account of the argument which was going on about the size of Untag's military component. It was then not until early March, and after further wrangling – for example, over whether Untag could purchase supplies in South Africa – that the full financial authorization was received from the Assembly.

This did not allow the time which the UN Secretariat had always said it needed to get Untag, and its considerable equipment, fully in place by 1 April. In view of financial constraints it was not considered possible to speed up the assembly of Untag, but the political situation was not thought to present the sort of difficulty which would have justified the postponement of the starting date of the whole operation. Thus when Untag became operational on 1 April only about 1,000 of its military personnel were in Namibia; they were not fully deployed; and the infantry battalions, on which the responsibility for border surveillance mainly fell, were represented only by advance parties. These circumstances may have helped to precipitate the crisis which ensued.

At that date, in a development which is still surrounded by some factual controversy, more than 1,000 PLAN fighters made an appearance in northern Namibia, allegedly having crossed from Angola. In the absence of a sizeable UN presence in the area, the South African Administrator-General of Namibia presented an urgent case for more resources to quash this infiltration, which, quite apart from its military significance, threatened to upset the diplomatic basis on which the whole peace process rested. On the recommendation of the UN Special Representative and Untag's Force Commander, the UN Secretary-General agreed that South African forces should be sent to counter the infiltration. (There was some measure of artificiality about this procedure, as in the absence of such a recommendation it is quite possible that South Africa would have acted unilaterally.) Heavy fighting followed between SADF and PLAN, and about 300 of the guerrillas were killed.

This dealt with the military threat to the consensus that all parties to the Namibian dispute should lay down their arms for the transition period. To alleviate the diplomatic threat which the episode presented to the peace process, the Joint Commission was called into urgent session, and held several special meetings, with Untag's participation.

To check on what was going on on the ground it also drew on the peacekeeping resources of the (reactivated) Joint Military Monitoring Commission (see Section J, above). There was a period of intensive diplomatic activity within the framework of the Joint Commission, and perhaps in part because of the contacts which had been developed over the previous ten years between South Africa and Untag's leading figures, together with the personal links which the United States-led peace process had established in the 1980s, the crisis was fairly quickly patched up.

A scheme was devised under which the PLAN fighters were to assemble at certain points under the supervision of Untag's Military Monitors, who would then arrange their return to Angola. As it happened, virtually nothing came of this, as the fighters preferred to return privately. But in any event, by the early weeks of May the Namibian operation was back on the rails, and Untag's military component was also by then fully in place. Untag had lost some of the time it intended to use for the complicated build-up to the elections. But the severe crisis of 1 April had been satisfactorily dealt with.

As a result of this episode swift measures were also taken, with Angola's full cooperation, to get Untag's arrangements in place for monitoring that state's promised restrictions on Swapo's PLAN fighters. Untag's Military Observers had opened a liaison office in the Angolan capital, Luanda, shortly before the crisis of 1 April. A strong outpost was now established at Lubango (also known as Sa da Bandeira), which was above the 16th parallel, and close to several PLAN camps. Between five and 30 of Untag's Military Observers (in this capacity called Monitors) were based there over the next nine months – the number fluctuating with the need – to check that there were no PLAN fighters below the 16th parallel, and that those above it were confined to their camps and disarmed. Allegations were often made by South Africa about improper PLAN activity, so that a lot of checking was involved. It was something of a cat and mouse game. But on the whole Untag's Lubango outpost worked successfully, in the sense that the situation was largely stabilized and presented no further threat to the transition process in Namibia.

SOVEREIGN NAMIBIA

With the 1 April crisis behind it, Untag's work was able to get properly under way. The demilitarization of the parties to the Namibian dispute went smoothly, with the SADF in particular cooperating fully with Untag. There were some problems over Koevoet's demobilization, but they were eventually sorted out. Untag's specific law and order tasks gave rise to no problems, and all the borders remained very quiet.

On the civilian side, the operation got fully into gear for its demanding tasks in relation to the elections. Untag's regional and district offices engaged in a vigorous campaign of political education and reconciliation. Much discussion took place with the Administrator-General regarding the repeal of restrictive or discriminatory laws. An amnesty had to be negotiated for returning Namibians and negotiations held regarding the release of political prisoners – both South African prisoners and Swapo detainees. Detailed arrangements had to be agreed with the Administrator-General regarding Untag's close scrutiny of the registration of voters. The Secretary-General's Special Representative negotiated a code of conduct with the political parties – no fewer than 10 – who were contesting the election. And Untag had to make provision for its large supervisory role in the actual elections.

Throughout this process Untag's police monitors were active in trying to ensure fair play. Their task was sometimes difficult, both on account of election fervour and because of the suspicion and even hostility with which they were sometimes viewed by the local police. But on the whole things went fairly smoothly, and the elections themselves were a huge success. Almost 700,000 voters were registered, and of these a truly remarkable 97 per cent actually voted, with only about 1.5 per cent of the votes cast (by a largely illiterate electorate) being declared invalid. The Special Representative certified that the electoral process had been free and fair and that the results were correct. Untag, amongst many, heaved a loud sigh of relief.

Of the 10 contesting parties, only two obtained more than four of the Constituent Assembly's 72 seats. They were Swapo, with 41 seats, and the Democratic Turnhalle Alliance with 21. This meant that Swapo had obtained the absolute majority which enabled it to form a provisional government. But it had not obtained the two-thirds majority which was necessary for the passage of the constitution. This suggested that some difficult bargaining might lie ahead regarding the terms of the constitution. But in the event the problems were many fewer than had been quite widely expected, and negotiations proceeded in a conciliatory and pragmatic spirit on all sides. It was thus being anticipated in January 1990 that independence would be achieved somewhat in advance of 1 April 1990 – which hitherto had been generally regarded as the target date. In the event, the chosen date was

21 March and adhered to. After an armed struggle of more than 20 years, and much international tribulation, sovereign Namibia was born. On the same day, Untag was formally wound up. The Provisional Namibian Government had earlier expressed interest in the possibility of some Untag military personnel staying on to assist in the protection of the new state, but the Security Council was not ready to agree to the UN playing that non-peacekeeping role. However, much of Untag's equipment was donated to Namibia, and in a bilateral arrangement Kenya agreed that her battalion might stay on for a while. Namibia also reached an agreement with Britain for the despatch of a Military Advisory Training Team to help build up the new Namibian Defence Force and establish a Defence Ministry.

There is no doubt that a peaceful transfer of power in Namibia could hardly have been envisaged without an involved peacekeeping operation. As with all such operations, it could get off the ground only with the cooperation of the disputing parties. For many years they were very far from agreement. But when South Africa eventually decided to relieve herself of what had become a considerable embarrassment, the way was open for Untag to provide a degree of assistance with the transition which was quite without precedent in the twentieth century history of decolonization. Accordingly, in any analysis of the events which led to Namibia's independence, the tool of international peacekeeping deserves a warm acknowledgement.

FURTHER READING

International Institute for Strategic Studies, *Strategic Survey 1988–1989* (Oxford: Brassey's, 1989).

Namibian Independence and Cuban Troop Withdrawal (Pretoria: Department of Foreign Affairs, Republic of South Africa, 1989).

André du Pisani, 'Whither Namibia?', in Dick Clark (ed.), *The Southern Africa Policy Forum* (Queenstown, Md: The Aspen Institute, 1989).

See also the Further Reading for Section J above.

Section L Vietnam's Withdrawal from Cambodia (1989–)

The communist Khmer Rouge regime which in the mid-1970s fought its way to power in Cambodia (also known, successively, as the Khmer Republic and Kampuchea, but now as Cambodia again) proved the most bestial of the post-war period. Estimates of the number of people slaughtered or starved to death vary between one and two million (out of a population of about seven million). When, therefore, neighbouring Vietnam invaded and overthrew the regime at the end of 1978 it might have been thought that few would mourn. But not so. For the Khmer Rouge was supported by China, whereas Vietnam's Great Power friend was the Soviet Union. Furthermore, local anxieties about the traditionally assertive Vietnamese were confirmed by the installation of a puppet government backed by about 200,000 Vietnamese troops. The exiled group was thus able to retain Cambodia's UN seat, and acquired further legitimacy by forming an alliance in 1982 with two non-communist resistance factions.

In 1985 Vietnam said she would withdraw from Cambodia by 1990, but the announcement was greeted with considerable scepticism. However, supporting the Cambodian regime was a considerable economic strain and had produced domestic divisions. The situation was, in fact, becoming Vietnam's Vietnam. The new Gorbachev regime in the Soviet Union also put in its word in favour of healing this running sore. The 1990 deadline was advanced to September 1989, and confirmed in April of that year. That Vietnam was serious was indicated by the fact that she proposed that the withdrawal of what were now said to be about 50,000 troops be supervised by Canada, India, and Poland – the three members of the earlier supervisory missions in Indo-China (see Section D above). The resistance coalition said it preferred the UN. But clearly the point of hard bargaining had been reached (see Map 42).

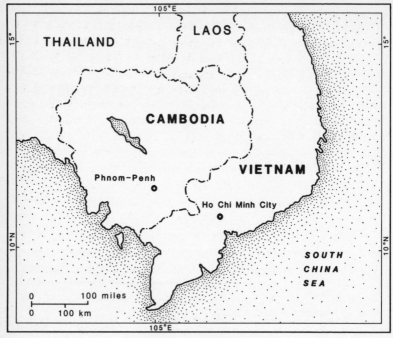

Map 42   Cambodia

At a 19-state international conference on the matter held in Paris in August 1989, which included the five major powers and all the Cambodian factions, it was agreed that a UN mission should go to Cambodia to plan for a possible peacekeeping operation. This was now conceived in relatively substantial terms, as its responsibilities were to include not just watching over the Vietnamese withdrawal but also the supervision of a cease-fire between the warring Cambodian groups and of the elections which would be necessary to legitimize a new government. Consensus was also reached on the addition of Australia, Cuba, and Indonesia to the three states originally proposed by Vietnam as members of the international control body.

But the conference failed. The Cambodian Government, no doubt because it was not allowed to hold the country's UN seat, objected to a peacekeeping role for the world Organization. More substantively, it also refused to contemplate the possibility of including the Khmer Rouge in the transitional government which would prepare for a national election. Clearly, in Cambodia there is a lot of history to overcome before a working compromise can be achieved.

Vietnam, however, kept to her withdrawal timetable, and the media confirmed that the last of her remaining 26,000 troops left Cambodia on the promised date of 26 September. There was still talk of an international mission to verify this, and one report said that the Cambodian Government had agreed to the UN playing such a role. But it had not happened by the end of 1989, and a more extensive peacekeeping operation of the kind which had been envisaged can only be sensibly embarked upon if all the Cambodian groups are willing to cooperate with it. Perhaps after a further period of civil war – which many observers anticipate and seemed actually to be developing in October and November – a more propitious context for peacekeeping will emerge.

Certainly, the deteriorating situation acted as a spur to diplomacy, so that in January 1990 there was much discussion of an ambitious Australian plan under which the UN would administer Cambodia for at least a year. Elections would then be held under its auspices to determine a new government. Japan was willing to consider helping with the huge, in UN terms, costs of such an operation, and in some other respects too the omens were not unfavourable. The United States was said to be reducing her support for the Khmer Rouge, and in the Gorbachev era Vietnam was less convincingly seen as a Soviet satellite. Thus the way was open for China to detach herself somewhat from the resistance coalition, and in mid-January 1990 the Australian plan was endorsed, in principle, by all five permanent members of the UN Security Council. Subsequently, in May, the 'permanent five' envisaged a lesser role for the UN. But ultimately, and as always, everything depends on the local factions, and in June 1990 they could not even agree on who should attend peace talks. It remains to be seen whether they will come to mirror the growing unity of the major powers regarding Cambodia. If they do, peacekeeping arrangements could become an important and even an essential part of the reconciling scene.

FURTHER READING

'Vietnam's September Song', *The Economist* (8 April 1989).
'Back to the battlefield for Cambodia', *The Economist* (2 September 1989).
International Institute for Strategic Studies, *Strategic Survey 1988–1989* (London: IISS, 1989).
John Pedler, 'Cambodia: danger and opportunity for the West', *The World Today*, 45 (2) (February 1989).

Part V
Dangerous Crossroads

Introduction: Controlling the Crossroads

When abroad on the international highway, states sometimes get involved in situations which are of a different order to those in which the principal repercussion is their own embarrassment or that of their friends. Instead, they may find themselves in, or even seek, a major confrontation with a long-standing adversary, or behave in a manner which could have that outcome. It is as if one or both parties were driving recklessly at a crossroads, with all the dangerous consequences which such behaviour can very easily entail. These consequences, moreover, could well involve a much wider company than the initial antagonists. For each of them might have close associates, of whom some, from more motives than one, might involve themselves in this way or that with the fortunes of their friend.

Not very long ago such happenings would have generally been seen as the business only of those states who were directly affected by the affray. If one state wanted or stumbled into war with another, and had not accepted any fetters on its legal freedom so to behave, the affair was regarded as entirely its own concern. If the conflict escalated, that too was just the bad – or possibly good – luck of those who were involved. War for states was a hazard roughly equivalent to the affliction of the individual by taxes – a seemingly inevitable concomitant of life.

The twentieth century, however, has seen a remarkable turnabout in the international aspect of this equation. In the theory of the matter, states are no longer free to threaten or use force against their fellows, so that resort to arms is now always presented in a defensive, or at most a pre-emptive, light. The international society at large is regarded as having a right to interest itself in outbreaks of inter-state violence, and to work for their limitation or conclusion. And since 1945 the development of bipolarity on the one hand and nuclear weapons on the other has resulted in great and understandable anxiety about the escalatory dangers of many conflicts.

Post-Second World War developments have given a further twist to the incidence of escalation and the extent of worries about it. The new norms about proper behaviour and the increasing practical difficulties of the matter have together produced a very marked diminution in

274

the despatch of armies across frontiers with a view to territorial aggrandizement. Deprived of this possible means of adding to their political realms, the superpowers have become even more concerned about the international orientation of third states, and this concern has been heightened by the ideological division of the times. In consequence, when lesser governments have appeared shaky there has sometimes been competitive activity to support or unseat them, or an apprehension about the possibility of such activity. Escalation has therefore sometimes seemed likely to occur not just as a consequence of an initially limited international dispute but also of internal political events which have attracted outside interest.

In the endeavour to control conflicts, and especially to prevent their escalation, use has quite often been made of the device of peacekeeping. And it is no coincidence that nine out of the eleven cases in which such means have found employment have been located in the Middle East. For that area's long historical experience as an important international crossroads has been given an even higher profile by four mid-century developments of a regionally-specific kind: firstly, the withdrawal from the Middle East of France and Britain; secondly, the volatility of many of the successor regimes and the fact that hardly any of them lined up clearly with either East or West; thirdly, the discovery that the region's oil resources were even larger than had been thought, and the financial interest in and economic dependence on them of many Western countries; and fourthly, the bitter Arab–Israeli conflict. When this heady scene is placed in the context of a keen competition between two ideologically-divided and nuclear-armed superpowers, both of whom have throughout shown a lively strategic interest in the affairs of the Middle East, it is not at all surprising that it has been the venue of a number of anti-escalatory operations of a peacekeeping kind.

The first was at a location which, in a very different local context, was to be the scene of much peacekeeping later on: Lebanon (Section B). In 1958, however, the problem arose out of the anxiety of its rightward-moving Government that externally-based left-wing forces were working for its overthrow; the initial sharing of that perception by the United States; and the scepticism of many other states about that analysis. The compromise outcome was the despatch of an observer group to see what was going on. Five years later, and in relation to (now North) Yemen, the first part of this scenario was reversed, and Egypt immediately sent large numers of troops to support the 'progressive' regime against its internal opponents, who were receiving help from Saudi Arabia (Section E). This activity rang many Western alarm bells; a disengagement agreement was negotiated; and a UN group sent to supervise its execution. In the event, however, and for reasons unconnected with the UN's peacekeeping work, it was not executed.

The next three peacekeeping bodies all attempted to defuse dangerous behaviour at the Arab–Israeli crossroads. After the Six Day War of 1967, in which Israel occupied much Arab land, UN Military Observers were posted on three of the four military fronts: on the Israeli–Syrian cease-fire line immediately after the War; on that between Egypt and Israel – which ran along the Suez Canal – shortly afterwards; and on Lebanon's side of her line with Israel in 1972 (Section F). They were all present when the war broke out in October 1973, and in varying ways still operate in these areas.

In the highly dangerous circumstances which developed on the Egyptian–Israeli front at the end of the 1973 War – when a superpower confrontation seemed imminent – first UN observers and then a UN Force were rushed to the scene (Section G). They stayed for six years, witnessing, and assisting in, a remarkable process of reconciliation. On the Israeli–Syrian front, too, UN observation was reinstituted at the end of the War, and in 1974 a stabilizing agreement provided for the despatch of a UN Force, which is still in place (Section H).

In 1975 civil war broke out in Lebanon, which immediately attracted the sharp concern of her two neighbours – Israel and Syria. As these two states composed the bitterest pair of Arab–Israeli enemies, and each had close links with a (different) superpower, the situation had considerable explosive potential. Over the next seven years it attracted no fewer than four operations which, at least at their start, had a peacekeeping character. In 1976 Syria intervened in strength to check the civil war, but had other fish to fry in Lebanon and is still trying to fry them (Section I). The UN sent an 'Interim' Force to south Lebanon in 1978, which is also still there (Section J). In 1982 a non-UN Force supervised the withdrawal of Palestinian fighters from Beirut, where they had been under siege by Israel (Section K). And immediately afterwards another Force of the same type tried to help the Lebanese Government restore its authority in its capital – but a good part of the Force ended up by participating, painfully, on the Governmental side in the resumed civil war (Section L).

Away from the Middle East, the UN deployed its largest-yet peacekeeping force in Congo (now Zaire) in 1960 (Section C). Much of the impetus behind the decision to establish this Force arose out of (arguably ill-founded) fears that the anarchy which existed in Congo might result in the state becoming a cockpit of the Cold War. The Force stayed for four years, arousing great controversy on two quite different counts: its relations with the host Government and its hostile behaviour towards the secessionist province of Katanga.

As well as helping to control incipient dangers at a crossroads, peacekeeping bodies can be used to assist in the winding down of conflicts which have occurred at such locations. Thus at the end of the Korean War of 1950–1953 (in which the UN was for the first, and thus far last, time a traditional combatant – an activity quite different from that which has come to be known as peacekeeping), the Organization was turned to for peacekeeping tasks (Section A). In a very tenuous form it conducts them still. In a rather similar way, the superpower parties to the Cuban Missile Crisis of 1962 looked to the UN to help them conclude the matter (Section D). But to their surprise and annoyance their plans were frustrated by the potential host state's outright refusal to accept the role which had been assigned to it. It was a reminder that while peacekeeping can be very useful, it is often far from popular with those who are, in a sense, on its receiving end.

Section A The Winding Down of the Korean War (1953–)

Following the 1950 attack by communist North Korea on the western-oriented South, a multinational (but chiefly American) UN army fought on the latter's behalf until an Armistice was agreed in July 1953. The boycott by the Soviet Union of the Security Council over the occupancy of China's seat by that state's Nationalist exiles, together with the dominance in the Organization of the United States and her associates, had enabled the West to use the UN for its own purposes. From one point of view the UN was keeping the peace. But the Organization's armed support of one side in this limited inter-bloc struggle meant that its activity was very far from what not long afterwards was to become known as peacekeeping.

Once an armistice was in sight, however, and with a view to improving the safety of this East–West crossroads, the way was, in principle, open for the use of the impartial and non-forceful mechanisms of peacekeeping. Two such bodies were set up by the Armistice Agreement, both based at Panmunjom. One was the Military Armistice Commission (MAC), composed of five officers from the UN Command (which included the United States and South Korea) and five from North Korea and China (who had intervened in support of the North Koreans), with a number of joint observer teams operating under its direction. The MAC's operational task was to preserve the integrity of the demilitarized zone which the Armistice had set up between the two sides. It was to do this by patrolling the zone's boundaries, investigating, at the request of either party, incidents whch occurred within the zone, and trying to settle any problems which arose regarding it. The fact that this stabilizing activity was to be done by the parties themselves might, on the face of it, seem unusual as peacekeeping is associated with the idea of third-party assistance. But erstwhile enemies have not infrequently established mixed commissions, for a variety of purposes. There is no

279

reason why, in appropriate circumstances, peacekeeping should not be one of them (see Map 43).

In Korea, however, the two sides remained so bitterly opposed to each other that there was little scope for the smooth operation of a peacekeeping mission. But its mere establishment probably helped in the achievement of the Armistice, and the MAC scheme did work after a fashion – reflecting the fact that both sides had an interest in the maintenance of the status quo. However, each side made, and continues to make, thousands of complaints each year about the other's alleged infringement of the demilitarized zone, and since 1967 North Korea has been uncooperative regarding requests for the use of joint observation teams. Moreover, each side sees the other as using the meetings of the MAC for the dissemination of propaganda rather than for serious business. But the fact that the MAC meets at all – in the late 1980s usually between two and four times a year at full level – is probably a useful safety valve, as well as being indicative of each side's continuing stake in the maintenance of the demilitarized zone and of overall

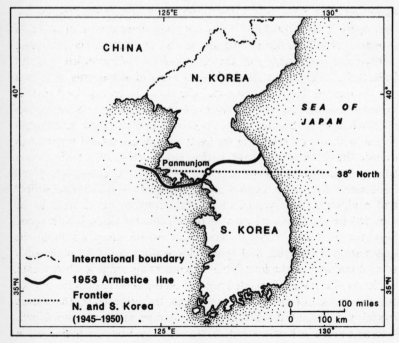

Map 43   Divided Korea

stability. Lower-level MAC meetings are also held from time to time, often to helpful effect. Five such meetings were held during 1988. Thus the MAC continues to have some defusing and stabilizing value in this tense situation, not least because it is the only official means of communication between the opposing military commanders.

Although South Korea is now backed on the ground only by United States forces, the Western side of the MAC is still, to the great annoyance of North Korea, called the UN Command. Fifteen other states fought in Korea on the Southern side, and this, too, continues to find expression in the MAC structure. Thus Canada, Philippines, and Thailand serve on the MAC on a rotational basis, together with two representatives from South Korea, one from the United States, and one from the United Kingdom. Britain's representative, a brigadier who is also the Defence Attaché at her Embassy to South Korea, acts for the other Commonwealth states who participated in the war – except, of course, that Canada acts in her own right when sitting on the MAC. The UK also provides the UN Command with an honour guard in the shape of a platoon of Gurkhas.

The other peacekeeping body which was set up by the Korean Armistice – the Neutral Nations Supervisory Commission (NNSC) – was, operationally speaking, never anything more than a charade. It consisted of officers from four states, the UN Command choosing Sweden and Switzerland and the communist side Czechoslovakia and Poland. Its task was to check that the level of armaments in Korea was not increased beyond that which existed at the time of the Amistice. Towards this end the NNSC was to establish 20 inspection teams, half of which were to be located at specified ports in North and South Korea, with the others being on hand to conduct special inspections outside the demilitarized zone at the request either of the MAC as a whole or of one of its sides. The NNSC was also to receive full information from each side on all replacements of military personnel and equipment. Any violations of the Armistice terms were to be reported to the MAC, which was responsible for dealing with them. However, the NNSC could do no more than ask questions about the information it received, and special inspections could be made only when a majority of the four NNSC members agreed to such requests.

Clearly, this system depended not just on the good faith of the parties but also on that of the NNSC's members. In both respects there were crucial and blatant shortcomings. In no time at all the five North Korean ports at which the NNSC was stationed were experiencing a mysterious lack of business, and the NNSC's Czech and Polish members usually thought the UN Command's requests for special inspections unworthy of acceptance. The North Korean armed forces also seemed to require remarkably little replenishment. In South Korea, by contrast, the NNSC was generally kept extremely busy. Charges and counter-charges followed, both within and outside the NNSC, and already in April 1954 the Swedish and Swiss delegates to the NNSC were suggesting that it be wound up. Early in 1955 the United States was agreeing with them. The NNSC members did not incur any additional expense through their participation, as the extra costs of the operation were the responsibility of the former belligerents. But much time and effort was being wasted, and only the communist delegations seemed satisfied with the position.

The outcome was that first the NNSC's strength was reduced. Then, in 1956, the UN Command suspended the activity of the remaining fixed teams in the South. In response, the NNSC withdrew all fixed teams, and the whole of its operational work came to a halt. Thus all that remained was a small group at its headquarters. In 1957 the United States, as the head of the UN Command, formally announced that it would no longer be bound by the Armistice provisions regarding the level of armaments in South Korea. A token NNSC group still sits at its headquarters, and holds weekly meetings, but has no substantive business. However, as an indirect means of communication between the two opposing sides, it is a useful supplement to the MAC. And it is, perhaps, an additional stabilizing influence. Like the MAC, therefore, the NNSC retains some vestigial peacekeeping functions.

In one sense the NNSC and the MAC were casualties of the Cold War. But in another sense they were not even that. For it is exceedingly unlikely that either side expected the scheme to work in the manner which was set out in the Armistice. The idea that the scene of a major East–West conflict which was superimposed on a particularly bitter local confrontation could be turned, cooperatively, into a relatively calm backwater was hardly realistic, especially at the height of the Cold War. It is very possible that the NNSC was seen as having some negative value, in that its failure would provide a credible ground – very necessary in the West – for the open rearmament of the two Koreas. But that was not a peacekeeping function.

There was, however, a very important way in which the NNSC certainly fulfilled one of the functions of peacekeeping. Korea was an East–West crossroads at which serious casualties were being incurred; the possibility of escalation could not be ruled out; and the conflict was also becoming a liability in the context of American politics. The

United States therefore wanted to 'bring the boys home' (or most of them), but the cessation of hostilities had to be on respectable terms. This requirement was met by providing for the stabilization of arms levels throughout Korea and for verification machinery of a superficially impartial and effective kind. These arrangements also appealed to the other side. The NNSC therefore supplied the parties, and particularly the West, with an acceptable basis on which the crisis could be defused from war to one of armed confrontation. This was no mean service.

FURTHER READING

Jacques Freymond, 'Supervising Agreements: The Korean Experience', *Foreign Affairs*, XXXVII (3) (April 1959).

Gene M. Lyons, *Military Policy and Economic Aid: The Korean Case, 1950–1953* (Columbus, Ohio: Ohio State University Press, 1961).

David W. Wainhouse *et al.*, *International Peace Observation* (Baltimore, Md: Johns Hopkins Press, 1966).

Section B The Flurry over Lebanon (1958)

THE HEART OF THE PROBLEM

Lebanon became a sovereign state in 1944 in the territorial shape which had been determined 20 years earlier by her overlord of the time, France. The boundaries which had then been drawn can now be seen as a major source of the state's current distress. For what France did, as the power also in control of the neighbouring territory to the east (Syria), was to enlarge the area which had traditionally been known as Lebanon so as to make it a more economically viable unit. This created a state in which the Christians of Mount Lebanon were joined by large numbers of Muslims – but care was taken to ensure that the Christians, who had long looked to France for protection, would be the majority group within the new boundaries. A census taken in 1932 – which, for political reasons, has never been updated – confirmed this by showing that the state contained six Christians for every five Muslims (with many sub-divisions on each side) (see Map 44).

Although, therefore, Lebanon was unquestionably Arab, it was a very special kind of Arab state, and it was recognized that with the coming of independence special measures would be necessary to safeguard its stability. This led to an unwritten National Covenant of 1943, in which it was agreed that the Christians would no longer bolster their internal position by appealing to France or any other Western country, and that the Muslims would not attempt to unite Lebanon with Syria or any other Arab state. It was also understood that while Lebanon would be a cooperative member of the Arab family, she would not take part in any of its quarrels. Furthermore, the President, who was the head of government as well as the head of state, was always to be a Maronite Christian (as was the head of the Army), the Prime Minister a Sunni Muslim, and the President of Parliament a Shia Muslim. Parliamentary elections were to be held in such a way as to ensure that six Christians were returned for every five Muslims. By these means it was hoped to satisfy all parties to the delicate internal distribution of power, and so provide a sufficient basis for a stable and prosperous national existence.

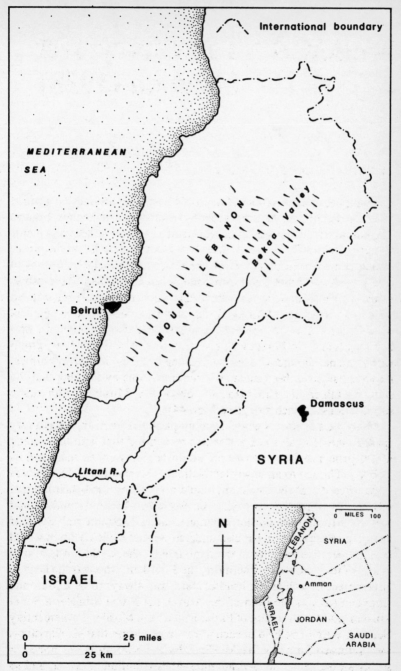

Map 44   Lebanon

It was later to become painfully clear that this scheme failed to take account not only of possible changes in the overall religious distribution of the population but also of the fact that beneath the surface of the state there was a veritable mosaic of powerful religious and political groups. Their members bore to each of them an allegiance which overrode any other, and as a result the foundation on which the state was built was dangerously flawed. But it was some time before Lebanon encountered the sort of challenge which was calculated to expose the rickety composition of her societal base. Meanwhile, in the early post-war years, and on the carefully-observed basis of the National Covenant, the state flourished.

But in 1958 there was a significant upset. Under President Chamoun the state had begun markedly to incline towards both the West and the monarchical Arab states who were opposed to the thrusting and controversial line being taken by Egypt's President Nasser. Lebanon's Muslim subjects, however, saw Nasserism more as something to be applauded than as a threat. The Christians in Lebanon, while sharing Chamoun's apprehension about militant Arab nationalism, were less than enthusiastic about some of his internal policies. Two matters drew this festering situation towards a crisis. One was the announcement, on 1 February 1958, that the two states of Egypt and Syria had merged into one – the United Arab Republic (UAR), with Nasser in command. This caused Chamoun great alarm. Secondly, at about the same time rumours began to spread that Chamoun was planning to amend the constitution to open the way to his re-election for a further six-year presidential term.

Early in May fighting broke out following the murder of a newspaper editor, and quickly spread. Just as quickly it was attributed by the Government to interference in Lebanon's affairs by the UAR, and complaints to this effect were lodged with both the Arab League and the UN. The League's conciliatory proposal was rejected by Chamoun and so he got what he seemed to want – a chance to air the matter at the UN, which at this time was Western-dominated. For this reason the Soviet Union wanted the UN to have nothing to do with the matter, but she was reluctant to veto a proposal in the Security Council for fear that the General Assembly would be more compliant. Chamoun, on the other hand, wanted a strong international presence which, directly or indirectly, would support his regime. The United States endorsed this approach, seeing the matter not just in terms of a threat to a friend but also as reflecting the subversive hand of international communism. However, too strong a proposal might have been difficult to sell, quite apart from the problem of a Soviet veto.

The way was therefore open for the compromise proposal that the UN should send an observer group to see what was really going on although, rather contradictatorily, the draft resolution also required the group to 'ensure' that there was no illegal infiltration of men or arms across Lebanon's borders. As Lebanon and the UAR found this acceptable, the Soviet Union did not veto it. Thus, on 11 June, the UN Observation Group in Lebanon (Unogil) was established. There was some uncertainty about the condition of the crossroads to which it was being sent, but some, at least, were convinced that a potentially-dangerous international conflict was in progress.

At Unogil's head was a three-man political–military team, under whom about 100 military observers from 21 states were quickly gathered. Unogil was also supplied with an air unit. Some observation posts were established, ground patrols instituted, and aerial reconnaissance begun. However, the long and rugged Lebanese frontier with Syria was controlled by rebel elements, and initially Unogil was prevented from entering the area or admitted in such a way as to minimize the value of its work. These and other problems were referred to in its first report, made at the beginning of July, which also said that it had not been possible to establish whether the rebels who had been observed had come from Syria. Nevertheless the Group felt justified in asserting that there was very little doubt that the majority of those actively opposing the Government were Lebanese.

This infuriated the Government, and some Western states also thought that more was going on than Unogil had seen, or allowed itself to see. Chamoun, however was comforted by United States' assurances that if the UN was unable to protect his regime she would do so. On 14 July it was decided that the hour for American intervention had come, for on that day the monarchy was overthrown in Iraq. The United States feared that this would set off a chain reaction against Western-oriented states in the Middle East, and that with Nasser's ready cooperation Soviet adventurism would be encouraged in the region, and maybe beyond. Over the next few days, therefore, 14,000 American troops landed in Lebanon and the entire Sixth Fleet, consisting of about 70 ships, was moved to the eastern Mediterranean.

At exactly this time, Unogil reported that, by agreement with the rebels, it would now have full and free access to all parts of the frontier with Syria. To take advantage of this situation it suggested that its existing strength of about 200 be increased, and in the Security Council the United States proposed that the Group be upgraded from an observer mission to a force. However, as the Soviet Union could not persuade the Council to call for the withdrawal of the United States from Lebanon, she vetoed this and all other proposals regarding Unogil.

As it happened, however, the crisis had exploded only to evaporate. The despatch of a senior American official to Lebanon in the wake of the troop landing resulted in a revision of the United States' interpretation of the situation. Now it was seen as a conflict which arose out of domestic rivalries and personality clashes, and subsequent developments in Lebanon were seen in that light. Talk of UAR infiltration and of the threat of Nasserism and communism was put on one side. The immediate internal problem in Lebanon also subsided. Although Chamoun had some time earlier said that he would not try to amend the Constitution, his ambitions could not be discounted until a successor had been chosen. With American assistance, a widely-acceptable candidate emerged – the Army Commander, General Chehab. He was prevailed upon to let his name go forward; was elected on 31 July; and although some tension remained, this brought the crisis to an effective end.

The issue which remained was the honourable extrication of the American troops. They had had difficulty in finding a role, and had agreed to a Unogil request that they stay in the camps which they had established near their landing places. The UN General Assembly, to which the problem of Lebanon had been passed, approached the matter on the assumption that there was still a difficulty which needed international treatment, and that the remedy was the replacement of the United States by the UN. After a leisurely debate it succeeded on 21 August in unanimously passing a resolution which embodied this bizarre idea. Thus, at a time when it was least necessary, and with the enthusiastic involvement of the Secretary-General, Unogil was rapidly increased in size, reaching a strength of 591 by mid-November. By this time the last of the American troops had already been withdrawn, so Unogil was immediately disbanded, the last of its personnel leaving Lebanon on 9 December.

It is very doubtful if the position on the ground in Lebanon in 1958 ever justified much international concern, let alone action. But the Western alliance, and particularly its superpower leader, did not at first see things that way. In consequence, the despatch of a peacekeeping mission served three stabilizing and resolving purposes. Firstly, it enabled the United States to postpone intervening for a while. Secondly,

Unogil's presence when intervention in fact took place discouraged the United States from rushing into what could have been provocative action inside Lebanon. Finally, when the United States realized that she had no good reason for being in Lebanon, Unogil's presence facilitated her withdrawal. It was all a rather crazy situation. But that did not prevent it from also carrying danger, and in that context the device of international peacekeeping was very useful.

JORDAN

King Hussein of Jordan ascended to his country's throne in 1952 at the age of only 17 and in very inauspicious circumstances. Throughout his still on-going reign confident forecasts of his early and violent overthrow have been made on numerous occasions. One such occasion was the Iraqi coup of July 1958. The King appealed to Britain – who had ruled the territory in the inter-war period – for help, and about 3,000 troops were quickly forthcoming. Like the American action in Lebanon, the move was intended to calm jittery nerves in a conservative sector of the Arab world, and warn the progressive forces that any attempt to repeat what was seen as their Iraqi success would be sternly rebuffed. In accordance with the tenor of the times, Britain said she would be delighted if the UN would relieve her of the responsibility she had felt obliged to undertake. And as the situation in the Middle East was quickly perceived to have calmed down, it did look as if some cosmetic arrangement to this effect would easily open the way to a British withdrawal.

This, however, was to reckon without Jordanian sensitivities about playing host to international peacekeepers, which may have been encouraged by UAR opposition to the idea. Neither a force, nor even an observer group, was acceptable. At most, Jordan was prepared to admit a sort of UN listening post, and this was the solution which was eventually found, easing the speedy withdrawal of the British force. A Special Representative of the UN Secretary-General was to be stationed in Jordan, and although he was soon noticeable much more for his absence than his presence, his mission remained formally in existence until the end of 1967. The episode was a reminder that although peacekeepers can be very useful, it does not follow that they are always welcome. Only if a state is in a very tight corner indeed is it usually agreeable to the idea that foreign military men should operate on its soil.

FURTHER READING

Gerald L. Curtis, 'The UN Observation Group in Lebanon', *International Organization*, XVIII (4) (Autumn 1964).

Rajeshwar Dayal, 'The 1958 Crisis in the Lebanon – the Role of the UN and the Great Powers', *India Quarterly*, 26 (April–June 1970).

Alan Dowty, *Middle East Crisis* (Berkeley, Calif: University of California Press, 1984).

Malcolm Kerr, 'The Lebanese Civil War', in Evan Luard (ed.), *The International Regulation of Civil Wars* (London: Thames & Hudson, 1972).

Robert Murphy, *Diplomat among Warriors* (London: Collins, 1964).

Brian Urquhart, *Hammarskjöld* (London: Bodley Head, 1972).

Section C The Congo Crisis (1960–1964)

BELGIAN INTERVENTION

Throughout virtually all of the 1950s the colonial powers took what then seemed a justifiably measured approach to the question of withdrawal from their African possessions, and Belgium's attitude was amongst the most leisurely. She had ruled the vast territory of the Congo (approximately the same size as West Europe) in a concerned but markedly paternalistic way, making no arrangements even for it to begin to stand on its own feet. Then, however, with Algeria providing an ominous example of what delay could mean, France began a sudden and wholesale retreat from Africa, and Britain looked as if she might stumblingly follow suit. In this atmosphere, Belgium changed her tune in a truly precipitous manner. In January 1960 she opened a conference with Congolese leaders with what for her was a dramatic proposal: independence in four years. She came out of the conference having agreed to independence in five months, on 30 June.

The deadline was met. However, not a week had elapsed before the new state was displaying its deficiencies. Soldiers of the National Army mutinied against their Belgian officers, and this began a quickly-spreading and violent disorder. Belgium tried to persuade Congo to let her use her locally-based troops to restore order, and in particular to protect the 100,000 Belgians who lived in the country, but without success. On 10 July she therefore took the matter into her own hands, beginning a series of interventions in various parts of Congo. As a result the Congolese Government sought international help, appealing first to the United States (who hastily declined) and then to the United Nations.

It was a request which by its very nature attracted much general support, including that of the two superpowers, each of whom was jousting for the friendship of this strategically-important new state. Moreover, at this time, under the enthusiastic Secretary-Generalship of Dag Hammarskjöld, the idea of a peacekeeping role for the UN was widely welcomed – although its implications were less than fully understood. The Security Council therefore had no difficulty in agreeing on 14 July that the UN should provide Congo with military assistance until her national security force was able to cope (although Britain and France abstained because the resolution made an unqualified call for Belgium's withdrawal). However, in an accompanying report it was stated very firmly that the UN Force was neither to become a party to any internal dispute nor to resort to force except in self-defence.

In this way the UN began what has, to date, been its largest peacekeeping operation – known, following its French acronym, as Onuc (Opération des Nations Unies au Congo). Within a week about 3,500 troops had arrived; by the end of 1960 they were five times that number; and at its numerical height in mid-1961 the Force was about 20,000 strong. During 1963 it was quickly run down in size, and withdrawn at the end of June 1964. By this time no fewer than 39 states had contributed military personnel, 17 of them – mostly African – supplying infantry battalions. None of the Security Council's permanent members were looked to for military help, but Britain, the Soviet Union, and – far and away the most important – the United States helped with

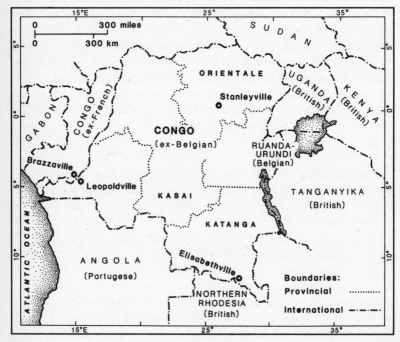

Map 45   Congo (1960)

the transport of troops, supplies, and equipment. The United States also bore a large part of the total cost. However, some other states – notably France and the Soviet Union – refused to pay their share. This meant that the grave political controversy to which the Operation gave rise was accompanied by a mounting financial crisis, which reached its peak shortly after the Force had been withdrawn. Together, these considerations resulted in the Operation becoming a watershed in the history of UN peacekeeping (see Map 45).

INTERNATIONAL DANGERS

Onuc's job was to help in the restoration of law and order – no mean task given the chaos which had engulfed Congo. The justification for the UN involving itself in this domestic matter was twofold. Firstly, even if Congo's charge of Belgian agression was denied, as it generally was in the West, there was no gainsaying the fact that the situation had been given an international dimension by Belgium's intervention. The arrival of a UN Force was therefore intended to defuse this aspect of the crisis, and it succeeded in doing so. As new contingents of UN troops arrived, they were deployed in areas occupied by Belgium, and negotiations were then held about the latter's early withdrawal. Such discussions went smoothly, and by the first week of September all regular Belgian troops had left Congo. Furthermore, all Belgian officers who had been attached to the Congolese Army had also been withdrawn by this date, save for those employed in the gendarmerie of what was now the secessionist Congolese province of Katanga.

The second justification for the mounting of a UN Force arose out of the Western perception that there was a likelihood of the Soviet Union becoming directly involved in Congo unless that country's disorder was speedily remedied. For on the one hand there was evidence that Congo herself was not averse to the issue of an invitation to the Soviets. Within a few days of the decision to establish Onuc, Congo threatened to ask for Soviet help unless the UN moved more firmly against Belgium. On the other hand, the Soviet Union said she was ready to supply the Government with lorries and transport planes, and in August she immediately responded to a request for the implementation of this offer, also providing the necessary technical staff. This was very far from direct involvement. But in the tense Cold War context of the time, with anxious talk of local conflicts escalating dangerously, it was easy for Western spokesmen to picture the Soviet Union as wanting to bring the East–West conflict to the heart of Africa, and it does seem that in official Western circles this was not all rhetoric.

A less dramatic appraisal, however, would have been more realistic. Without doubt, the Soviet Union would have been pleased to see the emergence of a Congolese regime sympathetic, or more, to the Communist bloc. But there was no evidence that, towards this end, she was contemplating military involvement in Congo, let alone hungering for it. That country was 5,000 miles away, had no sea coast or ports to speak of, and was surrounded by countries at least cool if not hostile to communism. Even obtaining access would therefore have presented formidable problems, and the supply and defence of a Soviet force would have been even more difficult given the likelihood of spoiling measures from the far better-placed United States. Moreover, there was no Congolese communist party, and its political elite could not be counted on for support. It was true that Congo's Prime Minister, Patrice Lumumba, was markedly of the left, but his chameleon-like nature detracted from his appeal as a potential ally. It was also the case that substantial intervention might not have easily been sold within the Soviet leadership, and probably would have found a sluggish market among the uncommitted states of Asia and Africa. While, therefore, Onuc's presence was doubtless a discouragement to adventurous behaviour, there was in any event little chance that the Soviet Union would have climbed out on this weak Congolese limb after an elusive prize of uncertain value.

Be that as it may, at least for the first six months of its life, and perhaps for its first year, Onuc was seen by the West as a very useful stabilizing agency at a potentially dangerous international crossroads. And even thereafter, on the basis that risks are better avoided, its value in this respect continued. For it provided some kind of bulwark against the contingency that some undesirable party might try to help in the restoration of order in Congo – for in that respect the UN Force had certainly been unable to work any immediate wonders.

LAW AND ORDER

The collapse of internal security in the new state and the consequential breakdown of public services reflected not just a lack of administrative training and experience but also the fractured social base on which Congo had been erected. There was no overriding sense of loyalty of the state. This, together with greed and some outside encouragement, accounts for the declared secession of Katanga, Congo's richest province, little more than a week after independence. A month later, and chiefly for tribal reasons, South Kasai did likewise. Meanwhile, Onuc was doing what it could to maintain order and to protect lives and property, but found itself harassed rather than helped by the Government. However, tribal and ideological factors were bringing the Government itself to the point of disintegration. On 5 September the President announced the deposition of the Prime Minister and the latter immediately responded in kind. Fearing even deeper disorder, Onuc closed the airport and radio station in the capital, Leopoldville.

As it happened, these actions worked very much in favour of the locally-based President, as he had no need to fly in extra supporters. The Prime Minister's base, by contrast, was in the distant province of Orientale. Furthermore, the President was able to obtain publicity for his case over the radio of the geographically and tribally contiguous foreign city of Brazzaville, capital of (ex-French) Congo. This led some to charge, expressed with particular venom by the Soviet Union, that the UN Secretariat had acted with the deliberate intent of ousting Lumumba, who had certainly caused the UN much frustration. But it does not necessarily follow, and probably does not in this case, that an act which favours one party was done with that intent: neutral acts can in all walks of life have unneutral consequences. A week later, in support of the President, the Congolese Army under Joseph Mobutu assumed power – with, it is often said, the encouragement and aid of the United States. The Army immediately ordered the closing of communist embassies in Leopoldville, so that the Soviets and their friends had hurriedly to depart.

For the next year Congo was without a government which was lawful in terms of the country's own constitution, and Lumumba's own province of Orientale, under his leading lieutenant, declared its secession. But on the ground it all made little difference, and for the Congolese life remained very uncertain and hazardous. Onuc continued to do what it could to help them by arranging cease-fires, neutral zones, and protected areas. But it was unable to protect Lumumba once he had left his house. He was arrested in the capital by the Government, handed over to his enemies in Katanga, and killed. This provoked the Security Council to pass a resolution in February 1961 authorizing Onuc to use force, as a last resort, to prevent civil war. But some states were withdrawing their contingents from the Force, out of dissatisfaction with the course of events in Congo or for other reasons. And the Council's resolution was viewed with considerable suspicion in Congo,

where the Government feared that it might presage an attempt by the
UN to take control of the country. A Conciliation Commission sent by
the UN General Assembly to Congo had also been ill received. However,
Onuc itself, in a low-key way, encouraged political reconciliation. With
its assistance a meeting of the Congolese Parliament was held, and out
of this a formally legitimate Government, termed one of national unity,
emerged in August 1961. It was led by a moderate who was sympathetic
to the West, and American persuasion, and money, was again said to
have been involved. This development led to cooperation between the
UN and the Government against the chief secessionist province of
Katanga.

KATANGA

The UN's efforts to maintain order were undoubtedly of great value
to many individual Congolese. (Furthermore, Onuc's civilian operations,
by providing a wide range of technical assistance, were helping to build
the infrastructure of the Congolese state.) But especially once the regular
Belgian forces had gone, and the perception of a Soviet threat had
subsided, it was hard to see an international political aspect to the
ongoing Congolese disorder. However, there was a keen desire on the
part of the UN's members to see a restoration of Congolese unity: the
principle of territorial integrity was one to which all states subscribed,
virtually by definition; a number of states found this concern sharpened
by their own internal fragility; the East and the neutralists were also
fired by the perception of 'neo-colonialist' hands behind Katanga's
relatively secure and prosperous de facto independence; and the West
was anxious to bolster the moderate central Government which had
emerged in August 1961. In Onuc a possible means of securing this
common goal was at hand.

It could hardly be said, however, that the legitimacy of the new
Government was generally acknowledged throughout Congo, as the
country was still plagued by serious internal disputes. This meant that
if Onuc helped the Government to assert its authority the UN would
not just be dealing with the sort of minor problems which come the
way of many governments but would be taking sides in a major domestic
conflict. There was also the consideration that such assistance would
almost certainly involve the positive use of force. This would be a double
departure from the basic values of peacekeeping, adherence to which
had been emphasized at the outset of the operation. It emerged, however,

and unsurprisingly, that the UN's member states were more interested in achieving their political goals than in adhering to the principles which had been enunciated in July 1960.

Things started cautiously, with the UN attempting at the end of August 1961 to expel all non-Congolese officers and mercenaries serving with the Katangan forces. Arrests were made without serious incident, but Onuc then agreed to suspend its activity so that the repatriation process could be continued voluntarily. However, this resulted in the operation losing its momentum and efficiency. Two weeks later, therefore, the UN troops in Katanga resumed their direct approach, and also armed themselves with warrants for the arrest of all the leading Katangan ministers. How far this move was endorsed at the top of the UN Secretariat, both in Congo and in New York, is unclear. In any event, it misfired, and fighting broke out. This produced strong criticism from a number of Western countries and led the UN Secretary-General to seek cease-fire talks. On his way to the venue for them in Northern Rhodesia (now Zambia) he was killed in an air crash.

His successor, U Thant, had fewer scruples about modifying the basis on which the Congo operation had been initiated. Moreover, international animosity towards Katanga was building up, evidenced by a Security Council resolution in November 1961 which condemned its secession and authorized the use of force to remove its foreign supporters. Skirmishing between its forces and Onuc led to larger-scale fighting in December, which ended with a renunciation of secession by Katanga's leader, Moise Tshombe. Shortly afterwards the Congolese Army, with some UN help, also brought the secession of Orientale Province to an end. Tshombe, however, announced that his agreement had to be ratified by the Katangan Parliament, and this led to a year-long stalemate. Thant introduced talk of economic sanctions, and, with American encouragement and Indian cooperation, strengthened the UN Force, the bulk of which was now deployed in Katanga. At the end of December 1962 fighting broke out once more, and this time Onuc did not stop until Tshombe had capitulated unconditionally. The secessionist regime had finally been brought down. The UN Force, greatly reduced in size, stayed on for a further 18 months but effectively its task had ended.

CONSEQUENCES

The UN's main achievement in Congo is usually seen as the holding together of the fragile Congolese state. This had not, however, been the intent with which Onuc had been established. There is no reason in principle why the purpose of an operation should not be changed with changing circumstances. But in this case the new functions assumed by Onuc bore little if any relationship to the calming or resolution of international difficulties, and their execution took the Force well beyond the distinctive ambit of what had come to be known as peacekeeping. It was an instance of the application to international relations of the thin-end-of-the-wedge phenomenon, and gave rise to much concern in West European circles. For the UN was seen as taking a cavalier attitude to an island of order just because those who controlled it happened to be widely unpopular.

Other groups of states were highly critical of earlier aspects of the operation. The Eastern bloc, for example, saw the deposition of Prime Minister Lumumba in September 1960 as the result of the UN Force being manipulated by the Western-oriented Secretariat. This coloured the Soviet approach to the use of peacekeeping troops in an internal context for at least a generation. Lumumba's ousting and his subsequent death was also sometimes viewed as a cautionary tale by leaders of states who found themselves considering whether to invite a UN peacekeeping force on to their soil. Furthermore, Onuc's role throughout its first year led to a lively apprehension, particularly in Africa, that UN peacekeeping forces could become overbearing guests. Signs of this distrust are still visible. And in many parts of the world the Congo operation was widely and unhappily pictured as a tool of United States' foreign policy.

One outcome of this dissatisfaction was a financial problem which has haunted UN peacekeeping ever since. Another was that in respect of future UN peacekeeping operations the role of the Secretary-General was much more circumscribed. A third was that all subsequent UN forces were put on a very short leash, in the sense that they were given a mandate which lasted, generally, only for a matter of months. This meant that the mandate had periodically to be renewed by the Security Council, which gave any of the Council's permanent members the opportunity to veto its extension. In theory, such an act could be circumvented by the UN General Assembly, but as a practical matter that was not likely.

A less precise but nonetheless important spillover effect of the UN's Congo operation was that it led many states to take a very hesitant approach towards the idea that the Organization should assume peacekeeping responsibilities of a law and order kind. The UN Secretariat also became very cautious about encouraging suggestions to that effect. This was very understandable. In such circumstances it can be enormously hard to give a force anything like a precise mandate. The situation to which it is despatched may well be fluid, so compounding the problem of how the force should react. And whatever it does it has a good change of running into controversy, in the shape of a vociferous domestic constituency taking offence at the behaviour of the force, and securing international backing for its complaint. Moreover, the withdrawal of a peacekeeping force which has met problems of this sort is by no means an uncomplicated matter. How much more straightforward is the task of a force which patrols a frontier area with the full cooperation of the states on both sides.

Nonetheless, domestic difficulties can have a very direct bearing on international tension, and it is unlikely that such situations will diminish in number. Quite the contrary. Accordingly, it is important that the very idiosyncratic condition of Congo (now Zaire) in the early 1960s should be clearly recognized: internally it was anarchical to an unusual degree; the amount of external controversy it aroused was equally high; and the UN was still feeling its way in the development of guidelines for its peacekeeping work. It is improbable that other internal situations which have international ramifications will generally present as difficult a combination of problems. Accordingly, they should not be seen as necessarily unsuitable for peacekeeping. Of course, the activity can always be abused through an abandonment by those in charge or on the spot of its basic values. But that is quite another matter.

FURTHER READING

Georges Abi-Saab, *The United Nations Operation in the Congo, 1960–1964* (Oxford: Oxford University Press, 1978).

D. N. Chatterjee, *Storm over the Congo* (New Delhi: Vikas, 1980).

Rajeshwar Dayal, *Mission for Hammarskjöld* (London: Oxford University Press, 1976).

Sarvepalli Gopal, *Jawaharlal Nehru: A Biography, Volume III* (London: Cape, 1984).

C. S. Jha, *From Bandung to Tashkent* (London: Sangam, 1983).

Ernest W. Lefever, *Uncertain Mandate* (Baltimore, Md: Johns Hopkins University Press, 1967).

Conor Cruise O'Brien, *To Katanga and Back* (London: Hutchinson, 1962).

K. P. Saksena, *The United Nations and Collective Security* (Delhi: D. K. Publications, 1974).

Stephen R. Weissman, *American Foreign Policy in the Congo, 1960–1964* (Ithaca, NY: Cornell University Press, 1974).

Section D The Cuban Missile Crisis (1962)

At the end of October 1962 the world's two superpowers engaged in a brief 'eyeball-to-eyeball' confrontation following the United States' discovery that the Soviet Union was in the process of installing nuclear-headed missiles in Cuba. The crisis was brought to an immediate end when the United States agreed to call off her naval quarantine of the island provided that the missiles were removed under UN supervision, and the Soviets assented to these terms. Plans were immediately put in motion at the UN for an observer team of between 40 and 50 officers drawn from neutral states, and the Secretary-General set off for Cuba to make the necessary arrangements. But on the next day he returned empty handed, Cuba having flatly refused to go along with the proposed scheme. This also meant the end of another idea, which would have led to the UN's aerial inspection of the island, using American planes (the markings of which had already been changed to those of the UN) and Canadian pilots. Like Egypt in 1956 and not entirely unlike India's later behaviour in 1965, Cuba was making up for the blow to her pride by being awkward about the UN's proposed peacekeeping involvement in the ending of the dispute (see Map 46).

The Soviet Union having failed to change her friend's mind, it was next suggested that the International Committee of the Red Cross should undertake the necessary inspection of the missile sites, but Cuba would have none of it. The same body was then advanced as a potential inspector on the high seas of ships going from and to Cuba, and the Cubans found the latter part of this idea acceptable. But this was to reckon without the Red Cross, which was troubled by the possibility that such work would compromise its standing as a purely humanitarian body. Eventually it agreed to provide about 30 inspectors, envisaging that they should be recruited from Switzerland's Army, but by then it was too late. For the superpowers had meanwhile settled on the necessary inspection being done by the United States, her warships drawing alongside departing Soviet ships and American helicopters keeping a close eye on the process from the air. So far as checking on

Map 46 Cuba

the missile sites was concerned, the United States simply announced that she would engage in the necessary aerial reconnaissance.

This episode was a sharp reminder of two important, and connected, matters. The first was that in a world of sovereign states the consent of the host state to a peacekeeping operation cannot be taken for granted. The second was that from the potential host's point of view peacekeeping is not an activity which is likely to receive an unqualified welcome. Its acceptance may be necessary to get out of a political jam, but even so it is always wise for those advocating such a scheme to take full account of the sensitivies of the intended host. The failure to do so in this case meant that, unusually, one of the principals found herself also playing a peacekeeping role.

FURTHER READING

James G. Blight and David A. Welch, *On the Brink* (New York: Hill and Wang, 1989).
Robert Kennedy, *13 Days* (London: Macmillan, 1969).
Theodore C. Sorensen, *Kennedy* (London: Hodder and Stoughton, 1965).
U. Thant, *View from the UN* (Newton Abbot: David and Charles, 1978).

Section E Egypt's Intervention in Yemen (1963–1964)

In September 1962 the traditional royalist regime in Yemen was overturned by republicans, but incompletely so. A civil war thereupon developed, which had threatening international links. For neighbouring Saudi Arabia was a source of both official and unofficial support for the royalists, whereas Egypt (then officially known as the United Arab Republic, UAR) immediately extended both diplomatic and military succour to the republicans. This involvement of the leading conservative and progressive states in the Arab world could conceivably have had even wider repercussions, as Saudi Arabia and Egypt were closely connected to the United States and the Soviet Union respectively. However, the United States, besides wanting to restore stability in this oil-rich part of the world, was at this time anxious to build up her standing in the eyes of the non-monarchical Arab regimes. She therefore bent her efforts in the direction of a dampening of the conflict at this troublesome Arab crossroads. The UN Secretary-General was also working towards that goal.

The outcome was an agreement of April 1963 in which Saudi Arabia promised to suspend her aid to the royalists and prohibit the use of her territory for the prosecution of the royalist cause. For her part, Egypt promised to withdraw her troops from Yemen, which were variously estimated to number between 15,000 and 30,000. It was also agreed that the demarcated part of the frontier between Saudi Arabia and Yemen, which was getting on for half its total length, should be demilitarized to a depth of 12 miles on each of its sides. Observers were to be stationed in this 200-mile-long zone and at other appropriate points to check on the implementation of the disengagement arrangement. A month later it was announced that agreement had been reached on the UN performing this observer function, and the parties were then persuaded to divide the cost of the operation equally between them for an initial period of two months. There was a slight hiccup as the Soviet Union insisted, not unreasonably, that the operation needed the authorization of the Security Council. But although she complained about the insufficient curbing of the party whom she saw as the aggressor, she did not veto the proposal, and the other Council members voted for it. Britain, for example, who was still in possession of the neighbouring colony and protectorates of Aden, was much in favour of this pacifying scheme (see Map 47).

The resulting UN Yemen Observer Mission (Unyom) was, in principle, a very important part of the disengagement package. Neither side had much faith in the mere word of the other, but neither was in a position to check on what the other was actually doing. The Yemeni royalists controlled much of the countryside, including the parts adjacent to Saudi Arabia, so that Egypt was unable to monitor border traffic. And although the Egyptian troops were relatively conspicuous, Saudi Arabia had no direct means of watching over their movements. Moreover, each side was likely to honour its promise only if it believed

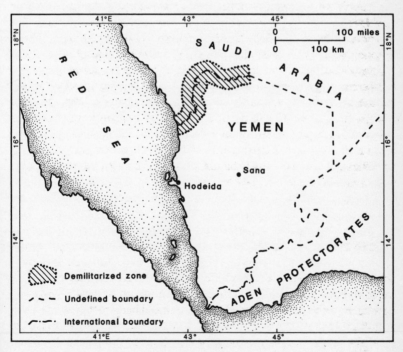

Map 47 Yemen

that the other was doing likewise. In consequence, the prospect of reports from an impartial third party was seen as a key element in securing the implementation on the ground of the agreement for defusing and resolving the crisis.

Unyom began its activity on 4 July 1963. The demilitarized zone was hard to supervise, on account of its size, rugged terrain, numerous tracks, and the fact that the latter were used for what was said to be normal commercial activity. To keep an eye on it Unyom had a Yugoslav reconnaissance unit of just over 100 officers and men and a Canadian air unit (of eight reconnaissance planes) of about half that size, each of them being deployed on both sides of the border. When manning checkpoints and on ground patrol the UN personnel carried arms for self-defence. Additionally, Unyom had six military observers stationed in Hodeida, the chief port, and Sana, the chief town and site of a military airfield. Egyptian troops moving into or out of the country were likely to pass through one of these centres, and thus Unyom anticipated that checking on their withdrawal would be a relatively easy matter.

Like all peacekeeping activity, this small Mission was premised on the assumption that the parties would honour their undertakings. The situation got off to a promising start, as following Unyom's arrival there appeared to be a reduction in Egyptian troops and a lessening of Saudi support for the royalists. With a view to maintaining the momentum, the parties agreed to extend their financing of Unyom for a further two months. But in fact the momentum was far from maintained, as the Egyptians in particular began to increase their support for their friends. Saudi Arabia retaliated by saying that she would not pay for a further extension of Unyom's life, but under American pressure agreed to do so. However, the Mission was changed in size and character. In effect it was recognized that there was no point in reporting on the non-implementation of the disengagement agreement, and that what was needed was a new commitment. Accordingly, the Yugoslav reconnaissance unit was withdrawn and the number of reconnaissance aircraft reduced to two. In partial compensation for this the number of military observers was increased to 21, drawn from nine countries. But Unyom's changed orientation was marked by it being given a civilian head.

On this basis Unyom's life was extended for several further periods of two months. But its presence had no discernible impact on the progress of the violent civil war in Yemen, and by April 1964 the number of Egyptian troops there was estimated by some to have increased to about 40,000. The UN Secretary-General was of the public view that Unyom's presence was a restraining influence on the parties, and to some extent that may have been so. But manifestly Unyom was not achieving anything of substance and the parties had no intention of remaking their original agreement. In this context the Secretary-General's reports on the operation exhibited increasing frustration, and when at the end of August 1964 Saudi Arabia said she would not pay for Unyom's continuation, she was not pressed to change her mind. Egypt did not object to its termination, and no one else urged a different course. Unyom was therefore wound up on 4 September.

It was sometimes implied that this undistinguished ending might have been averted had Unyom's mandate been stronger. But that is to mistake the nature of the problem. Outside intervention in the Yemeni civil war continued not because there were too many loopholes through which aid could be supplied but because one of the outsiders came to the view that the situation demanded not a cutting down but a building up of her assistance. In other words, in signing the disengagement agreement Egypt had misjudged the situation. She probably underestimated the extent of tribal support in Yemen for the royalists, and overestimated the strength of the republican regime. It did not take her long to realize her mistake, but by then she had agreed to leave. On that promise she therefore felt it necessary to renege. As both Egypt and the cause she was supporting were popular at the UN, she suffered little public embarrassment from her change of policy. But in private it was an extremely sensitive issue, and also costly. Moreover, in diplomatic terms it was a commitment from which it was difficult to withdraw. Not until her crushing defeat in the Arab–Israeli war of June 1967 did Egypt feel able to revise her position, signing a new disengagement agreement with Saudi Arabia in August of that year which this time she honoured.

There was, therefore, a clear sense in which the UN had failed in (what became North) Yemen. It had gone to witness a mutual withdrawal from that state, but departed without having done so. However, as the concept of 'failure' also implies a lack of capability and/or effort, the use of that term is not wholly appropriate for describing the UN's experience. For its servants did all they could to implement Unyom's mandate – but ultimately its implementation was never up to them. Unyom's job was to confirm that Egypt and Saudi Arabia were doing as they had promised. It was not its fault that Egypt decided that her promise was unwise. Thus this case served to underline the point that international peacekeeping is a secondary activity, dependent for its success on the cooperation of the principals. In Yemen one of the principals withdrew her cooperation, which resulted in the collapse of the disengagement agreement. The peacekeeping arrangement which had been set up on its basis was thereby made redundant.

FURTHER READING

Winston Burdett, *Encounter with the Middle East* (London: Deutsch, 1970).
Carl von Horn, *Soldiering for Peace* (London: Cassell, 1966).
Christopher J. McMullen, *Resolution of the Yemen Crisis, 1963* (Washington, DC: Georgetown University, 1980).
Dana Schmidt, 'The Civil War in Yemen', in Evan Luard (ed.), *The International Regulation of Civil Wars* (London: Thames and Hudson, 1972).

Section F The Maintenance of Calm in the Middle East since the Six Day War (1967–)

In the War which began on 5 June 1967, Israel inflicted crushing defeats on the three Arab neighbours with whom she fought, seizing the Sinai Desert from Egypt, the West Bank of the Jordan River from the state of that name, and the Golan Heights from Syria. During the next six years several small UN peacekeeping missions helped – when the parties were disposed to accept such help – to maintain calm on a number of these fronts (see Map 48).

ISRAEL–SYRIA

On the basis of a Security Council demand for compliance with its earlier call for a cease-fire, Military Observers from the UN Truce Supervision Organization (Untso) were, with the consent of the parties, immediately deployed along the new front lines on the Golan Heights (which were between one and three miles apart). Over the next few days the Observers demarcated the lines and secured the agreement of both combatants to them. Untso then set up observation posts on each side of what, de facto, was a buffer zone, seven such posts being established on the Israeli side and nine on the Syrian. It also began to conduct regular patrols along the cease-fire lines. These new stabilizing arrangements were endorsed by the Security Council, and by the end of June 110 Observers were involved in their operation.

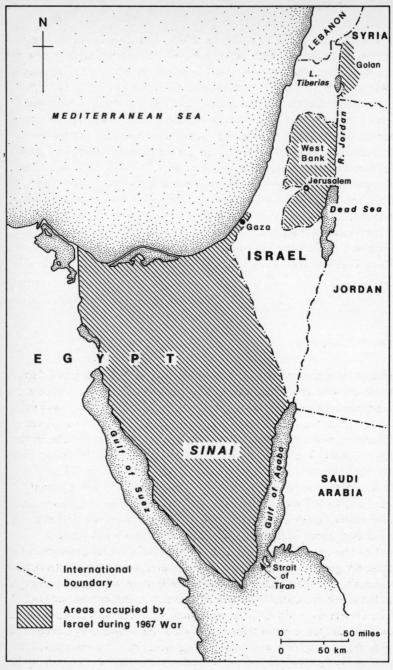

Map 48   Areas occupied by Israel as a result of the Six Day War of 1967

The effective use of this machinery was, of course, dependent on the parties, given that peacekeeping is a cooperative and not an authoritative activity. The significance of this principle was highlighted in August 1967 when Syria asked for the removal of all American personnel on the ground that the United States had consistently supported Israel. This meant that in future they could serve only on the Israeli side of the cease-fire line. Subsequently, Syria also asked for the removal of Canadian personnel, but Untso soon managed to change the host state's mind on that point. In all operational respects, however, the arrangements worked smoothly. Both sides had an interest in the maintenance of quiet, at least for a while, and the presence of impartial military personnel in observation posts and on patrol was a valuable aid to the achievement of this goal. The front was therefore stable until the sudden outbreak in October 1973 of another Arab–Israeli War – called the Yom Kippur War by the Israelis and the War of Ramadan by the Arabs.

EGYPT–ISRAEL

Except for a marshy area at its northern end, the 1967 Egyptian–Israeli cease-fire line ran along the Suez Canal. At first, no peacekeeping machinery was set up in this area. But with the rise of tension and firing in July, the Security Council authorized the deployment of Untso Observers in an effort to make the cease-fire more secure. The parties agreed, and before long 15 observation posts had been established, eight on the eastern (Israeli) side, and seven on the Egyptian. These arrangements required 90 Observers, but here too their nationalities gave rise to problems, both sides making objections to certain states. Eventually, agreement was reached on six states from which they might be drawn: Austria, Burma, Chile, Finland, France and Sweden.

For the next 18 months, and with Untso's useful assistance, the cease-fire generally held. Early in 1969, however, the situation deteriorated seriously, and from then until August 1970 there were huge exchanges of fire across the Canal – the War of Attrition as this episode was called. The Observers could do little more than sit it out, and because of the extreme danger some of their posts had to be temporarily closed. The War was brought to an end following American diplomatic activity, and thereafter the parties cooperated with Untso to maintain quiet until the outbreak of the next War in 1973.

ISRAEL–JORDAN

It was not long after the end of the Six Day War before tension began to increase on this front, but neither then nor later was a peacekeeping operation established there. The Secretary-General of the UN suggested on more than one occasion that observers should be posted along the cease-fire line, but due to the opposition of the states concerned nothing was done. Many Palestinian fighters were based in Jordan, which meant that incidents were quite likely. But whatever its real feelings about the matter, the Jordanian Government would have found it politically difficult to agree to anything which might obstruct the anti-Israeli activities of the Palestinians, and Israel did not want even the smallest of obstacles to the retaliation on which she might well embark. An additional, and important, reason for Jordan's reluctance was that she was most anxious not to give the cease-fire line the least semblance of permanence, for in terms of the value of the lost territory and the likelihood of getting it back, her position was probably worse than any other of Israel's truncated neighbours.

After one particularly large Israeli assault on Jordan in 1968, there was considerable encouragement in the Security Council for the idea that observers should be posted along the River Jordan. As the United States was among its supporters, it might be supposed that Israel would have gone along with the plan if it had received formal authorization. But Jordan was adamant in her opposition to it, and could rely, if necessary, on a Soviet veto. The matter was therefore dropped. Two years later, in a courageous move, Jordan succeeded in expelling the Palestinian fighters from her territory, and thereafter the front with Israel became much quieter – lessening the need for a peacekeeping presence. Jordan's gain, however, was Lebanon's loss, as the Palestinians moved in that direction.

ISRAEL–LEBANON

Lebanon had not participated in the 1967 War, but on the ground that she had claimed to be at war with Israel the latter denounced her 1949 Armistice Agreement with Lebanon. (Israel also denounced her Armistice Agreements with Jordan and Syria at this time, and had already, after the 1956 Suez War, denounced her Agreement with Egypt.) Untso derived some, but not all, of its functions from the Armistice Agreements (see Part III, Section C above), but the UN took the view that as an agreement could not, in law, be unilaterally denounced, Untso was still entitled to exercise those functions. As a practical matter, however, there can be very little by way of a peacekeeping role for a body if one side ignores it. The UN therefore merely maintained a skeleton Armistice structure in Lebanon after the 1967 War, as it did in the other states who had been signatories to the 1949 Agreements.

In the early 1970s, for the first time since Israel's creation, tension began to reach a serious level on the Israeli–Lebanese border, this being a direct consequence of the anti-Israeli activity of Palestinian fighters who were now based in South Lebanon in large numbers. Lebanon therefore asked the UN Security Council in 1972, on the basis of the 1949 Armistice Agreement, to station observers on her border with Israel, and the Council agreed to do so. In consequence, five observation posts were set up and manned by about three dozen Untso Military Observers, who also patrolled along the border. However, as Israel would have nothing to do with them, they served little purpose other than as the UN's reporters. They were able to keep a scorecard of Lebanon's complaints about Israel's violations of the frontier (still referred to by the UN as the Armistice Demarcation Line). But such activity had no stabilizing use, and might even have been counter-productive, given the impression it gave of partiality.

Lebanon (like Jordan) did not participate in the 1973 Arab–Israeli War. The UN presence at her southern border was therefore unaffected by it, and continued to operate in the same context as before until the Israeli invasion of Lebanon in 1978 (see Section J below). Thereafter, too, Untso continued to man the five observation posts, but the context was doubly changed: firstly because a UN Force was now in the region, with which the Untso personnel were operationally associated; and secondly because the posts themselves were located within the area in South Lebanon which has since 1978 been under one form or another of de facto Israeli control.

In some circumstances of the kind which existed between 1972 and 1978, the posting of impartial observers on just one side of a frontier may have some small deterrent effect. But in this case there was little evidence of any such influence either in respect of the Israelis or the Palestinians. Lebanon had, in effect, uttered a cry for help. But a small peacekeeping operation which was rejected by one party and ignored by the belligerent elements in what passed for the host state could have virtually no impact on the situation. This was therefore one case where the UN might have done better not to respond to the request for a peacekeeping mission, as circumstances dictated that its peacekeeping character was little more than superficial.

UNTSO's LATER ACTIVITY

Since the Arab–Israeli War of October 1973, Untso has, in operational terms, been reduced almost entirely to providing support for other, and larger, peacekeeping operations which were set up to try to control dangerous crossroads. In some other respects, however, it continues to fulfil several important functions of a general kind.

In Egypt, Untso Observers worked in conjunction with Unef II until that Force was wound up in 1979, being used chiefly to carry out inspections of the zones of limited forces and armaments (see Section G below). In these tasks American and Soviet Observers (the latter having joined Untso in 1973 in rather unusual circumstances – see below) sometimes found themselves operating in pairs on the Egyptian side of the UN buffer zone. This unusual feature could not occur on the Israeli side, as Israel refused to have dealings with the Soviets on the ground that their state was not in diplomatic relations with her. Egypt was also at first a bit wary of the Soviet officers, and after the 1975 Disengagement Agreement refused to allow them to operate in the area of the sensitive Abu Rudeis oilfield in southern Sinai. This resulted in the UN feeling obliged to avoid posting American officers to that area. However, in less than a year the UN managed to get Egypt to lift this ban, enabling Untso to use its superpower Observers throughout Egyptian-held Sinai.

After the withdrawal of Unef II in 1979, Untso continued to maintain a token UN presence in Sinai by manning five observation posts. Egypt was actively cooperative in this regard, seeing the UN as something of a counterweight to the heavy American representation in the non-UN peacekeeping bodies which now successively appeared in the area (see Part II, Sections J and K above). However, nationals of the permanent members of the Security Council were not initially used for this task as the Soviet Union would not allow her Observers to be employed in this way. She had supported the widespread Arab condemnation of the Egyptian–Israeli Peace Treaty, and no doubt wished to distance herself physically as well as diplomatically from the new peacekeeping bodies which were operating in Sinai directly in consequence of the Treaty. Soviet Observers would in any event have been of limited use because of Israel's refusal to cooperate with them. Account had to be taken of this view, as although Israel was not formally a host state she was still in occupation of much of Sinai. There was no objection from the United States to an equivalent restriction on the use of her Observers, and given the bigger role she was now playing in Sinai she may well have welcomed this aspect of the situation.

With Israel's final withdrawal from Egypt in 1982 one reason for this restriction was removed. But the Soviet Union still wished to keep her own UN Observers out of Sinai, so the existing policy remained in force. However, UN suggestions that Soviet and United States Observers might therefore be reduced in number fell on deaf ears. In 1985, with Mr Gorbachev now in power in the Soviet Union, the UN learnt that that state would no longer object to the posting of her Observers in Sinai. This was very welcome news, not least because of the dissatisfaction of the officers of the permanent members of the Security Council at having to kick their heels in Cairo. With Egypt's ready agreement, the lifting of the restriction was announced, and American Observers immediately began to help in manning the Sinai observation posts and patrolling between them. French Observers were similarly deployed later in the year. But it emerged that the UN had moved a bit too fast for the Soviet Union, advice being received that there should be some delay before Soviet Untso officers were redeployed. This delay lasted until 1987, which probably had something to do with the workings of the Soviet bureaucracy.

In Jordan, Untso maintains only a small holding office in Amman – its head formally being the chairman of the Israeli–Jordanian MAC. In recent years the Soviet members of Untso have been treated as eligible for this posting. There is also a small long-standing Untso office in Israeli-occupied Gaza, but it has no operational significance.

In Lebanon Untso has performed several tasks. It continues to man the five observation posts on the border, and since the establishment of the UN Interim Force in 1978 (see Section J below) a number of Untso Observers have been assigned to work with it. Mainly they operate in a liaison capacity with the various parties in the complex local scene. Additionally, since 1982 some Untso personnel have been constituted into an Observer Group in Beirut to monitor the situation and to engage in liaison work. In mid-1989 that Group was reduced to single figures because of the intensity of the fighting in Beirut. Chiefly because Israel will not deal with Observers from states who are not in diplomatic relations with her, Soviet officers are not used in Lebanon – and the Soviets are probably glad not to have their men in situations which might lead to some awkwardness with the PLO and Syria. The deteriorating security position in the mid- and late 1980s also resulted in restrictions being put on the use of American officers and the withdrawal of French officers, and early in 1989 the United States said that her Untso officers were not to be used anywhere in Lebanon.

Since the Israeli–Syrian Disengagement Agreement of 1974 (see Section H below), Untso personnel have been attached to the UN Observer Force between those two states, manning observation posts in the buffer zone and carrying out inspections of the zones of limited forces and armaments. The arrangements regarding the Force, however, provided that nationals of the permanent members of the Security Council would not be used, and the interpretation put on this has meant that such nationals cannot be employed operationally in this area on the tasks which are performed by Untso.

To conduct all these tasks, Untso, in August 1989, had 298 Military Observers, from the following 17 states: Argentina, Australia, Austria, Belgium, Canada, Chile, Denmark, Finland, France, Ireland, Italy, Netherlands, New Zealand, Norway, Sweden, the USSR, and the United States. The Soviets had more or less gatecrashed into Untso in 1973, following the confused and dramatic events which surounded the final stages of the October War. A limit was placed on Soviet participation of 36 Observers, which was the size of the then largest national group – Sweden. At that time the United States had only a handful of officers in Untso, but they were very smartly raised to 36. Soon afterwards, however, it was discovered that the number of Soviet officers with Untso was 72 – due, the Soviets explained, to the need for each of their Observers to be accompanied by an interpreter. This cut little ice with either the UN or the United States, and before long the 'interpreters' were withdrawn. The two super powers thus returned to a situation of equality in this respect, and as of August 1989 the number of their military officers in Untso was still 36 each. This is more than is operationally useful, for reasons which have been mentioned. But neither state is inclined to reduce the number of her Observers.

In November 1989 it was announced that, while Untso was not to increase in size or lose any of its contributor states, two additional states were to provide it with Military Observers: China and Switzerland. It was the first time that either state had contributed military personnel to UN peacekeeping. Given China's earlier suspicion of that activity, and Switzerland's non-membership in the UN for fear of jeopardizing her traditional neutrality, this development was a notable tribute to Untso, and more generally to the impartial and non-threatening nature of peacekeeping.

All the tasks which Untso conducts in support of UN Forces could, in principle, be done by the Forces themselves, and the jobs which Untso now does independently of other UN bodies are of virtually no immediate significance. However, on the assumption that the pacific functions of peacekeeping are also desirable, there are three grounds on which Untso's maintenance as an independent unit can be justified. Firstly, it provides an immediately available communications link between Israel and Jordan, which could be very useful in a crisis. Secondly, as its mandate is temporally open-ended, it can claim a foothold in the Middle East even if any of the UN Forces with which it is now associated, or for that matter the non-UN Multinational Force and Observers in Sinai, are withdrawn: especially as the circumstances of any such withdrawals are more likely to be dire than benign, the continued presence in the area of a body which would try to exert a defusing and stabilizing influence could be of considerable value.

Thirdly, Untso has since the mid-1950s served as a kind of instant resource body and training ground for UN peacekeeping. Whenever, since that time, a UN peacekeeping force or observer mission has been set up, some of its initial military staff have invariably come from Untso. Many commanders of such bodies have at one time or another served with Untso, as have some commanders of battalions assigned for service with the UN, and their experience with Untso has stood them in very good stead. When the UN sends out what is now called a technical mission to an area to which it looks as if a UN peacekeeping body might be sent, it is Untso, again, which is turned to for some of the necessary personnel. The availability of Untso for these purposes is undoubtedly a huge asset for the UN.

While, therefore, Untso's specific original purposes have long been left behind, and its current independent operational role is negligible, nonetheless it continues to serve some purposes which are of considerable value for peacekeeping, and which appear to command general support. If Untso did not exist it would be highly desirable to create it. But even in the improved international climate of the late 1980s, it is extremely unlikely that that would be done. Accordingly, Untso in its present form is much to be prized.

FURTHER READING

Odd Bull, *War and Peace in the Middle East* (London: Cooper, 1976).
United Nations, *The Blue Helmets* (New York: UN Department of Public Information, 1985).

Section G The Path to the Egyptian–Israeli Peace Treaty (1973–1979)

THE SECOND UN EMERGENCY FORCE

On 6 October 1973, which was the Jewish holy day of Yom Kippur, Egypt (and Syria) launched an attack on Israel which took her almost completely by surprise. It represented a remarkable failure of Israeli intelligence and, correspondingly, a conspicuous feather in Arab hats. Good military use was made of this circumstance, which meant that in the UN Security Council a common position did not emerge, for the Soviet Union did not wish to obstruct the progress of her Arab friends. Then, however, with massive American aid, the Israelis got a grip on the conflict. This brought all members of the Council (other than the non-participating China) together on 22 October in a call for a cease-fire. It was confirmed the next day, when the Secretary-General was also asked to send observers to the Egyptian–Israeli front.

But Israel did not desist, and encircled the Egyptian Third Army of 20,000 men on the east bank of the Suez Canal. Egypt then appealed to both superpowers to send troops to enforce the cease-fire. The prospect of Soviet troops in the Middle East was not at all to the liking of the United States, but the Soviet Union appeared to warm to the idea. She was also reported to have very large forces in the Mediterranean, and the United States had intelligence warnings that the Soviet Union was intending to transfer nuclear weapons to Egypt (intelligence which was not at the time passed on to her West European allies). The United States responded by putting her forces throughout the world on an ominous state of alert. Suddenly it looked as if the two nuclear giants were getting locked into a military confrontation, and a major war seemed more imminent than at any time since the Cuban missile crisis of 1962. Then on 25 October agreement was hurriedly reached in the

316

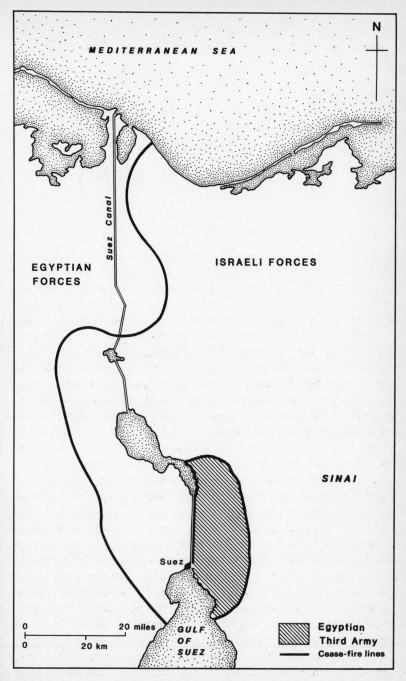

Map 49   Egyptian–Israeli cease-fire lines at the end of the October War of 1973

Security Council not just on a tough reiteration of the call for a cease-fire but also on the despatch of an interpositionary peacekeeping force to the area. Israel took the hint, and the crisis immediately subsided (see Map 49).

The Force which was so established took the same name as the one which had operated in the area from 1956 to 1967, and was thus called the UN Emergency Force (Unef II). It was given an initial mandate of six months and was to have a total strength of about 7,000. This figure was reached within four months, contingents being supplied by the following 12 states: Austria, Canada, Finland, Ghana, Indonesia, Ireland, Nepal, Panama, Peru, Poland, Senegal, and Sweden. The participation of the permanent members of the Security Council was specifically excluded, this representing the strongly-held view of the United States. But after much diplomatic wrangling, and over Israeli objections, an Eastern bloc state – Poland – was for the first time represented in a UN peacekeeping force. The overriding role of the Security Council in respect of all important matters concerning the Force was emphasized, and the Soviet Union drew attention to this in connection with her agreement that the expenses of the Force should be shared out amongst all UN members. The implied threat was clear, but it remained that the Soviets were more financially forthcoming than ever before in respect of a major UN peacekeeping operation. This also meant that the UN was able to get away from funding peacekeeping on a voluntary basis, which, most unsatisfactorily, it had had to do in the 1960s. Finally, it was laid down that, in accordance with the basic values of peacekeeping, Unef II would use force only in self-defence, and would act with complete impartiality.

Over the first two years of its life Unef II gradually declined to about 4,000 men. Then, following an enlargement of its responsibilities it was increased somewhat, but almost all the extra men were found to be unnecessary. The Force therefore declined again to little more than 4,000. At the time of its withdrawal in July 1979 it was almost exactly this size, and consisted of seven contingents. Six of the original contributors had left during the intervening years – Austria, Ireland, Nepal, Panama, Peru, and Senegal – and one new contribution had appeared in the shape of an Australian helicopter unit.

DEFUSION

The superpower crisis had seemingly been defused by the mere agreement that a peacekeeping force should go to the crossroads at which the more local conflagration was occurring. But the catalytic potential of the Egyptian–Israeli conflict had by no means been spent, and it was therefore of the utmost importance that immediate measures should be taken on the ground to bolster the fragile cease-fire. This was Unef II's initial job, and it was begun within 24 hours of the Security Council having decided to establish the Force. The first UN troops to arrive were immediately despatched to the front and interposed themselves wherever possible between the opposing forces. Observation posts and checkpoints were set up; patrolling was undertaken; attempts were made to persuade the parties not to make or maintain any forward movements; and complaints were investigated. This was no mean set of tasks. For notwithstanding the proclamation of the cease-fire, tension remained high and incidents could all too easily occur between the recently embattled and still closely interlocked troops. And there was no assurance that it would be possible to snuff out any local brush fires before they took a firm hold.

Unef II's speedy arrival, however, had the desired defusing effect. Of course, this was basically due to the fact that the parties had decided to stop fighting: the UN Force was not in the business of imposing a cease-fire. But without the help of the impartial peacekeepers it is very possible that the adversaries would not have been able to maintain calm. Peacekeeping had therefore shown its worth in an exceedingly dramatic context. The UN Force was also able to assist in defusing the immensely sensitive issue of the relief of Egypt's Third Army and the town of Suez which was caught up in its plight. First Unef II transported (non-military) supplies to the besieged troops and civilians, and then it also took over the Israeli checkpoints along the route. This agreement opened the way to the settlement of a matter which was of great significance to Israel – the exchange of prisoners. In the discussion of the implementation of these agreements, Unef II acted as a valuable go-between and enabler, as it did in respect of many day-to-day problems. In this way it made a further contribution to the immediate pacification of the conflict.

DISENGAGEMENT: I

The problem which gave rise to the greatest difficulty, however, was the disentangling of forces from the positions at which they had stopped fighting. The discussions which took place on this matter did so in the context of the Security Council's call for a return to the positions which had been held on 22 October, but no progress was made. It took an intensive bout of 'shuttle diplomacy' by Henry Kissinger, the American Secretary of State, to break the deadlock, and he did so in a relatively comprehensive way. The disengagement agreement signed by the parties on 18 January 1974 provided for the withdrawal of all Israeli forces from both the western and eastern banks of the Suez Canal, and the creation of three adjacent strips of territory immediately to the east of the Canal. Each strip averaged roughly six miles in width and ran more or less parallel to the Canal. The middle one was to be a buffer zone occupied and controlled by Unef II. Those to the west and east of it were to be occupied by Egypt and Israel respectively, but the forces they could maintain there were limited to prescribed levels and types. For a certain distance to the rear of these zones there was also a prohibition on anti-aircraft missiles and their launchers. Unef II was to check on the observance of these restrictions on forces and armaments, and make its reports available to the parties (see Map 50).

The details regarding the implementation of the agreement were worked out by the parties with Unef II. To minimize the likelihood of incidents, temporary buffer zones were to be established; and as Israel withdrew she was to hand the vacated territory over to Unef II, who was to hold it for a few hours before turning it over to Egypt. The UN Force was also responsible for the survey and marking of the lines of disengagement. The whole process went very smoothly, and was completed early in March a day ahead of the deadline.

The existence of a buffer zone between the two sides contributed notably to the stabilization of the situation, and the maintenance of the zone's integrity was dependent on the fact that it was occupied by a third-party force which was both impartial and non-threatening. Both sides were therefore able to accept the new situation, at least temporarily, and at the military level it became very quiet. Unef II established checkpoints and observation posts, and conducted mobile patrols throughout the territory which was now its responsibility. It also, with the assistance of Military Observers from the UN Truce Supervision Organization (Untso), carried out weekly inspections of the areas where there were restrictions on forces and armaments.

Unef II's operation, however, was not without political difficulties. One concerned its freedom of movement, on which the UN's guidelines for the Force insisted. But Israel refused to allow contingents and observers from states who did not recognize her to operate on territory which she controlled. As three of the five infantry battalions to which Unef II was soon reduced (those from Ghana, Indonesia, and Senegal) and one of its two logistic battalions (the Polish) were from states

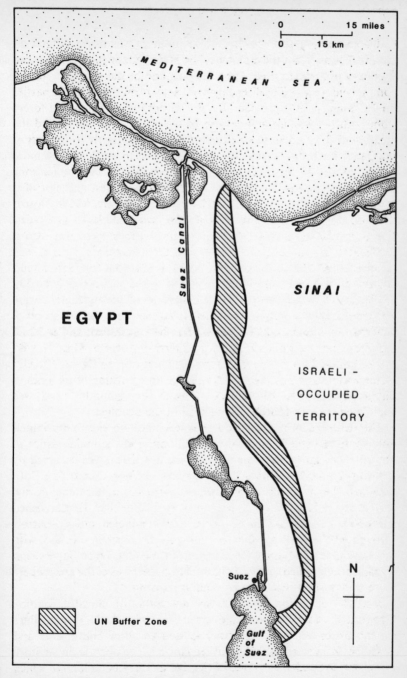

Map 50   The First Egyptian–Israeli Disengagement Agreement, January 1974

falling within the Israeli ban, the flexibility of the Force was considerably reduced.

Another problem concerned Unef II's very continuation. As a practical matter that required the consent of both parties. Israel offered no difficulties in this respect, for the shock of the Yom Kippur attack had changed her attitude to UN peacekeeping very markedly. Formerly her approach to it had been condescending; now, however, she valued any safeguards against attempts to alter the status quo. Unef II would not be a physical obstacle to a renewed Egyptian assault. But inasmuch as it expressed the desire of the international society, and particularly of the United States, for stability in the Middle East, Egypt was perhaps unlikely to brush it aside very lightly. Moreover, it obviated a face-to-face military situation, and the attendant likelihood of possibly dangerous incidents. Israel was thus very willing that Unef II should be maintained, and was also happy with its existing deployment well away from her home territory.

Egypt, however, took a different approach. Due to the exhilaration of the 1973 War and the subsequent running of the diplomatic tide in her favour, she felt that there was a real possibility of getting Israel back to, or at least well towards, her pre-1967 boundaries. Thus she often expressed the view – which internationally was the orthodox one – that the January 1974 disengagement agreement was but the first step along the road to a settlement, and towards that end she was willing to use Unef II as a bargaining counter; these rumblings came to a head in July 1975 when Egypt refused to agree to a renewal of its mandate. With a day to go she relented, and had her reward in a further bout of American diplomatic activity which resulted in the signature of a second disengagement agreement on 4 September.

DISENGAGEMENT: II

The new agreement provided for Israel's withdrawal from two further sectors of Egyptian territory which had been under her occupation since 1967. Firstly, it shifted the old disengagement arrangements eastwards across Sinai, but in an irregular fashion and with a number of complicated amendments and additions. Thus there was to be a new and much wider UN buffer zone. In the area between the western side of the zone and the Suez Canal certain specified restrictions were placed on Egyptian forces and armaments, and for a lesser distance to the east of the zone Israeli forces and armaments were to be limited as prescribed.

Each party agreed not to place anti-aircraft missiles nearer than six miles behind its limited armament zone, and not to place any weapon behind its zone which could reach the other side. Within the UN buffer zone Egypt and Israel were to have electronic early warning stations which were to be watched over by American civilians, who were also to maintain an independent United States early-warning system (see Part II, Section J above). The United States also undertook to continue her aerial supervision of the area covered by this part of the agreement, an activity which had been quietly taking place since the first disengagement agreement (see Map 51).

The second aspect of the agreement provided for Israel's withdrawal from a narrow strip of land along the eastern bank of the Gulf of Suez, running southwards from a point near its head for a distance of about 100 miles. It included an oil field at Abu Rudeis. This area was to be restored to Egyptian administration, except for two small UN buffer zones, and demilitarized. Unef II was to check on this last aspect of the matter, as also on the new limited forces and armaments provisions in respect of northern Sinai. It was agreed that the UN Force was an essential stabilizing element in the new arrangement, and that in future its mandate should be extended for a year at a time. This was an important Egyptian concession, as previously the renewal period had never been for more than six months, and twice had been for three months only.

Under the new agreement Unef II was responsible for supervising the redeployment of forces. Israel refused to sign the necessary implementing protocol until the United States Congress had agreed to that aspect of the scheme which would bring some American civilian technicians to Sinai. But once that had been done the disengagement process got smoothly under way and was completed by the end of February 1976, Unef II playing a role similar to its earlier one in respect of the implementation of the first disengagement agreement. Thereafter it assumed the longer-term funtions which had been assigned to it. In the south it checked on Egypt's observance of the demilitarization provisions by establishing checkpoints and observation posts and by patrolling throughout the area by both land and air. In its various buffer zones it used much the same means to ensure that no unauthorized persons had entered them. It provided escorts to and from the early-warning installations for the Americans, Egyptians, and Israelis who ran them. And, using Military Observers from Untso, it conducted fortnightly inspections within the areas of limited forces and armaments to see if the parties were honouring their undertakings. Once more the

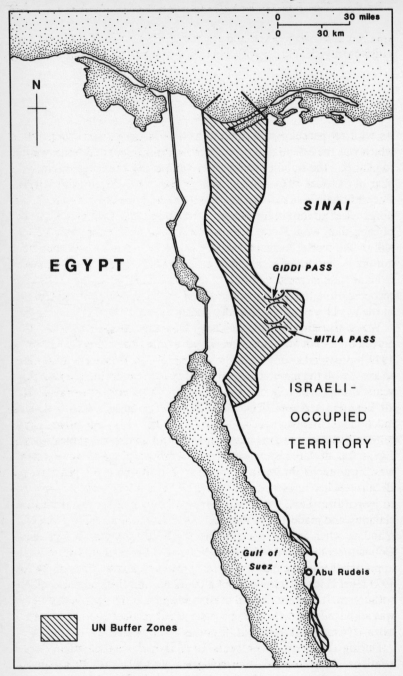

Map 51   The Second Egyptian–Israeli Disengagement Agreement, September
1975

area remained very quiet, and the few incidents which occurred were satisfactorily cleared up with the cooperation of the parties.

PEACE

As with all peacekeeping operations, it was the parties' cooperation which was the essential basis for success. Both Egypt and Israel wanted to maintain the stability which had so effectively been created since the War of October 1973, so they both worked very closely with Unef II. For although a subordinate element in the scheme of things, it was nonetheless an important element, providing a much greater assurance of calm than would have been possible without it. Even with the best will in the world, incidents might well have occurred, and then have got somewhat out of hand, had the forces of Egypt and Israel remained in immediate physical proximity – and although they were now bent on reconciliation, the history of their relationship meant that the best will in the world was only doubtfully present.

When, therefore, in 1978 at Camp David in the United States they agreed on a plan for peace, and signed a treaty to that effect in March 1979, it provided a continued role for Unef II. The Force was to continue to assist with the maintenance of stability in Sinai during the next three years, during which Israel was to conduct a phased withdrawal from all Egyptian territory. Then the UN was to be asked to help with indefinite security arrangements on both sides of the Egyptian–Israeli border. However, as she had sat down with Israel at the table of peace, Egypt was declared an enemy of the Arab people, and an anathema was pronounced on anything which had to do with the peace treaty. Because of her links with a number of Arab states, and her wish not to jeopardize them, the Soviet Union felt obliged to hearken to this clamour, and made it clear that she would veto an extension of Unef II's mandate when it next came before the Security Council. Her fellow Council members decided not to embarrass her further, and so at the appropriate time the matter was not pressed to a vote. Thus on 24 July 1979 Unef II found itself without a mandate, and the Force was quietly withdrawn. It was not the end of peacekeeping in the area as that device was adjudged still to be very necessary. But recourse had to be had to extra-UN means (see Part II, Sections J and K above).

During the previous six years Unef II had seen Egyptian–Israeli relations move from a fierce belligerency, which also threatened to precipitate a major world crisis, to what had widely been thought of as virtually impossible: a treaty of peace. The chief actor in this process, other than the immediate parties, was the United States. But the UN Force played a valuable minor role. This was particularly evident at the start of its life. Thereafter, too, the parties might well have stumbled had the way not been made smooth for them by the UN's impartial and non-threatening activity. Unef II's record therefore deserves a notable place in the history of peacekeeping.

FURTHER READING

E. D. Doyle, 'War and Peace in the Sinai', *An Cosantoir*, 39 (7 and 8) (July and August 1979).

Michael Harbottle, 'The October Middle East War: Lessons for UN Peace-keeping', *International Affairs*, 50 (4) (October 1974).

P. C. Harvey, *The Operational Effectiveness of UN Peace-Keeping Operations with particular reference to Unef II, October 1973–September 1975* (Keele: University of Keele, unpublished M. A. dissertation, 1977).

Henry Kissinger, *Years of Upheaval* (London: Weidenfeld and Nicolson and Michael Joseph, 1982).

N. A. Pelcovits, 'UN Peacekeeping and the 1973 Arab–Israeli Conflict', *Orbis*, XIX (1) (Spring 1975).

Nadav Safran, 'Engagement in the Middle East', *Foreign Affairs*, 53 (1) (October 1974).

Kurt Waldheim, *In the Eye of the Storm* (London: Weidenfeld and Nicolson, 1985).

Section H   The Israeli–Syrian Confrontation (1973–)

DISENGAGEMENT

The north-eastern corner of Israel is dominated by the precipitously-rising Golan Heights. From this commanding position Syria often made life miserable for the Israelis between 1948 and 1967, as relations between the two states were always poor, and often worse. In the Six Day War of June 1967 Israel succeeded in capturing the Heights, and so reversed the strategic position. For now it was a gentle descent of about 40 miles from the new Israeli front line to the Syrian capital, Damascus. In the Arab–Israeli War of October 1973 Syria initially pushed Israel back some way across the Golan. But the Israelis recovered, and not only regained the lost ground but in the north also pushed forward towards Saassa for a distance of about 15 miles – which meant that they were little more than 20 miles short of Damascus.

Military Observers from the UN Truce Supervision Organization (Untso) were, with the agreement of the parties, despatched to watch over the cease-fire line which emerged at the end of the war. But the line belied its name, being the frequent scene of massive exchanges of fire which the Observers managed only temporarily to halt. This lack of stability attracted international concern, not only because of its immediate implications but also because of the intimate connections which each side had with a super power. Syria was one of the Soviet Union's few close and reliable Middle Eastern friends, and Israel had very strong links with the United States at more than one level. Thus the continuing Israeli–Syrian tension could easily have become more than just a regional difficulty. It also threatened the furtherance of the disengagement process between Egypt and Israel (the first step in which had been taken in January 1974), which the United States was keenly sponsoring. Additionally, unless something was done about Syria's dissatisfaction, Arab pressure was likely to build up for a reimposition of the oil embargo against the West, which had had a telling effect immediately following the Yom Kippur War. Altogether, there was a lot of ground for the widespread anxiety over the inflammable condition of the Israeli–Syrian crossroads.

Accordingly, in May 1974, the United States Secretary of State, Henry Kissinger, embarked on what proved to be an exceedingly gruelling mediatory shuttle between Israel and Syria. The intractability of the problem and the intransigence of the parties often drove him to distraction. But on 31 May an agreement was signed, albeit in a frigid atmosphere. It fell into three parts.

Firstly it provided for a disengagement of forces. Israel was to withdraw to a line which was almost exactly similar to the one she had held after the 1967 War. Chief amongst the small but significant alterations to it were that she agreed to give up the town of Quneitra and the village of Rafid. Between the Israelis and the front line which was agreed for Syrian forces, a buffer zone was to be established. Secondly, for a distance of 15 miles on each side of this zone there were to be restrictions on forces and armaments, which would have the effect of thinning them out as the front lines were approached. Thirdly, the whole arrangement was to be supervised by a UN Disengagement Observer Force (Undof) of about 1,250 men. It was to patrol in the buffer zone and, through Untso's locally-based Military Observers, check on the observance of the agreed limitations on forces and armaments (see Map 52).

Syria had not been at all happy about the idea of a UN force occupying the buffer zone. States are almost always, of course, reluctant to admit a sizeable – or, indeed, any – peacekeeping group, as to do so hints at incapacity or chicanery on the part of the host. Furthermore, notwithstanding the disadvantageous way in which the war had ended for her, Syria was still somewhat elated by the progress she had made at its start against the supposedly invincible Israelis. She thus suggested that a few hundred observers would serve the required purpose. The outbreak and initial stages of the war, however, had caused Israel great psychological hurt, and her feeling of insecurity, together with her interest in the status quo, was evidenced by her arguing for a peacekeeping force no less than 3,000 strong. The outcome was a compromise, right down to the inclusion of both 'observer' and 'force' in the title of the peacekeeping group. (There is still some sensitivity in Syria about references to Undof as a 'force', and on some connected terminological matters.)

The UN Security Council had no difficulty in endorsing the proposal

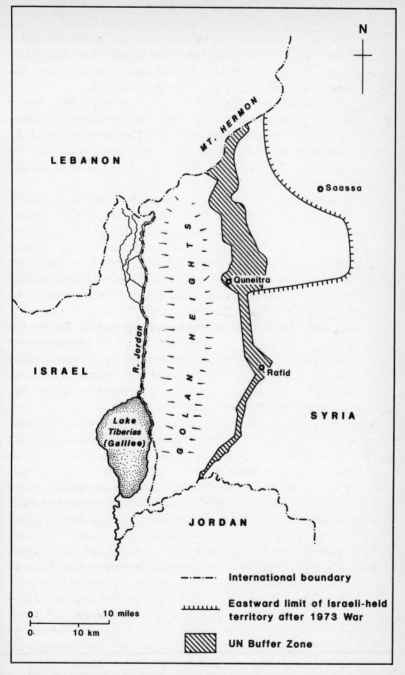

Map 52   The Israeli–Syrian Disengagement Agreement of May 1974

that the Organization should assist in the disengagement process. As was then her wont, China did not participate in the vote, and Iraq, on account of the deep antipathy between her own Arab socialist regime and that of neighbouring Syria, did likewise. But everyone else was much in favour of the scheme for defusing the current tension and bringing stability to the relationship. Indeed, the proposal was co-sponsored by the United States and the Soviet Union, the latter no doubt hoping to reinforce her sagging claim to be no less responsible than the United States for the Arab–Israeli peace process. This superpower harmony was also reflected in an agreement that Undof's costs were to be shared out amongst all member states.

Undof was initially established for a period of six months, and all its subsequent mandates have been for this length of time. Securing the first few renewals gave rise to appreciable difficulties, as Syria tried to use her agreement to Undof's continuation to obtain a further Israeli withdrawal. However, all she managed to achieve was the participation of the Palestine Liberation Organization (PLO) in a Security Council debate on Palestine, and by 1976 she seemed to have decided that she had wrung as much as she could out of the renewal issue. This conclusion may well have been assisted by Syria's increased interest in stability on Golan consequential upon the movement, in that year, of large numbers of her troops into Lebanon – where they remain still. Syria may also have been given pause by reports filtering out of Israel that influential cabinet members were arguing that their country no longer needed Undof. Certainly, since 1976 all renewals of Undof's mandate have gone through without the least hint of difficulty.

Following the initial Security Council resolution of 31 May 1974, contingents for Undof were supplied by four states: Austria and Peru provided infantry battalions and logistic units came from Canada and Poland. The Force was operational within a few days of the Council's decision, and by the middle of June had reached its full strength. Peru withdrew after a year and was replaced by Iran, who in turn was replaced by Finland in 1979. Since then there has been no change in Undof's national composition and hardly any in its size: as of November 1989 it is made up of 1334 men. As has been the case throughout its life, it is assisted by about 100 Untso Military Observers.

DEFUSION

After a war, the smooth redeployment of opposing forces within a limited area presents many difficulties. Troops who have recently been at each other's throats may still be ill-disposed towards each other and trigger-happy. Moreover, the withdrawing side may go with poor grace and the advancing side may be over-eager – each, for rather different reasons, wishing to display its continued virility. Accordingly, this kind of military disentanglement is likely to be considerably eased if a neutral third party is on hand to watch over and assist the process. This was a large part of Undof's initial job.

In accordance with plans worked out under its auspices, Undof first interposed itself between the opposing front lines with a view to helping to stabilize the cease fire. Next, in a series of moves, the Israeli troops redeployed across and away from the area they were to vacate. Each particular sector was handed over to Undof once their departure was complete, and then, after an interval (and usually on the next day) handed over by Undof to Syria – either to her military forces, if they were entitled to advance into it, or to her civilian administrators if the area in question was to be part of the buffer zone.

Alongside this operation was the far less tricky one of the thinning out of forces and armaments to the rear of the new front lines. This was to be done on a strictly reciprocal basis so that neither side would secure a temporary military advantage. To check on the honouring of their promises, and so provide each side with some assurance regarding the good faith of the other, Undof conducted inspections at the end of each phase of the activity. These, like the other disengagement procedures, went very smoothly, and all of them had been completed by the designated date of 26 June.

Thus, in less than a month an extremely hostile situation had been defused, and in the process the UN's impartial Force had played a notable part. The necessary things could no doubt have been done without the help of a third party. But they would have been much less easily done and exposed to many greater risks. All concerned, however, not least the interested bystanders, were most anxious that risks should be minimized. For that reason Undof's role was not just of considerable value but was also greatly appreciated.

STABILIZATION

If troops are within sight, sound, and reach of each other in a context of suspicion and hostility, it is all too easy for incidents to arise, no matter how big an attempt is made to maintain sharp discipline. It is also possible that a very local problem could lead to a wider conflagration.

A well-controlled army and a peacefully-inclined regime should be able to douse such flames very quickly. But the possibility of the situation getting out of hand cannot be excluded, perhaps because of military inefficiencies but more likely because of the political problem of finding the right time to call a halt. A buffer zone removes many of these hazards, but in itself it is insufficient, given the probability of suspicion than the other side is not playing fair. It is therefore exceedingly desirable that the zone should be watched over by an impartial third party.

Once the forces of Israel and Syria had redeployed, the supervision of the buffer zone which had been agreed upon became Undof's main task. The Force had to check that the zone remained free of the armed forces of the parties, and try to ensure that no other violations of the new status quo took place. It did this by establishing about three dozen positions from which constant observation takes place. These positions also act as the bases from which, as necessary, outposts are set up, and from which daily patrolling is done. Measures have been taken to try to prevent violations of the Israeli front line, most of which result from civilian activity, particularly that of shepherds in pursuit of their flocks. Violations of Syrian territory chiefly take the form of firing by Israeli troops, but it is rarely calculated or malicious. Both sides are notified by Undof's Commander of any violations which are adjudged to have occurred, and asked to rectify any inappropriate behaviour. Such behaviour, however, has hardly ever been of a serious nature, and neither side has shown any desire to inflate any aggravating incidents. The result has been a degree of calm in the buffer zone which contrasts very sharply with the preceding situation.

Another way in which Undof contributes to the stabilization of the region is through its checking of the areas in which forces and armaments are limited. Drawing on Untso's middle-ranking Military Observers, Undof makes inspections once every two weeks, and additional special inspections whenever requested to do so by either party. Its teams have not always been allowed complete freedom of movement, but except in respect of some surveillance stations, such problems have usually been quickly resolved. Generally, these inspections have gone smoothly, and Undof's reports – sent to both sides – have not given rise to any worries about possible breaches of the arms limitation agreements. These regular assurances, together with the little-used but always available possibility of snap inspections, are not in themselves of great significance. But they are a means of helping to keep anxiety at a somewhat lower level than it would otherwise reach, and as such are of value.

The same goal is served by the very fact of Undof's presence. For, on the one hand, it is indicative of some commitment by both parties to the maintenance of peace, at least in the short term; and on the other it displays the interest of the international society at large, in the shape of the UN Security Council, in the same goal. Each side might thus feel that the other is perhaps somewhat less likely to go to war than if there were no peacekeeping body between them, which in turn makes for a less tense atmosphere. This does not add up to very much. But it should not be wholly dismissed. One other possibly stabilizing factor which should not be discounted is the availability, and use, of Undof's Commander as a channel of communication between the two sides. As Israel and Syria are not in diplomatic relations with each other, the opportunity in an edgy situation to use this link as a kind of personal hot line could be of value. The Commander could also, of course, make his own representations.

Undof's stabilizing potential, however, depends entirely on the willingness of the parties to cooperate towards that end. It happens that since 1974 neither of them has wanted to make problems for the other on Golan. Israel has got the position she wants, and indeed in 1981 purported to annex the area. Syria is deeply dissatisfied with the status quo, but has not yet wanted to do anything about it. She has a large contingent of troops in Lebanon, a hostile Iraq on her eastern flank, and not inconsiderable internal problems. Both sides, therefore, have an interest in the maintenance of calm, and each has been able to ensure that this international goal is not undermined by domestic developments. For both of them are well-organized and tightly-administered states, with their armies under reasonably firm political control. Nor are there any quasi-official actors trying to muscle their way on to this particular stage, the quarter of a million Palestinians in and around Damascus not being allowed an independent political hand. Moreover, Israel and Syria are each supported by a superpower who wants to avoid the diplomatic, economic and conceivably military complications of another Arab–Israeli war.

Undof has therefore been operating in a context which is ideal for peacekeeping. In consequence, it has been able to get on with its job quietly and with considerable success. But if one side – Syria being the obvious candidate – wants war, Undof's presence will make no difference to the situation. Especially in the light of the way Syria has been building up her armed forces, it would be rash to expect that she will never make a physical attempt to regain the Golan. Meanwhile, Undof helps the parties to avoid an unsought war.

As that is the limit of Undof's task, it is improper to criticize it for not doing more. It would also be naive, given the depth both of the problem and of the distrust which each of the parties bears for the other. Of course, in politics the most unexpected things can happen, as the Egyptian–Israeli peace treaty testifies. If there were any chance of such a development on the Israeli–Syrian front, there is no ground for thinking that it would be obstructed by the presence of Undof. The idea that peacekeeping somehow takes the steam out of peacemaking has never been strongly based, and in this particular context is quite unsustainable. Without Undof, what would happen is that war would become rather more likely. With Undof, the chances of war are rather less. In the volatile context of the Middle East, this modest difference is widely seen as highly desirable.

FURTHER READING

Michael Comay, *UN Peace-Keeping in the Arab–Israeli Conflict, 1948–1975* (Jerusalem: Hebrew University, 1976).

Robert B. Houghton and Frank G. Trinka, *Multinational Peacekeeping in the Middle East* (Washington, DC: Foreign Service Institute, 1984).

Alan James, *The UN on Golan: Peacekeeping Paradox?* (Oslo: Norwegian Institute of International Affairs, 1986). Also published in an abbreviated form in *International Relations*, IX (1) (May 1987).

Henry Kissinger, *Years of Upheaval* (London: Weidenfeld & Nicolson and Michael Joseph, 1982).

Moshe Maoz and Avner Yaniv (eds), *Syria under Assad* (London: Croom Helm, 1986).

Section I   Syria's Intervention in Lebanon (1976–)

A year after its outbreak in 1975, Syria intervened powerfully in Lebanon's civil war (on the background to which, see Section B above). Claiming to be motivated by a wish to stabilize the situation, and thus promote a settlement, the force she sent in had before long reached getting on for 30,000 men. This move was made, however, only after indirect contacts with Israel, via the United States, had given Syria a ground for thinking that Israel would not respond militarily if Syrian forces kept north of a 'red line' which ran roughly from Rashaya in the east, through Jezzine, to Sidon on the coast. This limitation was observed very carefully by Syria, both initially and since – and as of June 1990 the Syrian force is still in Lebanon (see Map 53).

Syria's intervention was little welcomed in the rest of the Arab world. In an attempt to give the appearance of controlling the situation, the Arab League hastily established a symbolic Force in Lebanon, which included some of the Syrian troops, and later in 1976 transformed this body into an Arab Deterrent Force (ADF). The ADF included all the Syrian interventionary force and small contingents from Libya, Saudi Arab League hastily established a Symbolic Force in Lebanon, which and Saudi Arabia became its chief paymasters, with smaller contributions from Qatar and the United Arab Emirates. A Lebanese was appointed as its commander, and nominally the Force was under the authority of Lebanon's President. However, the non-Syrian contingents soon began to fall away, and all had gone by April 1979. In 1982 the periodic renewal of the ADF's mandate by the Arab League came to a halt, and in the following year Lebanon wound up the Command of the Force. But this made no difference to the position on the ground, where the Syrian troops remained in strength. Later, their presence was reluctantly accepted by the Lebanese Government.

The civil war in Lebanon could, and can, be said to be a matter of international concern. Quite apart from having facilitated Syria's intervention, the Government's lack of authority has permitted the

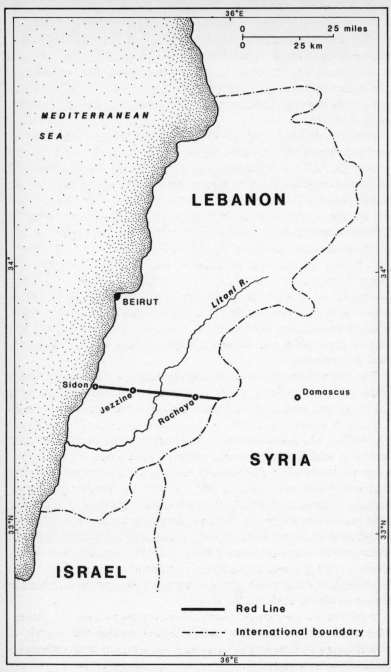

Map 53   The 'Red Line' in Lebanon

development of a situation in the southern part of the country which positively encourages Israeli intervention, with all its destabilizing consequences (see Sections J, K and L below). The area which now makes up Lebanon has always been something of an international crossroads, and since the Second World War it has been a particularly dangerous one.

This consideration, together with the formal legitimation of Syria's role in Lebanon by the Arab League, has caused some commentators to see the ADF as a peacekeeping force. In fact, the international authorization which Syria received for six years is of little relevance in this respect. For there is no reason in principle why a single state should not engage in activity which can properly and helpfully be described as international peacekeeping – although in practice there are almost always good reasons for trying to multilateralize such efforts. Furthermore, in the very special case of Lebanon, it is doubtful whether the Government's occasional complaints about the presence of Syrian troops should be regarded as destructive of the normal peacekeeping requirement of the host state's consent, as in reality the Government of Lebanon has since 1975 been little more than one party to the civil war – a point which was emphasized by the emergence in 1988 of two rival governments.

The real question marks about the peacekeeping character of Syria's intervention in Lebanon relate to its function and values. Ever since the two states became independent, Syria has had a grievance about Lebanon's separate existence, at least within her present boundaries. One way in which this has been expressed has been Syria's consistent refusal to establish an embassy in Beirut. While, therefore, in its intial stage her intervention undoubtedly had a stabilizing impact, and also had some subsequent value in this regard, it has increasingly seemed that she is more interested in controlling as much of Lebanon as possible than in restoring the pre-1975 status quo and so permitting her genuine withdrawal. This is not to imply that the restoration of stable government in Lebanon is a straightforward task. Quite the contrary! But Syria's desire for that goal seems conditional on Lebanon also remaining under her thumb. In other words, she is now more a party to the civil conflict than a would-be holder of the ring.

It follows that she cannot be seen as behaving impartially in Lebanon. Moreover, she has also frequently stepped outside the bounds of peacekeeping by behaving in a very aggressive way towards indigenous groups who were opposed to her presence, not least in the very serious fighting of 1989 which led to the virtual civilian depopulation of Beirut.

In regard to these events the Arab League, through a committee made up of Algeria, Morocco and Saudi Arabia, made efforts to establish an effective cease-fire and maintain it through the employment of its own supervisory peacekeeping device. Such a cease-fire was secured in September, and in the following month a plan for peace in Lebanon was reached in Saudi Arabia by Lebanon's remaining parliamentarians. Early in November they returned, under Syrian protection, to ratify it in their own country and elect a President. But these developments were accompanied neither by the appearance of peacekeepers nor by Syria's withdrawal.

They did, however, lead to the emergence of a government which received wide international recognition. But inside the country it was rejected by the alternative Christian government led by an Army General. His chief complaint concerned Syria's continuing role in Lebanon, and it was probably at his instigation that the new President was assassinated only 17 days after his election. It remains to be seen whether the General can retain the loyalty of his supporters in the light of this act and the distant prospect of peace in Lebanon which perhaps seemed to be emerging. (As of mid 1990 the Syrian-backed and internationally acknowledged Government was, internally, little more than a voice in a continuing wilderness: the militias of the Christian General and a confessional rival were regularly bombarding each other in Beirut, while periodic armed clashes also occurred between competing groups in the Muslim area of the city.) But what the events of 1989 certainly underlined was that although Syria's intervention had, at its beginning, something of a peacekeeping character, these credentials were fairly soon lost. Syria may have understandable reasons for cautiously but firmly trying to maintain a substantial foothold in Lebanon. But her activity there cannot be categorized as peacekeeping.

FURTHER READING

Yair Evron, *War and Intervention in Lebanon* (London: Croom Helm 1987).
Istvan Pogany, *The Arab League and Peacekeeping in the Lebanon* (Aldershot: Averbury, 1987).

Section J The Problem of South Lebanon (1978–)

To the in-built fragility of the Lebanese state (see Section B above) a further hazard was added as a result of the creation of Israel. For this led to numerous Palestinian refugees coming to Lebanon. Initially this additional Muslim presence was compatible with the state's stability, but in the late 1960s and early 1970s they became a seriously disturbing factor. Firstly, and chiefly on account of Israel's de facto expansion following the 1967 Arab–Israeli War, they swelled to as many as 400,000, out of a total population of about three million. Secondly, the Palestine Liberation Organization (PLO), which had been founded in 1964, more or less took over the southern part of Lebanon. After the expulsion of its fighters from Jordan in 1970, south Lebanon became the PLO's sole operational base for its struggle against Israel, and this led to a hitherto very quiet border becoming extremely tense.

In 1975 Lebanon's internal problems came to a head with the outbreak of civil war between the Christian and Muslim groups, and in the next year Syria tried to guarantee the latest cease-fire by sending about 30,000 troops into Lebanon. As Syria was, of Israel's four Arab neighbours, by far her bitterest enemy, and also had close links with the Soviet Union, this development caused Israel considerable concern. She made it clear that if necessary she would react against the Syrian force, but would desist provided that it remained well away from her northern border – to the north of a 'red line' running east to west across south Lebanon. However, that meant that the PLO still had a free hand to the south of the line, and it continued to harass Israel. In view of Israel's well-known policy of periodic retaliation in strength against hostile activity, the scene was being set for a substantial Israeli response at this potentially very volatile crossroads.

In March 1978, following the hijack of a tourist bus in Israel by Palestinian guerrillas, the Israel Defence Forces (IDF) moved into south Lebanon in strength, and within 24 hours had control of a zone six miles deep along the length of the Lebanese border. The United States was particularly annoyed by this, as it threatened to upset her early moves towards an Egyptian–Israeli peace treaty. The establishment of a peacekeeping force seemed the best way of speedily getting Israel out of Lebanon, and an American proposal to this effect was therefore put to the Security Council. The suggestion was that the force would supervise Israel's withdrawal and, it was hoped, help restore calm to the area. The UN Secretariat was far from happy about this idea, given the turbulent nature of the situation in south Lebanon. For different reasons the Soviet Union was also unenthusiastic about it, being caught between her desire not to support an American initiative and her wish to embarrass Israel. Accordingly, she abstained in the vote which established the UN Interim Force in Lebanon (Unifil) on 19 March.

Israel was greatly annoyed by this hasty development, not least because her opposition to it had been brushed aside by the United States, with whom she had always seen herself, correctly, as having a very special relationship. Perhaps partly as a means of signifying her displeasure, her immediate response was to push about another ten miles further into Lebanon – up to the Litani River. However, this move was probably also connected with the fact that the idea was gaining ground that Unifil should have an area of operation consisting of the area to be vacated by the IDF. Israel did not believe that a UN force would be able to control the PLO, but nevertheless thought that if there was to be something in the nature of a UN buffer zone, it was in her interests that it should be as deep as possible.

PHASE ONE: 1978–1982

The Eastern bloc and Austria declined the Secretary-General's invitation to participate in Unifil, not wishing to complicate their relations with the PLO, and the Latin American states also refused to contribute troops. But contingents from elsewhere were quickly assembled in south Lebanon. It had been anticipated that 4,000 men would be needed for the Force, but within a month an increase of its size to 6,000 had been approved. Early in 1982 the Security Council authorized a further increase to 7,000 men. During these four years troops were contributed to Unifil by the following 14 member states: Canada, Fiji, Finland, France, Ghana, Iran, Ireland, Italy, Nepal, Netherlands, Nigeria, Norway, Senegal and Sweden. At any one time the Force was usually made up of contingents from about nine or ten countries, and throughout it was assisted by between 30 and 90 Military Observers drawn from the UN Truce Supervision Organization (Untso). The participation of France – who had ruled Lebanon between the two World Wars and before that had had a special interest in the area – meant that for the second time (Britain's participation in the Cyprus Force being the first) a permanent member of the Security Council was contributing to a UN peacekeeping force.

The degree of unity amongst the major powers which this reflected also found expression in the agreement that Unifil's costs should be met by all UN members on the basis of an apportionment by the General Assembly. However, a number of states proved unwilling or unable to pay their shares – notably the Soviet Union until 1986 and the United States for some years thereafter. As a result the UN has fallen seriously behind in its reimbursement of states for the costs they have incurred in connection with Unifil.

A three-stage operation was envisaged for the UN Force. Firstly, the withdrawal of Israeli troops was to be supervised; secondly, the area was to be calmed and controlled; and thirdly, it was to be handed back to the Government of Lebanon – this last formulation glossing over the fact that the Government had not controlled the area for a number of years, and was in no condition to attempt to reassert its authority. The first stage began satisfactorily, with Israel handing over the territory from which she withdrew to Unifil. But on leaving the southernmost belt of Lebanese territory in June 1978 she turned it over to the local Christian militias led by Major Saad Haddad, which were hand in glove with Israel. Unifil did manage, through negotiations, to establish a number of positions within this area, which became known as the enclave. But it was in no sense under the UN Force's control, and in fact Unifil met with numerous difficulties there over the next four years. Within the enclave its personnel could not move freely, were regularly harassed, and frequently fired on. The fact that Unifil's headquarters had been established at Naqoura, which was within the enclave, only added to its problems. Haddad's forces also tried from time to time to encroach on the Unifil area. The IDF, by contrast, continued to move freely in the enclave. Thus the situation which had arisen from Israel's invasion was never fully defused (see Map 54).

Partly because of the enclave's existence and the provocation to which it gave rise, Unifil was also unable fully to stabilize the situation in its own area of operation. In the first place, it did not constitute a continuous buffer between Haddad's forces and the PLO's which had been driven north of the Litani River by the Israelis. For at one point the enclave ran along the River, and thus divided Unifil's area into

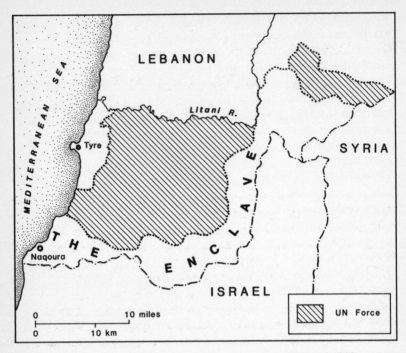

Map 54   The UN Force in Lebanon between 1978 and 1982

two. Secondly, on the ground that some Palestinian forces had held
their positions south of the Litani throughout the brief Israeli occupation,
Unifil agreed (and had little option but to do so) that some 300 of
them might remain within its area. Additionally, the PLO retained
control of the city of Tyre which was south of the Litani and to Unifil's
immediate north west.

Nonetheless, Unifil did form something in the nature of a neutral
zone across much of south Lebanon, and it tried to make it as secure
as possible against Palestinian and Lebanese armed elements opposed
to Israel. It did this by establishing roadblocks and checkpoints, setting
up observation posts along key infiltration routes, engaging in foot and
mobile patrols by day and night, organizing night-time listening posts
on a random basis, and deploying in relative density along the perimeter
of its area. When individuals or groups trying to infiltrate were
apprehended they were usually persuaded, by one non-forceful means
or another, to turn back, and sometimes their weapons were temporarily
confiscated.

However, attempts to enter the Unifil area from the north remained a recurring event, and hostile acts were periodically directed against Unifil personnel. Moreover, there were frequent exchanges of fire between the PLO and Haddad's forces, either directly across the gap in Unifil's deployment or over the Unifil area. These often escalated to involve Israel's forces, which led to further escalation as the PLO fired into Israel and the Israelis retaliated against PLO positions to the north of the Litani. Whenever possible Unifil tried to arrange cease-fires. On a larger canvas the UN and the United States succeeded in negotiating a general cease-fire in July 1981, which was maintained until April 1982.

Thus with Unifil's help an undue escalation of the continuing conflict was prevented. Unifil also helped to maintain a measure of relative calm within its operational area, evidenced by the return of large numbers of civilians who had left in 1978. And, with regard to them, it was able to engage in or facilitate a substantial amount of humanitarian work. Peace and security was by no means restored to the area, but without Unifil it is highly likely that the whole area would have been hugely more unstable. For in such a context the possibility of an Israeli–Syrian clash could not have been excluded. In turn, that development could have had very ominous repercussions, given that both Israel and Syria were strongly backed by a superpower. The Arab–Israeli dispute was indeed a dangerous international crossroads, so that small devices to increase its safety had a disproportionate value.

Unifil's successes and failures were basically a reflection of the extent and of the limits of the cooperation which the Force received from the parties. As a peacekeeping body, Unifil was neither equipped nor intended to keep the disputants in order. It could not impose itself on the situation, but had to operate within the parameters which were set by the principals. Accordingly, Unifil's inability to pacify the area was not due to its own deficiencies, but to the character of the situation in which it found itself. It did what it could, and was valuably instrumental in contributing towards a partial stabilization of south Lebanon between 1978 and 1982. But if either side decided that it was time for another major showdown, there was nothing which the UN Force could do to prevent it.

PHASE TWO: 1982–1985

In June 1982 Israel invaded Lebanon again, resolved to make a better job of smashing the PLO than it had done in 1978. As a reminder that it was the only authorized armed force in south Lebanon, Unifil offered some resistance, chiefly of a token and non-human kind – for example, by establishing road blocks. But it was no real obstacle to the invaders, who sped on right up to the outskirts of Lebanon's capital, Beirut. This time it was three years before they departed.

During this period Unifil was operating in occupied territory, from which the PLO had been expelled. The terms of its original mandate, which the Security Council left unchanged when periodically renewing the life of the Force, were thus even less applicable than they had ever been to the situation on the ground. Unifil's size was also maintained throughout this period at about 6,000 men. No doubt the Force was kept in place partly as a standing reproach to Israel, and as something of an obstacle to the de facto annexation of the area. It is also the case that the UN has always been loath to wind up an operation if there is a chance that it might be of some future use: an existing body can more easily be reactivated or expanded than a new one can be started from scratch.

More positively, Unifil was able to continue its humanitarian assistance to the locals, and was also able to afford them some protection – and large numbers of civilians returned to the area, or fled to it from the tribulations of other parts of the country. With regard to Israeli activity against alleged disturbers of the occupation, Unifil's presence was something of a moral restraint, and its members sometimes practised passive resistance in an effort to prevent violence to people and property. Additionally, Unifil tried to contain the activities of the local militias which were raised by the Israelis to patrol in the Unifil area. It also asserted itself in relation to any attempted encroachment into its area of Haddad's forces which, after his death in 1984, became reorganized as the South Lebanon Army (SLA).

It is very doubtful, however, if these tasks – none of which had any direct bearing on the maintenance of international peace – required a Force of anything like the size at which it was maintained. For various reasons, Nepal withdrew for a few years, and Nigeria and Senegal for good. The Netherlands reduced her representation during this period, and withdrew completely at the end of 1985. As a state traditionally sympathetic towards Israel, she had been dismayed to find (and was not the first so to do) that contact by her peacekeepers with Israel often induced an extremely critical attitude towards that country. All the other contributors maintained their contingents, however, and the Force as a whole hardly diminished at all in size.

Early in 1985 Israel announced that by the middle of the year she would have left Lebanon, opening the way for Unifil to resume its peacekeeping role. The years 1982–1985 should therefore be seen as a rather unusual interlude in its history. From the point of view of the local inhabitants, who increased markedly in number at this time, Unifil performed a number of very valuable services. But it was not engaged in peacekeeping.

PHASE THREE: 1985–

During this phase, Unifil has been faced with four major problems. The first of them arises from the fact that the IDF made an even less complete departure from south Lebanon that it had done in 1978. It was not to be expected that the old enclave and the puppet SLA would be abandoned. It emerged, however, that what Israel now called her 'security zone' in Lebanon was to be appreciably more extensive than the equivalent area had been prior to 1982. The new zone overlaps parts of what had hitherto been Unifil's exclusive western sector, and not only completely embraces its eastern sector but also covers extensive areas to its north. The IDF is not deployed in strength in its security zone, but is always available to support the SLA, leaving no doubt about who, at bottom, is in charge on the ground (see Map 55).

In Unifil's eastern sector, therefore, the situation has remained essentially the same as it was in 1982–1985. The Force is in Israeli-occupied territory. It does assert itself in what are deemed to be appropriate ways, especially in relation to the SLA alone. But it is not operating in a bilateral international context, and is therefore not engaged on peacekeeping. The logical thing for Unifil to do would be to withdraw from this area. But that would have the grave disadvantage of appearing to give in to Israel, and would thus be in accord neither with the current international orthodoxy that state territory is sacrosanct nor with the anti-Israel balance of political forces in the UN.

In respect of the old enclave – now the southernmost strip of the security zone – Unifil had by mid-1987 quietly withdrawn from most of its previous positions, which had always been inconveniently isolated and therefore difficult to maintain. It continued to regard this area as one where it was supposed to be exercising its functions. But it evidently, and sensibly, concluded that if one is simply in the business of flag waving, a lot of flags are not required. In that part of Unifil's western sector where there is now an overlap with the security zone, however, Unfil has been determined to assert its right to deploy full. This has

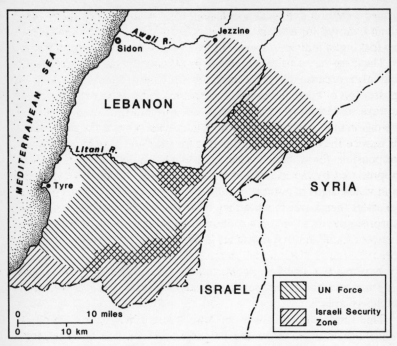

Map 55　The UN Force in Lebanon since 1985

led to a good deal of friction, and an uneasy and hazardous coexistence has developed.

Unifil's second main problem concerns its relationship with the indigenous forces of resistance to the continued de facto Israeli occupation of a good part of south Lebanon. On the one hand, the Force is supposed to ensure that its area is not used for any kind of hostile activity; on the other it is supposed to be supervising an Israeli withdrawal, which the resistance forces are trying to encourage. This conundrum has been resolved by Unifil not taking any physical action to stop fighting between the occupying and resistance forces which occurs in its exclusive area, and no action of any kind in respect of fighting in the area of overlap. But in its exclusive area it does what it can to ensure that only its personnel bear arms. Towards this end about 200 checkpoints and observation posts are manned, and there is regular and frequent patrolling. Unifil's detailed practice in this matter has varied, both between its contingents and over time. But outsiders are, at least in principle, not permitted to proceed into the Unifil area with armed weapons, and local people seen with weapons are liable to have them removed for a while. Vehicles are routinely searched, but there is no frisking of individuals, and Unifil is very reluctant to search houses.

These are very sensitive tasks, not just because of the political context but also because all adult males in Lebanon seem to regard the possession of a lethal weapon as a natural right. Moreover, Unifil has always to remember that while it can cajole, argue, and even bluff, neither in theory nor in practice does it have the powers of a government. It is, with the consent of what passes for the Government of Lebanon, responsible for a basic aspect of order, and its efforts are widely appreciated by the locals. But it lacks virtually all the usual outward and visible signs of authority, and this in a part where others are prone to assert themselves in what they believe to be an excellent cause. Not surprisingly, therefore, confrontations and incidents sometimes occur between Unifil and the resistance forces, and the area has by no means been cleared of illegitimate armaments. Nonetheless, Unifil does seem to have made a significant contribution towards reducing the number of arms, and has thus brought a reasonable measure of security to its exclusive area.

Thie third major problem for Unifil since 1985 stems from a split which has occurred within the indigenous resistance forces. The people of south Lebanon belong predominantly to the Shi'a branch of orthodox Islam, and although roughly equivalent in size to Lebanon's two other main politico-religious groupings, have until recently been very much the underdogs. In the 1970s, however, the balance began to change as a Shi'a movement called Amal (meaning, significantly, 'hope') gained ground, and received general support from Syria. Great animosity developed between it and the PLO, and with the latter's expulsion by the IDF, Amal became a kind of de facto government in the south.

However, in the 1980s a radical Shi'a group – Hezbollah, or 'party of God' – was established, with very close links with the extremist regime in (Shi'a) Iran. It quickly gathered support in the south, where it engaged in some dramatically offensive acts against the IDF. However, whereas Amal is not committed to anything more than an Israeli departure from Lebanon, and in practice is not always over-exercised about that, Hezbollah looks keenly forward to the day when the flag of Islam will fly over Jerusalem itself. From its point of view, therefore, Unifil is obstructing a just war by trying to prevent armed elements from entering or operating from its area. In response to Hezbollah's progress, Amal began to take a more aggressive line, thus contributing to a heightening of tension.

In August 1986 this produced a major crisis for Unifil, which rumbled on menacingly for about a month. A local Amal leader and his bodyguard were killed by a French sentry, which immediately led to a number of French positions coming under siege. A truce was arranged, but sporadic attacks continued as Hezbollah evidently got in on the act, which also had the consequence of widening the clashes to include other Unifil contingents and the SLA.

The reasons for the attacks on the French were fairly clear, the most immediate being revenge. They also no doubt represented the displeasure of Muslims at the recent pro-Christian role of France in the non-UN Multinational Force in Beirut (see Section L below). It may also have been remembered that France was the traditional protector of Lebanese Christians, which would not have done her any good. Finally, and very importantly, France was at this time Iraq's main supplier of arms in her war with Iran, thus attracting the enmity of Hezbollah. As a result of this situation there were large French withdrawals from Unifil, and not everyone was sad to see the French infantrymen go, as they sometimes seemed ill-attuned to the restrictive demands of peacekeeping. The whole episode was a reminder that while the peacekeeping troops of a major power might sometimes elicit more day-to-day respect than those of a mini-state, they can also cause gratuitous complications.

The crisis also, however, raised the question of whether the southern Shi'as were trying to break the UN Force. The very thought of that immediately rang some significant alarm bells. Syria weighed in with an expression of unequivocal support and no less a person than the Prime Minister of Israel commented on Unifil's usefulness as a stabilizing factor, ostentatiously moving forces to the north of Israel at the same time. Amal held a rally in Unifil's support, and, following diplomatic expressions of concern, calming words went out to Hezbollah from Iran. The danger passed, and subsequently the situation was eased by Hezbollah losing ground to Amal (and as of June 1990 Amal was still in essential control). The complexity and danger of the context in which Unifil is operating, however, had been firmly underlined.

A fourth, and final, complexity for Unifil is represented by the PLO. Many Palestinian fighters who had been expelled from south Lebanon by the IDF began to return to the area north of the Litani River after Israel's 1985 withdrawal, and tried to recruit in some large Palestinian refugee camps in that region. They received little by way of a welcome from any of the local parties but, especially with the growing momentum of the Intifada campaign on the Israeli-occupied West Bank and Gaza Strip, cannot be completely ignored. As of mid 1990 the PLO has not seriously tried to re-establish itself in the Unifil area. But the possibility that it might yet do so must be a chilling thought for the Force. For any such development would both heighten Unifil's immediate problems, and increase the hostile attention which would be directed towards its area by the SLA and the IDF.

UNIFIL'S PEACEKEEPING ROLE

In south Lebanon the host state is absent, an occupying state is present, various sub-groups are in battle with each other and the occupier, and there is agreement on hardly anything. But one matter on which there is a rough consensus is that Unifil's presence is a good thing. Those who are treated as spokesmen for the host state approve of it, as does Syria and, in a less open way, Israel. The SLA and Amal are probably glad that they do not have to confront each other more directly. Hezbollah and the PLO, it is true, do not welcome the restraints which Unifil places on them, but it is most unlikely that they are representative of the views of the local people. For, even amidst all its current tribulations, the area in which Unifil is stationed still enjoys a significantly higher degree of order and prosperity than it used to, and there can be little doubt that this is directly attributable to the activity of the UN Force. Most of the people of the area know that, and appreciate it. In a loose way, therefore, Unifil satisfies the peacekeeping requirement that its presence is based on consent.

It is also the case that since 1985 Unifil has, in an impartial and non-threatening manner, fulfilled a peacekeeping function. For even in the uneasy, fluid, and dangerous context of south Lebanon, it has been able to contribute towards the maintenance of international stability in two important ways. Firstly, as in its initial phase, Unifil provides something in the nature of a buffer between Israel and her immediate adversaries in Lebanon. It is neither complete nor impervious. But in the absence of the UN Force there would certainly be many more hostile acts directed towards the security zone, and hence more retaliation. Israel might, of course, respond to such a development by extending the zone, but that would hardly improve either the local situation or the wider international context.

This draws attention to Unifil's second stabilizing role – as a buffer between Israel and Syria. It has been clear ever since Syria's forces entered Lebanon in 1976 that neither she nor Israel wishes to tangle with the other in that country. In principle there is no reason why they should not continue to achieve this shared desire in the absence of Unifil, but it might well be more difficult. For there would necessarily be some competition for control of the ground vacated by Unifil, and however that was resolved tension would almost certainly increase in and around south Lebanon. Furthermore, and incidents between Israel and Syria could not fail to arouse the concern, and even the involvement in some way, of their superpower backers. The escalation of such developments could certainly, with good discipline, be prevented. But the situation would be a bit riskier, and at such an inflammable crossroads both Israel and Syria on the one hand and the Soviet Union and the United States on the other are anxious to minimize risk. All four states feel a little more comfortable with Unifil in place.

It is therefore very likely that the Security Council – in which, since 1986, the Soviet Union has joined the other permanent members in periodically voting for Unifil's extention – will wish to maintain the UN Force in south Lebanon. It is also, and consequentially, likely that enough money will be forthcoming for that to be done. Additionally, of course, it is necessary that contingents for the Force – which, as of January 1990 was 5876 strong – continue to be forthcoming. That, too, is likely, unless there is a dramatic increase in its casualties (which, for a peacekeeping force, are already not insignificant), for there have been no complete national withdrawals since the end of 1985. Unifil is in no way able to provide an answer to south Lebanon's problems. But it does help to prevent them from getting worse. That is never a negligible quality, and in south Lebanon's already unhappy condition, is one which has particular value.

FURTHER READING

Emmanuel A. Erskine, *Mission with UNIFIL* (London: Hurst, 1989).

David Gilmour, *Lebanon: The Fractured Country* (London: Sphere, revised edn 1984).

Alan James, 'Painful Peacekeeping: The UN in Lebanon, 1978–1982', *International Journal*, XXXVIII (4) (October 1983).

Alan James, *Interminable Interim: The UN Force in Lebanon* (London: Centre for Security and Conflict Studies, 1988).

Aharon Levran, 'UN Forces and Israel's Security', *Jerusalem Quarterly*, 37 (1986).

John Mackinlay, *The Peacekeepers* (London: Unwin Hyman, 1989).

Anthony McDermott and Kjell Skjelsbaek (eds), *A Thankless Task: The Role of UNIFIL in Southern Lebanon* (Oslo: Norwegian Institute of International Affairs, 1988).

Augustus Richard Norton, *Amal and the Shia* (Austin, Texas: University of Texas Press, 1987).

Bjorn Skogmo, *UNIFIL* (Boulder, Col.: Lynne Rienner, 1989).

Ramesh Thakur, *International Peacekeeping in Lebanon* (Boulder, Col.: Westview Press, 1987).

Naomi Joy Weinberger, 'Peacekeeping Options in Lebanon', *The Middle East Journal*, 37 (3) (Summer 1983).

Section K The Withdrawal of Palestinian Forces from Beirut (1982)

When Israel invaded Lebanon in June 1982 her forces swept to the very outskirts of Beirut. There they stopped, and laid siege to the western, Muslim, part of the city, where large numbers (thought to be 6,000–8,000) of Palestinian fighters had established positions amidst about half a million civilians. The object of the Israeli invasion had been to drive the Palestinians from Lebanon. But Israel's extremely heavy bombardment of West Beirut over the next two months failed to have this effect, and she was not disposed to take the heavy losses which would almost surely ensue if she sent her troops into the streets of the city. The political costs of her bombardment, which was brought to a wide international audience through television, were also mounting (see Map 56).

Meanwhile, American negotiators were trying to bring about a pacific resolution of the impasse. Israel's belligerence was not just embarrassing the United States but also, and worse, carried with it the possibility of escalatory clashes with the large Syrian force which was present in Lebanon (see Section I above). Eventually, in August, the American mediatory efforts bore fruit. The Palestine Liberation Organization (PLO) agreed that its men would leave Lebanon provided they could do so in a safe and not too obviously humiliating manner, and a number of Arab states agreed to take them. For her part, Israel was very willing to go along with this scheme provided she could be assured that all the fighters had really left, and also that the Syrian forces in West Beirut were redeployed outside the city. Clearly, what was called for was a peacekeeping mission to supervise what would be a very delicate operation.

On this occasion, however, the UN was not favoured with the task. Israel was opposed to that idea, largely because she suspected that the Organization's political partiality towards the PLO might find reflection

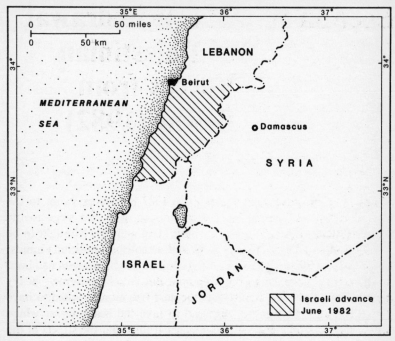

Map 56   Israel's 1982 advance into Lebanon

in its peacekeeping activity. Additionally, the recent establishment of
a non-UN peacekeeping force in Sinai (see Part II, Section K above)
had generated much enthusiasm in Israel for that approach and, more
particularly, for the closer involvement of the United States with
measures which bolstered Israeli security. Of course, formally speaking
Israel was not to be a host state in this instance, so her agreement
regarding the source and composition of the peacekeeping body was
not technically necessary. But as a practical matter it certainly was.
And Israel took the opportunity not only to veto the UN's involvement
but to say that her agreement to the proposed scheme was contingent
on American participation in the supervisory arrangements. The
Christian-dominated Lebanese Government also looked warmly on
this idea, like Israel being attracted by the thought of a close association
with the United States. And the PLO, too, saw virtue in the proposal
on the ground that its men would thereby be provided with the best
guarantee of a safe departure from Beirut.

The United States responded very cautiously to her sudden popularity.
Lebanon's formal invitation was required, and the United States also

sought, and received, assurances of cooperation from certain other Lebanese groups. A strict time limit of 30 days was placed on the operation. The American troops were to be prohibited from engaging in combat, except in self-defence. They were to remain under direct American command. Congress was assured that the situation contained no danger of imminent hostilities. And the troops were to leave immediately if the PLO failed to depart on schedule. It was also understood that the honour of participating in this, from most points of view, classic peacekeeping operation was to be shared with others – France and Italy agreeing to join in, at their own expense. A detailed plan for the PLO's departure was furnished, which satisfied all the interested parties, and the United States made it understood that the costs of the PLO evacuation would in one way or another be met. Thus all was set for the unveiling of the scheme on 20 August.

The body which resulted was called the Multinational Force (MNF – to which the number 'I' was soon added to distinguish it from its successor). However, it had no central command structure, and was not therefore a 'force' in the sense in which that word is usually employed. Instead, liaison and coordination arrangements were instituted between the 800 American, 800 French and 400 Italian troops who made up the MNF, and between them and the Lebanese Government and Army. The lack of a single commander and a common logistical system has often attracted the criticism of military men. But in this case it did not present any marked operational difficulties, as the three contingents knew exactly what they had to do, and the PLO and the Israelis played their allotted parts conscientiously.

An effective cease fire was declared, and the first members of the MNF began to arrive in Beirut as soon as 21 August. The PLO and Syrian forces immediately began to leave, in a manner which was much more suggestive of victory than defeat. They were closely supervised by the MNF, which arranged for the temporary clearing of such departure routes as ran through Israeli positions around the city. Everything went very smoothly, and what had been a tense and potentially explosive scene was effectively defused. To the surprise of many, the number of Palestinian fighters leaving Beirut was said to be about 14,400, together with getting on for half that number of Syrian troops. The last elements withdrew on 9 September, and three days later the MNF had also completed its departure. Lebanon still presented large and internationally alarming problems. But one very worrying aspect of the situation had, with the MNF's peacekeeping assistance, been defused and resolved, at least for a while.

FURTHER READING

Robert B. Houghton and Frank G. Trinka, *Multinational Peacekeeping in the Middle East* (Washington, DC: US Department of State, Foreign Service Institute, 1984).

Ramesh Thakur, *International Peacekeeping in Lebanon* (Boulder, Col.: Westview Press, 1987).

Section L   Big Powers in
Beirut
(1982–1984)

No sooner had the first Multinational Force (MNF I – see Section K above) left Beirut than events precipitated the creation of a second such Force – MNF II. In response to the assassination of the Lebanese President-elect on 14 September 1982, Israeli forces moved into West Beirut, to the considerable annoyance of many states, not least the United States. For in the light of Israel's support of Christian elements in Lebanon, this was a provocative act, West Beirut being the Muslim area of the city, divided from the Christian section by what had become known as the Green Line. This development had dramatic consequences. For the Israelis allowed right-wing Christian militia men to enter two Palestinian refugee camps at Sabra and Shatila, where they proceeded to butcher hundreds of civilians.

These events received wide international publicity, and elicited demands for a renewed international presence in Beirut. As one such group had only just left, it was not surprising that there was a general feeling in favour of its immediate return. In the emotional atmosphere of the moment, the United States was not disposed to prevaricate about this, and her two fellow members of MNF I, France and Italy, agreed to join her in a new peacekeeping body. There was some delay while Israel was persuaded to retire to her earlier positions, but by the end of September MNF II was in place.

The new Force, like its predecessor, had no central command structure. It started off at more than twice the size of MNF I, Italy and the United States contributing 1,400 troops each and France 1,500. Later the Italian element was increased to 2,200 and, in response to a good deal of otherwise unsuccessful canvassing, Britain supplied a small contingent of 100 men. Most of these troops carried heavier arms than in their earlier manifestation, but it was certainly not anticipated that MNF II would use them other than in self-defence. It was to be what could now be called a traditional peacekeeping force, dependent for its success on impartial and non-threatening activity in the context of cooperating parties (see Map 57).

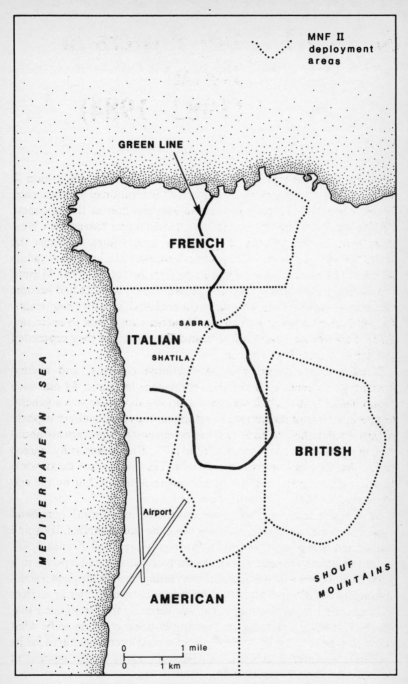

Map 57   The Second Multinational Force in Beirut

MNF II's mandate also reflected much earlier peacekeeping experience, having two associated aspects. Firstly, it was to interpose itself between Israel's forces and those of the Muslim Lebanese militias in Beirut, with a view to defusing the immediate tension. Secondly, and connectedly, but with a somewhat different aim in mind, MNF II was to support the Lebanese Army in the execution of its normal law and order tasks. The hope here was that such activity would contribute towards a restoration of the authority of the Government and its Army in the Beirut area, which in turn might assist in resolving the civil conflict which had not just plagued Lebanon for the previous six years but had also encouraged foreign interventions by both Syria and Israel. Caps were touched towards the customary idea in these circumstances that the help of the peacekeepers would not be needed for long. But, in a significant departure from MNF I's mandate, no time limit was set for MNF II. It was stated, however, that the contingents in the Force would be withdrawn at the request of the host state or when their own states judged that the time had come for them to leave. As before, each state contributing to MNF II was to meet the costs of its participation.

At first this operation went quite smoothly, exemplifying the idea of peacekeeping. MNF II members manned checkpoints jointly with the Lebanese Army but, wishing to build up the state's authority, did not themselves do the actual checking. They patrolled the city, accompanied by Lebanese liaison officers. And the American and French contingents participated in the training of the Lebanese Army – which, during the previous six years of civil war, had broken up into its confessional parts and as a unit had more or less disintegrated. (This last work supplemented the direct military assistance arrangements which France and the United States had instituted.) MNF II also performed many routine governmental functions and engaged in humanitarian work, clearing unexploded bombs, for example, and providing medical asistance – the Italian contingent being particularly notable for the latter. In all these matters the Force seemed to be generally welcome, and the situation to be acquiring an unaccustomed degree of stability.

It proved, however, to be the calm before the storm. The local Muslim militias, together with the Syrian interventionary force in Lebanon, continued to see the Government and the Christian militias as enemies, and the Lebanese Army as but one of these militias. France was still pictured in her traditional role as protector of the Lebanese Christians, and the United States as the close associate of Israel. Moreover, the United States exposed herself dangerously by engineering an agreement of May 1983 between Israel and Lebanon for an Israeli withdrawal –

subject to certain arrangements regarding Israel's security interests in southern Lebanon. The very fact of the agreement was widely seen as a Lebanese betrayal of the Arab cause, and Syria was particularly offended not just at being left out of the discussions but at being depicted as no less a foreign element in the Lebanese body politic than Israel. The underlying political situation was therefore as fractured as before, and the composition of MNF II brought with it the possibility of additional contention.

Military developments then proceeded to expose the Government's lack of legitimacy and the hazards of peacekeeping in such a situation. In April 1983 the American embassy in West Beirut was blown up, with much loss of life. In August, following the Lebanese Army's attempt to put down attacks on American and French positions, fighting broke out in Beirut between the Army and the Muslim militias. But it was in September that the situation went seriously downhill. Israel withdrew from the Beirut area, and fighting broke out between Government forces and Syrian-backed Muslim and Druze (a heretical Muslim sect) militias for the control of the strategically-important Shouf Mountains to the south east of the city. For whatever reason, the American and French positions began to suffer in the cross-fire; the Government failed in its initial attempt to take the Shouf; and the United States and France decided to support the governmental forces with heavy fire. Suicide bombing missions were made in October on the headquarters of the American and French MNF contingents, resulting in the death of 241 American and 58 French soliders. Retaliatory action followed.

In a short space of time two members of MNF II had thus moved from a peacekeeping to a participatory role. In this context there was no future for the Force as a peacekeeping body, and early in 1984 its contingents were one by one withdrawn. The Americans were the first and the French the last to decide on this course, while the Italian departure was distinguished from the others by the fact that it was discussed in detail with Untso's small Observer Group in Beirut (see Section F, above). Shortly before leaving, France proposed that MNF II be replaced by a UN force in which none of the Security Council's five permanent members would be represented. It would have the task of supervising a cease-fire and helping to protect civilians, but would have to abstain from intervention in Lebanon's internal affairs. Whether this programme contained a basic internal inconsistency was not put to the test – to the great relief of the likely contributors – for the proposal was vetoed by the Soviet Union. The Soviets, and their Syrian friends, may well have felt that with the Americans on the run and things seemingly going the Muslim way in Beirut, this was not the moment to introduce a body which might perhaps hamper the anti-Governmental campaign.

MNF II's inglorious end can easily be misunderstood. The fact that the Force was not acting in the name of the UN has no real bearing on the situation, for the basic factors which determine the success or failure of a peacekeeping body have to do with the context in which it operates and the way it actually behaves rather than the auspices under which it appears. Nor did the absence of a central command structure have a crucial impact on MNF II's fate. Undoubtedly this lack complicated some matters and facilitated individual rather than coordinated action. But if the participants had been set on marching in step, their liaison arrangements could perfectly well have implemented such an intention. It was equally the case that the vague mandate with which the Force was supplied – by no means a novelty for peacekeeping bodies – could have been interpreted in accordance with the values of peacekeeping had the contributing states so resolved.

The fundamental problem for MNF II was two-fold. The first part of it was that the political situation to which the Force was despatched was highly unsuitable for peacekeeping. What MNF II had been asked to do, basically, was to help maintain order with a view to the Government of Lebanon thereby reacquiring legitimacy. Law and order tasks, however, are always particularly delicate for peacekeepers due to the possibility of their actions, however impartially intended, being seen as favouring one internal party, and therefore disfavouring others. Problems of this kind can arise even in respect of a straightforward ring-holding mission in a political arena where the fairness of the constitution is not an issue. They get bigger where there is dispute about the basic provisions of the political system. And they are biggest of all where help is to be extended to an incumbent government whose legitimacy is seriously challenged. In such circumstances the peacekeeping body is virtually bound to be seen as involved in rather than above the fray. Those who set up MNF II hoped that some political alchemy would enable Lebanon's Government, with the aid of the Force, to be reaccepted as representative of the whole state. It was a very large hope. That is not uncommon in politics – but in this particular case it was quite without foundation.

The second part of MNF II's problem was revealed once it became apparent that Beirut in 1983 was not 'peacekeeping-friendly'; it concerned the Force's response to this situation. Instead of becoming even more insistent on behaviour which was in accord with the values of peacekeeping, even if that meant an acceptance of MNF II's inability to make any kind of contribution to the local scene, two of its members allowed their troops to get increasingly involved on one side of the redeveloping dispute. It is, of course, easier to make this comment with hindsight than at the time. One thing leads to another, and there is always the hope that the next blow will be decisive, so that in an escalating conflict it is hard to draw a line – in political as well as military terms. But the basic nature of the situation in Beirut was never unclear. Accordingly, it would have been possible for the participating states to make the limits of their role very plain to their contingents. And that is what they should have done. Having joined in a multilateral peacekeeping enterprise, each member had at the very least an obligation to its fellows to make sure that the character and extent of the commitment was sufficiently spelt out – and honoured. The failure to do so was not to the credit of those concerned; it led to some unnecessary confusion about the nature of peacekeeping; and it also proved to be without any political return.

It happened that France and the United States were particularly well placed to move to an interventionary role in the Lebanese conflict. Besides the quite considerable armaments (for peacekeepers) which their men had with them on the ground, both these states had very substantial naval and air resources offshore which could easily be called up. Their use was a reminder that while peacekeeping operations might sometimes draw much benefit from the involvement of the great powers, their role, to be effective in peacekeeping terms, also calls for great discipline.

FURTHER READING

Robert B. Houghton and Frank G. Trinka, *Multinational Peacekeeping in the Middle East* (Washington, DC: US Department of State, Foreign Service Institute, 1984).

Alan James, 'Options for Peace-Keeping', in Josephine O'Connor Howe (ed.), *Armed Peace: The Search for World Security* (London: Macmillan, 1984).

John Mackinlay, *The Peacekeepers* (London: Unwin Hyman, 1989).

Nathan A. Pelcovits, *Peacekeeping on Arab–Israeli Fronts* (Boulder, Col.: Westview Press, 1984).

Kjell Skjelsbaek and Anthony McDermott (eds), *The Multinational Force in Lebanon* (Oslo: Norwegian Institute of International Affairs, 1988).

Ramesh Thakur, *International Peacekeeping in Lebanon* (Boulder, Col.: Westview Press, 1987).

Conclusion: The Use of Peacekeeping

Contrary to what is often supposed, peacekeeping has proved its use in a very wide range of international disputes. As the 57 case studies in this book have shown, it can help to contain or resolve conflicts which extend from small back-yard problems to superpower confrontations. This statement should not surprise anyone who reasons from first principles and has some knowledge of politics and war. Impartial and non-threatening third parties can play a timely role in many walks of life. Where considerations of national honour and the need to save face are compounded by the antagonism of distrustful or recently-embattled states, such assistance can be of great value.

PEACEKEEPING AND INTERNATIONAL POLITICS

This book's analytical scheme has not resulted in the identification of a positive correlation between any of peacekeeping's aspects and the type of international context in which it has appeared. There is, for example, no suggestion of a link between the international character of a dispute and the size of the peacekeeping operation which it elicits. Most peacekeeping bodies consist of relatively small groups of observers, but the larger peacekeeping forces are to be found in four of the five categories into which international conflict has been divided (the exception being that which considers neighbourhood quarrels). Evidence is also lacking to support the idea that in terms of regularity and frequency some types of dispute achieve a higher peacekeeping score than others. The categories which deal with high-street embarrassments and dangerous crossroads do not, it is true, contain any instances from the period between the two World Wars. But each of them includes operations which were established in each of the four decades 1950–1989, and all the other three categories display a broad range of starting dates. So far as the length of peacekeeping missions is concerned, four of the five categories include operations of widely varying duration (back-yard problems being the exception). And all five categories provide instances of each type of peacekeeping function.

What does emerge from the employment of the analytical framework, however, are two general conclusions. The first is that peacekeeping is an activity which can be utilized in all types of international conflict. Those which have been termed clubhouse troubles, neighbourhood quarrels, and high-street embarrassments display a solid mixture of the three peacekeeping functions of defusion, stabilization and settlement. Dangerous crossroads have tended to elicit peacekeeping activity to defuse crises and stabilize situations, but have also given rise to operations designed to wind up disputes. The remaining category of back-yard problems has chiefly provided services of a stabilizing and settling kind, but crisis defusion has also been present. Clearly, peacekeeping is a versatile phenomenon.

The second conclusion is that the kind of international care and attention which peacekeepers offer can be in demand for long periods irrespective of the sort of issue to which they are applying their skills. Four of the five categories include one or more operations with a life of at least 15 years. Only in the case of back-yard problems have peacekeeping operations generally lasted for less than two years. No matter what the nature or apparent importance of the situation which leads to peacekeeping, it cannot be assumed that the resultant activity will be of short duration.

Clues to other general findings about peacekeeping may perhaps be found by placing it as a whole against the changing background of international politics. At one time, for example, it was thought by some that peacekeeping was an essentially post-colonial phenomenon – which would therefore greatly diminish once the adjustments entailed by the ending of overseas rule were complete. There was some apparent strength in this argument, inasmuch as a number of peacekeeping missions have had to do with or followed from the winding up of a colonial relationship. Further contemporary instances of the point can be found in the UN's operation in Namibia and in the discussion about how peacekeeping might be able to contribute to an ending of the Western Sahara problem.

There are, however, several difficulties about this proposition, the first of which is the inadequacy of its historical perspective. It is true that a number of inter-war instances of peacekeeping can be seen as post-imperial in that they arose out of the collapse of empires. But the empires in question were all intra-European, and the problems which they spawned were not at all the sort which were in the minds of those who saw peacekeeping as a response to the dismantling of overseas rule. Moreover, this period provides a number of examples of peacekeeping which had nothing to do with any kind of imperial edifice. Secondly, it is somewhat unrealistic to talk of, for example, Palestine, Kashmir, or Cyprus as post-colonial problems when 30 or 40 years have elapsed since the departure of the metropolitan power. A third, and much more basic inadequacy of this approach, however, is its assumption that the disputes which have followed the ending of colonialism, and attracted peacekeeping attention, have been typically and exclusively post-colonial in character. There is no ground for this assumption. Border tension, territorial disputes, intervention, minority problems, and civil disorder do not occur only as colonial legacies.

Another attempt to establish a link between peacekeeping and the ebb and flow of international politics is the suggestion that it has to a large extent been a reflection of the Cold War. The major powers, it is argued, might once have engaged in forceful action in the cause of international order – the role, indeed, which was envisaged for them by the UN Charter. Because, however, of the deep rift which developed between them after 1945, there has been no question of joint action of this kind, and they have been reluctant to act separately for fear of provoking a counter-intervention – and with it the danger of full-scale war. They have therefore turned to peacekeeping as a surrogate vehicle for ordering activity. This is certainly peacekeeping's overall purpose, which is greatly valued by the superpowers, as by many others. But the hypothesis that there is an intimate connection between peacekeeping and the Cold War immediately runs into a number of problems.

One is that this approach, like the previous one, suffers from a lack of historical perspective. As has been shown, peacekeeping antedates the Cold War. A second is that it is not easy to identify situations where the superpowers might have intervened but for the tensions of the Cold War and the availability of peacekeeping. One such case is that which occurred at the end of the October War of 1973, and there were also vague Soviet threats of intervention over the Suez crisis of 1956. But it is most unlikely that there was any substance to the latter. And other peacekeeping operations concerning the Arab–Israeli conflict have generally reflected the strong wish of the superpowers, for reasons which have had to do with much more than the Cold War, not to get closely involved. In relation to the Indo–Pakistani conflict over Kashmir there has been even less likelihood of the physical involvement of the superpowers. There was much talk of possible Soviet intervention in the Congo in 1960 but it does not seem that there was any real chance of soldiers with snow on their boots arriving in Central Africa. And sometimes peacekeeping has facilitated the departure of the superpowers from awkward situations, as in Vietnam and Afghanistan, rather than substituting for their arrival. There was an intervention problem in relation to Cyprus but not one which was related to the Cold War.

A third critical point in connection with this argument is that the burst of peacekeeping activity and proposals which took place in 1988 and 1989 occurred against a background of hugely-improved relations between the superpowers. This suggests, however, that the argument might be turned on its head, to the effect that peacekeeping is a reflection not of bad but of good relations between the great powers, and in particular between the superpowers. This both accords with contemporary developments and with the predominant experience of the inter-war period. Such a claim might also seem to be exemplified by those peacekeeping operations established by the UN Security Council (i.e., most UN operations), as they can be mounted only with at least the tacit acquiescence of all the Council's five permanent members.

However, on close examination this proposition is also less convincing than it might appear, for two reasons. Firstly, it is seriously undermined by the number of occasions since 1945 when operations have been established in contexts marked by superpower enmity rather than amity. In 1948 and 1949 the UN's observation groups in Palestine and Kashmir were being set up against the background of the Berlin crisis and the onset of the Cold War. In 1954 the establishment of the non-UN Control Commissions in Indo-China were a concomitant of poor East–West relations. In 1956 the UN's first peacekeeping force was sent to Suez a matter of days after the Soviet invasion of Hungary. In 1960 the UN's Congo operation was launched just a couple of months after the shooting down by the Soviets of a spying American aircraft had led to the breakdown of the summit meeting in Paris. In 1962 the UN's West New Guinea/West Irian operation was authorized just when the United States was getting suspicious about Soviet activities in Cuba. And the establishment in 1973 of the second UN Emergency Force in Egypt was a direct consequence of a major superpower confrontation.

Secondly, it cannot be assumed that the establishment of peacekeeping operations at a time of good superpower relations is indicative of a causal relationship between the two phenomena. Such a relationship may exist: the peacekeeping operations of the late 1980s regarding the withdrawal of Soviet troops from Afghanistan and of Cuban troops from Angola were certainly connected with the revised Soviet approch to the rest of the world in general and to the United States in particular. There were also links between this development and the setting up of a peacekeeping operation to oversee the transition of Namibia from South African rule to independence.

But other factors were also powerfully at work in these cases, especially the last. And in the remaining situations where peacekeeping operations have recently been established or seriously discussed, that activity does not appear to have been chiefly a consequence of the changed East–West atmosphere. Local considerations, rather, seem to have had a dominant influence on the arrangement of a cease-fire in the Iran–Iraq War, on the disposition of the parties to the Western Sahara dispute to contemplate a settlement, on the movement towards peace in Central America, and on the tentative talk about national reconciliation in Cambodia.

It follows from this and the earlier comments that undue prognostic weight should not be put on the sharp upsurge – perhaps the word 'explosion' is not too strong – in peacekeeping activity since the start of 1988, and of discussion about its possible use. Expectations that a trend in that direction has been established should be discouraged. Peacekeeping operations are not just a reflection of political ambience or fashion. Instead, they usually arise out of sudden crises or flagging militancy. The last phenomenon may perhaps to some extent be related to a more general development in international relations. But it need not be. Even less is it the case that a number of different crises can convincingly be linked to a single underlying cause. It is, rather, the entirely individual situation which tends to create the perceived need for a peacekeeping operation. Peacekeeping is thus chiefly the reflection of specific political circumstances, of a decision, in the light of the facts of the individual case, that third-party aid should be employed to help defuse a crisis, stabilize a situation, or move towards a settlement.

PEACEKEEPING AND THE DISPUTANTS

It is the disputing parties themselves who are primarily responsible for such decisions. They may decline the opportunity to make use of peacekeeping, notwithstanding the judgement of outsiders that the situation is highly appropriate for it. The prospect of cooperating with, and especially of playing host to, peacekeepers rarely generates much enthusiasm. But on a number of occasions disputants have been willing to do so. The term 'willing' has, in this context, a certain measure of elasticity. International politics, like all politics, is infused with constraints and pressures of various kinds, and sometimes these have made themselves felt in regard to peacekeeping. But at bottom the deployment and activity of peacekeepers is dependent on the cooperation of the disputants. Most obviously is this so in relation to the host state, from whom permission to operate, and to continue operating, must be received. But for a peacekeeping mission to achieve anything like its full purpose, the other party (or parties) must also be willing, in one way or another, to work with it.

This requirement is basic in both legal and political terms. In law, it is a concomitant of the fact that states, on account of their sovereignty – or constitutional independence – and except to the extent that they have accepted obligations specifically to the contrary, are entitled to take their own decisions on all matters concerning their territory and their policies. This arrangement, for better or ill, is the bedrock of international relations. It is hugely prized by all states, and is the aspiration of some dissident nationalist goups within states. So far as the political side of the equation is concerned, it is a fact of international life that it is enormously difficult to make states do what they are determined not to do. This may seem clear when their physical pacification or their ejection from foreign territory is in question, but it is no less the case in respect of getting them to adopt defusing or stabilizing measures, or to settle a dispute.

These considerations underline the significance of the non-threatening nature of peacekeeping. This characteristic reflects the fact that if a difficult international situation is to be eased with third-party help, that help needs to be locally acceptable. If it is not, it is most unlikely to be used. In that case it is also very improbable that the help will even be profferred. States are disinclined to engage in redundant activity, and are also reluctant to expose their personnel to the hazards which are inherent in a situation where they are unwelcome. It follows that states will be even less enamoured of any idea that they should try to impose help on an uncooperative disputant. Quite apart from the physical and political impracticalities of the scheme, they will also be mindful of the fact that it would breach the principle of non-intervention, to which all states pay obeisance.

This point deserves an extra emphasis, as in some Western circles it is often suggested that peacekeeping should be tougher. Whatever the intrinsic merits of greater 'toughness' in particular situations, its advocacy in the context of peacekeeping reflects a fundamental misconception of the nature of that phenomenon. It fails to take account of the importance for peacekeeping not just of a non-threatening approach but also of the inextricable connection between that approach and peacekeeping's other basic value of impartiality.

From one perspective, the use of force may sometimes appear completely impartial. But it may not look that way to those who are on its receiving end. And its employment in a contested situation is almost certainly going to have some impact on the relative strength of the parties. In these circumstances the disadvantaged party is hardly going to retain its confidence in the impartiality of the force-using body, which will thereby have effectively disqualified itself from the continued conduct of peacekeeping tasks. This is why, when peacekeepers help to maintain domestic order, the positive use of force is compatible with their basic role only if it is used in support of a government or a set of constitutional arrangements which receives general internal acceptance. Otherwise, as is inherently so in an inter-state context, the employment of force in a positive manner is going to favour one side at the expense of its opponent. Peacekeepers, to be of value in that capacity, have in all respects to stay out of the political fray.

Talk of tougher peacekeeping could also greatly diminish its initial acceptability. For there can be little doubt that states would be much less willing to invite peacekeepers on to their soil if there was a possibility of their not leaving when asked. And all parties to a dispute would become more wary of that kind of help if there was any question of the helpers taking the local situation by the scruff of the neck. In short, there is no viable half-way house between peacekeeping and enforcement. A peacekeeping mission which engages in the one-sided use of force loses its peacekeeping character. Moreover, such a development betokens a hierarchical approach which is at odds with the egalitarianism of the times besides being particularly unpopular with the potential consumers of peacekeeping.

THE USE OF PEACEKEEPING

If a peacekeeping mission is scrupulous in its attachment to impartial and non-threatening behaviour, and the parties are willing to cooperate with it, such a body can supply valuable, and maybe essential, help in defusing a crisis, stabilizing a situation (whether international or internal), or resolving a dispute. This book has identified no fewer than about 75 such missions, a good number of which served more than one peacekeeping function. There can be little question, therefore, that this device has been of considerable assistance in the maintenance of international peace. It has not served a primary role in this regard, as there is virtually no evidence to suggest that states are discouraged from warlike activity solely by the availability of peacekeeping bodies, or even by their presence. But if, for whatever reason, states are disposed towards peace, the implementation of that disposition can be considerably assisted by military personnel playing an untypical, peacekeeping, role. In that, secondary, sense peacekeeping deserves credit for its contribution towards making the twentieth century less battle-scarred than it might otherwise have been.

Possibly, by helping to prevent a recurrence of fighting, peacekeeping may sometimes have the side effect of contributing to the development of a more peaceful disposition in one or both of the parties. But that would be just a side effect. It is not the purpose of peacekeeping to create in the parties a genuinely conciliatory frame of mind. Rather, it aims to help in the implementation of an existing desire to avoid fighting – which, nowadays, is generally (albeit not always specifically) regarded as a highly desirable goal. It has been said that in doing this peacekeeping may sometimes get in the way of an improvement in the situation. Occasionally, indeed, it may reduce the feeling of urgency about the need for a settlement. But that is not at all the same as impairing the likelihood of a settlement. Peacekeepers often find themselves in the middle of conflicts which are peculiarly intractable. It is not their fault if the parties are in a far from pacific mood, nor can peacekeepers legitimately be blamed if the diplomatic pressure for inducing such an approach is insufficient. Of course, the peacekeepers may come in very handy as scapegoats. But peacekeeping is an activity which is distinct from peacemaking. To provide the one is not thereby to envision, or to downplay, the other, and throughout the post-1919 period the duality of (as well as the possible link between) what used to be called security and arbitration has been widely acknowledged.

The frequency of peacekeeping operations is likely to prove very variable. At times suitable opportunities may come thick and fast, but at other times years may go by without any new peacekeeping activity. Neither circumstance is a cause for either congratulation or despondency. There is no great merit, or demerit, about the incidence of peacekeeping. It is simply a device which states sometimes find helpful in calming, stabilizing, or settling their conflicts. It should not be assumed – with all the disappointing possibilities which may be built into that assumption – to be on the increase just because a number of new operations have appeared in recent times. Nor should too much be expected of it: it can succeed only to the extent to which the parties are willing to let it, for it is a derivative activity. But neither should it be undersold. On the premise that the discouragement of armed conflict is desirable, the tool of international peacekeeping has proved of immense worth. There is no reason to think that it will be of less use in the future. In relation to the control of international conflict, it is one of the more fruitful developments of the twentieth century.

Index

371